C000220232

Essential Virtual SAN (VSAN)

Administrator's Guide to VMware® Virtual SAN

Second Edition

VMware Press is the official publisher of VMware books and training materials, which provide guidance on the critical topics facing today's technology professionals and students. Enterprises, as well as small- and medium-sized organizations, adopt virtualization as a more agile way of scaling IT to meet business needs. VMware Press provides proven, technically accurate information that will help them meet their goals for customizing, building, and maintaining their virtual environment.

With books, certification and study guides, video training, and learning tools produced by world-class architects and IT experts, VMware Press helps IT professionals master a diverse range of topics on virtualization and cloud computing and is the official source of reference materials for preparing for the VMware Certified Professional examination.

VMware Press is also pleased to have localization partners that can publish its products into more than 42 languages, including, but not limited to, Chinese (Simplified), Chinese (Traditional), French, German, Greek, Hindi, Japanese, Korean, Polish, Russian, and Spanish.

For more information about VMware Press, please visit
http://www.vmwarepress.com.

vmware® PRESS

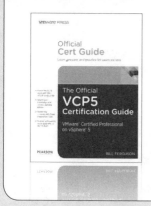

pearsonitcertification.com/vmwarepress

Complete list of products • Podcasts • Articles • Newsletters

VMware® Press is a publishing alliance between Pearson and VMware, and is the official publisher of VMware books and training materials that provide guidance for the critical topics facing today's technology professionals and students.

With books, certification and study guides, video training, and learning tools produced by world-class architects and IT experts, VMware Press helps IT professionals master a diverse range of topics on virtualization and cloud computing, and is the official source of reference materials for completing the VMware certification exams.

Make sure to connect with us!
informit.com/socialconnect

vmware® | PEARSON IT CERTIFICATION | Safari Books Online

ALWAYS LEARNING

PEARSON

Essential Virtual SAN (VSAN)

Administrator's Guide to VMware® Virtual SAN

Second Edition

Cormac Hogan

Duncan Epping

vmware® PRESS

Boston • Indianapolis • San Francisco
New York • Toronto • Montreal • London • Munich • Paris • Madrid
Capetown • Sydney • Tokyo • Singapore • Mexico City

Essential Virtual SAN (VSAN) Second Edition

Copyright © 2016 VMware, Inc

Published by Pearson Education, Inc.

Publishing as VMware Press

All rights reserved. Printed in the United States of America. This publication is protected by copyright, and permission must be obtained from the publisher prior to any prohibited reproduction, storage in a retrieval system, or transmission in any form or by any means, electronic, mechanical, photocopying, recording, or likewise.

ISBN-10: 0-13-451166-2

ISBN-13: 978-0-13-451166-5

Library of Congress Control Number: 2016903470

Printed in the United States of America

1   16

All terms mentioned in this book that are known to be trademarks or service marks have been appropriately capitalized. The publisher cannot attest to the accuracy of this information. Use of a term in this book should not be regarded as affecting the validity of any trademark or service mark.

VMware terms are trademarks or registered trademarks of VMware in the United States, other countries, or both.

Warning and Disclaimer

Every effort has been made to make this book as complete and as accurate as possible, but no warranty or fitness is implied. The information provided is on an as is basis. The authors, VMware Press, VMware, and the publisher shall have neither liability nor responsibility to any person or entity with respect to any loss or damages arising from the information contained in this book or from the use of any digital content or programs accompanying it.

The opinions expressed in this book belong to the author and are not necessarily those of VMware.

Special Sales

For information about buying this title in bulk quantities, or for special sales opportunities (which may include electronic versions; custom cover designs; and content particular to your business, training goals, marketing focus, or branding interests), please contact our corporate sales department at corpsales@pearsoned.com or (800) 382-3419.

For government sales inquiries, please contact governmentsales@pearsoned.com.

For questions about sales outside the United States, please contact intlcs@pearson.com

VMWARE PRESS PROGRAM MANAGER
Karl Childs

EXECUTIVE EDITOR
Mary Beth Ray

TECHNICAL EDITORS
Christian Dickmann
John Nicholson

SENIOR DEVELOPMENT EDITOR
Ellie Bru

MANAGING EDITOR
Sandra Schroeder

PROJECT EDITOR
Mandie Frank

COPY EDITOR
Cenveo® Publisher Services

PROOFREADER
Cenveo Publisher Services

INDEXER
Cenveo Publisher Services

EDITORIAL ASSISTANT
Vanessa Evans

DESIGNER
Chuti Prasertsith

COMPOSITOR
Cenveo Publisher Services

"I close my eyes, and think of home. Another city goes by in the night. Ain't it funny how it is, you never miss it 'til it has gone away. And my heart is lying there and will be 'til my dying day."

We would like to dedicate this book to the greatest band on earth, Iron Maiden.
—Cormac & Duncan

Contents

Foreword by Christos Karamanolis   xvii

About the Author   xix

About the Technical Reviewers   xxi

Acknowledgments   xxiii

We Want to Hear from You!   xxv

1   Introduction to VSAN   1

    Software-Defined Datacenter   1

    Software-Defined Storage   2

    Hyper-Convergence/Server SAN Solutions   3

    Introducing Virtual SAN   4

    What Is Virtual SAN?   6

    What Does VSAN Look Like to an Administrator?   9

    Summary   12

2   VSAN Prerequisites and Requirements for Deployment   13

    VMware vSphere   13

        ESXi   14

        Cache and Capacity Devices   14

        ESXi Boot Considerations   15

    VSAN Requirements   15

        VMware Hardware Compatibility Guide   16

        VSAN Ready Nodes   16

        Storage Controllers   17

        Capacity Tier Devices   19

        Cache Tier Devices   21

    Network Requirements   22

        Network Interface Cards   22

        Supported Virtual Switch Types   22

        Layer 2 or Layer 3   23

        VMkernel Network   23

        VSAN Network Traffic   24

        Jumbo Frames   24

        NIC Teaming   25

        Network I/O Control   25

    VSAN Stretched Cluster   25

    VSAN 2-Node Remote Office/Branch Office (ROBO)   26

        Firewall Ports   26

    Summary   26

3   VSAN Installation and Configuration   29

   VSAN Networking   29

   VMkernel Network for VSAN   30

   VSAN Network Configuration: VMware Standard Switch   31

   VSAN Network Configuration: vSphere Distributed Switch   32

      Step 1: Create the Distributed Switch   32

      Step 2: Create a Distributed Port Group   33

      Step 3: Build VMkernel Ports   34

   Possible Network Configuration Issues   38

   Network I/O Control Configuration Example   40

   Design Considerations: Distributed Switch and Network I/O Control   42

      Scenario 1: Redundant 10 GbE Switch Without "Link Aggregation" Capability   43

      Scenario 2: Redundant 10 GbE Switch with Link Aggregation Capability   45

   Creating a VSAN Cluster   48

   vSphere HA   49

      vSphere HA Communication Network   49

      vSphere HA Heartbeat Datastores   50

      vSphere HA Admission Control   50

      vSphere HA Isolation Response   51

      vSphere HA Component Protection   51

   The Role of Disk Groups   51

      Disk Group Maximums   52

      Why Configure Multiple Disk Groups in VSAN?   52

      Cache Device to Capacity Device Sizing Ratio   53

      Automatically Add Disks to VSAN Disk Groups   54

      Manually Adding Disks to a VSAN Disk Group   55

      Disk Group Creation Example   55

      VSAN Datastore Properties   58

   Summary   59

4   VM Storage Policies on VSAN   61

   Introducing Storage Policy-Based Management in a VSAN Environment   62

      Number of Failures to Tolerate   65

      Failure Tolerance Method   66

      Number of Disk Stripes Per Object   69

      IOPS Limit for Object   70

      Flash Read Cache Reservation   71

      Object Space Reservation   71

      Force Provisioning   71

      Disable Object Checksum   73

VASA Vendor Provider   73

> An Introduction to VASA   73

> Storage Providers   74

VSAN Storage Providers: Highly Available   75

> Changing VM Storage Policy On-the-Fly   75

> Objects, Components, and Witnesses   80

VM Storage Policies   80

> Enabling VM Storage Policies   81

> Creating VM Storage Policies   81

> Assigning a VM Storage Policy During VM Provisioning   81

Summary   82

5   Architectural Details   83

Distributed RAID   83

Objects and Components   86

> Component Limits   87

> Virtual Machine Storage Objects   88

> Namespace   89

> Virtual Machine Swap   90

> VMDKs and Deltas   90

> Witnesses and Replicas   90

> Object Layout   91

VSAN Software Components   94

> Component Management   95

> Data Paths for Objects   95

> Object Ownership   96

> Placement and Migration for Objects   96

> Cluster Monitoring, Membership, and Directory Services   97

> Host Roles (Master, Slave, Agent)   97

> Reliable Datagram Transport   98

On-Disk Formats   98

> Cache Devices   99

> Capacity Devices   99

VSAN I/O Flow   100

> Caching Algorithms   100

> The Role of the Cache Layer   100

> Anatomy of a VSAN Read on Hybrid VSAN   102

> Anatomy of a VSAN Read on All-Flash VSAN   103

> Anatomy of a VSAN Write on Hybrid VSAN   103

> Anatomy of a VSAN Write on All-Flash VSAN   104

Retiring Writes to Capacity Tier on Hybrid VSAN   105

Deduplication and Compression   105

Data Locality   107

Data Locality in VSAN Stretched Clusters   108

Storage Policy-Based Management   109

VSAN Capabilities   109

Number of Failures to Tolerate Policy Setting   110

Best Practice for Number of Failures to Tolerate   112

Stripe Width Policy Setting   113

RAID-0 Used When No Striping Specified in the Policy   117

Stripe Width Maximum   119

Stripe Width Configuration Error   120

Stripe Width Chunk Size   121

Stripe Width Best Practice   122

Flash Read Cache Reservation Policy Setting   122

Object Space Reservation Policy Setting   122

VM Home Namespace Revisited   123

VM Swap Revisited   123

How to Examine the VM Swap Storage Object   124

Delta Disk / Snapshot Caveat   126

Verifying How Much Space Is Actually Consumed   126

Force Provisioning Policy Setting   127

Witnesses and Replicas: Failure Scenarios   127

Data Integrity Through Checksum   130

Recovery from Failure   131

Problematic Device Handling   134

What About Stretching VSAN?   134

Summary   135

6   VM Storage Policies and Virtual Machine Provisioning   137

Policy Setting: Number of Failures to Tolerate = 1   137

Policy Setting: Failures to Tolerate = 1, Stripe Width = 2   144

Policy Setting: Failures to Tolerate = 2, Stripe Width = 2   148

Policy Setting: Failures to Tolerate = 1, Object Space Reservation = 50%   152

Policy Setting: Failures to Tolerate = 1, Object Space Reservation = 100%   155

Policy Setting: RAID-5   157

Policy Setting: RAID-6   158

Policy Setting: RAID-5/6 and Stripe Width = 2   159

Default Policy   160

Summary   164

7 Management and Maintenance   165

   Health Check   165

         Health Check Tests   165

         Proactive Health Checks   167

         Performance Service   168

   Host Management   169

         Adding Hosts to the Cluster   169

         Removing Hosts from the Cluster   170

         ESXCLI VSAN Cluster Commands   171

   Maintenance Mode   172

         Default Maintenance Mode/Decommission Mode   175

         Recommended Maintenance Mode Option for Updates and Patching   175

   Disk Management   177

         Adding a Disk Group   177

         Removing a Disk Group   178

         Adding Disks to the Disk Group   179

         Removing Disks from the Disk Group   180

   Wiping a Disk   182

         Blinking the LED on a Disk   183

         ESXCLI VSAN Disk Commands   184

   Failure Scenarios   185

         Capacity Device Failure   185

         Cache Device Failure   186

         Host Failure   187

         Network Partition   188

         Disk Full Scenario   193

   Thin Provisioning Considerations   194

   vCenter Management   195

         vCenter Server Failure Scenario   196

         Running vCenter Server on VSAN   196

         Bootstrapping vCenter Server   197

   Summary   199

8 Stretched Cluster   201

   What is a Stretched Cluster?   201

   Requirements and Constraints   203

   Networking and Latency Requirements   205

   New Concepts in VSAN Stretched Cluster   206

   Configuration of a Stretched Cluster   208

Failure Scenarios   216

Summary   224

9   Designing a VSAN Cluster   225

Ready Node Profiles   225

Sizing Constraints   227

Cache to Capacity Ratio   228

Designing for Performance   229

      Impact of the Disk Controller   231

VSAN Performance Capabilities   235

Design and Sizing Tools   236

Scenario 1: Server Virtualization—Hybrid   237

      Determining Your Host Configuration   238

Scenario 2—Server Virtualization—All-flash   241

Summary   244

10   Troubleshooting, Monitoring, and Performance   245

Health Check   246

      Ask VMware   246

      Health Check Categories   247

      Proactive Health Checks   253

ESXCLI   256

      esxcli vsan datastore   256

      esxcli vsan network   257

      esxcli vsan storage   258

      esxcli vsan cluster   262

      esxcli vsan faultdomain   263

      esxcli vsan maintenancemode   264

      esxcli vsan policy   264

      esxcli vsan trace   267

      Additional Non-ESXCLI Commands for Troubleshooting VSAN   268

Ruby vSphere Console   275

      VSAN Commands   276

      SPBM Commands   300

Troubleshooting VSAN on the ESXi   303

      Log Files   304

      VSAN Traces   304

      VSAN VMkernel Modules and Drivers   305

Performance Monitoring   305

      Introducing the Performance Service   305

ESXTOP Performance Counters for VSAN   308

vSphere Web Client Performance Counters for VSAN   309

VSAN Observer   310

Sample VSAN Observer Use Case   316

Summary   318

Index   319

Foreword by Christos Karamanolis

We are in the midst of a major evolution of hardware, especially storage technologies and networking. With NAND-based Flash, a single device can deliver 1M I/O operations a second. That's more than what a high-end disk array could deliver just a few years ago. With 10 Gbps networks becoming commodity, the industry is already eying 40 or even 100 Gbps Ethernet. Efficient protocols like RDMA and NVMe reduce the cycles CPUs need to consume to harness the capabilities of emerging storage and networking technologies. At the same time, CPU densities are doubling every two years.

It was within this technology forecast that I started the Virtual SAN project together with a handful of brilliant engineers back in 2010. We recognized that commodity servers have enough oomph to take over services like storage and networking traditionally offered by dedicated hardware appliances. We argued that software running on general-purpose (commodity) hardware is the way to go. Simply put, the technology evolution allows for the democratization of enterprise storage and networking. A software-defined architecture allows the customer to ride the wave of technology trends and offers enormous benefits—lower costs, flexibility with hardware choices, and, if it comes with the right tools, a unified way to manage one's infrastructure: compute, storage, network.

The operational complexity and scalability challenges of storage management have been amongst the biggest pain points of virtualization adopters. So, we focused on Software-Defined Storage at the same time that a little-known Stanford graduate, named Martin Casado, was making the case for Software-Defined Networks.

Fast forward to March 2016: VMware's Virtual SAN is in its fourth release (version 6.2), the most important release of the product since its debut in March 2014. With a panoply of data integrity, availability and space efficiency features, Virtual SAN stands tall against the most sophisticated storage products in the industry. By combining commodity hardware economics and a flexible, highly efficient software stack, VMware is making all-flash storage affordable and applicable to a broad range of use cases. With thousands of enterprise customers using VSAN for business-critical use cases that range from Hospitals to popular E-commerce platforms, and from oil rigs to aircraft carriers, Virtual SAN has the credentials to be deemed battle tested. And we proudly carry the scars that come with that!

However, if we focus entirely on the (impressive) storage features of Virtual SAN, we are missing an important point: the fundamental shift in the management paradigm that the product introduces. In the current instantiation of the technology, Virtual SAN is designed to be an ideal storage platform for hyper-converged infrastructures (HCI). The key benefit of HCI is its simple operational model that allows customers to manage the entire IT infrastructure with a single set of tools. Virtual SAN is blazing the path for VMware products and for the industry at large.

Since version 6.1, Virtual SAN has been offering a "Health Service" that monitors, probes and assists with remediation of hardware, configuration, and performance issues. With version 6.2, the management toolkit is extended with a "Performance Service", which provides advanced performance monitoring and analysis. Using these tools and data, the user has end-to-end visibility into the state of their infrastructure and the consumption of resources by different VMs and workloads. For example, one can do performance troubleshooting, pinpoint the root cause of any issues (whether compute, network or storage) and decide on remediation actions, while using a single tool set.

All management features of Virtual SAN including enablement, configuration, upgrades, as well as the health and performance services, are built using a scalable distributed architecture. They are fully supported through APIs, which are extensions of the very popular vSphere API. In the same spirit, all VSAN and HCI management features are natively integrated with the vSphere Web Client.

Virtual SAN is natively integrated with ESXi, the best hypervisor in the industry, to offer unmatched HCI efficiency and performance. The product works "out of the box" for vSphere customers. Moreover, the scale-out nature of its control plane opens the path for new use cases and applications in private and public clouds. We are just at the beginning of an exciting journey.

Much (digital) ink has been spilled describing Virtual SAN, its unique architecture, and the operational benefits it brings to customers. Not a day goes by without an article been published, without a friend or a foe expressing their opinion on the product and what it means for the customers. This book, however, is different. It is the most comprehensive and authoritative reference for Virtual SAN, the product and the technology behind it.

Duncan and Cormac have been on board since the early days of the project. They have contributed invaluable input during the design phases based on their personal experience and on customer feedback. Not only they are intimately familiar with the architecture of the product, but they also have extensive operational experience in the lab and with customer deployments around the world. As such, they approach the subject through the eyes of the IT professional.

I hope you find the book as informative as I have.

Christos Karamanolis
VMware Fellow. CTO, Storage and Availability Business Unit.

About the Authors

Cormac Hogan is a Senior Staff Engineer in the Office of the CTO in the Storage and Availability business unit at VMware. Cormac was one of the first VMware employees at the EMEA headquarters in Cork, Ireland, back in 2005, and has previously held roles in VMware's Technical Marketing, Integration Engineering and Support organizations. Cormac has written a number of storage-related white papers and has given numerous presentations on storage best practices and new features. Cormac is the owner of CormacHogan.com, a blog site dedicated to storage and virtualization.

He can be followed on twitter @CormacJHogan.

Duncan Epping is a Chief Technologist working for VMware in the Office of CTO of the Storage and Availability business unit. Duncan is responsible for ensuring VMware's future innovations align with essential customer needs, translating customer problems to opportunities, and function as the global lead evangelist for Storage and Availability. Duncan specializes in Software Defined Storage, hyper-converged infrastructures and business continuity/disaster recovery solutions. He has four patents pending and one granted on the topic of availability, storage and resource management. Duncan is the author/owner of VMware Virtualization blog Yellow-Bricks.com and has various books on the topic of VMware including the "vSphere Clustering Deepdive" series.

He can be followed on twitter @DuncanYB.

About the Technical Reviewers

Christian Dickmann is a Virtual SAN Architect and Sr. Staff Engineer in the Storage and Availability Business Unit at VMware. Besides system architecture, he currently focuses on management functionality for ease of use, troubleshooting, monitoring, installation, and lifecycle management. Since joining VMware in 2007, he worked on extensibility of the networking stack as well as built the vSphere R&D dev/test cloud from the ground up. The latter experience made him an avid user experience and customer advocate.

John Nicholson is a Senior Technical Marketing Manager in the Storage and Availability Business Unit. He focuses on delivering technical guidance around VMware Virtual SAN solutions. John previously worked for partners and customers in architecting and implementing enterprise storage and VDI solutions. He holds the VCP certification (VCP5-DT, VCP6-DCV) and is a member of the vExpert and Veeam Vanguard programs.

Acknowledgments

The authors of this book both work for VMware. The opinions expressed in the book are the authors' personal opinions and experience with the product. Statements made throughout the book do not necessarily reflect the views and opinions of VMware.

We would like to thank Christian Dickmann and John Nicholson for keeping us honest as our technical editors. Of course, we also want to thank the Virtual SAN engineering team for their help and patience. In particular, we want to call out a couple of individuals of the Storage and Availability BU, Christian Dickmann, Paudie O'Riordan and Christos Karamanolis, whose deep knowledge and understanding of VSAN, and storage technology in general, was leveraged throughout this book. We also want to thank William Lam for his contributions to the book.

Lastly, we want to thank our VMware management team (Yanbing Li, Christos Karamanolis) for supporting us on this and other projects.

Go VSAN!

Cormac Hogan and Duncan Epping

We Want to Hear from You!

As the reader of this book, *you* are our most important critic and commentator. We value your opinion and want to know what we're doing right, what we could do better, what areas you'd like to see us publish in, and any other words of wisdom you're willing to pass our way.

We welcome your comments. You can email or write us directly to let us know what you did or didn't like about this book—as well as what we can do to make our books better.

Please note that we cannot help you with technical problems related to the topic of this book.

When you write, please be sure to include this book's title and author as well as your name, email address, and phone number. We will carefully review your comments and share them with the author and editors who worked on the book.

Email: VMwarePress@vmware.com

Mail: VMware Press

        ATTN: Reader Feedback

        800 East 96th Street

        Indianapolis, IN 46240 USA

Reader Services

Register your copy of *Essential Virtual SAN (VSAN)* at www.informit.com for convenient access to downloads, updates, and corrections as they become available. To start the registration process, go to informit.com/register and log in or create an account*. Enter the product ISBN, 9780133854992, and click Submit. Once the process is complete, you will find any available bonus content under Registered Products.

*Be sure to check the box that you would like to hear from us in order to receive exclusive discounts on future editions of this product.

Introduction

When talking about virtualization and the underlying infrastructure that it runs on, one component that always comes up in conversation is storage. The reason for this is fairly simple: In many environments, storage is a pain point. Although the storage landscape has changed with the introduction of flash technologies that mitigate many of the traditional storage issues, many organizations have not yet adopted these new architectures and are still running into the same challenges.

Storage challenges range from operational effort or complexity to performance problems or even availability constraints. The majority of these problems stem from the same fundamental problem: legacy architecture. The reason is that most storage platform architectures were developed long before virtualization existed, and virtualization changed the way these shared storage platforms were used.

In a way, you could say that virtualization forced the storage industry to look for new ways of building storage systems. Instead of having a single server connect to a single storage device (also known as a logical unit or LUN for short), virtualization typically entails having one (or many) physical server(s) running many virtual machines connecting to one or multiple storage devices. This did not only increase the load on these storage systems, it also changed the workload patterns and increased the total capacity required.

As you can imagine, for most storage administrators, this required a major shift in thinking. What should the size of my LUN be? What are my performance requirements, and how many spindles will that result in? What kind of data services are required on these LUNs, and where will virtual machines be stored? Not only did it require a major shift in thinking, but it also required working in tandem with other IT teams. Whereas in the past server admins and network and storage admins could all live in their own isolated worlds, they now needed to communicate and work together to ensure availability of the platform they were building. Whereas in the past a mistake, such as a misconfiguration or underprovisioning, would only impact a single server, it could now impact many virtual machines.

There was a fundamental shift in how we collectively thought about how to operate and architect IT infrastructures when virtualization was introduced. Now another collective shift is happening all over again. This time it is due to the introduction of software-defined networking and software-defined storage. But let's not let history repeat itself, and let's avoid the mistakes we all made when virtualization first arrived. Let's all have frank and open discussions with our fellow datacenter administrators as we all aim to revolutionize datacenter architecture and operations!

You, the Reader

This book is targeted at IT professionals who are involved in the care and feeding of a VMware vSphere environment. Ideally, you have been working with VMware vSphere for some time and perhaps you have attended an authorized course in vSphere, such as the "Install, Configure, and Manage" class. This book is not a starters guide, but there should be enough in the book for administrators and architects of all levels.

How to Use This Book

This book is split into ten chapters, as described here:

- **Chapter 1, "Introduction to VSAN":** This chapter provides a high-level introduction to software-defined storage and VSAN.

- **Chapter 2, "VSAN Prerequisites and Requirements for Deployment":** This chapter describes the requirements from a physical and virtual perspective to safely implement VSAN.

- **Chapter 3, "VSAN Installation and Configuration":** This chapter goes over the steps needed to install and configure VSAN.

- **Chapter 4, "VM Storage Policies on VSAN":** This chapter explains the concept of storage policy-based management.

- **Chapter 5, "Architectural Details":** This chapter provides in-depth architectural details of VSAN.

- **Chapter 6, "VM Storage Policies and Virtual Machine Provisioning":** This chapter describes how VM storage policies can be used to simplify VM deployment.

- **Chapter 7, "Management and Maintenance":** This chapter describes the steps for most common management and maintenance tasks.

- **Chapter 8, "Stretched Clusters":** This chapter covers the operational and architectural aspects and design decisions around the introduction of VSAN stretched clusters.

- **Chapter 9, "Designing a VSAN Cluster":** This chapter provides various examples around designing a VSAN cluster, including sizing exercises.

- **Chapter 10, "Troubleshooting, Monitoring, and Performance":** This chapter covers the various (command line) tools available to troubleshoot and monitor VSAN.

## Chapter 1

Introduction to VSAN

This chapter introduces you to the world of software-defined datacenter (SDDC), but with a focus on the storage aspect. The chapter covers the basic premise of the software-defined datacenter and then delves deeper to cover the concept of software-defined storage and associated solutions such as the server storage-area network (server SAN) and hyper-converged infrastructure solutions.

Software-Defined Datacenter

VMworld, the VMware annual conferencing event, introduced VMware's vision for the software-defined datacenter (SDDC) in 2012. The SDDC is VMware's architecture for the public and private clouds where all pillars of the datacenter—computing, storaging, and networking (and the associated services)—are virtualized. Virtualizing datacenter components enables the IT team to be more flexible. If you lower the operational complexity and cost while increasing availability and agility, you will ultimately lower the time to market for new services.

To achieve all of that, virtualization of components by itself is not sufficient. The platform used must be capable of being installed and configured in a fully automated fashion. More importantly, the platform should enable you to manage and monitor your infrastructure in a smart and less operationally intense manner. That is what the SDDC is all about! Raghu Raghuram (VMware senior vice president) captured it in a single sentence: The essence of software-defined datacenter is "abstract, pool, and automate."

Abstraction, pooling, and automation are all achieved by introducing an additional layer on top of the physical resources. This layer is usually referred to as a *virtualization layer*. Everyone reading this book is probably familiar with the leading product for compute virtualization, VMware vSphere. Fewer people are probably familiar with network virtualization, sometimes referred to as software-defined network (SDN) solutions. VMware offers a solution named NSX that is based on the solution built by the acquired company Nicira. NSX does for networking what vSphere does for compute. These layers do not just virtualize the physical resources but also allow you to pool them and provide with an application-programming interface (API) that enables you to automate all operational aspects.

Automation is not just about scripting, however. A significant part of the automation of virtual machine (VM) provisioning (and its associated resources) is achieved through policy-based management. Predefined policies allow provisioning for VMs in a quick, easy, consistent, and repeatable manner. The resource characteristics specified on a resource pool or a vApp container exemplify a compute policy. These characteristics enable you to quantify resource policies for compute in terms of reservation, limit, and priority. Network policies can range from security to quality of service (QoS). Unfortunately, storage has thus far been limited to the characteristics provided by the physical storage device, which in many cases did not meet the expectations and requirements of many of our customers.

This book examines the storage component of VMware's SDDC. More specifically, the book covers how a product called Virtual SAN (VSAN), fits into this vision. You will learn how it has been implemented and integrated within the current platform and how you can leverage its capabilities and expand on some of the lower-level implementation details. Before going further, though, you want to have a generic understanding of where VSAN fits into the bigger software-defined storage picture.

Software-Defined Storage

Software-defined storage is a term that has been used and abused by many vendors. Because software-defined storage is currently defined in so many different ways, consider the following quote from VMware:

> Software Defined Storage is the automation and pooling of storage through a software control plane, and the ability to provide storage from industry standard servers. This offers a significant simplification to the way storage is provisioned and managed, and also paves the way for storage on industry standard servers at a fraction of the cost. (Source: http://cto .vmware.com/vmwares-strategy-for-software-defined-storage/)

A software-defined storage product is a solution that abstracts the hardware and allows you to easily pool all resources and provide them to the consumer using a user-friendly user interface (UI) and API. A software-defined storage solution allows you to both scale up and scale out, without increasing the operational effort.

Many hold that software-defined storage is about moving functionality from the traditional storage devices to the host. This trend was started by virtualized versions of storage devices such as HP's StoreVirtual VSA and evolved into solutions that were built to run on many different hardware platforms. One example of such a solution is Nexenta. These solutions were the start of a new era.

Hyper-Convergence/Server SAN Solutions

Over the last few years there have been many debates around what hyper-converged is versus a server SAN solution. In our opinion, the big difference between these two is the level of integration with the platform it is running on and the delivery model. When it comes to the delivery mode there are two distinct flavors:

- Appliance based
- Software only

An appliance-based solution is one where the hardware and the software are sold and delivered as a single bundle. It will come preinstalled with a hypervisor and usually requires little or no effort to configure. There is also a deep integration with the platform it sits on (or in) typically. This can range from leveraging the provided storage APIs to providing extensive data services to being embedded in the hypervisor.

In all of these cases local storage is aggregated into a large shared pool by leveraging a virtual storage appliance or a kernel-based storage stack. Typical examples of appliance-based solutions that are out there today include Nutanix, SimpliVity, and of course Virtual SAN. When one would ask the general audience what a typical "hyper-converged appliance" looks like, the answer would usually be: a 2U form factor with four hosts. However, hyper-convergence is not about a form factor in our opinion. It is about combining different components into a single solution. This solution needs to be easy to install, configure, manage, and monitor. It is fair to say, however, that traditionally most hyper-converged platforms were delivered in a 2U form factor with four hosts. Figure 1.1 shows what these appliances looked like, but make no mistake these are just generic x86 servers.

Figure 1.1 Commonly used hardware by hyper-converged storage vendors

You might ask, "If these are generic x86 servers with hypervisors installed and a virtual storage appliance or a kernel storage stack, what are the benefits over a traditional storage system?" The benefits of a hyper-converged platform are as follows:

- Time to market is short, less than 1 hour to install and deploy

- Ease of management and integration

- Able to scale out, both capacity and performance wise

- Lower total costs of acquisition compared to traditional environments

These solutions are sold as a single stock keeping unit (SKU), and typically a single point of contact for support is provided. This can make support discussions much easier. However, a hurdle for many companies is the fact that these solutions are tied to hardware and specific configurations. The hardware used by hyper-converged vendors is often not the same as the preferred hardware supplier you may already have. This can lead to operational challenges when it comes to updating/patching or even cabling and racking. In addition, a trust issue exists. Some people swear by server Vendor X and would never want to touch any other brand, whereas others won't come close to server Vendor X. Fortunately, most hyper-converged vendors these days offer the ability to buy their solution through different server hardware vendors. If that does not provide sufficient flexibility, then this is where the software-based storage solutions come into play.

Software-only storage solutions come in two flavors. The most common solution today is the virtual storage appliance (VSA). VSA solutions are deployed as a VM on top of a hypervisor installed on physical hardware. VSAs allow you to pool underlying physical resources into a shared storage device. Examples of VSAs include Maxta, HP's Store Virtual VSA, and EMC Scale IO. The big advantage of software-only solutions is that you can usually leverage existing hardware as long as it is on the hardware compatibility list (HCL). In the majority of cases, the HCL is similar to what the underlying hypervisor supports, except for key components like disk controllers and flash devices.

VSAN is also a software-only solution, but VSAN differs significantly from the VSAs listed. VSAN sits in a different layer and is not a VSA-based solution. On top of that, VSAN is typically combined with hardware by a vendor of choice. Hence, VMware refers to VSAN as a hyper-converged software solution as it is literally the enabler of many hyper-converged offerings.

Introducing Virtual SAN

VMware's plan for software-defined storage is to focus on a set of VMware initiatives related to local storage, shared storage, and storage/data services. In essence, VMware wants to make vSphere a platform for storage services.

Historically, storage was something that was configured and deployed at the start of a project, and was not changed during its life cycle. If there was a need to change some characteristics or features of the logical unit number (LUN) or volume that were being leveraged by VMs, in many cases the original LUN or volume was deleted and a new volume with the required features or characteristics was created. This was a very intrusive, risky, and time-consuming operation due to the requirement to migrate workloads between LUNs or volumes, which may have taken weeks to coordinate.

With software-defined storage, VM storage requirements can be dynamically instantiated. There is no need to repurpose LUNs or volumes. VM workloads and requirements may change over time, and the underlying storage can be adapted to the workload at any time. VSAN aims to provide storage services and service-level agreement *automation* through a software layer on the hosts that *integrates* with, *abstracts*, and *pools* the underlying hardware.

A key factor for software-defined storage is storage policy-based management (SPBM). SPBM can be thought of as the next generation of VMware's storage profile feature that was introduced with vSphere 5.0. Where as the initial focus of storage profiles was more about ensuring VMs were provisioned to the correct storage device, in vSphere 6.x., SPBM is a critical component to how VMware is implementing software-defined storage.

Using SPBM and vSphere APIs, the underlying storage technology surfaces an abstracted pool of storage space with various capabilities that is presented to vSphere administrators for VM provisioning. The capabilities can relate to performance, availability, or storage services such as thin provisioning, compression, replication, and more. A vSphere administrator can then create a *VM storage policy* (or profile) using a subset of the capabilities that are required by the application running in the VM. During deployment time, the vSphere administrator selects a VM storage policy. SPBM pushes the VM storage policy down to the storage layer, and datastores that understand the requirements placed in the VM storage policy will be made available for selection. This means that the VM is always instantiated on appropriate underlying storage based on the requirements placed in the VM storage policy and that the VM is provisioned with just the right amount of resources and, the required services from the abstracted pool of storage resources.

Should the VM's workload, availability requirement, or I/O pattern change over time, it is simply a matter of applying a new VM storage policy with requirements and characteristics that reflect the new workload to that specific VM, or even virtual disk, after which the policy will be seamlessly applied without any manual intervention from the administrator (in contrast to many legacy storage systems, where a manual migration of VMs or virtual disks to a different datastore would be required). VSAN has been developed to seamlessly integrate with vSphere and the SPBM functionality it offers.

What Is Virtual SAN?

VSAN is a storage solution from VMware, released as a beta version in 2013, made generally available to the public in March 2014, and reached version 6.2 in March 2016. VSAN is fully integrated with vSphere. It is an object-based storage system and a platform for VM storage policies that aims to simplify VM storage placement decisions for vSphere administrators. It fully supports and is integrated with core vSphere features such as vSphere high availability (HA), vSphere distributed resource scheduler (DRS), and vMotion, as illustrated in Figure 1.2.

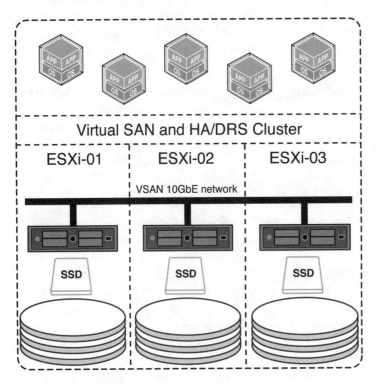

Figure 1.2   Simple overview of a VSAN cluster

VSAN's goal is to provide both resiliency and scale-out storage functionality. It can also be thought of in the context of QoS in so far as VM storage policies can be created that define the level of performance and availability required on a per-VM, or even virtual disk, basis.

VSAN is a software-based distributed storage solution that is built directly in the hypervisor. Although not a virtual appliance like many of the other solutions out there, a VSAN can be best thought of as a kernel-based solution that is included with the hypervisor. Technically, however, this is not completely accurate because components critical for performance and responsiveness such as the data path and clustering are in the kernel, while other components that can be collectively considered part of the "control plane" are implemented as native user-space agents. Nevertheless, with VSAN there is no need to install anything other than the software you are already familiar with: VMware vSphere.

VSAN is about simplicity, and when we say *simplicity*, we do mean simplicity. Want to try out VSAN? It is truly as simple as creating a VMkernel network interface card (NIC) for VSAN traffic and enabling it on a cluster level, as shown in Figure 1.3. Of course, there are certain recommendations and requirements to optimize your experience, as described in further detail in Chapter 2, "VSAN Prerequisites and Requirements for Deployment."

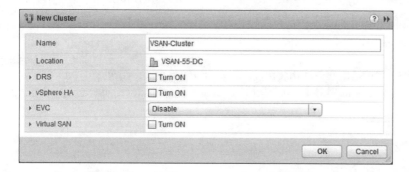

Figure 1.3   Two-click enablement

Now that you know it is easy to use and simple to configure, what are the benefits of a solution like VSAN? What are the key selling points?

- **Software defined:** Use industry standard hardware
- **Flexible:** Scale as needed and when needed, both scale up and scale out
- **Simple:** Ridiculously easy to manage and operate
- **Automated:** Per-VM and disk policy-based management
- **Hyper-converged:** Enables you to create dense/building-block-style solutions

That sounds compelling, doesn't it? You may ask: where does VSAN fit, what are the use cases, and are there situations where it doesn't fit today? Today, the use cases are as follows:

- **Business critical apps:** Stable storage platform with all data services required to run business critical workloads, whether that is Microsoft Exchange, SQL, Oracle, etc.

- **Virtual desktops:** Scale-out model using predictive and repeatable infrastructure blocks that lowers costs and simplifies operations.

- **Test and dev:** Avoids acquisition of expensive storage (lowers total cost of ownership [TCO]), fast time to provision.

- **Management or DMZ infrastructure:** Fully isolated, resulting in increased security and no dependencies on the resources it is potentially managing.

- **Disaster recovery target:** Inexpensive disaster recovery solution, enabled through a feature like vSphere replication that allows you to replicate to any storage platform.

- **Remote office/branch office (ROBO):** With the ability to start with as little as two hosts, centrally managed, VSAN is the ideal fit for ROBO environments.

- **Stretched cluster:** Providing very high availability across remote sites for a wide range of potential workloads.

Now that you know what VSAN is and that it is ready for any type of workload, let's have a brief look at what was introduced in terms of functionality with each release.

- **Virtual SAN 1.0: March 2014**

  - Initial release

- **Virtual SAN 6.0: March 2015**

  - All-flash configurations

  - 64 host cluster scalability

  - 2x performance increase for hybrid configurations

  - New snapshot mechanism

  - Enhanced cloning mechanism

  - Fault domain/rack awareness

- **Virtual SAN 6.1: September 2016**

  - Stretched clustering across a max of 5 ms (milliseconds) RTT

  - 2-node VSAN for remote office, branch office (ROBO) solutions

  - vRealize operations management pack

  - vSphere replication—5 minutes RPO

  - Health monitoring

- **Virtual SAN 6.2: March 2016**

    - RAID 5 and 6 over the network (erasure coding)

    - Space efficiency (deduplication and compression)

    - QoS–IOPS limits

    - Software checksums

    - IPv6 support

    - Performance monitoring

Hopefully, that gives a quick overview of all the capabilities introduced and available in each of the releases. There are many items listed, but that does not mean Virtual SAN is complex to configure, manage, and monitor. Let's take a look from an administrator perspective; what does VSAN look like?

What Does VSAN Look Like to an Administrator?

When VSAN is enabled, a single shared datastore is presented to all hosts that are part of the VSAN-enabled cluster. This is the strength of VSAN; it is presented as a datastore. Just like any other storage solution out there, this datastore can be used as a destination for VMs and all associated components, such as virtual disks, swap files, and VM configuration files. When you deploy a new VM, you will see the familiar interface and a list of available datastores, including your VSAN-based datastore, as shown in Figure 1.4.

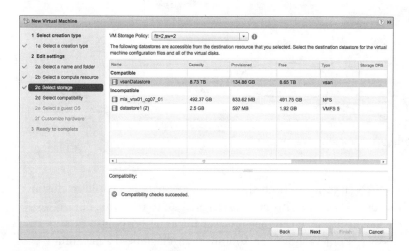

Figure 1.4　Just a normal datastore

This VSAN datastore is formed out of host local storage resources. Typically, all hosts within a VSAN-enabled cluster will contribute performance (flash) and capacity (magnetic disks or flash) to this shared datastore. This means that when your cluster grows, your datastore will grow with it. VSAN is what is called a scale-out storage system (adding hosts to a cluster), but it also allows scaling up (adding resources to a host).

Each host that wants to contribute storage capacity to the VSAN cluster will require at least one flash device and one capacity device (magnetic disk or flash). At a minimum, VSAN requires three hosts in your cluster to contribute storage (or two hosts if you decide to use a witness host, which is a common configuration for ROBO); other hosts in your cluster could leverage these storage resources without contributing storage resources to the cluster itself. Figure 1.5 shows a cluster that has four hosts, of which three (esxi-01, esxi-02, and esxi-03) contribute storage and a fourth does not contribute but only consumes storage resources. Although it is technically possible to have a non-uniform cluster and have a host not contributing storage, VMware highly recommend creating a uniform cluster and having all hosts contributing storage for overall better utilization, performance, and availability.

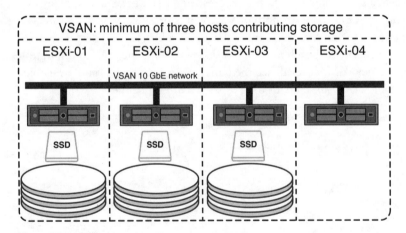

Figure 1.5   Nonuniform VSAN cluster example

Today's boundary for VSAN in terms of both size and connectivity is a vSphere cluster. This means that VSAN supports single cluster/datastores of up to 64 hosts, but of course a single vCenter Server instance can manage as many as 64 host clusters. It is a common practice for most customers, however, to limit their clusters to a maximum size of around 20 hosts. This is for operational considerations like the time it takes to update a full cluster. Each host can run a supported maximum of 200 VMs, allowing for a total combined of 6,400 VMs within a 64-host VSAN cluster. As you can imagine with a storage system at this scale, performance and responsiveness are of utmost importance. VSAN was designed to take advantage of flash to provide the experience that users expect in today's world. Flash resources are used for all writes, and depending on the type of hardware configuration used (all-flash or hybrid) reads will typically also be served from flash.

To ensure VMs can be deployed with certain characteristics, VSAN enables you to set policies on a per-virtual disk or a per-VM basis. These policies help you meet the defined service-level objectives (SLOs) for your workload. These can be performance-related characteristics such as read caching or disk striping, but can also be availability-related characteristics that ensure strategic replica placement of your VM's disks (and other important files).

If you have worked with VM storage policies in the past, you might now wonder whether all VMs stored on the same VSAN datastore will need to have the same VM storage policy assigned. The answer is no. VSAN allows you to have different policies for VMs provisioned to the same datastore and even different policies for disks from the same VM.

As stated earlier, by leveraging policies, the level of resiliency can be configured on a per-virtual disk granular level. How many hosts and disks a mirror copy will reside on depends on the selected policy. Because VSAN can use mirror copies (RAID-1) or erasure coding (RAID-5/6) defined by policy to provide resiliency, it does not require a local RAID set. In other words, hosts contributing to VSAN storage capacity should simply provide a set of disks to VSAN.

Whether you have defined a policy to tolerate a single host failure or, for instance, a policy that will tolerate up to three hosts failing, VSAN will ensure that enough replicas of your objects are created. The following example illustrates how this is an important aspect of VSAN and one of the major differentiators between VSAN and most other virtual storage solutions out there.

EXAMPLE: We have configured a policy that can tolerate one failure and created a new virtual disk. We have chosen to go with a number of failures to tolerate =1, which results in a RAID-1 configuration. This means that VSAN will create two identical storage objects and a witness. The witness is a component tied to the VM that allows VSAN to determine who should win ownership in the case of a failure. If you are familiar with clustering technologies, think of the witness as a quorum object that will arbitrate ownership in the event of a failure. Figure 1.6 may help clarify these sometimes-difficult-to-understand concepts. This figure illustrates what it would look like on a high level for a VM with a virtual disk that can tolerate one failure. This can be the failure of a host, NICs, disk, or flash device, for instance.

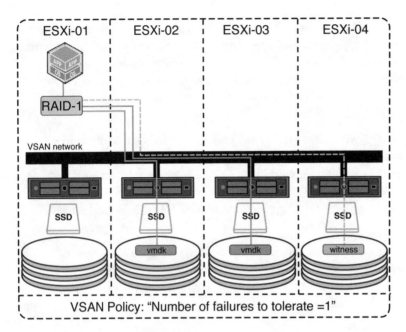

Figure 1.6   VSAN failures to tolerate

In Figure 1.6, the VM's compute resides on the first host (ESXi-01) and its virtual disks reside on the other hosts (ESXi-02 and ESXi-03) in the cluster. In this scenario, the VSAN network is used for storage I/O, allowing for the VM to freely move around the cluster without the need for storage components to be migrated with the compute. This does, however, result in the first requirement to implement VSAN. VSAN requires a minimum one dedicated 1 Gbps NIC port, but VMware recommends a 10 GbE for the VSAN network.

Yes, this might still sound complex, but in all fairness, VSAN masks away all the complexity, as you will learn as you progress through the various chapters in this book.

Summary

To conclude, vSphere Virtual SAN (VSAN) is a market leading, hypervisor-based distributed storage platform that enables convergence of compute and storage resources, typically referred to as hyper-converged software. It enables you to define VM-level granular SLOs through policy-based management. It allows you to control availability and performance in a way never seen before, simply and efficiently.

This chapter just scratched the surface. Now it's time to take it to the next level. Chapter 2 describes the requirements for installing and configuring VSAN.

## Chapter 2

VSAN Prerequisites and Requirements for Deployment

Before delving into the installation and configuration of virtual storage area network (VSAN), it is necessary to discuss the requirements and the prerequisites. VMware vSphere is the foundation of every VSAN-based virtual infrastructure.

VMware vSphere

VSAN was first released with VMware vSphere 5.5 U1. Additional versions of VSAN were released with VMware vSphere 6.0 (VSAN 6.0), VMware vSphere 6.0 U1 (VSAN 6.1), and VMware vSphere 6.0 U2 (VSAN 6.2). Each of these releases included additional VSAN features, which will be discussed at various stages of this book and were listed in Chapter 1, "Introduction to VSAN."

VMware vSphere consists of two major components: the vCenter Server management tool and the ESXi hypervisor. To install and configure VSAN, both vCenter Server and ESXi are required.

VMware vCenter Server provides a centralized management platform for VMware vSphere environments. It is the solution used to provision new virtual machines (VMs), configure hosts, and perform many other operational tasks associated with managing a virtualized infrastructure.

To run a fully supported VSAN environment, the vCenter Server 5.5 U1 platform is the minimum requirement, although VMware strongly recommends using the latest version of vSphere where possible. VSAN can be managed by both the Windows version of vCenter Server and the vCenter Server appliance (VCSA). VSAN is configured and monitored via the vSphere Web Client, and this also needs a minimum version of 5.5 U1 for support.

VSAN can also be fully configured and managed through the command-line interface (CLI) and the vSphere application programming interface (API) for those wanting to automate some (or all) of the aspects of VSAN configuration, monitoring, or management. Although a single cluster can contain only one VSAN datastore, a vCenter Server can manage multiple VSAN and compute clusters.

ESXi

VMware ESXi is an enterprise-grade virtualization product that allows you to run multiple instances of an operating system in a fully isolated fashion on a single server. It is a bare-metal solution, meaning that it does not require a guest-OS and has an extremely thin footprint. ESXi is the foundation for the large majority of virtualized environments worldwide.

For standard datacenter deployments, VSAN requires a minimum of three ESXi hosts (where each host has local storage and is contributing this storage to the VSAN datastore) to form a *supported* VSAN cluster. This is to allow the cluster to meet the minimum availability requirements of tolerating at least one host failure.

With VSAN 6.1 (released with vSphere 6.0 U1), VMware introduced the concept of a 2-node VSAN cluster primarily for remote office/branch office deployments. There are some additional considerations around the use of a 2-node VSAN cluster, including the concept of a witness host, which will be discussed in more detail in Chapter 8, "Stretched Clusters."

As of VSAN 6.0, a maximum of 64 ESXi hosts in a cluster are supported, a significant increase from the 32 hosts that were supported in the initial VSAN release that was part of vSphere 5.5; from here on will be referred to as VSAN 5.5. The ESXi hosts must be running version 6.0 at a minimum to support 64 hosts however.

At a minimum, it is recommended that a host must have at least 6 GB of memory. If you configure a host to contain the maximum number of disk groups, we recommend that the host be configured with a minimum of 32 GB of memory. VSAN does not consume all of this memory, but it is required for the maximum configuration. The VSAN host memory requirement is directly related to the number of physical disks in the host and the number of disk groups configured on the host. You will learn more about this in Chapter 9, "Designing a VSAN Cluster." In all cases we recommend to go with more than 32 GB per host to ensure that your workloads, VSAN, and the hypervisor have sufficient resources to ensure an optimal user experience.

Cache and Capacity Devices

With the release of VSAN 6.0, VMware introduced the new all-flash version of VSAN. VSAN was only available as a hybrid configuration with version 5.5. A hybrid configuration is where the cache tier is made up of flash-based devices and the capacity tier is made up of magnetic disks. In the all-flash version, both the cache tier and capacity tier are made up of flash devices. The flash devices of the cache and capacity tier are typically a different grade flash device in terms of performance and endurance. This allows you, under certain circumstances, to create all-flash configurations at the cost of SAS-based magnetic disk configurations.

ESXi Boot Considerations

When it comes to installing an ESXi for a VSAN-based infrastructure, there are various options to consider regarding where to place the ESXi image. ESXi can be installed on a local magnetic disk, USB flash drive, SD card, or SATADOM devices. Note that SATADOM support only appeared in VSAN 6.0; these devices were not supported in the initial VSAN release. At the time of writing (VSAN 6.2) stateless booting of ESXi (auto-deploy) is not supported. By deploying ESXi to a USB flash drive or SD card, you have the added advantage of not consuming a magnetic disk for the image. This disk can then be consumed by VSAN to create the distributed, shared VSAN datastore used for deploying VMs. However, there are some drawbacks to this approach, such as lack of space for storing log files and VSAN trace files.

For hosts with 512 GB or less memory, booting the ESXi image from USB/SD devices is supported. For hosts with a memory configuration larger than 512 GB, ESXi needs to be installed on a local disk or a SATADOM device. This is discussed in more detail in Chapter 10, "Troubleshooting, Monitoring, and Performance." When installing ESXi on USB or SD, note that you should use a device that has a minimum capacity of 8 GB.

If the host does not have USB/SD and a local disk is used to install ESXi, this disk cannot be part of a disk group and therefore cannot be used to contribute storage to the VSAN datastore. Therefore, in an environment where the number of disk slots is a constraint, it is recommended to use USB/SD or SATADOM.

VSAN Requirements

Before enabling VSAN, it is highly recommended that the vSphere administrator validates that the environment meets all the prerequisites and requirements. To enhance resilience, this list also includes recommendations from an infrastructure perspective:

- Minimum of three ESXi hosts for standard datacenter deployments. Minimum of two ESXi hosts and a witness host for the smallest deployment, for example, remote office/branch office.

- Minimum of 6 GB memory per host to install ESXi.

- VMware vCenter Server.

- At least one device for the capacity tier. One hard disk for hosts contributing storage to VSAN datastore in a hybrid configuration; one flash device for hosts contributing storage to VSAN datastore in an all-flash configuration.

- At least one flash device for the cache tier for hosts contributing storage to VSAN datastore, whether hybrid or all-flash.

- One boot device to install ESXi.

- At least one disk controller. Pass-through/JBOD mode capable disk controller preferred.

- Dedicated network port for VSAN–VMkernel interface. 10 GbE preferred, but 1 GbE supports smaller hybrid configurations. With 10 GbE, the adapter does not need to be dedicated to VSAN traffic, but can be shared with other traffic types, such as management traffic, vMotion traffic, etc.

- L2 or L3 multicast is required on the VSAN network.

VMware Hardware Compatibility Guide

Before installing and configuring ESXi, validate that your configuration is on the official VMware compatibility guide for VSAN, which you can find at the following website:

> http://vmwa.re/vsanhcl

With the release of VSAN 6.0, a new health check tool was made available which examines the state of your VSAN cluster, amongst other features. One of the health checks validates that your VSAN cluster disk controller hardware is supported as per the VMware compatibility guide. Administrators can download a file that contains the latest version of the hardware, driver, and firmware versions, and the health check tool verifies that the configuration is correct.

VSAN has strict requirements when it comes to disks, flash devices, and disk controllers. With all the various options, configuring the perfect VSAN host can be a complex exercise. Before reading about all the components, you will want to learn about an alternative: VSAN ready nodes.

VSAN Ready Nodes

VSAN ready nodes are a great alternative to manually selecting components. Ready nodes would also be the preferred way of building a VSAN configuration. Various vendors have gone through the exercise and created configurations that are called *VSAN ready nodes*.

These nodes consist of tested and certified hardware only and, in our opinion, provide an additional guarantee. VSAN ready nodes are also listed in the compatibility guide, as shown in Figure 2.1.

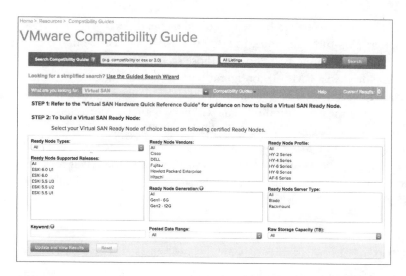

Figure 2.1   Virtual SAN ready nodes configurations

For the more adventurous types, or those who prefer a particular server model or vendor that is not currently listed in the VSAN ready nodes compatibility guide, some specifics for the various components, such as storage controllers and disk drives, must be called out. The sections that follow highlight these considerations in more detail.

Storage Controllers

Each ESXi host participating in the VSAN cluster requires a disk controller. It is recommended that this disk controller is capable of running in what is commonly referred to as *pass-through mode*, *HBA mode*, or *JBOD mode*. In other words, the disk controller should provide the capability to pass up the underlying magnetic disks and solid-state disks (SSDs) as individual disk drives without a layer of redundant array of inexpensive disks (RAID) sitting on top. The result of this is that ESXi can perform operations directly on the disk without those operations being intercepted and interpreted by the controller. VSAN will take care of any RAID configuration when policy attributes such as availability and performance for virtual machines are defined. The VSAN compatibility guide will call out the disk controllers that have successfully passed testing.

Every server vendor has many different disk controllers that can be selected when configuring a new server. The compatibility guide lists a number of controllers for the most commonly used server brands, as well as a couple of generic LSI disk controllers that are often used with brands like SuperMicro and Quanta. There are over 70 different disk controllers on the VSAN compatibility guide, providing an unlimited number of options in terms of hardware configurations.

In some scenarios, hardware may have already been acquired or the disk controllers that are available do not support pass-through mode. In other words, the devices behind these controllers are not directly visible to the ESXi host. In those scenarios, administrators must place each individual drive in a RAID-0 configuration and then the devices become visible to the ESXi host. However, you must ensure that this is a valid configuration for the controller. Once again, the compatibility guide will list whether a controller is supported in pass-through mode, RAID-0 mode, or indeed both. Make sure to validate the compatibility guide before configuring your disk controller in a specific way. Also note that the compatibility guide lists both the supported firmware and the driver for each individual disk controller. Validate these versions and upgrade if needed before deploying any virtual machines.

Disk Controller RAID-0

For disk controllers that do not support pass-through/HBA/JBOD mode, VSAN supports disk drives presented via a RAID-0 configuration. Volumes can be used by VSAN if they are created using a RAID-0 configuration that contains only a single drive. This needs to be done for both the magnetic disks and the SSDs. This can be done using the disk controller software/firmware. Administrators need to understand, however, that when SSDs are exposed to a VSAN leveraging a RAID-0 configuration, in many cases the drive is not recognized as a flash device because these characteristics are masked by the RAID-0 configuration. If this occurs, you will need to mark the drive as a flash device. This can be done via the vSphere Web Client. Simply select the device in question, and click on the appropriate disk services icon to toggle a device between SSD and hard disk drive (HDD), as shown in Figure 2.2.

There is also an example that shows how to address another common device presentation issue: how to mark a device as local. In some environments, devices can be recognized as shared volumes even though they are local to the ESXi host. This is because some SAS controllers allow devices to be accessed from more than one host. In this case, the devices, although local, are shown as shared (not local).

If you wish to mark a device as flash device, or mark a device as local, as of VSAN 6.0 this is now also possible via the vSphere Web Client, as shown in Figure 2.2. Depending on the type of device and how it is currently marked, the menu and the icons will change accordingly. Note that it is only possible to use this functionality when the appropriate license key has been entered.

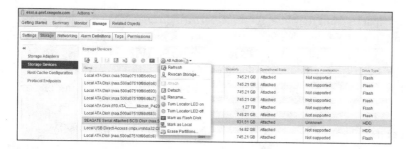

Figure 2.2 Marking Storage Devices

When using RAID-0 instead of pass-through, you must take into consideration certain operational impacts. When pass-through is used, drives are (in most scenarios) instantly recognized, and there is no need to configure the drives as local/SSD. On top of that, when a RAID-0 set is used, the drive is bound to that RAID-0 configuration. This means that the RAID-0 set has a 1:1 relationship with a given drive. If this drive fails and needs to be replaced with a new drive, this relationship is broken and a new RAID-0 set with a new drive must be manually created. The effort involved will differ per RAID controller used, whereas with a disk controller in pass-through mode, replacing the drive is a matter of removing and inserting. However, depending on the RAID controller, vendor-specific tools might be required to make the device "active" once more. In fact, new RAID-0 volumes may have to be created to allow VSAN to consume the replacement device.

Performance and RAID Caching

VMware has carried out many performance tests using various types of disk controllers and RAID controllers. In most cases, the performance difference between pass-through and RAID-0 configurations was negligible. The VMware compatibility guide for VSAN lists the functionality that should be enabled or disabled per controller.

When utilizing RAID-0 configurations, you should disable the storage controllers write cache so as to provide VSAN full control. When the storage controller cache cannot be completely disabled in a RAID-0 configuration, you should configure the storage controller cache for 100% read cache, effectively disabling the write cache. The main reason for this is because VSAN has its own caching mechanism and we want to ensure that IOs which are acknowledged back to the guest OS has actually been stored on persistent storage (write buffer) rather than stored on disk controller cache which is outside of what VSAN controls.

Capacity Tier Devices

Each ESXi host that is participating in a hybrid VSAN cluster and contributing storage to the VSAN datastore must have at least one capacity device. Additional capacity devices will obviously increase capacity, and may also increase performance as VM storage objects can be striped across multiple devices. Also for consideration, a higher number of capacity devices will lead to a larger number of capacity balancing options. When a disk has reached 80% of its capacity VSAN will automatically try to move components on that disk to other disks in the host, or disks on other hosts, to prevent that disk from running out of capacity.

For ESXi hosts that are participating in an all-flash VSAN configuration, flash devices are also used for the capacity tier.

Each capacity tier device will be part of a disk group. At most, a VSAN host can have five disk groups, each containing seven capacity devices, resulting in a maximum of 35 capacity devices, as depicted in Figure 2.3.

VSAN supports various types of magnetic disks, ranging from SATA 7200 RPM up to SAS 15K RPM, and these are listed on the compatibility guide. A large portion of VM storage I/O performance will be met by flash devices in the cache tier, but note that any I/O that needs to come from the capacity tier will be bound by the performance characteristics of those devices. A 7200 RPM SATA magnetic disk will provide a different experience than a high performance flash device, but usually will also come at a different price point, depending on the hardware vendor used. Chapter 9 provides various examples that demonstrate the impact of choosing magnetic disk devices and also provides an example of an all-flash configuration.

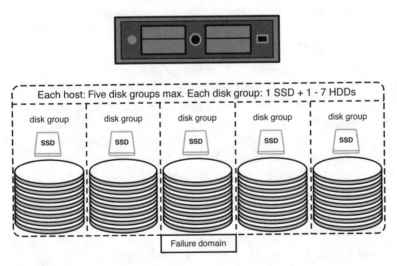

Figure 2.3   Maximum disks and disk group configuration

Cache Tier Devices

Each ESXi host, whether it is in a hybrid configuration or an all-flash configuration, must have at least one flash device when that host is contributing capacity to a VSAN cluster. This flash device, in hybrid configurations, is utilized by VSAN as both a write buffer and a read cache. In an all-flash configuration, the flash device acts as a write cache only but tends to have a much higher endurance specification than the capacity tier flash devices. There is no need for a dedicated read cache in all-flash configurations, since reading from the capacity tier (which is also flash) is extremely fast.

The flash cache device in VSAN sits in front of a group of capacity devices. Each disk group requires one flash device. Because VSAN can have a maximum of five disk groups per host, the maximum number of flash devices per host used for the cache tier is also five. The more flash capacity in a host, the greater will be the performance, because more I/O can be cached/buffered.

For the best VSAN performance, choose a high specification flash device. VMware supports various types of flash, ranging from SSDs to PCIe flash devices. VMware has published a list of supported PCIe flash devices, SSDs, and NVMe devices in the VMware compatibility guide. Before procuring new equipment, review the VMware compatibility guide to ensure that your configuration is a supported configuration.

The designated flash device performance classes specified within the VMware compatibility guide are as follows:

- ~~Class A: 2,500–5,000 writes per second~~ (no longer on the VCG)
- **Class B:** 5,000–10,000 writes per second
- **Class C**: 10,000–20,000 writes per second
- **Class D**: 20,000–30,000 writes per second
- **Class D**: 30,000–100,000 writes per second
- **Class E**: 100,000+ writes per second

This question often arises: "Can I use a consumer grade SSD and will VSAN work?" From a technical point of view, VSAN works perfectly fine with a consumer grade SSD; however, in most cases, consumer-grade SSDs have much lower endurance guarantees, different (lower) performance characteristics, unpredictable latency spikes ranging from milliseconds to seconds, and this is the main reason why Class A devices have been removed from the compatibility guide. Although it might be attractive from a price point to use a consumer-grade SSD, we like to stress that VSAN is dependent on flash for both buffering and caching; when your drive fails, this will impact the disk group to which this SSD is bound. When the flash device fails, the disk group is marked as unhealthy. This brings us to the second important column on the compatibility guide page, which is the flash device endurance class, which is as follows:

- **Class A**: >= 365 TBW

- **Class B**: >= 1825 TBW

- **Class C**: >= 3650 TBW

- **Class D**: >= 7300 TBW

The higher the class, the more reliable and longer the lifetime of the average device in this case. For those who are not aware, TBW stands for "terrabytes written" and is the number of writes the device is guaranteed to be able to endure.

After having looked at the various SSDs and PCIe flash devices, we have concluded that it is almost impossible to recommend a brand or type of flash to use. This decision should be driven by the budgetary constraints, server platform vendor support, and more importantly by the requirements of the applications that you plan to deploy in your VMs running on VSAN.

Network Requirements

This section covers the requirements and prerequisites from a networking perspective for VSAN. VSAN is a distributed storage solution and therefore heavily leans on the network for intra-host communication. Consistency and reliability are the keys.

Network Interface Cards

Each ESXi host must have at least one 1 GbE network interface card (NIC) dedicated to VSAN hybrid configurations. For all-flash configurations, 10 GbE NICs are required. However, as a best practice, VMware and the authors of this book are recommending 10 GbE NICs for all configurations. For redundancy, you can configure a team of NICs on a per-host basis. We consider this as a best practice, but it is not necessary to build a fully functional VSAN cluster.

Supported Virtual Switch Types

VSAN is supported on both VMware vSphere Distributed Switches (VDS) and VMware standard switches (VSS). There are some advantages to using a Distributed Switch that will be covered in Chapter 3, "VSAN Installation and Configuration." No other virtual switch types have been explicitly tested with VSAN. A license for the use of VDS is included with Virtual SAN.

Layer 2 or Layer 3

VSAN is supported over layer 2 (L2) (switched) or layer 3 (L3) (routed) networks. In the initial release, there was no L3 support. However, full support for L3 was introduced in version 6.0. Do note that VSAN relies on the availability of multicast traffic. This means that in both cases (L2 and L3) multicast traffic will need to be allowed and, in the case of L3, it must also be routed between the networks. We have noticed during the many conversations we have had with customers over the past 2 years that multicast traffic is usually not allowed by default, so make sure to talk to your networking team before configuring VSAN.

VMkernel Network

On each ESXi host that wants to participate in a VSAN cluster, a VMkernel port for VSAN communication must be created. The VMkernel port is labeled Virtual SAN traffic and was introduced in vSphere 5.5. This VMkernel port is used for intra-cluster node communication. It is also used for reads and writes when one of the ESXi hosts in the cluster owns a particular VM, but the actual data blocks that make up the VM files are located on a different ESXi host in the cluster. In this case, I/O will need to traverse the network configured between the hosts in the cluster, as depicted in Figure 2.4, where VMkernel interface vmk2 is used for VSAN traffic by all the hosts in the VSAN cluster. The VM residing on ESXi-01 does all of its reads and writes leveraging the VSAN network.

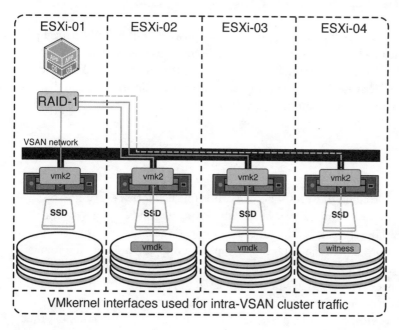

Figure 2.4 VSAN traffic

VSAN Network Traffic

The protocol used by VSAN is a proprietary protocol. VMware has not published a specification of the protocol. This is similar to the approach taken for other VMware products and features such as vMotion, Fault Tolerance, vSphere Replication, and other VMware proprietary protocols, where VMware deems the information proprietary. The VSAN network is used for three different traffic types. It is important to know these because they introduce a requirement for your physical network switch configuration:

- **Multicast heartbeats:** These are used to discover all participating VSAN hosts in the cluster, as well as to determine the state of a host. Compared to other traffic types, multicast heartbeats generate very few packets.

- **Multicast and unicast packets from the clustering service (CMMDS):** This traffic does metadata updates like object placement and statistics. These generate more network traffic than the heartbeats, but it's still a very small percentage.

- **Storage traffic (e.g., reads, writes):** This is the majority of network traffic. Any host within the cluster can talk to any other host over unicast.

To ensure that VSAN hosts can communicate properly, it is required that multicast traffic is enabled on the physical switch. If multicast communication is not possible between the ESXi hosts in the VSAN cluster over the VSAN traffic network, the VSAN cluster will not form correctly.

Although multicast is just a small percentage of the total network traffic, it is a critical part. The majority of traffic in a VSAN cluster will be storage traffic as storage read and write I/O go over the network. Ensuring optimal network bandwidth is important. VMware recommends that physical switches that support real multicast traffic are used and that lower-end switches that convert the multicast traffic into broadcast traffic be avoided, if possible.

Jumbo Frames

Jumbo frames are supported on the VSAN network. It is our belief that every VSAN deployment is different, both from a server hardware perspective and from a network hardware perspective. Therefore, it is difficult to recommend for or against the use of jumbo frames. In addition, there is an operational impact in implementing jumbo frames on non greenfield sites. When jumbo frames are not consistently configured end-to-end, network problems may occur. Tests have been conducted to prove the benefits of jumbo frames, but results so far have been inconclusive. In some scenarios, a performance improvement of 15% is measured and a decrease of CPU utilization is observed. In other scenarios, no performance increase or CPU utilization decrease has been measured.

In an operationally mature environment where a consistent implementation can be guaranteed, the use of jumbo frames is left to the administrator's discretion.

NIC Teaming

Another potential way of optimizing network performance is teaming of NICs. NIC teaming in ESXi is transparent to VSAN. You can team NICs in various ways. To allow VSAN to use multiple physical NIC ports, it is possible to implement either physical teaming (LACP) or create multiple VSAN VMkernel interfaces. Chapter 3 covers the configuration details and parameters in more detail. Note, however, that there is no guarantee that VSAN network traffic will be able to utilize the full bandwidth of multiple physical NICs at the same time; various factors play a part, including the size of the cluster, the number of NICs, and the number of different IP addresses used.

Network I/O Control

Although it is recommended to use 10 GbE NICs, there is no requirement to solely dedicate these cards to the VSAN network. NICs can be shared with other traffic types; however, you might consider using network I/O control (NIOC) to ensure that the VSAN traffic is guaranteed a certain amount of bandwidth over the network in the case where congestion of the network arises. This is especially true if a 10 GbE NIC is shared with (for instance) vMotion traffic, which is infamous for utilizing all available bandwidth when possible. NIOC requires the creation of a VDS because NIOC is not available with VSS. Luckily, the Distributed Switch is included with the VSAN license.

Chapter 3 provides various examples of how NIOC can be configured for the various types of network configurations.

VSAN Stretched Cluster

VSAN stretched cluster functionality was introduced with VSAN 6.1. This feature allows virtual machine components to be deployed across sites in different data centers, and if one site or data center fails, virtual machines can be restarted on the surviving site. There are a number of considerations to take into account for VSAN stretched cluster, including latency and bandwidth, not only between the data center sites, but also to the witness site. These will be covered in greater detail in the *VSAN Stretched Cluster* section, later in this book (Chapter 8), but we will list some of the basic guidelines here for your convenience:

- Maximum of 5 ms RTT latency between data sites (requirement)
- Maximum of 200 ms RTT between data sites and the witness site (requirement)

- 10 Gbps between data sites
- 100 Mbps from data sites to witness site

VSAN 2-Node Remote Office/Branch Office (ROBO)

In much the same way as there are specific network requirement for VSAN stretched cluster, there are also network requirements around latency and bandwidth for 2-node ROBO deployments. With VSAN 6.1, 2-node/ROBO configurations were also introduced. For ROBO configurations the following general guidelines apply:

- Maximum of 500 ms RTT between ROBO location and central witness (requirement)
- 1 Mbps from ROBO location to central witness
- 1 Gbps network connection between hosts on ROBO location

Firewall Ports

When you are enabling VSAN, a number of ESXi firewall ports are automatically opened (both ingoing and outgoing) on each ESXi host that participates in the VSAN cluster. The ports are used for inter-cluster host communication and for communication with the storage provider on the ESXi hosts. Table 2.1 provides a list of VSAN-specific network ports. Let it be clear that 98% (or more) of all traffic in a VSAN cluster will be RDT traffic on port 2233.

Table 2.1 ESXi Ports and Protocols Opened by VSAN

Name	Port	Protocol
Cmmds	12345, 23451	UDP
RDT	2233	TCP
Vsanvp	8080	TCP
Health check	443	TCP

Summary

Although configuring VSAN literally takes a couple of clicks, it is important to take the time to ensure that all requirements are met and to ensure that all prerequisites are in place. A stable storage platform starts at the foundation, the infrastructure on which it is enabled. Before moving on to Chapter 3, you should run through this checklist to confirm that all requirements have been met:

- vSphere 6.0 U2 recommended.

- Three hosts minimum.

- 6 GB memory per host minimum, 32 GB recommended minimum.

- When exceeding 512 GB of host memory, it is required to install ESXi on magnetic disk. USB flash drives or SD cards are not supported.

- Certified disk controller.

- At least one certified flash device per host for caching.

- At least one certified magnetic drive or flash device per host for capacity.

- Dedicated 1 GbE NIC port or shared 10 GbE NIC port for VSAN.

- Multicast enabled on VSAN network (layer 2 or layer 3).

The following list identifies additional recommendations, which are not requirements for a fully functional VSAN but which might be desirable from a production standpoint:

- Network switch redundancy for VSAN

- NIC redundancy for VSAN

- Jumbo frames consistently implemented end-to-end

- NIOC to provide QoS to VSAN traffic

VSAN Installation and Configuration

This chapter describes in detail the installation and configuration process, as well as all initial preparation steps that you might need to consider before proceeding with a virtual storage area network (VSAN) cluster deployment. You will find information on how to correctly set up network and storage devices, as well as some helpful tips and tricks on how to deploy the most optimal VSAN configuration.

VSAN Networking

Network connectivity is the heart of any VSAN cluster. VSAN cluster hosts use the network for virtual machine (VM) I/O and also communicate their state between one another. Consistent and correct network configuration is key to a successful VSAN deployment. Because the majority of disk I/O will either come from a remote host, or will need to go to a remote host, VMware recommends leveraging a 10 GbE infrastructure. Note that although 1 GbE is fully supported in hybrid configurations, it could become a bottleneck in large-scale deployments.

VMware vSphere provides two different types of virtual switch, both of which are fully supported with VSAN:

- The VMware standard virtual switch (VSS) provides connectivity from VMs and VMkernel ports to external networks but is local to an ESXi host.

- A vSphere Distributed Switch (VDS) gives central control of virtual switch administration across multiple ESXi hosts. A VDS can also provide additional networking features over and above what a VSS can offer, such as network I/O control (NIOC) that can provide quality of service (QoS) on your network. Although a VDS normally requires a particular vSphere edition, VSAN includes a VDS independent license of the vSphere edition you are running.

VMkernel Network for VSAN

All ESXi hosts participating in a VSAN network need to communicate with one another. A new VMkernel type called Virtual SAN traffic was introduced in vSphere 5.5. A VSAN cluster will not successfully form until a VSAN–VMkernel port is available on each ESXi host participating in the VSAN cluster. The vSphere administrator must create a VSAN–VMkernel port on each ESXi host in the cluster before the VSAN cluster forms (see Figure 3.1).

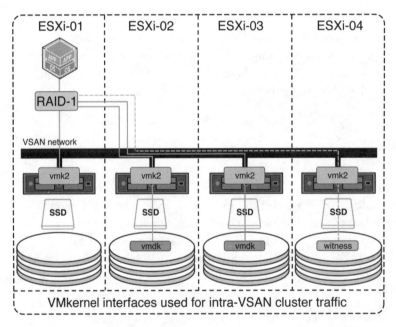

Figure 3.1   VMkernel interfaces used for intra-VSAN cluster traffic

Without a VMkernel network for VSAN, the cluster will not form successfully. If communication is not possible between the ESXi hosts in the VSAN cluster, only one ESXi host will join the VSAN cluster. Other ESXi hosts will not be able to join. This will still result in a single VSAN datastore, but each host can only see itself as part of that datastore. A warning message will display when there are communication difficulties between ESXi hosts in the cluster. If the cluster is created before the VMkernel ports are created, a warning message is also displayed regarding communication difficulties between the ESXi hosts. Once the VMkernel ports are created and communication is established, the cluster will form successfully.

VSAN Network Configuration: VMware Standard Switch

With a VSS, creating a port group for VSAN network traffic is relatively straightforward. By virtue of installing an ESXi host, a VSS is automatically created to carry ESXi network management traffic and VM traffic. You can use an already-existing standard switch and its associated uplinks to external networks to create a new VMkernel port for VSAN traffic. Alternatively, you may choose to create a new standard switch for the VSAN network traffic VMkernel port (see Figure 3.2) by selecting some new uplinks for the new standard switch.

Figure 3.2   Add networking wizard: virtual switch selection/creation

In this example, we have decided to create a new standard switch or vSwitch. As you progress through the "add networking" wizard, after selecting the appropriate uplinks for this new standard switch, you will get to the port properties shown in Figure 3.3. This is where the appropriate network service for the VMkernel port is selected. For VSAN the "Virtual SAN traffic" service should be enabled.

Figure 3.3   Enabling the Virtual SAN traffic service on a port

Complete the wizard and you will have a standard switch configured with a VMkernel port group to carry the VSAN traffic. Of course, this step will have to be repeated for every ESXi host in the VSAN cluster.

VSAN Network Configuration: vSphere Distributed Switch

In the case of a VDS, a distributed port group needs to be configured to carry the VSAN traffic. Once the distributed port group is created, VMkernel interfaces on the individual ESXi hosts can then be created to use that distributed port group. The sections that follow describe this process in greater detail.

Step 1: Create the Distributed Switch

Although the official VMware documentation makes no distinction regarding which versions of Distributed Switch you should be using, the authors recommend using the latest version of the Distributed Switch with VSAN. This is the version that the authors used in their VSAN tests. Note that all ESXi hosts attaching to this Distributed Switch must be running the same version of ESXi when a given Distributed Switch version has been selected, preferably the version of the selected Distributed Switch should be the same as the ESXi/vSphere version. Earlier versions of ESXi will not be able to utilize this Distributed Switch.

One of the steps when creating a Distributed Switch is to check whether NIOC is enabled or disabled. We recommend leaving this at the default option of enabled. Later on, we discuss the value of NIOC in a VSAN environment.

Step 2: Create a Distributed Port Group

The steps to create a distributed port group are relatively straightforward:

1. Using the vSphere Web Client, navigate to the VDS object in the vCenter Server inventory.

2. Select the option to create a new distributed port group.

3. Provide a name for the distributed port group.

4. Set the characteristics of the port group, such as the type VLAN, the VLAN ID, the type of binding, allocation, and the number of ports that can be attached to the port group, as shown in Figure 3.4.

Figure 3.4   Distributed port group settings

One important consideration with the creation of the port group is the port allocation settings and the number of ports associated with the port group. Note that the default number of ports is eight and that the allocation setting is elastic by default. This means that when all ports are assigned, a new set of eight ports is created. A port group with an allocation type of elastic can automatically increase the number of ports as more devices are allocated. With the port binding set to static, a port is assigned to the VMkernel port when it connects to the distributed port group. If you plan to have a 16-host or larger VSAN cluster, you could consider configuring a greater number of ports for the port group instead of the default of eight. This means that in times of maintenance and outages, the ports always stay available for the host until such time as it is ready to rejoin the cluster, and it means that the switch doesn't incur any overhead by having to delete and re-add the ports.

When creating a Distributed Switch and distributed port groups, there are a lot of additional options to choose from, such as port binding type. These options are well documented in the official VMware vSphere documentation, and although we discussed port allocation in a little detail here, most of the settings are beyond the scope of this book. Readers who are unfamiliar with these options can find explanations in the official VMware vSphere documentation. However, you can simply leave these Distributed Switch and port groups at the default settings and VSAN will deploy just fine with those settings.

Step 3: Build VMkernel Ports

Once the distributed port group has been created, you can now proceed with building the VMkernel ports on the ESXi hosts. The first step when adding networking to an ESXi host is to select an appropriate connection type. For VSAN network traffic, **VMkernel network adapter** is the connection type, as shown in Figure 3.5.

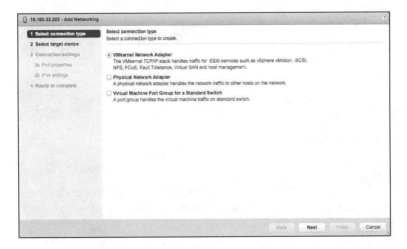

Figure 3.5 VMkernel connection type

The next step is to select the correct port group or distributed port group with which to associate this VMkernel network adapter. We have previously created a distributed port group, so we select that distributed port group, as shown in Figure 3.7.

Once the distributed port group has been selected, it is now time to select the appropriate connection settings for this VMkernel port. In the first part of the connection
settings, the port properties are populated. This is where the services associated
with the VMkernel port are selected. In this case, we are creating a VMkernel port
for VSAN traffic, so that would be the service that should be selected, as shown in
Figure 3.8. By default, there are three TCP/IP stacks to choose from when creating
a VMkernel adapter. However, only one TCP/IP stack, namely the default TCP/IP
stack, can be used for the VSAN network. The TCP/IP provisioning stack can only
be used for provisioning traffic and the vMotion TCP/IP stack can only be used for
vMotion. You will not be able to select these stacks for virtual SAN traffic. Options
for configuring different network stacks may be found in official VMware documentation and are beyond the scope of this book, but suffice to say that different network
stacks can be configured on the ESXi host and have different properties such as default
gateways associated with each network stack. The different TCP/IP stacks are shown in
Figure 3.6.

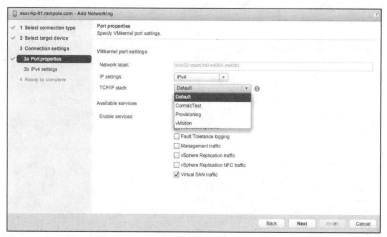

Figure 3.6   VMkernel

Currently there is no dedicated TCP/IP stack for Virtual SAN traffic. There is also
no support for the creation of a customer Virtual SAN TCP/IP stack. During normal
VSAN configurations, this does not need consideration. However, when stretched
clusters are discussed in Chapter 8, we will talk about virtual SAN network considerations in more detail, and how ESXi hosts in a stretched VSAN cluster can communicate
over L3 networks.

Figure 3.7   VMkernel target device

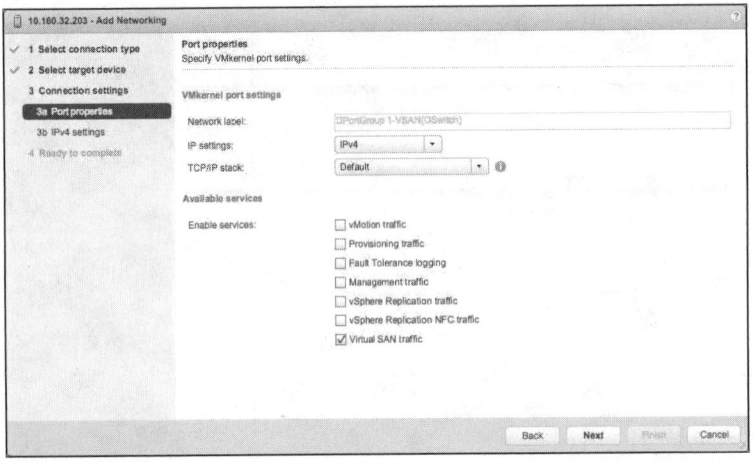

Figure 3.8   VMkernel port properties

Once the correct service (**Virtual SAN traffic**) has been chosen, the next step is to populate the IPv4 settings of the VMkernel adapter, as shown in Figure 3.9. IPv6 is fully supported as of VSAN 6.2. You have two options available for both IPv4 and IPv6 settings: DHCP or static. The dynamic host configuration protocol (DHCP) is a standardized network protocol that is used to provide network configuration details to other devices over the network. If DHCP is chosen, a valid DHCP server needs to exist on the network to provide valid IPv4/IPv6 information to the ESXi host for this VMkernel port. In this example, we have chosen to go with a static IPv4 configuration, as that is most common, so a valid IP address and subnet mask must be provided.

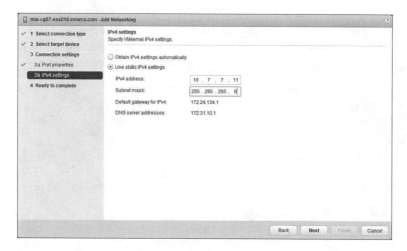

Figure 3.9   VMkernel IPv4 settings

With all the details provided for the VMkernel port, you can double-check the configuration before finally creating the port, as illustrated in Figure 3.10.

This VMkernel port configuration must be repeated for each of the ESXi hosts in the VSAN cluster. When this configuration is complete, the network configuration is now in place to allow for the successful formation of the VSAN cluster.

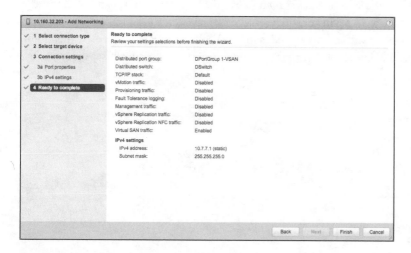

Figure 3.10   VMkernel ready to complete

Possible Network Configuration Issues

If the VSAN VMkernel is not properly configured, a warning will be displayed in the Virtual
SAN > health section on the monitor tab of your VSAN cluster object. If you click the
warning for the particular tests that have failed, further details related to the network status
of all hosts in the cluster will display, as shown in Figure 3.11. In this scenario a single host in
an eight-host cluster is part of a different IP subnet, causing connectivity issues as expected.

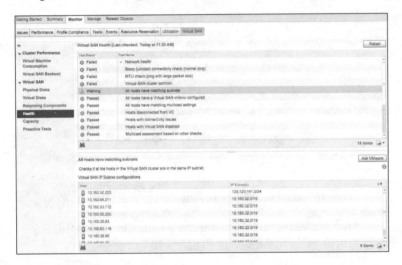

Figure 3.11   Network configuration warning

For VSAN 6.1 and earlier versions, another place to observe VSAN communication issues is
in the summary view of the ESXi host, as shown in Figure 3.12. If the host cannot communicate with the rest of the VSAN cluster, the message displayed in the summary tab reads:
"Host cannot communicate with all other nodes in the VSAN enabled cluster." At this point,
you need to revisit the VMkernel port properties and ensure that it has been set up correctly.

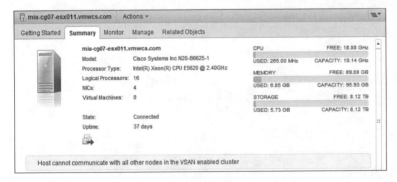

Figure 3.12   Host cannot communicate

Another issue that has surprised a number of customers is the reliance on multicast traffic. One of the requirements for VSAN is to allow multicast traffic on the VSAN network between the ESXi hosts participating in the VSAN cluster; however, multicast is used only for relatively infrequent operations. For example, multicast is used for the initial discovery of hosts in the VSAN cluster and for the ongoing "liveness" checks among the hosts in the cluster.

So, how does this lack of multicast support on the network manifest itself? Well, what you will see after enabling VSAN on the cluster is that a warning is shown on a cluster level. If you go to Virtual SAN > health section on the monitor tab of your VSAN cluster object and look at the network health test, it will display a warning on "Multicast assessment based on other checks" and/or "All hosts have matching multicast settings," even though you can ping/vmkping all the VSAN interfaces on all the hosts. Another symptom is that you may find multiple single host VSAN clusters formed, with a single ESXi host in its own unique cluster partition.

How do you resolve it? Well, a number of our VSAN customers discussed some options on the VMware community forum for VSAN, and these were the recommendations:

- **Option 1**: Disable internet group management protocol (IGMP) snooping for the VSAN traffic VLAN. Now this will allow *all* multicast traffic through; but if the only traffic is VSAN, this should be a negligible amount of traffic and should be safe to use.

- **Option 2**: Configure IGMP snooping querier. If there is other multicast traffic and you are concerned that disabling IGMP snooping might open the network up to a flood of multicast traffic, this is a preferred option.

Customers who ran into this situation stated that both methods worked for them; however, we recommend that you refer to your switch provider documentation on how to handle multicast configurations. Some switches convert multicasts to broadcasts, and the packets will be sent to all ports. VMware recommends that customers should avoid using these switches with VSAN if at all possible. The smarter switches that use IGMP snooping have the capability to send the multicast packets on ports where the multicast has been requested, and these switches are more desirable in VSAN deployments. The reason for this recommendation is that simple switches that turn multicast traffic into broadcast traffic can flood a network and affect other non-VSAN hosts attached to the switch.

One final point is to explain how you can figure out which host or hosts are partitioned from the cluster. The easiest way is to use the disk management view under the VSAN manage tab and then the disk groups view. This contains a column called network partition groups. This column will show a group number to highlight which partition a particular host resides in. If the cluster is successfully formed and all hosts are communicating, all hosts in this view will have the same network partition number as shown in the example in Figure 3.13. Note that it also shows whether the hosts are healthy and currently connected to the VSAN cluster.

Figure 3.13   Network partition group

Network I/O Control Configuration Example

As previously mentioned, NIOC can be used to guarantee bandwidth for VSAN cluster communication and I/O. NIOC is available only on VDS, not on VSS. Indeed, VDS is only available with some of the higher vSphere editions; however, VSAN includes VDS irrespective of the vSphere edition used.

If you are using an earlier version of a Distributed Switch prior to your vSphere version, although not explicitly called out in the vSphere documentation, we recommend upgrading to the most recent version of the Distributed Switch if you plan to use it with VSAN. This is simply a cautionary recommendation as we did all of our VSAN testing with the most recent version of Distributed Switch.

As of vSphere 5.5, NIOC has a traffic type called *Virtual SAN traffic*, and thus provides QoS on VSAN traffic. Although this QoS configuration might not be necessary in most VSAN cluster environments, it is a good feature to have available if VSAN traffic appears to be impacted by other traffic types sharing the same 10 GbE network interface card (NIC). An example of a traffic type that could impact VSAN is *vMotion*. By its very nature, vMotion traffic is "bursty" and might claim the full available bandwidth on a NIC port, impacting other traffic types sharing the NIC, including VSAN traffic. Leveraging NIOC in those situations will avoid a self-imposed denial-of-service (DoS) attack.

Setting up NIOC is quite straightforward, and once configured it will guarantee a certain bandwidth for the VSAN traffic between all hosts. NIOC is enabled by default when a VDS is created. If the feature was disabled during the initial creation of the Distributed Switch, it may be enabled once again by editing the Distributed Switch properties via the vSphere Web Client. To begin with, use the vSphere Web Client to select the VDS in the vCenter Server inventory. From there, navigate to the manage tab and select the resource allocation view. This displays the NIOC configuration options, as shown in Figure 3.14.

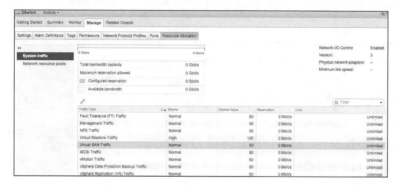

Figure 3.14   NIOC resource allocation

To change the resource allocation for the VSAN traffic in NIOC, simply edit the properties of the VSAN traffic network resource pool. Figure 3.15 shows the modifiable configuration options.

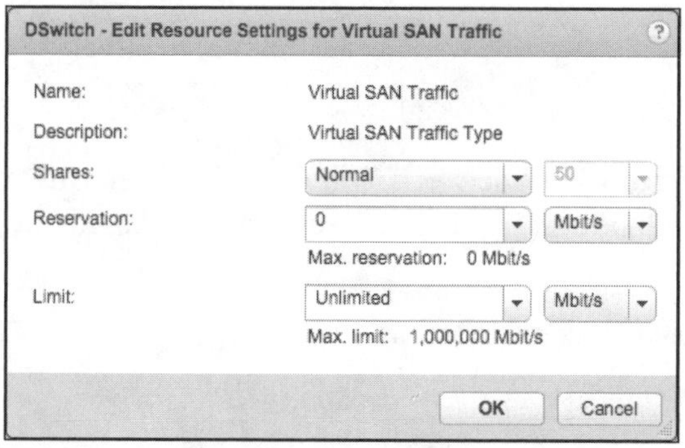

Figure 3.15   NIOC configuration

By default, the limit is set to unlimited, physical adapter shares are set to 50, and there is no reservation. The unlimited value means that VSAN network traffic is allowed to consume all the network bandwidth when there is no congestion. With a reservation you can configure the minimum bandwidth that needs to be available for this particular traffic stream, which must not exceed 75% of available bandwidth. We recommend leaving this untouched and prefer using the shares mechanism. If congestion arises, the physical adapter shares come into place. These shares are compared with the share values assigned to other traffic types to determine which traffic type gets priority.

With VSAN deployments, VMware is recommending a 10 GbE network infrastructure. In these deployments, two 10 GbE network ports are usually used, and are connected to two physical 10 GbE capable switches to provide availability. The various types of traffic will need to share this network capacity, and this is where NIOC can prove invaluable.

We do not recommend setting a limit on the VSAN traffic. The reason for this is because a limit is a "hard" setting. In other words, if a 2 Gbps limit is configured on VSAN traffic, the traffic will be limited even when additional bandwidth is available on the network. Therefore, you should not use limits because of this behavior. Instead, you should use shares and "artificially limit" your traffic types based on resource usage and demand.

Design Considerations: Distributed Switch and Network I/O Control

To provide QoS and performance predictability, VSAN and NIOC should go hand in hand. Before discussing the configuration options, the following types of networks are being considered:

- Management network
- vMotion network
- Virtual SAN network
- VM network

This design consideration assumes 10 GbE redundant networking links and a redundant switch pair for availability. Two scenarios will be described. These scenarios are based on the type of network switch used:

1. Redundant 10 GbE switch setup *without* "link aggregation" capability
2. Redundant 10 GbE switch setup *with* "link aggregation" capability

NOTE

Link aggregation (IEEE 802.3ad) allows users to use more than one connection between network devices. It basically combines multiple physical connections into one logical connection, and provides a level of redundancy and bandwidth improvement.

In both configurations, recommended practice dictates that you create the following port groups and VMkernel interfaces:

- 1 × management network VMkernel interface
- 1 × vMotion VMkernel interface (with all interfaces in the same subnet)

- 1 × VSAN VMkernel interface
- 1 × VM port group

To simplify the configuration, you should have a single VSAN and vMotion VMkernel interface.

To ensure traffic types are separated on different physical ports, we will leverage standard Distributed Switch capabilities. We will also show how to use shares to avoid noisy neighbor scenarios.

Scenario 1: Redundant 10 GbE Switch Without "Link Aggregation" Capability

In this configuration, two individual 10 GbE uplinks are available. It is recommended to separate traffic and designate a single 10 GbE uplink to VSAN for simplicity reasons. The recommended minimum amount of bandwidth per traffic type is as follows:

- **Management network**: 1 GbE
- **vMotion VMkernel interface**: 5 GbE
- **VM network**: 2 GbE
- **VSAN VMkernel interface**: 10 GbE

Various traffic types will share the same uplink. The management network, VM network, and vMotion network traffic are configured to share uplink 1, and VSAN traffic is configured to use uplink 2. With the network configuration done this way, sufficient bandwidth exists for all the various types of traffic when the VSAN cluster is in a normal or standard operating state.

To make sure that no single traffic type can impact other traffic types during times of contention, NIOC is configured, and the shares mechanism is deployed.

When defining traffic type network shares, this scenario works under the assumption that there is only one physical port available and that all traffic types share that same physical port for this exercise.

This scenario also takes a worst-case scenario approach into consideration. This will guarantee performance even when a failure has occurred. By taking this approach, we can ensure that VSAN always has 50% of the bandwidth at its disposal while leaving the remaining traffic types with sufficient bandwidth to avoid a potential self-inflicted DoS.

Table 3.1 outlines the recommendations for configuring shares for the traffic types.

Table 3.1   Recommended Share Configuration by Traffic Type (Scenario 1)

Traffic Type	Shares	Limit
Management Network	20	N/A
vMotion VMkernel Interface	50	N/A
VM Port Group	30	N/A
Virtual SAN VMkernel Interface	100	N/A

When selecting the uplinks used for the various types of traffic, you should separate traffic types to provide predictability and avoid noisy neighbor scenarios. The following configuration is recommended:

- Management network VMkernel interface = Explicit failover order = Uplink 1 active/Uplink 2 standby

- vMotion VMkernel interface = Explicit failover order = Uplink 1 active/Uplink 2 standby

- VM port group = Explicit failover order = Uplink 1 active/Uplink 2 standby

- Virtual SAN VMkernel interface = Explicit failover order = Uplink 2 active/Uplink 1 standby

Setting an explicit failover order in the teaming and failover section of the port groups is recommended for predictability (see Figure 3.16). The explicit failover order always uses the highest-order uplink from the list of active adapters that passes failover detection criteria.

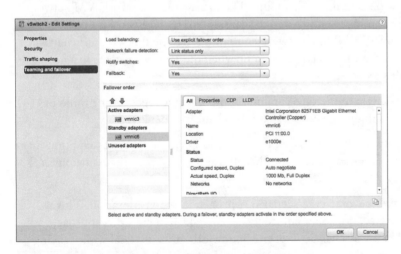

Figure 3.16   Using explicit failover order

Separating traffic types allows for optimal storage performance while also providing sufficient bandwidth for the vMotion and VM traffic (see Figure 3.17). Although this could also be achieved by using the load-based teaming (LBT) mechanism, note that the LBT load balancing period is 30 seconds, potentially causing a short period of contention when "bursty" traffic share the same uplinks. Also note that when troubleshooting network issues arise, it might be difficult to keep track of the relationship between the physical NIC port and VMkernel interface. Therefore, this approach also provides a level of simplicity to the network configuration.

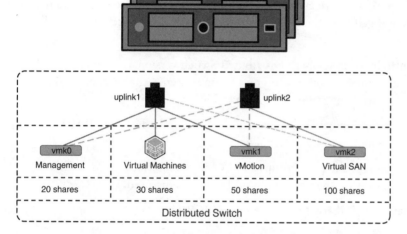

Figure 3.17   DistributedsSwitch, failover order, and NIOC configuration

Scenario 2: Redundant 10 GbE Switch with Link Aggregation Capability

In this next scenario, there are two 10 GbE uplinks set up in a teamed configuration (often referred to as EtherChannel or link aggregation). Because of the physical switch capabilities, the configuration of the virtual layer will be extremely simple. We will take the previous recommended minimum bandwidth requirements into consideration for the design:

- **Management network**: 1 GbE
- **vMotion VMkernel**: 5 GbE
- **VM port group**: 2 GbE
- **VSAN VMkernel interface**: 10 GbE

When the physical uplinks are teamed (link aggregation), the Distributed Switch load-balancing mechanism is required to be configured with one of the following configuration options:

- IP-Hash
- Link aggregation control protocol (LACP)

IP-Hash is a load-balancing option available to VMkernel interfaces that are connected to multiple uplinks on an ESXi host. An uplink is chosen based on a hash of the source and destination IP addresses of each packet. For non-IP packets, whatever is located at those IP address offsets in the packet is used to compute the hash.

LACP is supported on vSphere 5.5 and higher distributed switches. This feature allows you to connect ESXi hosts to physical switches by means of dynamic link aggregation. Link aggregation groups (LAGs) are created on the Distributed Switch to aggregate the bandwidth of the physical NICs on the ESXi hosts that are in turn connected to LACP port channels.

LACP support was introduced in vSphere Distributed Switch version 5.1, but enhanced support was introduced in the 5.5 versions. If you are running an earlier version of the Distributed Switch, you should upgrade to the 5.5 versions at a minimum.

The official vSphere networking guide has much more detail on IP-hash and LACP support and should be referenced for additional details.

It is recommended to configure all port groups and VMkernel interfaces to use either LACP or IP-Hash depending on the type of physical switch being used:

- Management network VMkernel interface = LACP/IP-Hash
- vMotion VMkernel interface = LACP/IP-Hash
- VM port group = LACP/IP-Hash
- VSAN VMkernel interface = LACP/IP-Hash

Because various traffic types will share the same uplinks, you also want to make sure that no traffic type can affect other types of traffic during times of contention. For that, the NIOC shared mechanism is once again used.

Working under the same assumptions as before that there is only one physical port available and that all traffic types share the same physical port, we once again take a worst-case scenario approach into consideration. This approach will guarantee performance even in a failure scenario. By taking this approach, we can ensure that VSAN always has 50% of the bandwidth at its disposal while giving the other traffic types sufficient bandwidth to avoid a potential self-inflicted DoS situation arising.

When both uplinks are available, this will equate to 10 GbE for VSAN traffic. When only one uplink is available (due to NIC failure or maintenance reasons), the bandwidth is also cut in half, giving a 5 GbE bandwidth.

Table 3.2 outlines the recommendations for configuring shares for the traffic types.

Table 3.2 Recommended Share Configuration by Traffic Type (Scenario 2)

Traffic Type	Shares	Limit
Management Network	20	N/A
vMotion VMkernel Interface	50	N/A
VM Port Group	30	N/A
VSAN VMkernel Interface	100	N/A

Figure 3.18 depicts this configuration scenario.

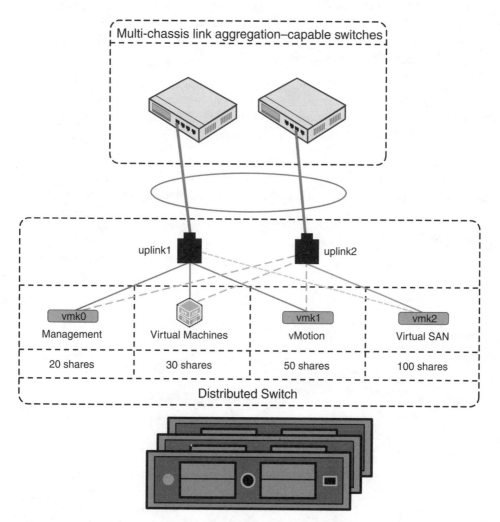

Figure 3.18 Distributed switch configuration for link aggregation

Either of the scenarios discussed here should provide an optimal network configuration for your VSAN cluster.

Creating a VSAN Cluster

The creation of a VSAN cluster is identical in many respects to how a vSphere administrator might set up a vSphere Distributed Resource Scheduler (DRS) or vSphere High Availability (HA) cluster. A cluster object is created in the vCenter Server inventory, and one can either choose to enable the VSAN cluster functionality and then add in the hosts to the cluster, or add the hosts first and then enable VSAN on the cluster. The net result from enabling VSAN on a cluster is to have all of the ESXi hosts in the VSAN cluster access a shared, distributed VSAN datastore. At the time of writing in VSAN, only a single VSAN datastore can be created on a single cluster. Therefore, all local storage is consumed by this single VSAN datastore.

The VSAN datastore is made up from the local storage of each of the ESXi hosts in the cluster. The size of the VSAN datastore is entirely dependent on the number of hosts in the VSAN cluster and the number of magnetic disks (hybrid) or flash devices used for capacity (all-flash) in the ESXi hosts participating in the VSAN cluster.

When you enabled the initial version of VSAN, only a single option was displayed asking the administrator to choose a manual or automatic cluster. As of version 6.2, additional options are displayed during the initial configuration of VSAN, as shown in Figure 3.19.

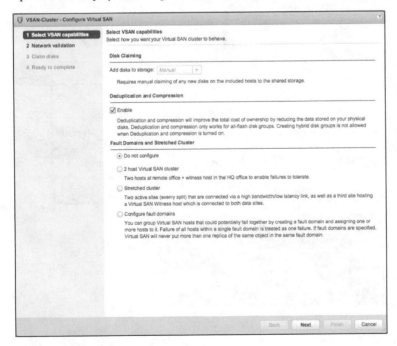

Figure 3.19   New VSAN configuration screen

The automatic or manual aspect of disk claiming is still available in version 6.2. If you enable "Deduplication and Compression" however, the selection for this option will always be "manual." Disk claiming refers to whether the vSphere administrator would like VSAN to discover all the local disks on the hosts and automatically add them to the VSAN datastore or if the vSphere administrator would like to manually select which disks to add to the cluster. Note that when configuring VSAN on an existing cluster, vSphere HA needs to be disabled before enabling VSAN. Before we look at all the different VSAN constructs and configuration aspects, let's take a side step first and look at what changes for vSphere HA with the introduction of VSAN and discuss some configuration options which are recommended for VSAN.

vSphere HA

vSphere HA is fully supported on a VSAN cluster to provide additional availability to VMs deployed in the cluster; however, a number of significant changes have been made to vSphere HA to ensure correct interoperability with VSAN. These changes are important to understand as they will impact the way you configure vSphere HA.

vSphere HA Communication Network

In non-VSAN deployments, vSphere HA agents communication takes place over the management network. In a VSAN environment, vSphere HA agents communicate over the VSAN network. The reasoning behind this is that in the event of a network failure we want vSphere HA and VSAN hosts to be part of the same partition. This avoids possible conflicts when vSphere HA and VSAN observe different partitions when a failure occurs, with different partitions holding subsets of the storage components and objects.

vSphere HA in VSAN environments by default continues to use the management network's default gateway for isolation detection. We suspect that most VSAN environments will more than likely have the management network and the VSAN network sharing the same physical infrastructure (especially in 10 GbE environments). However, if the VSAN and management networks are on a different physical infrastructure, it is recommended to change the default vSphere HA isolation address from the management network to the VSAN network. By default, the isolation address is the default gateway of the management network as previously mentioned. VMware's recommendation when using vSphere HA with VSAN is to use an IP address on the VSAN network as an isolation address. To prevent vSphere HA from using the default gateway and to use an IP address on the VSAN network, the following settings must be changed in the advanced options for vSphere HA:

- das.useDefaultIsolationAddress=false
- das.isolationAddress0=<ip address on VSAN network>

However, if there is no suitable isolation address on the VSAN network, then leave the isolation address on the management network as per the default.

One other notable difference relates to network reconfiguration. Changes are not automatically detected by vSphere HA if they are made at the VSAN layer to the VSAN networks. Therefore, a vSphere HA cluster reconfiguration must be manually initiated by the vSphere administrator for these changes to be detected.

vSphere HA Heartbeat Datastores

Another noticeable difference with vSphere HA on VSAN is that the VSAN datastore cannot be used for datastore heartbeats. These heartbeats play a significant role in determining VM ownership in the event of a vSphere HA cluster partition with traditional SAN or NAS datastores. This feature is very advantageous when vSphere HA is deployed on traditional shared storage (SAN/NAS) because it allows some level of coordination between partitions. vSphere HA does not use the VSAN datastore for heart-beating and won't let a user designate it as a heartbeat datastore. VSAN instead uses the clustering service over the network that allows for very fast failure detection. The key reason for this is that VSAN typically leverages the same network interfaces and switches as vSphere HA would; as such the result of datastore heartbeats and network heartbeats would be the same.

Note, however, that if ESXi hosts participating in a VSAN cluster also have access to shared storage, either virtual machine file system (VMFS) or network file system (NFS), these traditional datastores are used for vSphere HA heartbeats.

vSphere HA Admission Control

There is another consideration to discuss regarding vSphere HA and VSAN interoperability. When configuring vSphere HA, one of the decisions that need to be made is about admission control. Admission control ensures that vSphere HA has sufficient resources at its disposal to restart VMs after a failure by setting aside resources.

Note that VSAN is not admission control-aware when it comes to failure recovery. There is no way to automatically set aside spare resources like this on VSAN to ensure that overcommitment does not occur.

If a failure occurs, VSAN will try to use all the remaining space on the remaining nodes in the cluster to bring the VMs to a compliant state. Caution and advanced planning is imperative on VSAN with vSphere HA, as multiple failures in the VSAN cluster may fill up all the available space on the VSAN datastore due to overcommitment of resources.

Recommended practice dictates that you take "rebuild capacity" into consideration when planning and designing a VSAN environment. In Chapter 9, "Designing a VSAN Cluster," you learn how to achieve this. For simplicity reasons, it is recommended to align this form of VSAN (manual) admission control with the selected vSphere HA admission control settings. Do note that the health check section in the Web Client does inform the current state of the cluster, and the state after a full host failure.

vSphere HA Isolation Response

When a host isolation event occurs in a VSAN cluster with vSphere HA enabled, vSphere HA will apply the configured isolation response. With vSphere HA, you can select three different types of responses to an isolation event:

- Leave power on

- Power off, then fail over

- Shut down, then fail over

The recommendation is to have vSphere HA automatically power off the VMs running on that host when a host isolation event occurs. Therefore, the "isolation response" should be set to "power off, then fail over" and not the default setting that is leave powered on.

Note that "power off, then fail over" is similar to pulling the power cable from a physical host. The VM process is literally stopped—this is not a clean shutdown. In the case of an isolation event, however, it is unlikely that VSAN can write to the disks on the isolated host and as such powering off is recommended. If the ESXi host is partitioned, it is also unlikely that the VM will be able to access a quorum of components of the storage object.

vSphere HA Component Protection

In a traditional environment it is possible to configure a response to an all paths down (APD) and permanent device loss (PDL) scenario within HA. This is part of new functionality that was introduced with vSphere 6.0 called VM Component Protection. In the current version this is not supported for VSAN and as such a response to APD and/or PDL does not have to be configured for vSphere HA in a VSAN only cluster.

Now that we know what has changed for vSphere HA, let's take a look at some core constructs of VSAN.

The Role of Disk Groups

VSAN uses the concept of a disk group as a container for magnetic disks and flash devices. VMs that have their storage deployed on a device in a particular disk group will leverage the caching capabilities of the flash device in the same disk group only. The disk group can be thought of as an aggregate of storage devices that uses flash for performance and magnetic disk drives or flash for capacity. You must take into account a number of considerations for disk groups, which we will look at in detail now. In the future, when we refer to a cache device in the context of VSAN disk groups, we refer to SSDs, PCIe flash, and NVMe flash devices. When we refer to a capacity device we refer to magnetic disks (SATA, SAS or NL-SAS), SSDs, PCIe flash, and NVMe flash devices.

Disk Group Maximums

In VSAN 6.2, there are a maximum number of five disk groups per host. Each disk group will contain at least one caching device and one capacity device to persistently store VMs. VSAN supports both hybrid and all-flash configurations but a single VSAN cluster cannot mix hybrid and all-flash disk groups at the time of writing.

Each of these disk groups can contain a maximum of one caching device and seven capacity devices. This means that the VSAN datastore maximum size is seven capacity devices × five disk groups × number of ESXi hosts in the cluster × size of the capacity device. As you see, this is quite scalable and can produce a very large distributed datastore.

Why Configure Multiple Disk Groups in VSAN?

Disk groups allow a vSphere administrator to define a failure domain and a deduplication/ compression domain in the case of an all-flash configuration. How deduplication and compression work are described in Chapter 5, "Architectural Details." For now it is sufficient to understand that it happens on a per disk group basis as it can impact the design of your host and the disk groups within the host.

There are different ways of designing a disk group, and the most important factor here is whether the VSAN cluster is all-flash or hybrid-based. For both, however, the failure domain concept applies. Let's look at that first.

With multiple disk groups with a single caching device and a few capacity devices, should the caching device in a disk group fail, the failure domain is limited to only those capacity devices in that particular disk group. With one very large disk group containing lots of capacity devices, a caching device failure can impact a greater number of VMs as it will impact the full disk group. The failure domain should be a consideration when designing disk group configurations.

Figure 3.20 shows two VSAN hosts. The first VSAN host contains two disk groups, each with one caching device and three capacity devices. The second VSAN host contains a single disk group with one caching device and six capacity devices. In the case of the first host, when the caching device fails it does not impact the other disk group in this host, which means that 50% of the capacity and performance is still available. The second VSAN host will be impacted to a greater extent. In that case all six capacity devices would be unavailable when the caching device has failed. This is what we mean when we say that a disk group can be used to define a failure domain.

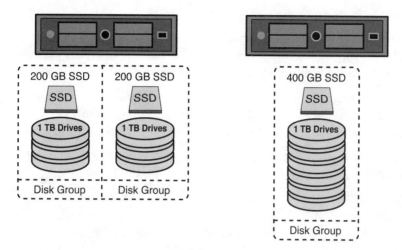

Figure 3.20   Disk groups define failure domains

In most cases the failure domain or the performance aspects arguments will lead to multiple disk groups instead of a single disk group. There is however another interesting discussion when it comes to this. For all-flash configurations on a per-cluster level space efficiency functionality (deduplication and compression) can be enabled. Although enabled on a per-cluster basis, deduplication and compression happen on a per-disk group basis. This means that for any given block that needs to be stored on a capacity device in an all-flash cluster, VSAN will see if an identical block has been stored already on that particular disk group. If that is the case then there is no need to store it, else VSAN will compress the data and store it as a new unique block on the disk group. This also means that in an all-flash configuration, depending on your workload, it may be beneficial to create a few larger disk groups over many smaller disk groups, as the deduplication process will be more effective with a larger group. But this needs to be considered along with the fact that when deduplication and compression are enabled on a disk group, a failure of any of the devices in that disk group, be it a cache device or capacity device, impacts the whole of the disk group. This is because the space efficiency metadata is distributed across all the capacity devices in the disk group. As always, this is up to the administrator to decide, and a balance between risk and benefit will need to be found.

Cache Device to Capacity Device Sizing Ratio

When designing your VSAN environment from a hardware perspective, realize that VSAN heavily relies on your caching device (flash) for performance. As a rule of thumb, VMware recommends 10% cache capacity of the expected consumed total virtual disk capacity before "failures to tolerate" has been taken into account. VMware also supports lower ratios. Larger ratios will, in fact, improve the performance of VMs by virtue of the fact that more I/O can be cached. SSDs will function as read cache and write buffer capacity for VMs in VSAN. For the moment, it is sufficient to understand that in a hybrid

VSAN cluster 70% of your caching device will be used as a read cache and 30% as a write buffer. In an all-flash configuration 100% of the caching device will be used as a write-buffer and the 10% rule also applies, but increasing the size will not lead to greater performance as all IOs are already served from cache.

The 10% value is based on the assumption that the majority of working data sets are about 10%. Using this rule of thumb (and it is just a rule of thumb) to cover the majority of workloads means that live data from the application running in your VM should be in flash.

For example, assume that we have 100 VMs. Each VM has a 100 GB virtual disk, of which anticipated usage is 50 GB on average. In this scenario, this would result in the following:

10% of (100 × 50 GB) = 500 GB

This total amount of cache capacity should be divided by the number of ESXi hosts in the VSAN cluster. If you have five hosts, in this example that would lead to 100 GB of cache capacity recommended per host.

Automatically Add Disks to VSAN Disk Groups

Automatic versus manual mode has been a topic of hot debate over the past releases. We have found that in the majority of cases customers like to keep control over which device is used for what and part of which disk group. Manual mode allows you to do this. In some cases customers, however, prefer to have VSAN handle disk management, and this is fully supported.

If automatic mode is chosen during the VSAN cluster creation workflow, VSAN will automatically discover local magnetic disks and local SSDs on each host and build disk groups on each host in the cluster. Note that these SSDs and magnetic disks will be claimed by VSAN only if they are empty and contain no partition information. VSAN will not claim disks that are already being used or have been used in the past and contain residual data. For VSAN to claim these disks, they will first have to be wiped clean.

Each host with valid storage will have a disk group containing their local magnetic disks and/or SSDs. Suffice it to say that a disk group can be thought of as a container of magnetic disks and/or SSDs. As stated previously, each disk group can only contain a single caching device and a maximum of seven capacity devices, but there may be multiple disk groups defined per ESXi host. Finally, after all of this is completed, the VSAN datastore is created, and its size reflects the capacity of all the capacity devices across all the hosts in the cluster, less some metadata overhead.

ESXi hosts that are part of the VSAN cluster but do not contribute storage to the VSAN datastore can still access the VSAN datastore. This is a very advantageous feature of VSAN, because a VSAN cluster can now be scaled not just on storage requirements, but also on compute requirements. Note, however, that VMware recommends uniformly configured clusters for better load balancing, availability, and overall performance.

Although automatic mode will claim "local" disks, most ESXi hosts with SAS controllers will have their disks show up as "remote," and VSAN will not auto-claim these disks. In this case, the vSphere administrator must manually create the disk groups, even though the cluster is set up in automatic mode, as explained in Chapter 2, "VSAN Prerequisites and Requirements for Deployment."

Manually Adding Disks to a VSAN Disk Group

As mentioned earlier, as you create the VSAN cluster, you have the option to manually add disks. If this option is selected, administrators are given the opportunity to select multiple cache devices and multiple capacity devices manually via the VSAN configuration wizard. The administrator can select between one and seven capacity devices per disk group and at most one caching device to each of the disk groups. After each disk group is created on a per-host basis, the size of the VSAN datastore will grow according to the amount of capacity devices that is added. Note that the SSDs function as caching devices and are not included in the capacity of the VSAN datastore.

You might wonder when this manual option would be used. First and foremost, it is a requirement for all-flash environments. This is to ensure that the right type of flash is selected for the caching layer and the capacity layer. Another possible reason could be that when VSAN constructs disk groups it will always try to do this in a consistent manner; however, due to many different server configurations, especially those using SAS for disk connectivity, the manual method may be an important approach over the automatic method. SAS reports devices with unique identifiers instead of on a port-by-port basis. Therefore, a disk in disk slot 1 of one host may be part of disk group 1 in ESXi host 1, while disk in disk slot 1 may become part of disk group 2 in ESXi host 2. When disks need to be replaced for whatever reason, it is of utmost importance that the correct disk is removed and replaced with a new one. Therefore, a vSphere administrator may want to manually configure the disk groups so that the disks are easily identifiable and we have found that this is what most VSAN customers do as it may make life easier during replacement of devices. When using an all-flash configuration though and functionality like deduplication and compression is enabled, all disks should be claimed at the same time and not one by one.

Disk Group Creation Example

Disk group creation is necessary only if the cluster is created in manual mode. If the cluster is created in automatic mode, the disk groups are automatically created for you, using all available disks on the host. The mechanism to create a disk group is quite straightforward. You need to remember some restrictions, however, as mentioned previously:

- At most, there can be one caching device per disk group.

- At most, there can be seven capacity devices per disk group.

Multiple disk groups may be created if a host has more than seven capacity devices or more than one caching device. To create a disk group, the cluster must first of all be configured in manual mode, as shown in Figure 3.21. This can be done during the configuration of VSAN, but can also be changed to manual after the configuration of VSAN.

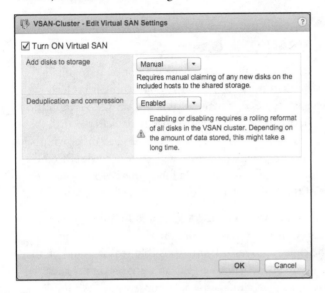

Figure 3.21 Turning on VSAN

Once the cluster is in manual mode, there will be no storage devices claimed by VSAN. The next step is to manually create disk groups. Navigate to the disk management section under VSAN management in the vSphere Web Client. From here, you select a host in the cluster and click the icon to create a new disk group. This will display all available disks (SSD and magnetic disks) in the host, as shown in Figure 3.22.

Figure 3.22 VSAN Disk Management

At this point, vSphere administrators have a number of options available. They can decide to claim all disk from all hosts if they want, or they can individually build disk groups one host at a time. The first option is useful if disks show up as not local, such as disks that may be behind a SAS controller. For more granular control, however, administrators may like to set up disk groups one host at a time for more control.

When you decide to configure disk groups manually, the vSphere Web Client provides a very intuitive user interface (UI) to do this. From the UI, you can select the capacity devices and flash devices that form the disk group in a single step, as shown in Figure 3.23.

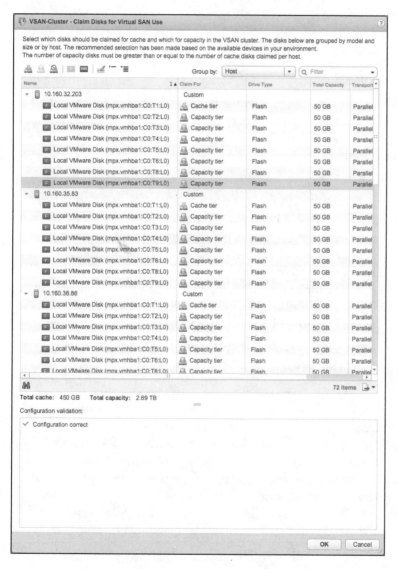

Figure 3.23 Claiming disks for VSAN

If the first icon (claim disks) is chosen, all hosts and disks may be selected in one step. If the second icon (create disk groups) is chosen, this steps through the hosts one at a time, claiming disks for that host only. Note the guidance provided in the wizard. Hosts that contribute storage to the VSAN must contribute at least one caching device and one capacity device. In reality, you would expect a much higher number of capacity devices compared to caching devices. And just to reiterate the configuration maximums for VSAN, a disk group may contain only one caching device but up to seven capacity devices.

After the disk groups have been created, the VSAN datastore is created. This VSAN datastore can now be used for the deployment of VM.

VSAN Datastore Properties

The raw size of a VSAN datastore is governed by the number of capacity devices per ESXi host and the number of ESXi hosts in the cluster. There is some metadata overhead to also consider. For example, if a host has seven × 2 TB magnetic disks in the cluster, and there are eight hosts in the cluster, the raw capacity is as follows:

$7 \times 2 \text{ TB} \times 8 = 112 \text{ TB raw capacity}$

Now that we know how to calculate how much raw capacity will be available, how do we know how much effective capacity we will have? Well, this depends on various factors, but it all begins with the hardware configuration, all-flash or hybrid. When creating your VSAN cluster, depending on whether you have an all-flash or hybrid configuration, you have the option to enable "deduplication and compression." Deduplication and compression will play a big factor in available capacity for an all-flash configuration. Note that these data services are not available in a hybrid configuration. We will discuss deduplication and compression in more detail in Chapter 5.

But not just deduplication and compression, there is also the number of copies of the VM that we need to factor in. This is enabled through the policy-based management framework.

After creating the disk groups, your VSAN is configured. Once the VSAN datastore is formed, a number of datastore capabilities are surfaced up into vCenter Server. These capabilities will be used to create the appropriate VM storage policies for VMs and their associated virtual machine disk (VMDK) storage objects deployed on the VSAN datastore. These include stripe width, number of failures to tolerate, force provisioning, provisioned capacity, and if the replication mechanism needs to be optimized for performance or for capacity. Before deploying VMs, however, you first need to understand how to create appropriate VM storage policies that meet the requirements of the application running in the VM.

VM storage policies and VSAN capabilities will be discussed in greater detail later in Chapter 4, "VM Storage Policies on VSAN," but suffice it to know for now that these capabilities form the VM policy requirements. These allow a vSphere administrator to specify requirements based on performance, availability, and data services when it comes to VM provisioning. The next chapter discusses VM storage policies in the context of VSAN and how to correctly deploy a VM using VSAN capabilities.

Summary

If everything is configured and working as designed, VSAN can be configured in just a few clicks. However, it is vitally important that the infrastructure is ready in advance. Identifying appropriate magnetic disk drives for capacity, sizing your flash resources for performance, and verifying that your networking is configured to provide the best availability and performance are all tasks that must be configured and designed up front.

Now the VSAN cluster is up and running, let's makes use of it. We touched on the topic of VM storage policies. These should be created to reflect the requirements of the application running in your VM. We look at how to do this in the next chapter.

## Chapter 4

VM Storage Policies on VSAN

In vSphere 5.0, VMware introduced a feature called profile-driven storage. Profile-driven storage is a feature that allows vSphere administrators to easily select the correct datastore on which to deploy virtual machines (VMs). The selection of the datastore is based on the capabilities of that datastore, or to be more specific, the underlying capabilities of the storage array that have been assigned to this datastore. Examples of the capabilities are RAID level, thin provisioning, deduplication, encryption, replication, etc. The capabilities are completely dependent on the storage array.

Throughout the life cycle of the VM, profile-driven storage allows the administrator to check whether its underlying storage is still *compatible*. In other words, does the datastore on which the VM resides still have the correct capabilities for this VM? The reason why this is useful is because if the VM is migrated to a different datastore for whatever reason, the administrator can ensure that it has moved to a datastore that continues to meet its requirements. If the VM is migrated to a datastore without paying attention to the capabilities of the destination storage, the administrator can still check the compliance of the VM storage from the vSphere client at any time and take corrective actions if it no longer resides on a datastore that meets its storage requirements (in other words, move it back to a compliant datastore).

However, VM storage policies and storage policy-based management (SPBM) have taken this a step further. In the previous paragraph, we described a sort of storage quality of service driven by the storage. All VMs residing on the same datastore would inherit the capabilities of the datastore. With VSAN, the storage quality of service no longer resides with the datastore; instead, it resides with the VM and is enforced by the VM storage policy associated with the VM and the VM disks (VMDKs). Once the policy is pushed down to the storage layer, in this case VSAN, the underlying storage is then responsible for creating storage for the VM that meets the requirements placed in the policy.

Introducing Storage Policy-Based Management in a VSAN Environment

VSAN leverages this approach to VM deployment, using an updated method called storage policy-based management (SPBM). All VMs deployed to a VSAN datastore must use a VM storage policy, although if one is not specifically created, a default one that is associated with the datastore is assigned to the VM. The VM storage policy contains one or more VSAN capabilities. This chapter will describe the VSAN capabilities. After the VSAN cluster has been configured and the VSAN datastore has been created, VSAN surfaces up a set of capabilities to the vCenter Server. These capabilities, which are surfaced by the vSphere APIs for Storage Awareness (VASA) storage provider (more on this shortly) when the cluster is configured successfully, are used to set the availability, capacity, and performance policies on a per-VM (and per-VMDK) basis when that VM is deployed on the VSAN datastore.

As previously mentioned, this differs significantly from the previous VM storage profile mechanism that we had in vSphere in the past. With the VM storage profile feature, the capabilities were associated with datastores, and were used for VM placement decisions. Now, through SPBM, administrators create a policy defining the storage requirements for the VM, and this policy is pushed out to the storage, which in turn instantiates per-VM (and per-VMDK) storage for virtual machines. In vSphere 6.0, VMware introduced Virtual Volumes (VVols). Storage policy-based management for VMs using VVols is very similar to storage policy-based management for VMs deployed on VSAN. In other words, administrators no longer need to carve up logical unit numbers (LUNs) or volumes for virtual machine storage. Instead, the underlying storage infrastructure instantiates the virtual machine storage based on the contents of the policy. What we have now with SPBM is a mechanism whereby we can specify the requirements of the VM, and the VMDKs. These requirements are then used to create a policy. This policy is then sent to the storage layer [in the case of VVols, this is a SAN or network-attached storage (NAS) storage array] asking it to build a storage object for this VM that meets these policy requirements. In fact, a VM can have multiple policies associated with it, different policies for different VMDKs.

By way of explaining capabilities, policies, and profiles, capabilities are what the underlying storage is capable of providing by way of availability, performance, and reliability. These capabilities are visible in vCenter Server. The capabilities are then used to create a VM storage policy (or just policy for short). A policy may contain one or more capabilities, and these capabilities reflect the requirements of your VM or application running in a VM. Previous versions of vSphere used the term *profiles*, but these are now known as *policies*.

Deploying VMs on a VSAN datastore is very different from previous approaches in vSphere. In the past, an administrator would present a LUN or volume to a group of ESXi hosts and in the case of block storage partition, format, and build a VMFS file system to create a datastore for storing VM files. In the case of network-attached storage (NAS), a network file system (NFS) volume is mounted to the ESXi host, and once again a VM is created on the datastore. There is no way to specify a RAID-0 stripe width for these VMDKs, nor is there any way to specify a RAID-1 replica for the VMDK.

In the case of VSAN (and now VVols), the approach to deploying VMs is quite different. Consideration must be given to the availability, performance, and reliability factors of the application running in the VM. Based on these requirements, an appropriate VM storage policy must be created and associated with the VM during deployment.

There were five capabilities in the initial release of VSAN, as illustrated in Figure 4.1.

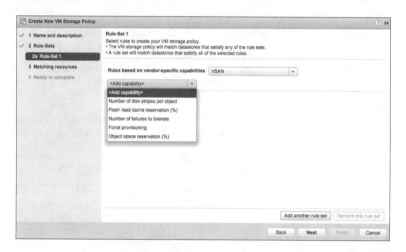

Figure 4.1   VSAN capabilities that can be used for VM storage policies

In VSAN 6.2, the number of capabilities is increased to support a number of new features. These features include the ability to implement RAID-5 and RAID-6 configurations for virtual machine objects deployed on an all-flash VSAN configuration, alongside the existing RAID-0 and RAID-1 configurations. With RAID-5 and RAID-6, it now allows VMs to tolerate one or two failures, but it means that the amount of space consumed is much less than a RAID-1 configuration to tolerate a similar amount of failures. There is also a new policy for software checksum. Checksum is enabled by default, but it can be disabled through policies if an administrator wishes to disable it. The last capability relates to quality of service and provides the ability to limit the number of input/output operations per second (IOPS) for a particular object.

You can select the capabilities when a VM storage policy is created. Note that certain capabilities are applicable to hybrid VSAN configurations (e.g., flash read cache reservation), while other capabilities are applicable to all-flash VSAN configurations (e.g., failure tolerance method set to performance).

VM storage policies are essential in VSAN deployments because they define how a VM is deployed on a VSAN datastore. Using VM storage policies, you can define the capabilities that can provide the number of VMDK RAID-0 stripe components or the number of

RAID-1 mirror copies of a VMDK. If an administrator desires a VM to tolerate one failure but does not want to consume as much capacity as a RAID-1 mirror, a RAID-5 configuration can be used. This requires a minimum of four hosts in the cluster and implements a distributed parity mechanism across the storage of all four hosts. If this configuration would be implemented with RAID-1, the amount of capacity consumed would be 200% the size of the VMDK. If this is implemented with RAID-5, the amount of capacity consumed would be 133% the size of the VMDK.

Similarly, if an administrator desires a VM to tolerate two failures using a RAID-1 mirroring configuration, there would need to be three copies of the VMDK, meaning the amount of capacity consumed would be 300% the size of the VMDK. With a RAID-6 implementation, a double parity is implemented, which is also distributed across all the hosts. For RAID-6, there must be a minimum of six hosts in the cluster. RAID-6 also allows a VM to tolerate two failures, but only consumes capacity equivalent to 150% the size of the VMDK.

Figure 4.2 shows the new policies introduced in VSAN 6.2.

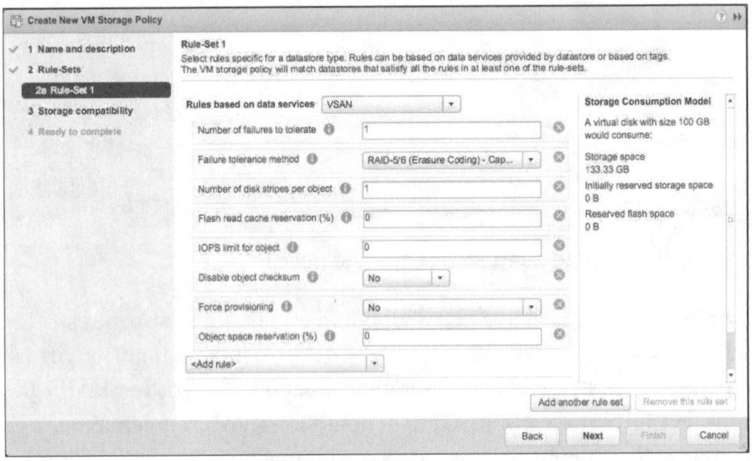

Figure 4.2   New VSAN capabilities

The sections that follow highlight where you should use these capabilities when creating a VM storage policy and when to tune these values to something other than the default. Remember that a VM storage policy will contain one or more capabilities.

In the initial release of VSAN, five capabilities were available for selection to be part of the VM storage policy. In VSAN 6.2, as previously highlighted, additional policies were introduced. As an administrator, you can decide which of these capabilities can be added to the policy, but this is, of course, dependent on the requirements of your VM. For example, what performance and availability requirements does the VM have? The capabilities are as follows:

- Number of failures to tolerate
- Number of disk stripes per object

- Failure tolerance method

- IOPS limit for object

- Disable object checksum

- Flash read cache reservation (hybrid configurations only)

- Object space reservation

- Force provisioning

The sections that follow describe the VSAN capabilities in detail.

Number of Failures to Tolerate

In this section, *number of failures to tolerate* is described having *failure tolerance method* set to its default value that is *Performance*. Later on we will describe a different scenario when *failure tolerance method* is set to *Capacity*.

This capability sets a requirement on the storage object to tolerate at least *n* number of failures in the cluster. This is the number of concurrent host, network, or disk failures that may occur in the cluster and still ensure the availability of the object. When the *failure tolerance method* is set to its default value of *RAID-1*, the VM's storage objects are mirrored; however, the mirroring is done across ESXi hosts, as shown in Figure 4.3.

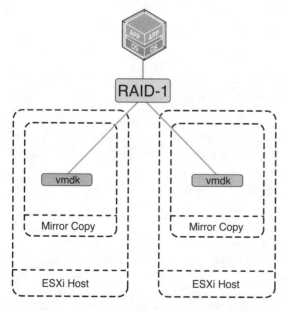

Figure 4.3   Number of failures to tolerate results in a RAID-1 configuration

When this capability is set to a value of n, it specifies that the VSAN configuration must contain at least $n + 1$ replicas (copies of the data); this also implies that there are $2n + 1$ hosts in the cluster.

Note that this requirement will create a configuration for the VM objects that may also contain an additional number of witness components being instantiated to ensure that the VM remains available even in the presence of up to *number of failures to tolerate* concurrent failures (see Table 4.1). Witnesses provide a quorum when failures occur in the cluster or a decision has to be made when a split-brain situation arises. These witnesses will be discussed in much greater detail later in the book, but suffice it to say that witness components play an integral part in maintaining VM availability during failures and maintenance tasks.

One aspect worth noting is that any disk failure on a single host is treated as a "failure" for this metric (although multiple disk failures on the same host are also treated as a single host failure). Therefore, the VM may not persist (remain accessible) if there is a disk failure on host A and a host failure of host B when number of failures to tolerate is set to 1.

Table 4.1 Witness and hosts required to meet number of failures to tolerate requirement

Number of Failures to Tolerate	Mirror Copies/ Replicas	Witness Objects	Minimum Number of ESXi Hosts
0	1	0	1
1	2	1	3
2	3	2	5
3	4	3	7

Table 4.1 is true if the number of disk objects to stripe is set to 1. The behavior is subtly different if there is a stripe width greater than 1. The number of disk stripes per object will be discussed in more detail shortly.

If no policy is chosen when a VM is deployed, the default policy associated with the VSAN datastore is chosen, which in turn sets the number of failures to tolerate to 1. When a new policy is created, the default value of number of failures to tolerate is also 1. This means that even if this capability is not explicitly specified in the policy, it is implied.

Failure Tolerance Method

This is a new capability introduced in VSAN 6.2 and is how administrators can choose either RAID-1 or RAID-5/6 configuration for their virtual machine objects. The *failure tolerance method* is used in conjunction with *number of failures to tolerate*. The purpose of this setting is to allow administrators to choose between performance and capacity. If performance is the absolute end goal for administrators, then RAID-1 (which is still the default) is the tolerance method that should be used. If administrators do not need maximum performance and are more concerned with capacity usage, then RAID-5/6 is the tolerance method that should be used. The easiest way to explain the behavior is to display the various policy settings and the resulting object configuration, as shown in Table 4.2.

As can be seen from Table 4.2, when the *failure tolerance method* RAID5/6 is selected, either RAID-5 or RAID-6 is implemented depending on the number of failures that you wish to tolerate (although it only supports a maximum setting of two for *number of failures to tolerate*). If performance is still the desired capability, then the traditional RAID-1 configuration is implemented, with the understanding that this uses mirror copies of the objects, and thus consumes significantly more space.

One might ask why RAID-5/6 less performing than RAID-1. The reason lies in I/O amplification. In steady state, where there are no failures in the cluster, there is no read amplification when using RAID-5/6 versus RAID-1. However, there is write amplification. This is because the parity component needs to be updated every time there is a write to the associated data components. So in the case of RAID-5, we need to read the component that is going to be updated with additional write data, read the current parity, merge the new write data with the current data, write this back, calculate the new parity value, and write this back also. In essence, a single write operation can amplify into two reads and two

Table 4.2 Object configuration when number of failures to tolerate and failure tolerance method are set

Number of Failures to Tolerate	Failure Tolerance Method	Object Configuration	Number of ESXi Hosts Required
0	RAID5/6 (Erasure Coding)	RAID-0	1
0	RAID-1 (mirroring)	RAID-0	1
1	RAID5/6 (Erasure Coding)	RAID-5	4
1	RAID-1 (mirroring)	RAID-1	3
2	RAID5/6 (Erasure Coding)	RAID-6	6
2	RAID-1 (mirroring)	RAID-1	5
3	RAID5/6 (Erasure Coding)	N/A	N/A
3	RAID-1 (mirroring)	RAID-1	7

writes. With RAID-6, which has double parity, a single write can amplify into three reads and three writes.

And indeed, when there is a failure of some component in the RAID-5 and RAID-6 objects, and data needs to be determined using parity, then the I/O amplification is even higher. These are the considerations an administrator needs to evaluate when deciding on the *failure tolerance method*.

One item to keep in mind is that even though *failure tolerance method* set to RAID5/6 consumes less capacity, it does require more hosts than the traditional RAID-1 approach and is only supported (in this release) on an all-flash VSAN configuration. When using RAID-1, the rule is that to tolerate *n* failures, there must be *2n* + 1 hosts for the mirrors/ replicas and witness. So to tolerate one failure, there must be three hosts; to tolerate two failures, there must be five hosts; or to tolerate three failures, there must be seven hosts in the cluster, all contributing storage to the VSAN datastore. With *failure tolerance method* set to RAID5/6, four hosts are needed to tolerate one failure and six hosts are needed to tolerate two failures, even though less space is consumed on each host. Figure 4.4 shows an example of a RAID-5 configuration for an object, deployed across four hosts with a distributed parity.

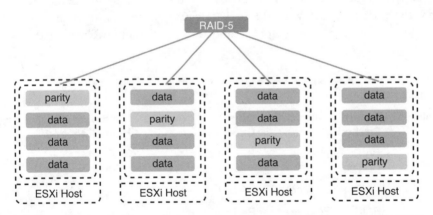

Figure 4.4 RAID-5 configuration, a result of *failure tolerance method* RAID5/6 and number of failures to tolerate set to 1

The RAID-5 or RAID-6 configurations also work with *number of disk stripes per object*. If stripe width is also specified as part of the policy along with *failure tolerance method* set to RAID5/6 each of the components on each host is striped in a RAID-0 configuration, and these are in turn placed in either a RAID-5 or-6 configuration.

One final note is in relation to having a number of failures to tolerate setting of zero or three. If you deploy a VM with this policy setting, which includes a *failure tolerance method*

RAID5/6 setting, the VM provisioning wizard will display a warning stating that this policy setting is only effective when the number of failures to tolerate is set to either one or two. You can still proceed with the deployment, but the object is deployed as a single RAID-0 object.

Number of Disk Stripes Per Object

This capability defines the number of physical disks across which each replica of a storage object (e.g., VMDK) is striped. When *failure tolerance method* is set to performance, this policy setting can be considered in the context of a RAID-0 configuration on each RAID-1 mirror/replica where I/O traverses a number of physical disk spindles. When *failure tolerance method* is set to capacity, each component of the RAID-5 or RAID-6 stripe may also be configured as a RAID-0 stripe. Typically, when the number of disk stripes per object is defined, the number of failures to tolerate is also defined. Figure 4.5 shows what a combination of these two capabilities could result in, once again assuming that the new VSAN 6.2 policy setting of *failure tolerance method* is set to its default value *RAID-1*.

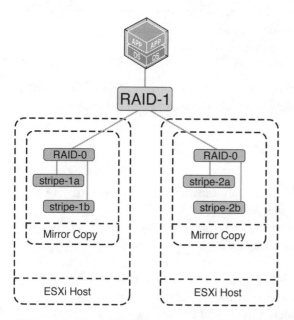

Figure 4.5   Storage object configuration when stripe width set is to 2 and failures to tolerate is set to 1 and replication method optimizes for is not set

To understand the impact of stripe width, let's examine it first in the context of write operations and then in the context of read operations.

Because all writes go to the cache device write buffer, the value of an increased stripe width may or may not improve performance. This is because there is no guarantee that the new stripe will use a different cache device; the new stripe may be placed on a capacity device in the same disk group, and thus the new stripe will use the same cache device. If the new stripe is placed in a different disk group, either on the same host or on a different host, and thus leverages a different cache device, performance might improve. However, you as the vSphere administrator have no control over this behavior. The only occasion where an increased stripe width could definitely add value is when there is a large amount of data to destage from the cache tier to the capacity tier. In this case, having a stripe could improve destage performance.

From a read perspective, an increased stripe width will help when you are experiencing many read cache misses, but note that this is a consideration in hybrid configurations only. All-flash VSAN considerations do not have a read cache. Consider the example of a VM deployed on a hybrid VSAN consuming 2,000 read operations per second and experiencing a hit rate of 90%. In this case, there are still 200 read operations that need to be serviced from magnetic disk in the capacity tier. If we make the assumption that a single magnetic disk can provide 150 input/output operations per second (IOPS), then it is obvious that it is not able to service all of those read operations, so an increase in stripe width would help on this occasion to meet the VM I/O requirements. In an all-flash VSAN, which is extremely read intensive, striping across multiple capacity flash devices can also improve performance.

In general, the default stripe width of 1 should meet most, if not all VM workloads. Stripe width is a capability that should change only when write destaging or read cache misses are identified as a performance constraint.

IOPS Limit for Object

IOPS limit for object is a new Quality of Service (QoS) capability introduced with VSAN 6.2. This allows administrators to ensure that an object, such as a VMDK, does not generate more than a predefined number of I/O operations per second. This is a great way of ensuring that a "noisy neighbor" virtual machine does not impact other virtual machine components in the same disk group by consuming more than its fair share of resources. By default, VSAN uses an I/O size of 32 KB as a base. **This means that a 64 KB I/O will therefore represent two I/O operations in the limits calculation**. I/Os that are less than or equal to 32 KB will be considered single I/O operations. For example, 2 × 4 KB I/Os are considered as two distinct I/Os. It should also be noted that both read and write IOPS are regarded as equivalent. Neither cache hit rate nor sequential I/O are taken into account. If the IOPS limit threshold is passed, the I/O is throttled back to bring the IOPS value back under the threshold. The default value for this capability is 0, meaning that there is no IOPS limit threshold and VMs can consume as many IOPS as they want, subject to available resources.

Flash Read Cache Reservation

This capability is applicable to hybrid VSAN configurations only. It is the amount of flash capacity reserved on the cache tier device as read cache for the storage object. It is specified as a percentage of the logical size of the storage object (i.e., VMDK). This is specified as a percentage value (%), with up to four decimal places. This fine granular unit size is needed so that administrators can express sub 1% units. Take the example of a 1 TB VMDK. If you limited the read cache reservation to 1% increments, this would mean cache reservations in increments of 10 GB, which in most cases is far too much for a single VM.

Note that you do not have to set a reservation to allow a storage object to use cache. All VMs equally share the read cache of cache devices. The reservation should be left unset (default) unless you are trying to solve a real performance problem and you believe dedicating read cache is the solution. If you add this capability to the VM storage policy and set it to a value 0 (zero), however, you will not have any read cache reserved to the VM that uses this policy. In the current version of VSAN, there is no proportional share mechanism for this resource when multiple VMs are consuming read cache, so every VM consuming read cache will share it equally.

Object Space Reservation

All objects deployed on VSAN are thinly provisioned. This means that no space is reserved at VM deployment time, but rather space is consumed as the VM uses storage. The object space reservation capability defines the percentage of the logical size of the VM storage object that may be reserved during initialization. The object space reservation is the amount of space to reserve specified as a percentage of the total object address space. This is a property used for specifying a thick provisioned storage object. If object space reservation is set to 100%, all of the storage capacity requirements of the VM storage are reserved up front (thick). This will be lazy zeroed thick (LZT) format and not eager zeroed thick (EZT). The difference between LZT and EZT is that EZT virtual disks are zeroed out at creation time; LZT virtual disks are zeroed out gradually at first write time.

One thing to bring to the readers' attention is the special case of using object space reservation when deduplication and compression are enabled on the VSAN cluster. When deduplication and compression are enabled, any objects that wish to use object space reservation in a policy must have it set to either 0% (no space reservation) or 100% (fully reserved). Values between 1% and 99% are not allowed. Any existing objects that have object space reservation between 1% and 99% will need to be reconfigured with 0% or 100% prior to enabling deduplication and compression on the cluster.

Force Provisioning

If the force provisioning parameter is set to a nonzero value, the object that has this setting in its policy will be provisioned even if the requirements specified in the VM storage policy cannot be satisfied by the VSAN datastore. The VM will be shown as noncompliant in the VM summary tab and relevant VM storage policy views in the vSphere client. If there is not enough space in the cluster to satisfy the reservation requirements of at least one replica, however, the provisioning will fail even if force provisioning is turned on. When additional resources become available in the cluster, VSAN will bring this object to a compliant state.

One thing that might not be well understood regarding *force provisioning* is that if a policy cannot be met, it attempts a much simpler placement with requirements which reduces to *number of failures to tolerate* to 0, *number of disk stripes per object* to 1, and *flash read cache reservation* to 0 (on hybrid configurations). This means Virtual SAN will attempt to create an object with just a single copy of data. Any *object space reservation (OSR)* policy setting is still honored. Therefore there is no gradual reduction in capabilities as VSAN tries to find a placement for an object. For example, if policy contains *number of failures to tolerate* = 2, VSAN won't attempt an object placement using *number of failures to tolerate* = 1. Instead, it immediately looks to implement *number of failures to tolerate* = 0.

Similarly, if the requirement was *number of failures to tolerate* = 1, number of *disk stripes per object* = 4, but Virtual SAN doesn't have enough capacity devices to accommodate *number of disk stripes per object* = 4, then it will fall back to *number of failures to tolerate* = 0, *number of disk stripes per object* = 1, even though a policy of *number of failures to tolerate* = 1, *number of disk stripes per object* = 2 or *number of failures to tolerate* = 1, *number of disk stripes per object* = 3 may have succeeded.

Caution should be exercised if this policy setting is implemented. Since this allows VMs to be provisioned with no protection, it can lead to scenarios where VMs and data are at risk.

Administrators who use this option to force provision virtual machines need to be aware that although virtual machine objects may be provisioned with only one replica copy (perhaps due to lack of space), once additional resources become available in the cluster, VSAN may immediately consume these resources to try to satisfy the policy settings of virtual machines.

Some commonly used cases where force provisioning is used are (a) when boot-strapping a VSAN management cluster, starting with a single node that will host the vCenter Server, which is then used to configure a larger VSAN cluster, and (b) when allowing the provisioning of virtual machine/desktops when a cluster is under maintenance, such as a virtual desktop infrastructure (VDI) running on VSAN.

Remember that this parameter should be used only when *absolutely* needed and as an exception. When used by default, this could easily lead to scenarios where VMs, and all data associated with it, are at risk. Use with caution!

Disable Object Checksum

VSAN 6.2 introduced this new capability. This feature, which is enabled by default, is looking for data corruption (bit rot), and if found, automatically corrects it. Checksum is validated on the complete I/O path, which means that when writing data the checksum is calculated and automatically stored. Upon a read the checksum of the data is validated, and if there is a mismatch, the data is repaired. VSAN 6.2 also includes a scrubber mechanism. This mechanism is configured to run once a year (by default) to check all data on the VSAN datastore; however, this value can be changed by setting an advanced host setting. We recommend leaving this configured to the default value of once a year. In some cases you may desire to disable checksums completely. The reason for this could be performance, although the overhead is negligible and most customers prefer data integrity over a 1% to 3% performance increase. However in some cases, this performance increase may be desired. Another reason for disabling checksums is in the situation where the application already provides a checksum mechanism, or the workload does not require checksum. If that is the case, then checksums can be disabled through the "disable object checksum capability," which should be set to "Yes" to disable it.

That completes the capabilities overview. Let's now look at some other aspects of the storage policy-based management mechanism.

VASA Vendor Provider

As part of the VSAN cluster creation step, each ESXi host has a VSAN storage provider registered with vCenter. This uses the vSphere APIs for Storage Awareness (VASA) to surface up the VSAN capabilities to the vCenter Server. The capabilities can then be used to create VM storage policies for the VMs deployed on the VSAN datastore. If you are familiar with VASA and have used it with traditional storage environments, you'll find this functionality familiar; however, with traditional storage environments that leverage VASA, some configuration work needs to be done to add the storage provider for that particular storage. In the context of VSAN, a vSphere administrator does not need to worry about registering these; these are automatically registered when a VSAN cluster is created.

An Introduction to VASA

VASA allows storage vendors to publish the capabilities of their storage to vCenter Server, which in turn can display these capabilities in the vSphere Web Client. VASA may also provide information about storage health status, configuration info, capacity and thin provisioning info, and so on. VASA enables VMware to have an end-to-end story regarding storage. Traditionally, this enabled storage arrays to inform the VASA storage provider of capabilities, and then the storage provider informed vCenter Server, so now users can see storage array capabilities from vSphere Web Client. Through VM storage policies, these storage capabilities are used in the vSphere Web Client to assist administrators in choosing the right storage in terms of space, performance, and service-level agreement (SLA) requirements. This was true for both traditional storage arrays, and now it is true for VSAN also. Prior to the release of virtual volumes (VVols), there was a notable difference in workflow when using VASA and VM storage policies when comparing traditional storage to VSAN. With traditional storage, VASA historically surfaced information about the datastore capabilities, and a vSphere administrator had to choose the appropriate storage on which to place the VM. With VSAN, and now VVols, you define the capabilities you want to have for your VM storage in a VM storage policy. This policy information is then pushed down to the storage layer, basically informing it that these are the requirements you have for storage. VASA will then tell you whether the underlying storage (e.g., VSAN) can meet these requirements, effectively communicating compliance information on a per-storage object basis. The major difference is that this functionality is now working in a bidirectional mode. Previously, VASA would just surface up capabilities. Now it not only surfaces up capabilities but also verifies whether a VM's storage requirements are being met based on the contents of the policy.

Storage Providers

Figure 4.6 illustrates an example of what the storage provider looks like. When a VSAN cluster is created, the VASA storage provider from every ESXi host in the cluster is registered to the vCenter Server. In a four-node VSAN cluster, the VASA VSAN storage provider configuration would look similar to this.

Figure 4.6 VSAN storage providers, added when the VSAN cluster is created

You can always check the status of the storage providers by navigating in the Web Client to the vCenter Server inventory item, selecting the **Manage** tab and then the **Storage Providers** view. One VSAN provider should always be online. The other storage providers should be in standby mode. This is all done automatically by VSAN. There is typically no management of the VASA providers required by administrators.

In VSAN clusters that have more than eight ESXi hosts, and thus more than eight VASA storage providers, the list of storage providers is shortened to eight in the user interface (UI) for display purposes. The number of standby storage providers is still displayed correctly; you simply won't be able to interrogate them.

VSAN Storage Providers: Highly Available

You might ask why every ESXi host registers this storage provider. The reason for this is high availability. Should one ESXi host fail, another ESXi host in the cluster can take over the presentation of these VSAN capabilities. If you examine the storage providers shown in Figure 4.6, you will see that only one of the VSAN providers is online. The other storage providers from the other two ESXi hosts in this three-node cluster are in a standby state. Should the storage provider that is currently active go offline or fail for whatever reason (most likely because of a host failure), one of the standby providers will be promoted to active.

There is very little work that a vSphere administrator needs to do with storage providers to create a VSAN cluster. This is simply for your own reference. However, if you do run into a situation where the VSAN capabilities are not surfacing up in the VM storage policies section, it is worth visiting this part of the configuration and verifying that at least one of the storage providers is active. If you have no active storage providers, you will not discover any VSAN capabilities when trying to build a VM storage policy. At this point, as a troubleshooting step, you could consider doing a refresh of the storage providers by clicking on the refresh icon (orange circular arrows) in the storage provider screen.

What should be noted is that the VASA storage providers do not play any role in the data path for VSAN. If storage providers fail, this has no impact on VMs running on the VSAN datastore. The impact of not having a storage provider is lack of visibility into the underlying capabilities, so you will not be able to create new storage policies. However, already running VMs and policies are unaffected.

Changing VM Storage Policy On-the-Fly

Being able to change a VM storage policy on-the-fly is quite a unique aspect of VSAN. We will use an example to explain the concept of how you can change a VM storage policy on-the-fly and how it changes the layout of a VM without impacting the application or the guest operating system running in the VM.

Consider the following scenario, briefly mentioned earlier in the context of stripe width. A vSphere administrator has deployed a VM on a hybrid VSAN configuration with the default VM storage policy, which is that the VM storage objects should have no disk striping and should tolerate one failure. The layout of the VM disk file would look something like Figure 4.7.

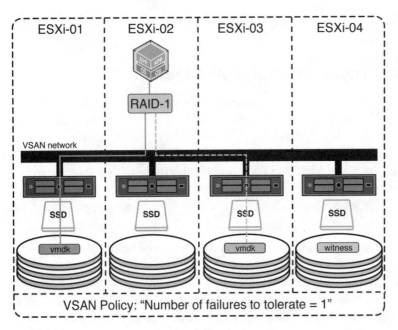

Figure 4.7 VSAN policy with the capability number of failures to tolerate = 1

The VM and its associated applications initially appeared to perform satisfactorily with a 100% cache hit rate; however, over time, an increasing number of VMs were added to the VSAN cluster. The vSphere administrator starts to notice that the VM deployed on VSAN is getting a 90% read cache hit rate. This implies that 10% of reads need to be serviced from magnetic disk/capacity tier. At peak time, this VM is doing 2,000 read operations per second. Therefore, there are 200 reads that need to be serviced from magnetic disk (the 10% of reads that are cache misses). The specifications on the magnetic disks imply that each disk can do 150 IOPS, meaning that a single disk cannot service these additional 200 IOPS. To meet the I/O requirements of the VM, the vSphere administrator correctly decides to create a RAID-0 stripe across two disks.

On VSAN, the vSphere administrator has two options to address this.

The first option is to simply modify the VM storage policy currently associated with the VM and add a stripe width requirement to the policy; however, this would change the storage layout of all the other VMs using this same policy.

Another approach is to create a brand-new policy that is identical to the previous policy but has an additional capability for stripe width. This new policy can then be attached to the VM (and VMDKs) suffering from cache misses. Once the new policy is associated with the VM, the administrator can synchronize the new/updated policy with the VM. This can be done immediately, or can be deferred to a maintenance window if necessary. If it is deferred, the VM is shown as noncompliant with its new policy. When the policy change is implemented, VSAN takes care of changing the underlying VM storage layout required to meet the new policy, *while the VM is still running* without the loss of any failure protection. It does this by mirroring the new storage objects with the additional components (in this case additional RAID-0 stripe width) to the original storage objects.

As seen, the workflow to change the VM storage policy can be done in two ways; either the original current VM storage policy can be edited to include the new capability of a stripe width = 2 or a new VM storage policy can be created that contains the failures to tolerate = 1 and stripe width = 2. The latter is probably more desirable because you may have other VMs using the original policy, and editing that policy will affect all VMs using it. When the new policy is created, this can be associated with the VM and the storage objects in a number of places in the vSphere Web Client. In fact, policies can be changed at the granularity of individual VM storage objects (e.g., VMDK) if necessary.

After making the change, the new components reflecting the new configuration (e.g., a RAID-0 stripe) will enter a state of reconfiguring. This will temporarily build out additional replicas or components, in addition to keeping the original replicas/components, so additional space will be needed on the VSAN datastore to accommodate this on-the-fly change. When the new replicas or components are ready and the configuration is completed, the original replicas/components are discarded.

Note that not all policy changes require the creation of new replicas or components. For example, adding an IOPS limit, or reducing the number of failures to tolerate, or reducing space reservation does not require this. However, in many cases, policy changes will trigger the creation of new replicas or components.

Your VM storage objects may now reflect the changes in the Web Client, for example, a RAID-0 stripe as well as a RAID-1 replica configuration, as shown in Figure 4.8.

Compare this to the tasks you may have to perform on many traditional storage arrays to achieve this. It would involve, at the very least, the following:

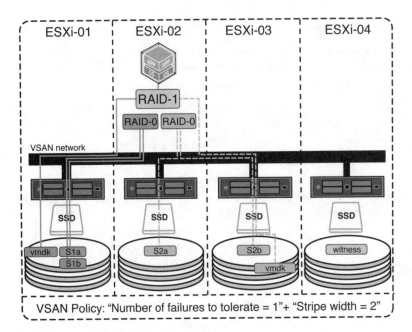

Figure 4.8   VSAN RAID-0 and RAID-1 configuration

- The migration of VMs from the original datastore.

- The decommissioning of the said LUN/volume.

- The creation of a new LUN with the new storage requirements (different RAID level).

- Possibly the reformatting of the LUN with VMFS in the case of block storage.

- Finally, you have to migrate your VMs back to the new datastore.

In the case of VSAN, after the new storage replicas or components have been created and synchronized, the older storage replicas and/or components will be automatically removed. Note that VSAN is capable of striping across disks, disk groups, and hosts when required, as depicted in Figure 4.8, where stripes S1a and S1b are located on the same host but stripes S2a and S2b are located on different hosts. It should also be noted that VSAN can create the new replicas or components without the need to move any data between hosts; in many cases the new components can be instantiated on the same storage on the same host.

We have not shown that there are, of course, additional witness components that could be created with such a change to the configuration. For a VM to continue to access all its components, a full replica copy of the data must be available and more than 50% of the components (votes) of that object must also be available in the cluster. Therefore, changes to the VM storage policy could result in additional witness components being created, or indeed, in the case of introducing a policy with less requirements, there could be fewer witnesses.

You can actually see the configuration changes taking place in the vSphere UI during this process. Select the VM that is being changed, click its **manage** tab, and then choose the **VM storage policies** view, as shown in Figure 4.9. Although this view does not show all the VM storage objects, it does display the VM home namespace, and the VMDKs are visible.

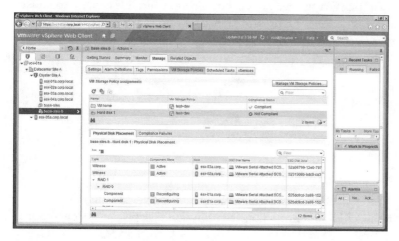

Figure 4.9   VM Storage Policy view in the vSphere client showing component reconfiguration

In VSAN 6.0, there is also a way to examine all resyncing components. Select the VSAN cluster object in the vCenter inventory, then select monitor, Virtual SAN, and finally "resyncing components" in the menu. This will display all components that are currently resyncing/rebuilding. Figure 4.10 shows the resyncing dashboard view, albeit without any resyncing activity taking place.

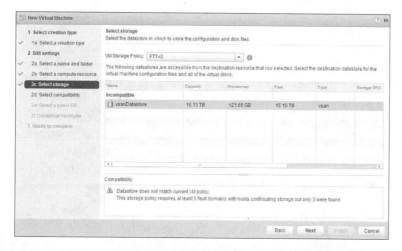

Figure 4.10   Resyncing activity as seen from the vSphere Web Client

Objects, Components, and Witnesses

A number of new concepts have been introduced in this chapter so far, including some new terminology. Chapter 5, "Architectural Details," covers in greater detail objects, components, and indeed witness disks, as well as which VM storage objects are impacted by a particular capability in the VM storage policy. For the moment, it is enough to understand that on VSAN, a VM is no longer represented by a set of files but rather a set of storage objects. There are five types of storage objects:

- VM home namespace
- VMDKs
- VM swap
- Snapshot delta disks
- Snapshot memory

Although the vSphere Web Client displays only the VM home namespace and the VMDKs (hard disks) in the VM > monitor > policies > physical disk placement, snapshot deltas and VM swap can be viewed in the cluster > monitor > Virtual SAN > virtual disks view. We will also show ways of looking at detailed views of all the storage objects, namely delta and VM swap, in Chapter 10, "Troubleshooting, Monitoring, and Performance," when we look at various monitoring tools available to VSAN.

VM Storage Policies

VM storage policies work in an identical fashion to storage profiles introduced in vSphere 5.0, insofar as you simply build a policy containing your VM provisioning requirements. There is a major difference in how storage policies work when compared to the original storage profiles feature. With storage profiles, you simply used the requirements in the policy to select an appropriate datastore when provisioning the VM. The storage policies not only select the appropriate datastore, but also inform the underlying storage layer that there are also certain availability and performance requirements associated with this VM. So while the VSAN datastore may be the destination datastore when the VM is provisioned with a VM storage policy, settings within the policy will stipulate additional requirements. For example, it may state that this VM has a requirement for a number of replica copies of the VM files for availability, a stripe width and read cache requirement for high performance, and a thin provisioning requirement.

VM storage policies are held inside VSAN, as well as being stored in the vCenter inventory database. Every object stores its policy inside its own metadata. This means that vCenter is not required for VM storage policy enforcement. So if for some reason the vCenter Server is unavailable, policies can continue to be enforced.

Enabling VM Storage Policies

In the initial release of VSAN, VM storage policies could be enabled or disabled via the UI. This option is not available in later releases. However, VM storage policies are automatically enabled on a cluster when VSAN is enabled on the cluster. Although VM storage policies are normally only available with certain vSphere editions, a VSAN license will also provide this feature.

Creating VM Storage Policies

vSphere administrators have the ability to create multiple policies. As already mentioned, a number of VSAN capabilities are surfaced up by VASA related to availability and performance, and it is at this point that the administrator must decide what the requirements are for the applications running inside of the VMs from a performance and availability perspective. For example, how many component failures (hosts, network, and disk drives) does the administrator require this VM to tolerate and continue to function? Also, is the application running in this VM demanding from an IOPS perspective? If so, an adequate read cache should be provided as a possible requirement so that the performance requirement is met. Other considerations include whether the VM should be thinly provisioned or thickly provisioned, if RAID-5 or RAID-6 configurations are desired to save storage space, if checksum should be disabled, or if an IOPS limit is required for a particular VM to avoid a "noisy neighbor" situation.

Another point to note is that since vSphere 5.5, policies also support the use of tags for provisioning. Therefore, instead of using VSAN datastore capabilities for the creation of requirements within a VM storage policy, tag-based policies may also be created. The use of tag-based policies is outside the scope of this book, but further information may be found in the generic vSphere storage documentation.

Assigning a VM Storage Policy During VM Provisioning

The assignment of a VM storage policy is done during the VM provisioning. At the point where the vSphere administrator must select a destination datastore, the appropriate policy is selected from the drop-down menu of the available VM storage policies. The datastores are then separated into compatible and incompatible datastores, allowing the vSphere administrator to make the appropriate and correct choice for VM placement.

This matching of datastores does not necessarily mean that the datastore will meet the requirements in the VM storage policy. What it means is that the datastore understands the set of requirements placed in the policy. It may still fail to provision this VM if there are not enough resources available to meet the requirements placed in the policy. However, if a policy cannot be met, the compatibility section in the lower part of the screen displays a warning that states why a policy may not be met.

This three-node cluster example shows a policy that contains a *number of failures to tolerate* = 2. A three-node cluster cannot meet this policy, but when the policy was originally created, the VSAN datastore shows up as a matching resource as it understood the contents of the policy. However, on trying to use this policy when deploying a VM, the VSAN datastore shows up as noncompliant, as Figure 4.11 demonstrates.

Figure 4.11 The VSAN datastore is shown as noncompliant when a policy cannot be met

This is an important point to keep in mind: Just because VSAN tells you it is compatible with a particular policy when that policy is originally created, this in no way implies that it can deploy a VM that uses the policy.

Summary

You may have used VM storage profiles in the past. VM storage policies differ significantly. Although we continue to use VASA, the vSphere APIs for Storage Awareness, VM storage policies have allowed us to switch the storage characteristics away from datastores and to the VMs. VMs, or more specifically the applications running in VMs, can now specify their own requirements using a policy that contains underlying storage capabilities around performance, reliability, and availability.

## Chapter 5

Architectural Details

This chapter examines some of the underlying architectural details of Virtual SAN (VSAN). We have already touched on a number of these aspects of VSAN, including the use of flash devices for caching I/O, the role of VASA in surfacing up VSAN capabilities, VM storage policies, witness disks, the desire for pass-through storage controllers, and so on.

This chapter covers these features in detail, in addition to the new architectural concepts and terminology that is introduced by VSAN. Although most vSphere administrators will never see many of these low-level constructs, it will be useful to have a generic understanding of the services that make up VSAN when troubleshooting or when analyzing log files. Before examining some of the lower-level details, here is one concept that we need to discuss first as it is the core of VSAN: distributed redundant array of inexpensive disks (RAID).

Distributed RAID

VSAN is able to provide highly available and excellent performing VMs through the use of distributed RAID, or to put another way, RAID over the network. From an availability perspective, distributed RAID simply implies that the VSAN environment can withstand the failure of one or more ESXi hosts (or components in that host, such as a disk drive) and continue to provide complete functionality for all your VMs. To ensure that VMs perform optimally, VSAN distributed RAID provides the ability to divide virtual disks across multiple physical disks and hosts.

A point to note, however, is that VM availability and performance is now defined on a per-VM basis through the use of storage policies. Actually, to be more accurate, it is defined on a per-virtual disk basis. Using a storage policy, administrators can now define how many host or disk failures a VM can tolerate in a VSAN cluster and across how many hosts and disks a virtual disk is deployed. If you explicitly choose not to set an availability requirement in the storage policy by setting *number of failures to tolerate* equal to zero, a host or disk failure can certainly impact your VM's availability.

In the earlier releases, VSAN uses RAID-1 (synchronous mirroring) exclusively across hosts to meet the availability and reliability requirement of storage objects deployed on the system. The number of mirror copies (replicas) of the VM storage objects depended on the VM's storage policy, in particular the *number of failures to tolerate* requirement. Depending on the VM storage policy, you could have up to three replicas of a VM disk (VMDK) across a VSAN cluster for availability. By default, VSAN always deploys VMs with *number of failures to tolerate* equal to 1; there is always a replica copy of the VM storage objects for every VM deployed on the VSAN datastore. This is the default policy associated with VSAN datastores. This can be changed based on the policy selected during VM provisioning.

In VSAN 6.2 two new RAID types are introduced. The first of these is RAID-5 and the second is RAID-6. These are created when the *failure tolerance method* capability setting is set to capacity in the VM storage policy rather than performance (which is the default). The purpose of introducing these additional distributed RAID types is to save on capacity usage. Both RAID-5 and RAID-6 use a distributed parity mechanism rather than mirrors to protect the data. With RAID-5, the data is distributed across three disks on three ESXi hosts, and then the parity of this data is calculated and stored on a fourth disk on a fourth ESXi host. The parity is not always stored on the same disk or on the same host. It is distributed, as shown in Figure 5.1.

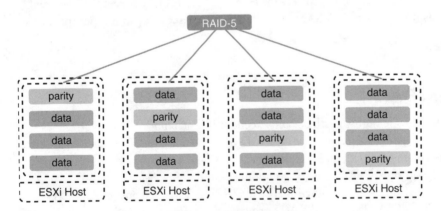

Figure 5.1 RAID-5 deployment with distributed parity

A RAID-5 configuration can tolerate at least one host failure. RAID-6 is designed to tolerate two host failures. In a RAID-6 configuration, data is distributed across four disks on four ESXi hosts, and when the parity is calculated, it is stored on two additional disks on two additional ESXi hosts. Therefore, if you wish to utilize a RAID-6 configuration, a total of six ESXi hosts are required. Once again the parity is distributed, as shown in Figure 5.2.

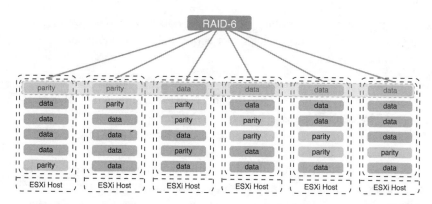

Figure 5.2   RAID-6 deployment with distributed parity

The space savings can be calculated as follows. If you deploy a 100 GB VMDK object and wish to tolerate one failure using a RAID-1 configuration, a total of 200 GB of capacity would be consumed on the VSAN datastore. With RAID-5, a total of 133.33 GB would be consumed. Similarly, if you deploy the same 100 GB VMDK object and wish to tolerate two failures using a RAID-1 configuration, a total of 300 GB of capacity would be consumed on the VSAN datastore. With RAID-6, a total of 150 GB would be consumed.

As discussed in Chapter 4, "VM Storage Policies on VSAN," administrators may now choose between performance and capacity. If performance is the absolute end goal for administrators, then RAID-1 (which is still the default) is the *failure tolerance method* that should be used. If administrators do not need maximum performance, and are more concerned with capacity usage, then RAID-5/6 as the failure tolerance method may be used.

Depending on the number of disk stripes per object policy setting, a VM disk object may be "striped" across a number of disk spindles to achieve a desired performance. Performance of VM storage objects can be improved via a RAID-0 configuration; however, a stripe configuration does not always necessitate an improvement in performance. The section "Stripe Width Policy Setting," later in this chapter, explains the reasons for this as well as when it is useful to increase the stripe width of a VMDK in the VM storage policy.

Objects and Components

It is important to understand the concept that the VSAN datastore is an *object storage system* and that VMs are now made up of a number of different storage objects. This is a new concept for vSphere administrators as traditionally a VM is made up of a set of files on a logical unit number (LUN) or volume.

We have not spoken in great detail about object and components so far, so before we go into detail about the various types of objects, let's start with the definition and concepts of an object and component on VSAN.

An *object* is an individual storage block device, compatible with SCSI semantics that resides on the VSAN datastore. It may be created on demand and at any size, although VMDKs were limited to 2 TB–512 bytes in the initial release of VSAN version 5.5. Since the release of VSAN 6.0, VMDKs of up to 62 TB are now supported, in line with virtual machine file system (VMFS) and network file system (NFS) datastores. Objects now replace LUNs as the main unit of storage on VSAN. In VSAN, the objects that make up a virtual machine are VMDKs, VM home namespace, and VM swap. Of course, if a snapshot is taken of the virtual machine, then a delta disk object is also created. If the snapshot includes the memory of the virtual machine, this is also instantiated as an object, so a snapshot could be made up of either one or two objects, depending on the snapshot type. Each "object" in VSAN has its own RAID tree that turns the requirements into an actual layout on physical devices. When a VM storage policy is selected during VM deployment, the requirement around availability and performance in the policy applies to the VM objects.

Components are leaves of the object's RAID trees—that is, a "piece" of an object that is stored on a particular "cache device + capacity device" combination (in a physical disk group). A component gets transparent caching/buffering from the cache device (which is always flash), with its data "at rest" on a capacity device (which could be flash in all-flash VSAN configurations or magnetic disk in hybrid VSAN configurations).

A VM can have five different types of objects on a VSAN datastore as follows, keeping in mind that each VM may have multiples of some of these objects associated with it:

- The VM home or "namespace directory"
- A swap object (if the VM is powered on)
- Virtual disks/VMDKs
- Delta disks (each an object) created for snapshots
- Snapshot memory (each an object) optionally created for snapshots

Of the five objects, the VM namespace may need a little further explanation. All VMs files, excluding VMDKs, deltas (snapshots), memory (snapshots) and swap, reside in an area called the *VM namespace* on VSAN. The typical files found in the VM home namespace are the .vmx, the .log files, .vmdk descriptor files, and snapshot deltas descriptors files, and everything else one would expect to find in a VM home directory.

Each storage object is deployed on VSAN as a RAID tree, and each leaf of the tree is said to be a component. For instance, if I choose to deploy a VMDK with a stripe width of 2, but did not wish to tolerate any failures (for whatever reason), a RAID-0 stripe would be configured across a minimum of two disks for this VMDK. The VMDK would be the object, and each of the stripes would be a component of that object.

Similarly, if I specified that my VMDK should be able to tolerate at least one failure in the cluster (host, disk, or network), and left all the other policy settings at their defaults, a RAID-1 mirror of the VMDK object would be created with one replica component on one host and another replica component on another host in my VSAN cluster. Finally, if my policy included a requirement for both striping and availability, my striped components would be mirrored across hosts, giving me a RAID 0+1 configuration. This would result in four components making up my single object, with two striped components in each replica.

Note that delta disks are created when a snapshot is taken of a VM. A delta disk inherits the same policy as the parent disk (stripe width, replicas, and so on).

The swap object is created only when the VM is powered on.

There is another component called the witness. The witness component is very important and special. Although it does not directly contribute toward VM storage, it is nonetheless an important component required to determine a quorum for a VM's storage objects in the event of a failure in the cluster. We will return to the witness component shortly, but for the moment let's concentrate on VM storage objects.

Component Limits

One major limit applies in relation to components in VSAN. It is important to understand this because it is a hard limit and essentially will limit the number of VMs you can run on a single host and in your cluster. The limitations of the original VSAN 5.5 were as follows:

- **Maximum number of components per host limit**: 3,000

In VSAN 6.0, the number of components per host limit was increased, as a new on-disk format was introduced.

- **Maximum number of components per host limit**: 9,000

Components per host include components from powered-off VMs, unregistered VMs, and templates. VSAN distributes components across the various hosts in the cluster and will always try to achieve an even distribution of components for balance. However, some hosts may have more components than others, which is why VMware recommends, as a best practice, that hosts participating in a VSAN cluster be similarly or identically configured. Components are a significant sizing consideration when designing and deploying VSAN clusters, as discussed in further detail in Chapter 9, "Designing a VSAN Cluster."

The vSphere Web Client enables administrators to interrogate objects and components of the VM home namespace and the VMDKs of a VM. Figure 5.3 provides an example of one such layout. The VM has one hard disk, which is mirrored across two different hosts, as you can see in the "hosts" column, where it shows the location of the components.

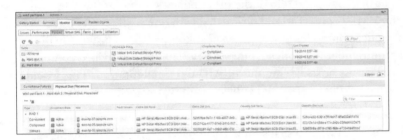

Figure 5.3   Physical disk placement

Virtual Machine Storage Objects

As stated earlier, the five storage objects are VM home namespace, VM Swap, VMDK, delta disks, and snapshot memory, as illustrated in Figure 5.4. We will ignore Snapshot Memory for the moment, and discuss the other objects in a little more detail.

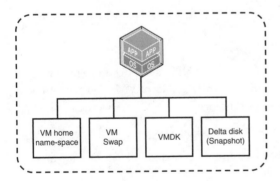

Figure 5.4   VM storage objects

We will now look at how characteristics defined in the VM storage policy impact these storage objects. Note that not all of the VM storage objects implement these policies.

Namespace

Virtual machines use the namespace object as their VM home, and use it to store all of the virtual machine files that are not dedicated objects in their own right. So, for example, this includes, but is not limited to, the following:

- The .vmx, .vmdk (the descriptor portion), .log files that the VMX uses.

- Digest files for content-based read cache (CBRC) for VMware horizon view. This feature is referred to as the view storage accelerator. Virtual desktop infrastructure (VDI) is a significant use case for VSAN.

- vSphere Replication and Site Recovery Manager files.

- Guest customization files.

- Files created by other solutions.

These are unique objects and there is one per VM. VSAN leverages VMFS as the file system within the namespace object to store all the files of the VM. This is a fully fleshed, vanilla VMFS. That is, it includes the cluster capabilities, so that we can support all the solutions that use locks on VMFS (e.g., vMotion, vSphere High Availability [HA]). This appears as an auto-mounted subdirectory when you examine the ESXi hosts' file systems. However, although it is a vanilla VMFS being used, it does not have the same limitations as VMFS has in other environments because the number of hosts connected to these VM home namespace VMFS volumes is at most two (e.g., during a vMotion), whereas in traditional environments the same VMFS volume could be shared between dozens of hosts. In other words, VSAN leverages these vanilla VMFS volumes in a completely different way, allowing for greater scale and better performance.

For the VM home, a special VM storage policy is used. For the most part, the VM home storage object does not inherit all of the same policy requirements as the VMDKs. If you think about it, why would you want to give something like the VM home namespace a percentage of flash read cache (hybrid only) or a stripe width? You wouldn't, which is why the VM home namespace does not have these settings applied even when they are in the policy associated with the virtual machine. The VM home namespace does, however, inherit the *number of failures to tolerate* setting. This allows the VM to survive multiple hardware failures in the cluster. With the release of VSAN 6.2, it also inherits the *failure tolerance method* policy setting, which means that the VM home namespace could be deployed as a RAID-5 or RAID-6 configuration, not just a RAID-1 configuration, as was the case in prior versions of VSAN.

So, because high performance is not a major requirement for the VM home namespace storage object, VSAN overwrites the inherited policy settings so that stripe width is always set to 1 and read cache reservation is always set to 0%. It also has object space reservation set to 0% so that it is always thinly provisioned. This avoids the VM home namespace object consuming unnecessary resources, and makes these resources available to objects that might need them, such as VMDKs.

One other important note is that if force provisioning is set in the policy, the VM home namespace object also inherits that, meaning that the VM will be deployed even if the full complement of resources is not available.

In VSAN 6.2, a new performance service was introduced. This service aggregates performance information from all of the ESXi hosts in the cluster and stores the metrics in a stats database on the VSAN datastore. The object in which the "stats DB" is stored is also a namespace object. Therefore, the use of namespace objects is not limited to virtual machines, although this is the most common use.

Virtual Machine Swap

The VM swap object also has its own special policy settings. For the VM swap object, its policy always has number of failures to tolerate set to 1. The main reason for this is that swap does not need to persist when a virtual machine is restarted. Therefore, if HA restarts the virtual machine on another host elsewhere in the cluster, a new swap object is created. Therefore, there is no need to add additional protection above tolerating one failure.

By default, swap objects are provisioned 100% up front, without the need to set object space reservation to 100% in the policy. This means, in terms of admission control, VSAN will not deploy the VM unless there is enough disk space to accommodate the full size of the VM swap object. In VSAN 6.2, a new advanced host option $SwapThickProvision-Disabled$ has been created to allow the VM swap option to be provisioned as a thin object. If this advanced setting is set to true, the VM swap objects will be thinly provisioned.

VMDKs and Deltas

As you have seen, VM home namespace and VM swap have their own default policies when a VM is deployed and do not adhere to all of the capabilities set in the policy. Therefore, it is only the VMDKs and snapshot files (delta disks) of these disk files that obey all the capabilities that are set in the VM storage policies.

Because VSAN objects may be made up of multiple components, each VMDK and delta has its own RAID tree configuration when deployed on VSAN.

Witnesses and Replicas

As part of the RAID-1 tree, each object usually has multiple replicas, which as we have seen, could be made up of one or more components. We would like to mention here that when we create VM storage objects, one or more witness components *may* also get created. Witnesses are part of each and every object in the RAID-1 tree. They are components that make up a leaf of the RAID-1 tree, but they contain only metadata. They are there to be tiebreakers and are used for quorum determination in the event of failures in the VSAN cluster.

Let's take the easiest case to explain their purpose: Suppose, for example, that we have deployed a VM that has a stripe width setting of 1 and it also has number of failures to tolerate setting of 1. We do not wish to use RAID-5 or RAID-6 in this example. In this case, two replica copies of the VM need to be created. Effectively, this is a RAID-1 with two replicas; however, with two replicas, there is no way to differentiate between a network partition and a host failure. Therefore, a third entity called the witness is added to the configuration. For an object on VSAN to be available, two conditions have to be met:

- The RAID tree must allow for data access. (With a RAID-1 configuration, at least one full replica needs to be intact. With a RAID-0 configuration, all stripes need to be intact.) With the new RAID-5 and RAID-6 configurations, three out of four RAID-5 components must still be available, and four out of the six RAID-6 components must still be available.

- In the earlier versions of VSAN, the rule was that there must be more than 50% of all components available. With the introduction of votes associated with components in VSAN 6.0, this rule changed to having more than 50% of the votes available.

In the preceding example, only when there is access to one replica copy and a witness, or indeed two replica copies (and no witness), you would be able to access the object. That way, at most one part of the cluster can ever access an object in the event of a network partition.

A common question is whether the witness consumes any space on the VSAN datastore. In the original VSAN version 5.5, which uses VMFS as the on-disk format, a witness consumes about 2 MB of space for metadata on the VSAN datastore. With the release of VSAN version 6.0, which uses VSANFS as the on-disk format, a witness consumes about 4 MB of space for metadata on the VSAN datastore. Although insignificant when compared to most, it could be something to consider when running through design, sizing, and scaling exercises while planning to deploy many VMs with many VMDKs on VSAN.

Object Layout

The next question people usually ask is how objects are laid out in a VSAN environment. As mentioned, the VM home namespace for storing the VM configuration files is formatted with VMFS. All other VM disk objects (whether VMDKs or snapshots) are instantiated as distributed storage objects in their own right.

Although VSAN takes care of object placement to meet the *number of failure to tolerate* and *failure tolerance method* requirements and an administrator should not worry about these placement decisions, we understand that with a new solution you may have the desire to have a better understanding of physical placement of components and objects. VMware expected that administrators would have this desire; therefore, the vSphere user interface (UI) allows vSphere administrators to interrogate the layout of a VM object and see where each component (stripes, replicas, and witnesses) that make up a storage object resides, as shown in Figure 5.5.

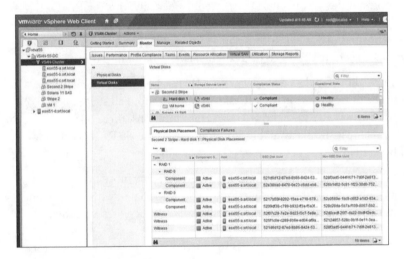

Figure 5.5   RAID-1, RAID-0, and witnesses

VSAN will never let components of different replicas (mirrors) share the same host for availability purposes.

Note that in versions prior to VSAN 6.2, we do not see the VM swap file objects. This was because the swap file's universally unique identifier (UUID) was not available through the virtual infrastructure management (VIM) application programming interface (API), so neither the Ruby vSphere console (also known as RVC, covered later in Chapter 10, "Troubleshooting, Monitoring, and Performance") nor the vSphere Web Client can show this information. However, there is a method to retrieve swap file information in the previous version of VSAN, as demonstrated shortly. Snapshot/delta disk objects are not visible in the vSphere UI either in versions of VSAN prior to 6.2, but these objects implicitly inherit the same policy settings as the VMDK base disk against which the snapshot is taken.

In VSAN 6.2, both the VM swap objects and snapshot deltas are visible via the vSphere Web Client. If administrators navigate to the VSAN cluster > monitor tab, and select virtual disks, the objects are listed there. We have been talking about the concept of VM storage policies for a while now; let's now consider this further.

Default VM Storage Policy

VMware encourages administrators to create their own policies with VSAN and not to rely on the default policy settings. However, if you decide to deploy a VM on a VSAN datastore without selecting a policy, a default policy is applied. The default policy, called Virtual SAN default storage policy, has been created with very specific characteristics to prevent administrators from unintentionally putting VMs and the associated data at risk when, for whatever reason, a policy is not selected. We have seen this happening fairly often in the earlier version of VSAN when administrators create VMs in a hurry and simply forget to select a policy. However, we do need to stress that VMware strongly encourages administrators to create their own VM storage policies, even when the requirements are the same as those in the default policy. For one thing, it enables the administrator to do meaningful compliance reporting.

The default policy can be observed from the vSphere Web Client. Let's inspect it in Figure 5.6.

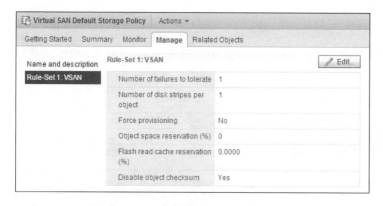

Figure 5.6   Virtual SAN default storage policy

From this, we can deduce that the storage objects will always be deployed with a *number of failures to tolerate* set to 1. What is missing from the view in Figure 5.6 is *failure tolerance method* policy setting, which by default is set to *RAID-1 (mirroring) performance*. This means that RAID-5 (not RAID-6) configurations are not used. In other words, this storage object will be deployed in a RAID-1 mirror. If the *failure tolerance method* policy is set to *RAID-5/6 (erasure coding)—capacity*, then RAID-5 or RAID-6 is implemented, based on the value of *number of failures to tolerate*. This relationship is discussed in detail in Chapter 4. Figure 5.7 shows the various settings that the fault tolerance method can take in a policy.

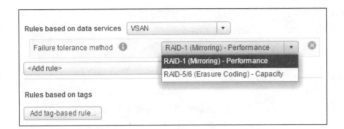

Figure 5.7   Fault tolerance method

Another point to make about the default policy is that checksum will be enabled; in other words the capability *disable checksum* will be set to *false*.

A final point is related to force provisioning. By default, *force* `provisioning` is set to "No"; it is only explicitly enabled for the VM swap object. If we would like to, for instance, bootstrap a vCenter Server onto a single-host VSAN cluster, then it would not be possible with the current policy settings. This is because the creation of the VM will fail since the default policy has *number of failures to tolerate* set to 1, and since only a single host is available in the VSAN cluster, VSAN cannot adhere to these requirements. To allow for this to work, a change in default profile is needed, and *force provisioning* will need to be set to "Yes" in the default policy.

Now we will shortly take a look at what an administrator can define in a policy other than using the default policy.

VSAN Software Components

This section briefly outlines some of the software components that make up the distributed software layer.

Much of this information will not be of particular use to vSphere administrators on a day-to-day basis. All of these complexities are hidden away based on how VMware has implemented the installation and configuration of VSAN by a few simple mouse clicks. However, we did want to highlight some of the major components behind the scenes for you because, as mentioned in the introduction, you may see messages from time-to-time related to these components appearing in the vSphere UI and the VMkernel logs, and we want to provide you with some background on what is the function of these components. Also, when you begin to use the RVC in Chapter 10, a number of the outputs will refer to these software components, which is another reason why we are including this brief outline.

The VSAN architecture consists of four major components, as illustrated in Figure 5.8 and is described in more depth in the sections that follow.

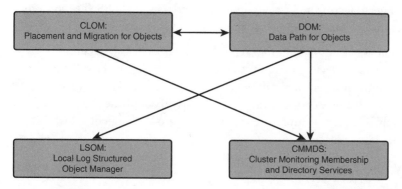

Figure 5.8 VSAN software components

Component Management

The VSAN local log structured object manager (LSOM) works at the physical disk level. It is the LSOM that provides storage for the VM storage object components in the local disks of the ESXi hosts, and it includes both the read caching (for hybrid configurations) and write buffering (for both hybrid and all-flash configuration) for these objects. When we talk in terms of components, we are talking about one of the striped components that make up a RAID-0 configuration, or one of the replicas that makes up a RAID-1 configuration. It could also be a data or parity segment for RAID-5 or RAID-6 configurations. Therefore, LSOM works with the magnetic disks, solid-state disks (SSDs), and flash devices on the ESXi hosts.

Another way of describing the LSOM is to state that it is responsible for providing persistence of storage for the VSAN cluster. By this, we mean that it stores the components that make up VM storage objects as well as any configuration information and the VM storage policy.

LSOM reports events for these devices, for example, if a device has become unhealthy. The LSOM is also responsible for retrying I/O if transient device errors occur.

LSOM also aids in the recovery of objects. On every ESXi host boot, LSOM performs an SSD log recovery. This entails a read of the entire log that ensures that the in-memory state is up-to-date and correct. This means that a reboot of an ESXi host that is participating in a VSAN cluster can take longer than an ESXi host that is not participating in a VSAN cluster.

Data Paths for Objects

The distributed object manager (DOM) provides distributed data access paths to objects built from local (LSOM) components. The DOM is responsible for the creation of reliable, fault-tolerant VM storage objects from local components across multiple ESXi hosts in the VSAN cluster. It does this by implementing distributed RAID types for objects.

DOM is also responsible for handling different types of failures such as I/O failing from a device and unable to contact a host. In the event of an unexpected host failure, during recovery DOM must resynchronize all the components that make up every object. Components publish a bytesToSync value periodically to show the progress of a synchronize operation. This can be monitored via the vSphere Web Client UI when recovery operations are taking place.

Object Ownership

We discuss object owners from time to time in this chapter. Let's elaborate a little more about what object ownership is. For every storage object in the cluster, VSAN elects an owner for the object. The owner can be considered the storage head responsible for coordinating (internally within VSAN) who can do I/O to the object. The owner basically is the entity that ensures consistent data on the distributed object by performing a transaction for every operation that modifies the data/metadata of the object.

As an analogy, in NFS configurations, consider the concept of NFS server and NFS client. Only certain clients can communicate successfully with the server. In this case, the VSAN storage object owner can be considered along the same lines as an NFS server, determining which clients can do I/O and which clients cannot. The final part of object ownership is the concept of a component manager. The component manager can be thought of as the network front end of LSOM (in other words, how a storage object in VSAN can be accessed).

An object owner communicates to the component manager to find the leaves on the RAID tree that contain the components of the storage object. Typically, there is only one client accessing the object. However, in the case of a vMotion operation, multiple clients may be accessing the same object. In the vast majority of cases, the owner entity and client co-reside on the same node in the VSAN cluster.

Placement and Migration for Objects

The cluster level object manager (CLOM) is responsible for ensuring that an object has a configuration that matches its policy (i.e., the requested stripe width is implemented or that there are a sufficient number of mirrors/replicas in place to meet the availability requirement of the VM). Effectively, CLOM takes the policy assigned to an object and applies a variety of heuristics to find a configuration in the current cluster that will meet that policy. It does this while also load balancing the resource utilization across all the nodes in the VSAN cluster.

DOM then applies a configuration as dictated by CLOM. CLOM distributes components across the various ESXi hosts in the cluster. CLOM tries to create some sort of balance, but it is not unusual for some hosts to have more components, capacity used/reserved, or flash read cache used/reserved than others.

Each node in a VSAN cluster runs an instance of CLOM, called *clomd*. Each instance of CLOM is responsible for the configurations and policy compliance of the objects owned by the DOM on the ESXi host, where if it runs so it needs to communicate with cluster monitoring, membership, and directory service (CMMDS) to be aware of ownership transitions. CLOM only communicates with entities on the node where it runs. It does not use the network.

Cluster Monitoring, Membership, and Directory Services

The purpose of cluster monitoring, membership, and directory services (CMMDS) is to discover, establish, and maintain a cluster of networked node members. It manages the physical cluster resources inventory of items such as hosts, devices, and networks and stores object metadata information such as policies, distributed RAID configuration, and so on in an in-memory database. The object metadata is always also persisted on disk. It is also responsible for the detection of failures in nodes and network paths.

Other software components browse the directory and subscribe to updates to learn of changes in cluster topology and object configuration. For instance, DOM can use the content of the directory to determine the nodes storing the components of an object and the paths by which those nodes are reachable.

Note that CMMDS forms a cluster (and elects a master) only if there is multicast network connectivity between the hosts.

CMMDS is used to elect "owners" for objects. The owner of an object will perform all the RAID tasks for a particular object, as discussed earlier.

Host Roles (Master, Slave, Agent)

When a VSAN cluster is formed, you may notice through `esxcli` commands that each ESXi host in a VSAN cluster has a particular role. These roles are for the VSAN clustering service *only*. The clustering service (CMMDS) is responsible for maintaining an updated directory of disks, disk groups, and objects that resides on each ESXi host in the VSAN cluster. This has nothing to do with managing objects in the cluster or doing I/O to an object by the way; this is simply to allow nodes in the cluster to keep track of one another. The **clustering service** is based on a master (with a backup) and agents, where all nodes send updates to the master and the master then redistributes them to the agents, using a reliable ordered multicast protocol that is specific to VSAN. This is the reason why the VSAN network must be able to handle multicast traffic, as discussed in the earlier chapters of this book. Roles are applied during a cluster discover, at which time the ESXi hosts participating in the VSAN cluster elect the master. A vSphere administrator has no control over which role a cluster member takes.

A common question is why a backup role is needed. The reason for this is since the ESXi host that is currently in the master role suffers a catastrophic failure and there is no backup, all ESXi hosts must reconcile their entire view of the directory with the newly elected master. This would mean that all the nodes in the cluster might be sending all their directory contents from their respective view of the cluster to the new master. By having a backup, this negates the requirement to send all of this information over the network, and thus speed up the process of electing a new master node.

In the case of VSAN stretched clusters, a configuration introduced in VSAN 6.1 that allows nodes in a VSAN cluster to be geographically dispersed across different sites, the master node will reside on one site whilst the backup node will reside on the other site.

An important point to make is that, to a user or even for a vSphere administrator, the ESXi node that is elected for the role of master has no special features or other visible differences. Because the master is automatically elected, even on failures, and given that the node has no user visible difference in abilities, doing operations on a master node versus any other node doesn't matter at all.

Reliable Datagram Transport

The reliable datagram transport (RDT) is the communication mechanism within VSAN. It uses transmission control protocol (TCP) at the transport layer. It creates and tears down TCP connections (sockets) on demand.

RDT is built on top of the VSAN clustering service. The clustering service uses heartbeats to determine link state. If a link failure is detected, RDT will drop connections on the path and choose a different healthy path.

When an operation needs to be performed on a VSAN object, DOM uses RDT to talk to the owner of the VSAN object. Because the RDT promises reliable delivery, users of the RDT can rely on it to retry requests after path or node failures, which may result in a change of object ownership and hence a new path to the owner of the object. The CMMDS (via its heart beating and monitoring functions) and the RDT are responsible for handling timeouts and path failures.

On-Disk Formats

Before looking at the various I/O-related flows, let's briefly discuss the on-disk formats used by VSAN.

Cache Devices

VMware uses its own proprietary on-disk format for the flash devices used in the cache layer by VSAN. In hybrid configurations, which has both a read cache and a write buffer, the read cache portion of the flash device has its own on-disk format, and there is also a log-structured format for the write buffer portion of the flash device. In the case of all-flash configuration, there is only a write buffer; there is no read cache. Both formats are specially designed to boost the endurance of the flash device beyond the basic functionality provided by the flash device firmware.

Capacity Devices

It may come as a surprise to some, but in the original VSAN 5.5 release, VMware used the VMFS as the on-disk format for VSAN. However, this was not the traditional VMFS. Instead, there is a new format unique to VSAN called VMFS local (VMFS-L). VMFS-L is the on-disk file system format of the local storage on each ESXi host in VSAN. The standard VMFS is specifically designed to work in clustered environments where many hosts are sharing a datastore. It was not designed with single-host/local disk environments in mind, and certainly not distributed datastores. VMFS-L was introduced for use cases like distributed storage. Primarily, the clustered on-disk locking and associated heartbeats on VMFS were removed. These are necessary only when many hosts share the file system. They are unnecessary when only a single host is using it. Now instead of placing a SCSI reservation on the volume to place a lock on the metadata, a new lock manager is implemented that avoids using SCSI reservation completely. VMFS-L does not require on-disk heartbeating either. Now it simply updates an in-memory copy of the heartbeat (because no other host needs to know about the lock). Tests have shown that VMFS-L can provide disks in about half the time of standard VMFS with these changes incorporated.

In VSAN 6.0, a new on-disk format was introduced. This was based on the VirstoFS, a high performance, sparse file system from a company called Virsto that VMware acquired. This is referred to as the v2 format, and improved the performance of snapshots (through a new vsanSparse format) and clones on VSAN 6.0. Customers could upgrade from VMFS-L (v1) to VSANFS (v2) through a seamless rolling upgrade process, where the content of each host's disk group was evacuated elsewhere in the cluster; the disk group on the host was removed and recreated with the new v2 on-disk format, and this process was repeated until all disk groups were upgraded.

In VSAN 6.2, to accommodate new features and functionality such as deduplication, compression, and checksum, another on-disk format (v3) is introduced. This continues to be based on VSANFS, but has some additional features for the new functionality.

VSAN I/O Flow

In the next couple of paragraphs, we will trace the I/O flow on both a read and a write operation from an application within a guest OS when the VM is deployed on a VSAN datastore. We will look at a read operation when the stripe width value is set to 2, and we will look at a write operation when the number of failures to tolerate is set to 1 using RAID-1. This will give you an understanding of the underlying I/O flow, and this can be leveraged to get an understanding of the I/O flows when other capability values are specified. We will also discuss the destaging to the capacity layer, as this is where deduplication and compression comes into play. Before we do, let's first look at the role of flash in the I/O path.

Caching Algorithms

There are different caching algorithms in place for the hybrid configurations and the all-flash configurations. In a nutshell, the caching algorithm on hybrid configurations is concerned with optimally destaging blocks from the cache tier to the capacity tier, whilst the caching algorithm on all-flash configurations is concerned with ensuring that hot blocks (data that is live) are held in the caching tier while cold blocks (data that is not being accessed) are held in the capacity tier.

The Role of the Cache Layer

As mentioned in the previous section, SSDs (and by that we also mean flash devices) have two purposes in VSAN when they are used in the caching layer on hybrid configurations; they act as both a read cache and a write buffer. This dramatically improves the performance of VMs. In some respect, VSAN can be compared to a number of "hybrid" storage solutions in the market, which also use a combination of SSD and magnetic disks to increase the performance of the I/O, but which have the ability to scale out capacity based on low-cost SATA or SAS magnetic disk drives.

There is no read cache in all-flash VSAN configurations; the caching tier acts as a write buffer only.

Purpose of Read Cache

The purpose of the read cache in hybrid configurations is to maintain a list of commonly accessed disk blocks by VMs. This reduces the I/O read latency in the event of a cache hit; that is, the disk block is in cache and does not have to be retrieved from magnetic disk. The actual block that is being read by the application running in the VM may not be on the same ESXi host where the VM is running. In this case, DOM picks a mirror for a given read (based on offset) and sends it to the correct component. This is then sent to

LSOM to find whether the block is in the cache. If it transpires that there is a cache miss, the data are retrieved directly from magnetic disk in the capacity tier, but of course this will incur a latency penalty and could also impact the number of input/output operations per second (IOPS) achievable by VSAN. This is the purpose of having a read cache on hybrid VSAN configurations, as it reduces the number of IOPS that need to be sent to magnetic disks. The goal is to have a minimum read cache hit rate of 90%. VSAN also has a read ahead cache optimization where 1 MB of data around the data block being read is also brought into cache.

VSAN always tries to make sure that it sends a given read request to the same mirror so that the block only gets cached once in the cluster; in other words, it is cached only on one cache device, and that cache device is on the ESXi host that contains the mirror where the read requests are sent. Because cache space is relatively expensive, this mechanism optimizes how much cache you require for VSAN. Correctly sizing VSAN cache has a very significant impact on performance in steady state.

Why There Is No Read Cache in All-Flash VSAN Configurations?

In all-flash VSAN configurations, since the capacity layer is also flash, if there would be a read cache miss, fetching the data block from the capacity tier would not be as expensive as fetching a data block from the capacity tier in a hybrid solution which uses spinning disk. Instead, it is actually a very quick (typically sub-millisecond) operation. Therefore, it is not necessary to have a flash-based read cache in all-flash VSAN configurations since the capacity tier can handle reads effectively. By not implementing a read cache, we also free up the cache tier for more writes, boosting overall performance.

Purpose of Write Cache

The write cache behaves as a write-back buffer in both all-flash and hybrid VSAN configurations. Writes are acknowledged when they enter the prepare stage on flash devices used in the cache tier. The fact that we can use flash devices for writes in hybrid configurations reduces significantly the latency for write operations since the writes do not have to be destaged to the capacity tier before they are acknowledged.

Because the writes go to the cache tier flash devices, we must ensure that there is a copy of the data block elsewhere in the VSAN cluster. All VMs deployed to VSAN have an availability policy setting that ensures at least one additional copy of virtual machine data is available (unless, of course, administrators explicitly override the default policy and choose a failure to tolerate setting of 0). This availability policy includes the write cache contents. Once a write is initiated by the application running inside of the guest OS, the write is sent to all replicas in parallel. Writes are buffered in the cache tier flash device associated with the disk group where the components of the VMDK storage object reside.

This means that in the event of a host failure, we also have a copy of the in-cache data and so no corruption will happen to the data; the virtual machine will simply reuse the replicated copy of the cache as well as the replicated disk data.

Note that all-flash VSAN configurations continue to use the cache tier as a write buffer, and all virtual machine writes land first on this cache device, same as in hybrid configurations. The major algorithm change here is how the write cache is used. The write cache is now used to hold "hot" blocks of data (data that is in a state of change). Only when the blocks become "cold" (no longer updated/written) they are moved to the capacity tier.

Anatomy of a VSAN Read on Hybrid VSAN

For an object placed on a VSAN datastore, when using a RAID-1 configuration, it is possible that there are multiple replicas when the number of failures to tolerate value is set to a value greater than 0 in the VM storage policy. Reads may now be spread across the replicas. Different reads may be sent to different replicas according to their logical block address (LBA) on disk. This is to ensure that VSAN does not necessarily consume more read cache than necessary, and avoids caching the same data in multiple locations.

Taking the example of an application in issuing a read request, the cluster service (CMMDS) is first consulted to determine the owner of the data. The owner, using the logical block address (LBA), determines which component will service the request and sends it there. This then goes to LSOM to determine if the block is in read cache. If the block is present in read cache, the read is serviced from that read cache. If a read cache miss occurs, and the block is not in cache, the next step is to read the data from the capacity tier, and on hybrid VSAN configurations, the capacity tier will be made up of magnetic disks.

As mentioned, the owner of the object splits the reads across the components that go to make up that object, so that a given block is cached on at most one node, maximizing the effectiveness of the cache tier. In many cases, the data may have to be transferred over the network if the data is on the storage of a different ESXi host. Once the data are retrieved, it is returned to the requesting ESXi host and the read is served up to the application.

Figure 5.9 gives an idea of the steps involved in a read operation on hybrid VSAN. In this particular example, the stripe width setting is 2, and the VM's storage object is striped across disks that reside on different hosts. (Each stripe is therefore a component, to use the correct VSAN terminology.) Note that Stripe-1a and Stripe-1b reside on the same host, while Stripe-2a and Stripe-2b reside on different hosts. In this scenario, our read needs to come from Stripe-2b. If the owner does not have the block that the application within the VM wants to read, the read will go over the 10 GbE network to retrieve the data block.

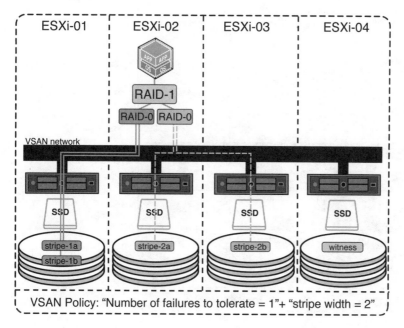

Figure 5.9   VSAN I/O flow: Failures to tolerate = 1 + stripe width = 2

Anatomy of a VSAN Read on All-Flash VSAN

Since there is no read cache in all-flash VSAN clusters, the I/O flow is subtlety different when compared to a read operation on hybrid configurations. On an all-flash VSAN, when a read is issued, the write buffer is first checked to see if the block is present (i.e., is it a hot block?). The same is done on hybrid, FYI. If the block being read is in the write buffer, it will be fetched from there. If the requested block is not in the write buffer, the block is fetched from the capacity tier. Now remember that the capacity tier is also flash in an all-flash VSAN, so the latency overhead in first checking the cache tier, and then having to retrieve the block from the capacity tier is minimal. This is the reason why we have not implemented a read cache for all-flash VSAN configurations, and the cache tier is totally dedicated as a write buffer. By not implementing a read cache, as mentioned earlier, we free up the cache tier for more writes, boosting overall IOPS performance.

Anatomy of a VSAN Write on Hybrid VSAN

Now that we know how a read works, let's take a look at a write operation. When a new VM is deployed, its components are stored on multiple hosts. VSAN does not have the notion of data locality and as such it could be possible that your VM runs on ESXi-01 from a CPU and memory perspective, while the components of the VM are stored on both ESXi-02 and ESXi-03, as shown in Figure 5.10.

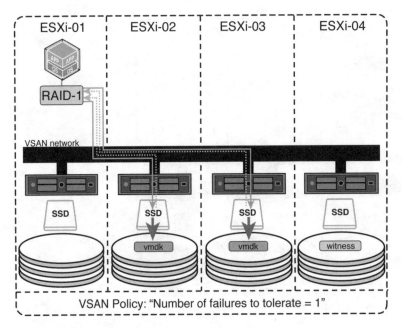

Figure 5.10   VSAN I/O flow: Write acknowledgment

When an application within a VM issues a write operation, the owner of the object clones the write operation. The write is sent to the write cache (SSD flash device) on ESXi-02 and to the write cache (SSD flash device) on ESXi-03 in *parallel*. The write is acknowledged when the write reaches the cache, and the prepare operation on the SSD is completed. The owner waits for ACK from both hosts and completes I/O. Later, the write will be destaged as part of a batch commit to magnetic disk. This happens independent from each other. In other words, ESXi-02 may destage writes at a different time than ESXi-03. This is not coordinated because it depends on various things such as how fast the write buffer is filling up, how much capacity is left, and where data are stored on magnetic disks.

Anatomy of a VSAN Write on All-Flash VSAN

A write operation on an all-flash VSAN is very similar to how writes are done in hybrid VSAN configurations. In hybrid configurations, only 30% of the cache tier is dedicated to the write buffer, and the other 70% is assigned to the read cache. Since there is no read cache in all-flash configurations, the full 100% of the cache tier is assigned to the write buffer (up to a maximum of 600 GB in the current version of VSAN). However, the authors understand that this limitation should be increased in the near future.

The role of the cache tier is also subtlety different between hybrid and all-flash. As we have seen, the write buffer in hybrid VSAN improves performance since writes do not need to go to the capacity tier made up of magnetic disks, thus improving latency. In all-flash VSAN, the purpose of the write buffer is endurance. A design goal of all-flash VSAN is to place high endurance flash devices in the cache tier so that they can handle the most amounts of I/O. This allows the capacity tier to use a lower specification flash device, and they do not need to handle the same amount of writes as the cache tier.

Having said that, write operations for all-flash are still very similar to hybrid in so far as that only when the block being written is in the write buffer of all of the replicas is the write acknowledged.

Retiring Writes to Capacity Tier on Hybrid VSAN

Writes across virtual disks from applications and guest OSs running inside a VM deployed on VSAN accumulate in the flash tier over time. On hybrid VSAN configuration, that is, VSAN configurations that use flash devices for the cache tier and magnetic disks for the capacity tier, VSAN has an elevator algorithm implemented that periodically flushes the data in the write buffer in cache to magnetic disk in address order. The write buffer of the SSD is split into a number of "buckets." Data blocks, as they are written, are assigned to buckets in increasing logical block address (LBA) order. When destaging occurs, perhaps due to resource constraints, the data in the oldest bucket is destaged first.

VSAN enables write buffering on the magnetic disks to maximize performance. The magnetic disk write buffers are flushed before discarding writes from SSD, however. As mentioned earlier, when destaging writes, VSAN considers the location of the I/O. The data accumulated on a per bucket basis provides a sequential (proximal) workload for the magnetic disk. In other words, the LBAs in close proximity to one another on the magnetic disk are destaged together for improved performance. In fact, this proximal mechanism also provides improved throughput on the capacity tier flash devices for all-flash VSAN configurations.

The heuristics used for this are sophisticated and take into account many parameters such as rate of incoming I/O, queues, disk utilization, and optimal batching. This is a self-tuning algorithm that decides how often writes on the SSD destage to magnetic disk.

Deduplication and Compression

VSAN 6.2 introduces two new data reduction features, deduplication and compression. When enabled on a cluster level, Virtual SAN will aim to deduplicate each block and compress the result before destaging the block to the capacity layer. These features are only available for all-flash VSAN. Compression and deduplication cannot be enabled separately; they are either disabled or enabled together. Deduplication and compression work on a disk group level. In other words, only objects deployed on the same disk group can contribute toward space savings. If components from different but identical VMs are deployed to different disk groups, there will not be any deduplication of identical blocks of data. However, deduplication and compression are cluster-wide features they are either on or off. You cannot choose in which virtual machines, or in which disk groups, to enable them on.

For components deployed on the same disk group that have deduplication and compression enabled, deduplication will be done to a 4 KB block level. A disk group will only use one copy of that 4 KB block and all duplicate blocks will be eliminated as shown in Figure 5.11.

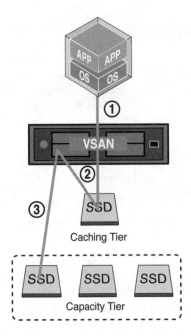

Figure 5.11 Deduplicating blocks

The process of deduplication is done when the block is being destaged from the cache tier to the capacity tier. To track the deduplicated blocks, hash tables are used. The deduplicated data and hash table metadata are spread across the capacity devices that make up the disk group.

Deduplication does not differentiate between the components in the disk group. It may deduplicate blocks in the VM home namespace, VM swap, VMDK object, or snapshot delta object.

If a disk group begins to fill up capacity wise, VSAN examines the footprint of the deduplicated components, and moves the ones which will make the most significant difference to the capacity used in the disk group.

Please note however that if deduplication and compression are enabled on a disk group, a single device failure will make the entire disk group appear unhealthy.

Once the block has been deduplicated, VSAN looks to compress that 4 KB block down to 2 KB or less. If VSAN can compress a block down to <=2 KB, it keeps the compressed copy. Otherwise the uncompressed block is kept.

The process for this is relatively straightforward, as shown in Figure 5.12. At step 1 the VM writes data to VSAN that lands on the caching tier. When the data becomes cold and needs to be destaged, VSAN reads the block into memory (step 2). It will compute the hashes, eliminate the duplicates, and compress the remaining blocks before writing it to the capacity tier (step 3).

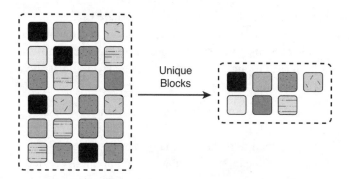

Figure 5.12   Deduplication and compression process

For those interested, VSAN currently uses SHA1 for the deduplication hash and uses LZ4 for the compression. Of course, this may change in future releases.

Data Locality

A question that usually comes now is this: What about data locality? Is cache (for instance) kept local to the VM? Does the VM cache and the VMDK storage object need to travel with the VM each time vSphere Distributed Resource Scheduler (DRS) migrates a VM due to a compute imbalance? Prior to VSAN 6.2 the answer for a standard VSAN deployments was "no"; VSAN does not have the concept of data locality. However, with VSAN 6.2 some changes have been introduced to the architecture. There are different layers of cache, let's list those first to explain where "locality" applies and where not.

- Flash-based write cache
- Flash-based read cache (with hybrid)
- Memory-based read cache

For flash-based caches there is no locality principle. The reason for this is straightforward: Considering that read I/O is at most one network hop away and that the latency incurred on 10 GbE is minimal compared to, for instance, flash latency and even kernel latency, the cost of moving data around simply does not weigh up against the benefits. This is especially true when you consider the fact that by default vSphere DRS runs once every 5 minutes at a minimum which can result in VMs being migrated to a different host every 5 minutes. Considering the cost of flash and the size of flash-based caches, moving around data in these flash-based cache tiers is simply not cost-effective. VSAN instead focused on load balancing of storage resources across the cluster in the most efficient and optimal way, because this is more beneficial and cost-effective to VSAN.

Having said that, as of version 6.2 VSAN also has a small in-memory read cache. Small in this case means 0.4% of a host's memory capacity, up to a max of 1 GB per host. This in-memory cache is a client-side cache, meaning that the blocks of a VM are cached in memory on the host where the VM is located. When the VM migrates, the cache will need to be warmed up again as the client-side cache is invalidated. Note, though, that in most cases hot data already resides in the flash read cache or in the write cache layer and as such the performance impact is low.

If there is a specific requirement to provide an additional form of data locality, however, it is good to know that VSAN integrates with CBRC (in memory read cache for VMware View), and this can be enabled without the need to make any changes to your VSAN configuration. Note that the CBRC does not need a specific object or component created on the VSAN datastore; the CBRC digests are stored in the VM home namespace object.

Data Locality in VSAN Stretched Clusters

There is a caveat to this treatment of data locality, and it is when considering a VSAN stretched cluster deployment. VSAN stretched clusters were introduced in VSAN 6.1. These clusters allow hosts in a VSAN cluster to be deployed at different, geographically dispersed sites. In a VSAN stretched cluster, one mirror of the data is located at site 1 and the other mirror is located at site 2 (VSAN stretched cluster only supports RAID-1 currently). Previously we mentioned that VSAN implements a sort of round-robin policy when it comes to reading from mirrors. This would not be suitable for VSAN stretched clusters as 50% of the reads would need to traverse the link to the remote site. Since VMware supports latency of up to 5 ms between the sites, this would have an adverse effect on the performance of the virtual machine. Rather than continuing to read in a round-robin, block offset fashion, VSAN now has the smarts to figure out which site a VM is running on in a stretched cluster configuration, and change its read algorithm to do 100% of its read from the mirror/replica on the local site. This means that there are no reads done across the link during steady-state operations. It also means that all of the caching is done on the local site, or even on the local host using the in-memory cache. This avoids incurring any additional latency, as reads do not have to traverse the inter-site link. Note that this is not read locality on a per-host basis. It is read locality on a per-site basis. On the same site, the VM's computation could be on any of the ESXi hosts while its local data object could be on any other ESXi host.

Storage Policy-Based Management

In the introduction of the book, you learned that storage policy-based management (SPBM) now plays a major role in the policies and automation for VMware's software-defined storage vision. Chapter 4 covered some of the basics of SPBM in combination with VSAN and showed that by using SPBM administrators could specify a set of requirements for a virtual machine. More specifically, it defines a set of requirements for the application running in the virtual machine. This set of requirements is pushed down to the storage layer, and the storage layer now checks if the storage objects for this virtual machine can be instantiated with this set of requirements. For instance, is there an available number of physical disks to meet the number of stripe widths if this is a requirement placed in the policy? Or are there enough hosts in the cluster to meet the number of failures to tolerate if this is a requirement placed in the policy? If the requirements are understood, the VSAN datastore is said to be a matching resource, and is highlighted as such in the provisioning wizard. Later, when the virtual machine is deployed, administrators can check if the virtual machine is compliant from a storage perspective in its own summary window. If the VSAN datastore is overcommitted, or cannot meet the striping performance requirement, it is not shown as a matching resource in the deployment wizard. If the virtual machine is still deployed to the VSAN datastore even though it shows up as not matching (perhaps through force provisioning), the VM will be displayed as noncompliant in its summary window. The VM may also show up as noncompliant if a failure has occurred in the cluster, and the policy requirements can no longer be met, such as *number of failures to tolerate*.

To summarize, SPBM provides an automated policy-driven mechanism for selecting an appropriate datastore for virtual machines in a traditional environment based on the requirements placed in the VM's storage policy. Within a VSAN-enabled environment, SPBM determines how virtual machines are provisioned and laid out.

Let's now take a closer look at the concept of SPBM for VSAN-based infrastructures.

VSAN Capabilities

This section examines the VSAN capabilities that can be placed in a VM storage policy. These capabilities, which are surfaced by the VASA provider for the VSAN datastore when the cluster is configured successfully, highlight the availability and performance policies that can be set on a per-object basis. We explicitly did not say virtual machine as policies can be set at a per virtual disk granularity.

If you overcommit on the capabilities (i.e., put a capability in the policy that cannot be met by the VSAN datastore), the VSAN datastore will no longer appear as a matching resource during provisioning, and the VM will also show noncompliant in its summary tab even if you successfully deploy.

While on the subject of VSAN capabilities, let's revisit them and discuss them in more detail.

Number of Failures to Tolerate Policy Setting

In Chapter 4, we looked at which of the VM storage policy settings affect VM storage objects. With that in mind, let's look at number of failures to tolerate (FTT for short) in greater detail; this is probably the most used capability VSAN has to offer.

This capability sets a requirement on the storage object to tolerate at least n failures. In this case, n refers to the number of concurrent host, network, or disk failures that may occur in the cluster while still ensuring the availability of the VM's storage objects, and thus allowing the virtual machine to continue to run or be restarted by vSphere HA depending on the type of failure that occurred. If this property is populated in the VM storage policy, and RAID-1 is the chosen configuration over RAID-5 and RAID-6, then the storage objects must contain at least $n + 1$ replicas.

Note that a virtual machine will remain accessible on a VSAN datastore only as long as its storage objects remain available. To recap what has been discussed before, a virtual machine deployed on the VSAN datastore will have a number of storage objects such as VM home namespace, VM swap, VMDK, snapshot deltas, and snapshot memory. For the virtual machine to remain accessible, more than 50% of the components that make up the VM's storage objects must be available.

Let's take a simple policy example to clarify. If you deploy a virtual machine that has number of failures to tolerate = 1 as the only policy setting (implying a RAID-1 configuration), you may see the VMDK storage object deployed, as shown in Figure 5.13.

Physical Disk Placement	Compliance Failures			
150GB-VM - Hard disk 1 : Physical Disk Placement				Q Filter
Type	1▲ Component State	Host	SSD Disk Name	SSD Disk Uuid
▾ RAID 1				
Component	■ Active	🖥 10.20.177.17	💿 Local ATA Disk (naa.500151...	52871f6f-d28a-d243-6
Component	■ Active	🖥 10.20.177.19	💿 Local ATA Disk (naa.500151...	5201336c-8c4b-3bee-
Witness	■ Active	🖥 10.20.177.18	💿 Local ATA Disk (naa.500151...	52637483-6029-c086-
				4 items

Figure 5.13   Simple physical disk placement example with failures to tolerate = 1

It is important to understand that storage objects are made up of components. There are two components making up the RAID-1 mirrored storage object—one on host 17 and the other on host 19. These are the mirror replicas of the data that make failure tolerance possible. But what is this witness component on host 18? Well, remember that 50% of the components (votes) must remain available. In this example, if you didn't have a witness and host 17 failed, you would lose one component (50%). Even though you still had a valid replica available, more than 50% of the components (votes) would not be available. This is the reason for the witness disk. The witness is also used to determine who is still in the cluster in the case of split-brain scenarios.

The witness itself is essentially a piece of metadata; it is only about 4 MB in size, and so it doesn't consume a lot of space. As you create storage objects with more and more components, additional witnesses may get created, as shown in Figure 5.14. This is entirely dependent on the RAID-1 configuration and how VSAN decides to place components.

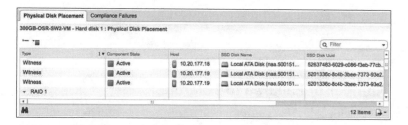

Figure 5.14   Additional witnesses may get created

Now that you understand the concept of the witness, the next question is this: How many hosts do you need in the VSAN cluster to accommodate n number of failures to tolerate with RAID-1? Table 5.1 outlines this solution.

Table 5.1   Relationship between failures to tolerate, replicas, and hosts required

Number of Failures to Tolerate (n)	Number of RAID-1 Replicas ($n + 1$)	Number of Hosts Required in VSAN Cluster ($2n + 1$)
1	2	3
2	3	5
3	4	7

If you try to specify a number of failures to tolerate value that is greater than that which can be accommodated by the VSAN cluster, you will not be allowed to do so. Figure 5.15 depicts an example of trying to set number of failures to tolerate to 2 in a three-node cluster.

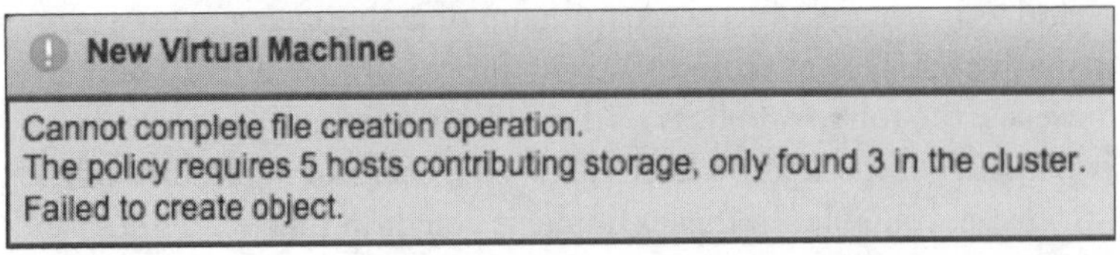

> ⓘ **New Virtual Machine**
>
> Cannot complete file creation operation.
> The policy requires 5 hosts contributing storage, only found 3 in the cluster.
> Failed to create object.

Figure 5.15   Failures to tolerate requires a specific number of hosts

Note that the other RAID types introduced in VSAN 6.2, namely RAID-5 and RAID-6, have a pre-defined number of hosts and a pre-defined number of failures to tolerate, as shown in Table 5.2.

Table 5.2   Relationship between failures to tolerate and hosts required with RAID-5 and RAID-6

RAID Configuration	Number of Failures to Tolerate (n)	Number of Hosts Required in VSAN Cluster
RAID-5	1	4
RAID-6	2	6

Best Practice for Number of Failures to Tolerate

The recommended practice (with RAID-1 configurations) for number of failures to tolerate is 1, unless you have a pressing concern to provide additional availability to allow VMs to tolerate more than one failure. Note that the increasing number of failures to tolerate would require additional disk capacity to be available for the creation of the extra replicas.

VSAN has multiple management workflows to warn/protect against accidental decommissioning of hosts that could result in VSAN's being unable to meet the number of failures to tolerate policy of given VMs. This includes a noncompliant state being shown in the VM summary tab.

Then the question arises: What is the minimal number of hosts for a VSAN cluster? In VSAN 6.1, a new 2-node configuration for remote office/branch office solutions was introduced, but this also required a witness appliance. If we omit the 2-node configuration for the moment, customers would for the most part require three ESXi hosts to deploy VSAN. However, what about scenarios where you need to do maintenance and want to maintain the same level of availability during maintenance hours?

To comply with a number of failures to tolerate = 1 policy, you need three hosts at a minimum at all times. Even if one host fails, you can still access your data, because with three hosts and two mirror copies and a witness, you will still have more than 50% of your components (votes) available. But what happens when you place one of those hosts in maintenance mode, as shown in Figure 5.16?

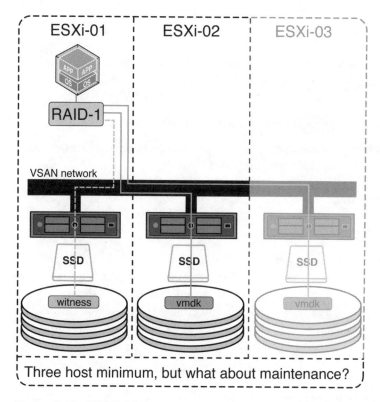

Figure 5.16   VSAN: Minimum number of hosts

When both remaining hosts keep functioning as expected, all VMs will continue to run. If another host fails or gets placed into maintenance mode, you have a challenge as at this point the remaining host will have less than 50% of the components of your VM. As a result, VMs cannot be restarted (nor do any I/O) because the component will not have an owner.

Stripe Width Policy Setting

The second most popular capability is definitely number of disk stripes per object. We will refer to this as stripe width for the purposes of keeping things simple. The first thing to discuss is when striping can be beneficial to virtual machines in a VSAN environment. The reason we are bringing this up is that you need to be aware that all I/O in VSAN go to the cache tier that is made up of flash. To be more correct, all writes go to the write buffer on flash, and on hybrid configurations, we try to service all reads from the read cache on the cache tier, too. Some reads may have to be serviced by magnetic disk if the data is not in cache (read cache miss), however.

So, where can a stripe width increase help?

- It may be possible to improve write performance of a VM's storage objects if they are striped across different disk groups or indeed striped to a capacity device located on another host.

- When there are read cache misses in hybrid configurations.

- Possible performance improvements during destaging of blocks from cache tier flash devices to magnetic disk in hybrid configurations.

Let's elaborate on these a bit more.

Performance: Writes

Because all writes go to the cache tier (write buffer), the value of an increased stripe width may or may not improve performance for your virtual machine I/O. This is because there is no guarantee that the new stripe will use a different cache tier device; the new stripe may be placed on a capacity device in the same disk group, and thus the new stripe will use the same cache tier. This is applicable to both all-flash and hybrid configurations.

There are three different scenarios for stripes:

- **Striping across hosts**: Improved performance with different cache tier flash devices

- **Striping across disk groups**: Improved performance with different cache tier flash devices

- **Striping in the same disk group**: No improved performance (using same cache tier flash device).

At the moment, VSAN does not have data gravity/locality of reference outside of VSAN stretched clusters, so it is not possible to stipulate where a particular component belonging to a storage object should be placed. This is left up to the VSAN component placement algorithms, which try to place storage components down on disk in a balanced fashion across all nodes in the cluster.

Therefore, in conclusion, adding a stripe width may not result in any improved write performance for VM I/O, but allows for the potential of improved performance.

Performance: Read Cache Misses in Hybrid Configurations

Let's look at the next reason for increasing the stripe width policy setting; this is probably the primary reason for doing so. In situations where the data set of a virtual machine is too big or the workload is so random that the read cache miss rates can overwhelm the throughput of a single magnetic disk in a hybrid configuration, it can be beneficial to ensure that multiple magnetic disks are used when reading. This can be achieved by setting a stripe width.

From a read perspective, an increased stripe width helps when you are experiencing many read cache misses. If you consider the example of a virtual machine consuming 2,000 read operations per second and experiencing a hit rate of 90%, there are 200 read operations that need to be serviced from magnetic disk. In this case, a single magnetic disk that can provide 150 IOPS cannot service all of those read operations, so an increase in stripe width would help on this occasion to meet the VM I/O requirements.

How can you tell whether you have read cache misses? In earlier versions of VSAN, this information was not available within vSphere Web Client. However, the RVC VSAN observer tool provides a lot of detailed information, including read cache hit rate, as shown in Figure 5.17. In this case, the read cache hit rate is 100%, meaning that there is no point in increasing the stripe width, because all I/O are being served by flash.

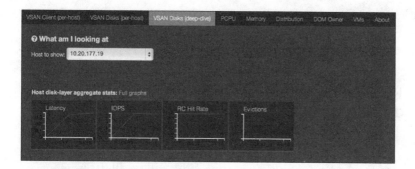

Figure 5.17   100%, no evictions

In VSAN 6.2, a new performance service was introduced that placed information regarding the performance of the VSAN cluster in the vSphere Web Client. Now you no longer need to launch tools such as RVC to examine this information. In Figure 5.18, there is a 0% read cache hit rate. Either this is a very idle system, or it is an all-flash VSAN that does not use read cache. In fact, it is both.

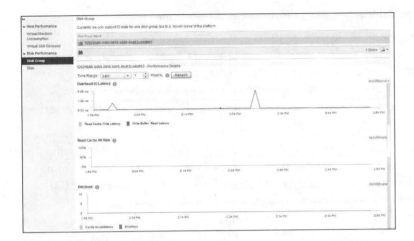

Figure 5.18   Performance service

To summarize, if read cache misses were occurring in your VSAN, increasing the stripe width may improve the performance for I/O that needs to be serviced from magnetic disk, if a single spindle was not enough to handle the requests. The RVC, VSAN observer, and the new performance service are discussed in detail in Chapter 10.

Performance: Cache Tier Destaging

The final reason for increasing the stripe width relates to destaging blocks from cache to magnetic disk. There is an important consideration regarding cache destaging: What sorts of workloads are running on VSAN?

By way of an example, if you are doing virtual desktop infrastructure (VDI) deployment and you have hundreds of virtual machines, then it is likely that VSAN needs to destage to all parts of the capacity tier. Changing the stripe width on the policy may not help since it is likely that all of the magnetic disks are already in use through destaging.

In a situation where there are 99 virtual machines doing mostly reads and almost no writes, there will be very little destaging. So increasing the stripe width will have little benefit. However, if there are few virtual machines doing a very large number of writes and thus incurring a lot of destaging, then a performance improvement might be expected during destage if those few virtual machines are configured with a higher stripe width.

How can you tell whether your cache tier has lots of blocks to be destaged? In earlier versions of VSAN, administrators need to use the VSAN observer tool, available with vCenter Server 5.5 U1 and later. The VSAN observer tool is part of the RVC, and the view shown in Figure 5.19 is taken from the VSAN disks (deep-dive): Device-level stats option. Once again, Chapter 10 covers both RVC and the VSAN observer in detail.

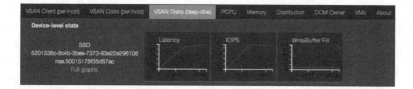

Figure 5.19   VSAN observer write buffer fill info

With the availability of VSAN 6.2 and the new performance service, this information is now readily available in the vSphere Web Client. Figure 5.20, taken once again from the disk group view, shows the write buffer free percentage.

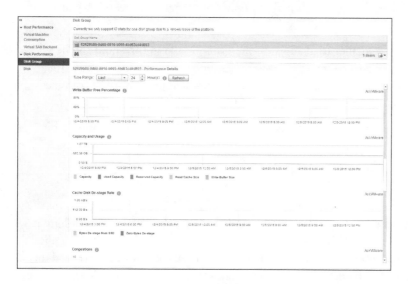

Figure 5.20   Write buffer free percentage via the performance service

RAID-0 Used When No Striping Specified in the Policy

Those who have been looking at the Web Client regularly, where you can see the placement of components, may have noticed that VSAN appears to create a RAID-0 for your VMDK even when you did not explicitly ask it to. Or perhaps you have requested a stripe width of two in your policy and then observed what appears to be a stripe width of three being created. VSAN will split objects as it sees fit when there are space constraints. This is not striping per se, since component can end up on the same physical capacity device. Instead, we can refer to it as chunking. VSAN will use this chunking method on certain occasions. The first of these is when a virtual disk (VMDK) is larger than any single chunk of free space. Essentially, VSAN hides the fact that even when there are small capacity devices on the hosts, administrators can still create very large VMDKs. Therefore, it is not uncommon to see large VMDKs split into multiple components, even when no stripe width is specified in the VM storage policy. VSAN will use this chunking method when a virtual disk (VMDK) is larger than any capacity device.

There is another occasion where this chunking may occur. By default, an object will also be split if its size is greater than 255 GB (the maximum component size). An object might appear to be made up of multiple 255 GB chunks even though striping may not have been a policy requirement. It can be split even before it reaches 255 GB when free disk space makes VSAN think that there is a benefit in doing so. Note that just because there is a standard split at 255 GB, it doesn't mean all new chunks will go onto different magnetic disks. In fact, since this is not striping per se, multiple chunks may be placed on the same physical capacity device. It may, or may not, depend on overall balance and free capacity.

If the capacity devices are smaller than 255 GB, then this chunking threshold can be modified via the advanced parameter VSAN.ClomMaxComponentSizeGB. (Consult the official VSAN documentation or VMware support before changing this ESXi advanced setting.)

Let's look at what some of our tests that have been done, as that may make things a bit clearer for you.

Test 1

On a hybrid configuration, we created a 150 GB VM on a VSAN datastore (which had 136 GB magnetic disks as its capacity devices) with a policy of number of failures to tolerate (FTT) = 1. We got a simple RAID-1 for our VMDK with two components, each replica having just one component (so no RAID-0). Now this is because the VM is deployed on the VSAN datastore as thin by default, so even though we created a 150 GB VM, because it is thin it can sit on a single 136 GB magnetic disk, as demonstrated in Figure 5.21.

Physical Disk Placement	Compliance Failures			
150GB-VM - Hard disk 1 : Physical Disk Placement				
Type	1 ▲ Component State	Host	SSD Disk Name	SSD Disk Uuid
▼ RAID 1				
Component	Active	10.20.177.17	Local ATA Disk (naa.500151...	52871f6f-d28a-d243-6
Component	Active	10.20.177.19	Local ATA Disk (naa.500151...	5201336c-8c4b-3bee-
Witness	Active	10.20.177.18	Local ATA Disk (naa.500151...	52637483-6029-c086-
				4 items

Figure 5.21   Simple physical disk placement: Single witness component

Test 2

On the same cluster, we created a 150 GB VM, with a policy of FTT = 1 and object space reservation (OSR) = 100%. Now we get another RAID-1 of our VMDK, but each replica is made up of a RAID-0 with two components. OSR is essentially specifying a thickness for the VM. Because we are guaranteeing space, our VM needs to span at least two magnetic disks, and therefore a stripe is being used.

Test 3

We created a 300 GB VM, with a policy of FTT = 1, OSR = 100%, and stripe width (SW) = 2. We got another RAID-1 of our VMDK as before, but now each replica is made up of a RAID-0 with *three* components. Here, even with a SW = 2 setting, our VMDK requirement is still too large to span two magnetic disks. A third capacity device is required in this case, as shown in Figure 5.22.

We can conclude that multiple components in a RAID-0 configuration are used for VMDKs that are larger than a single magnetic disk, even if a stripe width is not specified in the policy.

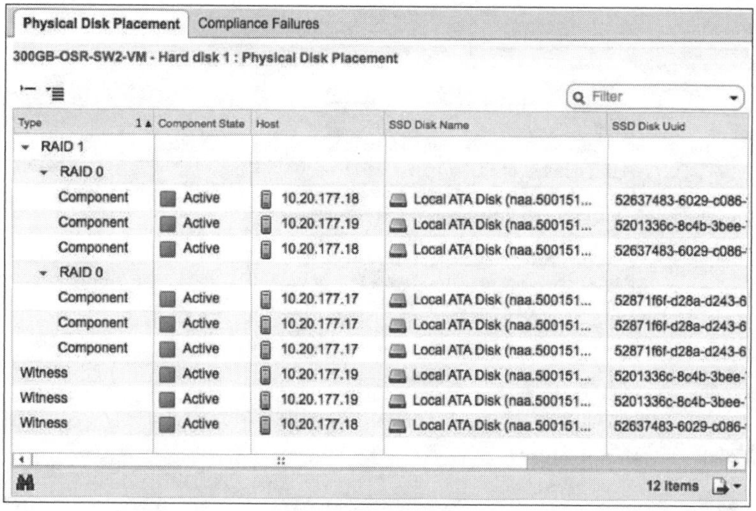

Figure 5.22   More complex deployment: Multiple witness components needed

Stripe Width Maximum

In VSAN, the maximum stripe width that can be defined is 12. This can be striping across magnetic disks in the same host, or across hosts. Remember that when you specify a stripe width and failures to tolerate (FTT) value, and the *failure tolerance method* is left at the default of performance for RAID-1, there has to be at least stripe width (SW) × (FTT+1) number of capacity devices before VSAN is able to satisfy the policy requirement, ignoring for the moment that additional devices will be needed to host the witness component(s). This means that the larger the number of FTT and SW, the more complex the placement of object and associated components will become. The number of disk stripes per object setting in the VM storage policy means stripe across "at least" this number of magnetic disks per mirror. VSAN may, when it sees fit, use additional stripes.

Figure 5.23 shows a screenshot taken for a VM storage policy screen, with the information icon selected for further details. The reference to HDD in the help screen actually stands for hard disk drive, what we have been calling magnetic disks in this book. Of course, HDDs are only used in hybrid configurations, so this is taken from VSAN 5.5, before support for all-flash was introduced. However, the guidance is the same for both models. Note that RAID-5 and RAID-6 can also implement a RAID-0 stripe width. Each chunk of the RAID-5 or RAID-6 object may be striped across multiple capacity tier devices, if stripe width is specified in the VM Storage policy, and *failure tolerance method* is set to capacity.

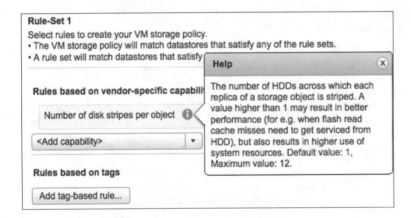

Figure 5.23   Number of disk stripes per object

Stripe Width Configuration Error

You may ask yourself what happens if a vSphere administrator requests the VSAN cluster to meet a stripe width policy setting that is not available or achievable. Figure 5.24, taken from the first release of VSAN, shows the resulting error. Basically, the deployment of the VM fails, stating that there were not sufficient capacity devices found to meet the requirements of the defined policy. A similar error is displayed in all versions of VSAN.

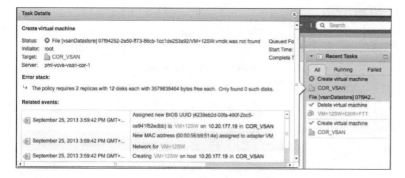

Figure 5.24   Task failed: Only found 0 such disks

Stripe Width Chunk Size

A question that then often arises after the stripe width discussion is whether there is a specific segment size. In other words, when the stripe width is defined using the VM storage policies, which increment do the components use to grow? VSAN uses a stripe segment size of 1 MB. As depicted in Figure 5.25, "1 MB stripe segment 1" will go to ESXi-02, and when the next 1 MB is written, the "1 MB stripe segment 2" will go to ESXi-03, and so on.

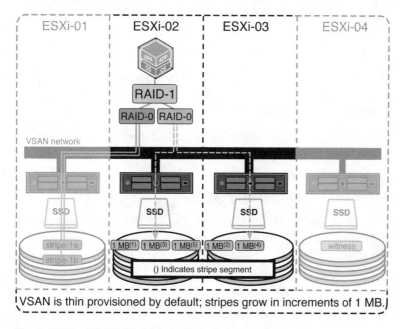

Figure 5.25   VSAN I/O flow: 1 MB increment striping

Stripe Width Best Practice

After reading this section, you could more clearly understand that increasing the stripe width could potentially complicate placement. VSAN has a lot of logic built in to handle smart placement of objects. We recommend not increasing the stripe width *unless* you have identified a pressing performance issue such as read cache misses during destaging.

Remember that all I/O should go to the flash layer first. All writes certainly go to flash first, and in the case of hybrid configurations, they are later destaged to magnetic disks. For reads, the operation is first attempted in the flash layer. If a read cache miss occurs, the block is read from magnetic disk in hybrid configurations and from flash capacity devices in all-flash configurations. Therefore, if all of your reads are being satisfied by the cache tier, there is no point in increasing the stripe width as it does not give any benefits. Doing the math correctly beforehand is much more effective, leading to proper sizing of the flash-based cache tier, rather than trying to increase the stripe width after the VM has been deployed!

Flash Read Cache Reservation Policy Setting

This policy setting, applicable to hybrid configurations only, is the amount of flash capacity reserved on the cache tier as read cache for the storage object. It is specified as a percentage of the logical size of the storage object, up to four decimal places. This fine granular unit size is needed so that administrators can express sub 1% units. Take the example of a 1 TB VMDK. If we limited the read cache reservation to 1% increments, this would mean cache reservations in increments of 10 GB, which in most cases is far too much for a single VM.

Note that you do not have to set a reservation to get cache. The reservation should be set to 0, meaning it is equally shared amongst all virtual machines, unless you are trying to solve a real performance problem for a particular VM or group of VMs.

There is no proportional share mechanism for this resource, which is what vSphere administrators will be familiar with from other vSphere features.

Object Space Reservation Policy Setting

All objects deployed on VSAN are thin provisioned by default. The object space reservation capability defines the percentage of the logical size of the storage object that may be reserved during initialization. To be clear, the OSR is the amount of space to reserve, specified as a percentage of the total object address space. You can use this property for specifying what is akin to a thick provisioned storage object, albeit it is not quite the same.

If OSR is set to 100%, all the storage capacity requirements of the VM are reserved up front. Note that although the object itself will still be thin provisioned, the space it can claim is reserved explicitly for this object so that the VSAN datastore cannot run out of disk space for this VM.

Note that if deduplication and compression are enabled as data reduction features in VSAN 6.2, OSR may only be set to 0% or 100%. Values of between 1% and 99% cannot be used.

You may remember that certain storage objects (notably VM namespace and VM Swap) do not adhere to certain policy settings. One of these is object space reservation. Let's take a look at these two special objects.

VM Home Namespace Revisited

The VM namespace on VSAN is a *255 GB thin object*. The namespace is a per-VM object. As you can imagine, if we allocated policy settings to the VM home namespace, such as proportional capacity and flash read cache reservation, much of the magnetic disk and flash resources could be wasted. To that end, the VM home namespace has its own special policy, as follows:

Number of disk stripes per object: 1

Number of failures to tolerate: <as-per-policy>

Flash read cache reservation: 0%

Force provisioning: Off

Object space reservation: 0% (thin)

Failure tolerance method: <as-per-policy>

Checksum disabled: <as-per-policy>

IOPS limit for object: <as-per-policy>

The number of failures to tolerate policy setting is the only setting inherited from the VM storage policy. So, if a customer creates a VM storage policy with an FTT setting, the VM home namespace will be deployed with the ability to tolerate the number failures specified in that policy.

VM Swap Revisited

The VM swap follows much the same conventions as the VM home namespace. It has the same default policy as the VM home namespace, which is 1 disk stripe, and 0% read cache reservation. However, it does have a 100% object space reservation.

Note that the VM swap has an FTT setting of 1. It does not inherit the FTT from the VM storage policy.

Number of disk stripes per object: 1

Number of failures to tolerate: 1

Flash read cache reservation: 0%

Force provisioning: On

Object space reservation: 100%

Failure tolerance method: Performance

Checksum disabled: No (e.g., enabled)

IOPS limit for object: Disabled

There is one additional point in relation to FTT; that is, it has force provisioning set to 1. This means that if some of the policy requirements cannot be met, such as number of failures to tolerate, the VM swap is still created.

VM swap is also not limited in the way the VM home namespace is limited to a 255 GB thin object.

The default values for VM swap are not overridden by VM storage policy entries either. However, as highlighted previously, the advanced parameter *SwapThickProvisionDisabled* can be used to make the VM swap object deployed as thin rather than fully reserved (thick).

The swap object is always deployed as a RAID-1 configuration. It is never deployed with RAID-5 or RAID-6, even if *failure tolerance method* is set to capacity in the policy associated with the VM. However, having said that, this could be overridden by modifying the default policy for swap via *esxcli* commands. However, we don't expect many readers to do this. If you really have a desire to do something like this for the VM swap, refer to the official VMware documentation.

How to Examine the VM Swap Storage Object

As we have seen, the VM swap is one of the objects that make up the set of VM objects, along with the VM home namespace, VMDKs, snapshot delta, and snapshot memory. Unfortunately in versions of VSAN prior to 6.2, you will not see the VM swap file represented in the list of VM objects in the vSphere Web Client. This leads inevitably to the question regarding how you go about checking and verifying the policy and resource consumption of a VM's swap object.

This is in fact quite tricky, because even if you try to use the RVC command, `vsan.vm_object_info`, you only get information about VM home namespace, VMDKs, deltas, and snapshot memory. Chapter 10 covers RVC commands in extensive detail. Again, there is no information displayed for the VM swap. To get information about the VM swap, you first have to retrieve the UUID information from the VM's swap descriptor file. One way of doing this is to SSH onto an ESXi host that is participating in the VSAN cluster and use the cat command in the ESXi shell to display the contents of the VM swap descriptor file. You are looking for the objectID entry. Here is an example:

```
# cat Auto-Perf-Tool-0b43d77a.vswp
# Object DescriptorFile
version = "1"

objectID = "vsan://4f386056-1874-0983-b93e-ecf4bbd58600"
object.class = "vmswap"
```

Once you have the descriptor, this can then be used in RVC to display information about the actual swap object. The command to do this is vsan.object_info. This RVC command takes two arguments. The first argument shown in Example 5.1 is the cluster, and the second argument is the UUID:

Example 5.1   Using vsan.object_info to Display Information about the Swap Object

```
/vcsa-05/Datacenter/computers> ls
0 VSAN (cluster): cpu 134 GHz, memory 306 GB
/vcsa-05/Datacenter/computers> vsan.object_info 0 4f386056-1874-0983-b93e-
ecf4bbd58600
DOM Object: 4f386056-1874-0983-b93e-ecf4bbd58600 (v4, owner: esxi-b-pref.
rainpole.com, policy: hostFailuresToTolerate = 1, forceProvisioning = 1,
proportionalCapacity = 100)
  RAID_1
    Component: 4f386056-4f12-6a83-25fd-ecf4bbd58600 (state: ACTIVE (5),
host: esxi-b-pref.rainpole.com, md: naa.500a07510f86d686, ssd: t10.ATA_____
Micron_P420m2DMTFDGAR1T4MAX___ votes: 1, usage: 8.0 GB)
    Component: 4f386056-f50d-6b83-7493-ecf4bbd58600 (state: ACTIVE (5),
host: esxi-a-pref.rainpole.com, md: naa.500a07510f86d693, ssd: t10.ATA_____
Micron_P420m2DMTFDGAR1T4MAX___ votes: 1, usage: 8.0 GB)
  Witness: 4f386056-4fda-6b83-b6e1-ecf4bbd58600 (state: ACTIVE (5), host:
esxi-c-scnd.rainpole.com, md: naa.500a07510f86d6cf, ssd: t10.ATA_____
Micron_P420m2DMTFDGAR1T4MAX_____ votes: 1, usage: 0.0 GB)
  Extended attributes:
    Address space: 8589934592B (8.00 GB)
    Object class: vmswap
    Object path: /vmfs/volumes/vsan:5204d7ce46d435a6-
81ba22b8f602a826/07386056-e16e-d37d-6536-ecf4bbd58600/Auto-Perf-Tool-
0b43d77a.vswp
    Object capabilities: NONE
```

Now that we have the VM swap object info, we can see a number of things:

- `hostFailuresToTolerate` for VM Swap is set to 1. This gives us a RAID-1 (mirror) configuration for VM Swap.

- `forceProvisioning` for VM Swap is set to 1. This means that even if the current policy cannot be met we should always provision the VM swap object.

- `ProportionalCapacity` for VM swap is set to 100%. This means that the space needed for swap is indeed fully reserved.

What can be deduced from this is that from a space utilization standpoint, the VM swap of a VM deployed on VSAN will consume (Configured memory–Memory reservation) * (FTT + 1) amount of space on disk. In most environments, this basically means that on disk you will consume twice the provisioned VM memory by default, because the majority of customers do not set reservations.

Of course, the plan is to eventually get this information more easily accessible, but for now, this method should allow you to gather this information should you need it. The VM swap (.vswp) is an important consideration when sizing your VSAN storage, so make sure to consider this. Chapter 9 provides a formula to do so. The new capacity views in VSAN 6.2 can also provide an insight into how much space is being consumed by the various objects that got to make up a virtual machine deployed on VSAN, including the VM swap objects.

Delta Disk / Snapshot Caveat

For the most part, a delta VMDK (or snapshot, as it's often referred to) will always inherit the policy associated with the base disk. In VSAN, a vSphere administrator can also specify a VM storage policy for a linked clone. In the case of linked clones, the policy is applied just to the linked clone (top-level delta disk), not the base disk. This is not visible through the UI, however. Both VMware Horizon View and VMware vCloud Director use this capability through the vSphere API.

Now since you know that you can reserve space and disks are thin provisioned, you are probably wondering where you can find out how much space a VM consumes and how much is reserved.

Verifying How Much Space Is Actually Consumed

When you select the VSAN datastore in the UI, then the monitor tab, and then click **storage reports**, you can get a nice view of how much space is being consumed by each of the VMs, as illustrated in Figure 5.26. Note that the default view does not automatically show these columns. You have to add these columns to view via the user interface.

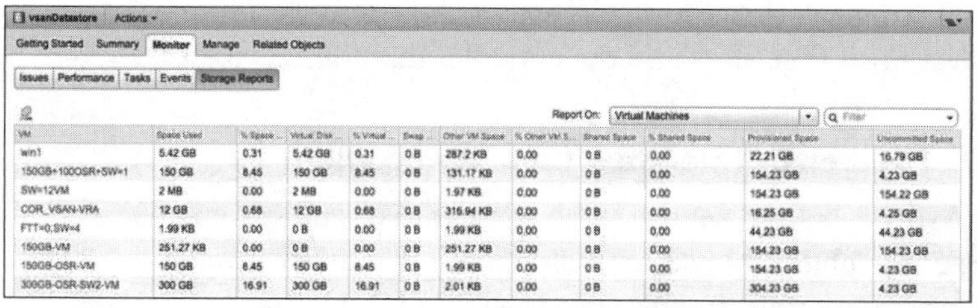

Figure 5.26 How much space is being consumed on the VSAN datastore

There are a few interesting pieces of output here with regard to OSR. As stated, all VMs deployed to VSAN are thin in nature. In the example in Figure 5.26, we deployed a VM called 150 GB VM that did not use OSR. You can see that the size of the virtual disk for this VM is 0 bytes.

In a second example, we deployed a VM called 150 GB-OSR-VM, which has 100% OSR. In this example, you can see that the virtual disk size is 150 GB since VSAN has reserved (but not consumed) 100% of the space required by this object.

Force Provisioning Policy Setting

We have already mentioned this capability various times: force provisioning. If this parameter is set to a non zero value, the object will be provisioned even if the policy specified in the VM storage policy is not satisfied by VSAN. However, if there is not enough space in the cluster to satisfy the reservation requirements of at least one replica, then the provisioning will fail even if force provisioning is turned on!

Now that we know what the various capabilities do, let's take a look on how VSAN leverages these in failure scenarios.

Witnesses and Replicas: Failure Scenarios

Failure scenarios are often a hot topic of discussion when it comes to VSAN. What should one configure, and how do we expect VSAN to respond? This section runs through some simple scenarios to demonstrate what you can expect of VSAN in certain situations.

The following examples use a four-host VSAN cluster and use a RAID-1 mirroring configuration. We will examine various *number of failures to tolerate* and *stripe width* settings and discuss the behavior in the event of a host failure. You should understand that the examples shown here are for illustrative purposes only. These are simply to explain some of the decisions that VSAN *might* make when it comes to object placement. VSAN may choose any configuration as long as it satisfies the customer requirements (i.e., number of failures to tolerate and stripe width). For example, with higher numbers of number of failures to tolerate and stripe width, we have placement choices to use more or less witnesses and more or less hosts than shown in the examples that follow.

Example 1: Number of Failures to Tolerate = 1 and Stripe Width = 1

In this first example, the stripe width is set to 1. Therefore, there is no striping per se, simply a single instance of the object. However, the requirements are that we must tolerate a single disk or host failure, so we must instantiate a replica (a RAID-1 mirror of the component). However, a witness is also required in this configuration to avoid a split-brain situation. A split-brain is when ESXi-01 and ESXi-03 continue to operate, but no longer communicate to each other. Whichever of the hosts can communicate with the witness is the host that has the valid copy of the data in that scenario. Data placement in these configurations may look like Figure 5.27.

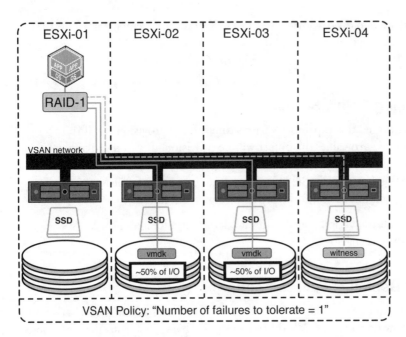

Figure 5.27   Number of failures to tolerate = 1

In Figure 5.27, the data remains accessible in the event of a host or disk failure. If ESXi-04 has a failure, ESXi-02 and ESXi-03 continue to provide access to the data as a quorum continues to exist. However, if ESXi-03 and ESXi-04 both suffer failures, there is no longer a quorum, so data becomes inaccessible. Note that in this scenario the VM is running, from a compute perspective, on ESXi-01, while the components of the objects are stored on ESXi-02/03/04.

Example 2: Number of Failures to Tolerate = 1 and Stripe Width = 2

Turning to another example, this time the stripe width is increased to 2. This means that each component must be striped across two spindles at minimum; however, VSAN may decide to stripe across magnetic disks on the same host or across magnetic disks on different hosts. Figure 5.28 shows one possible distribution of storage objects.

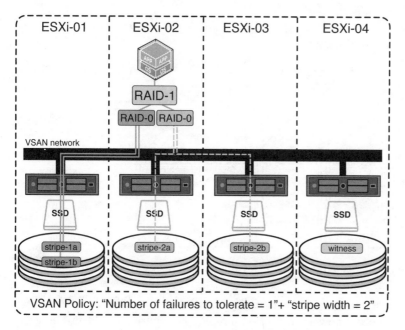

Figure 5.28   Number of failures to tolerate = 1 and stripe width = 2

As you can see, VSAN in this example has chosen to keep the components for the first stripe (RAID-0) on ESXi-01 but has placed the components for the second stripe across ESXi-02 and ESXi-03. Once again, with number of failures to tolerate set to 1, we mirror using RAID-1. In this configuration, a witness is also used. Why might a witness be required in this example? Consider the case where ESXi-01 has a failure. This impacts both the components on ESXi-01. Now we have two components failed and two components still working on ESXi-02 and ESXi-03. In this case, we still require a witness to attain quorum.

Note that if one component in each of the RAID-0 configuration fails, the data would be inaccessible because both sides of the RAID-1 are impacted. Therefore, a disk failure in ESXi-01 and a disk failure in ESXi-02 can make the VM inaccessible until the disk faults are rectified. Because a witness contains no data, it cannot help in these situations. Note that this is more than one failure, however, and our policy is set to tolerate only one failure.

Example 3: Number of Failures to Tolerate = 2 and Stripe Width = 2

In this last example, the number of failures to tolerate is set to 2, meaning another replica is required. And because each replica is made up of two striped components, an additional two components must be deployed on the VSAN datastore. Again, a possible deployment might look like Figure 5.29.

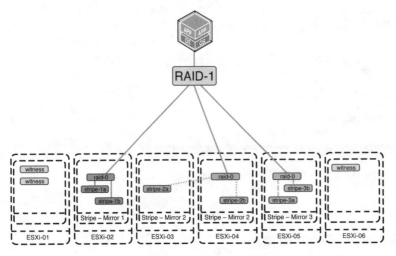

Figure 5.29   Number of failures to tolerate = 2 and stripe width = 2

The components per stripe width have been explained previously, and should be clear. Similarly, the fact that there is now a third RAID-0 replica configured should also be self-explanatory at this stage. But what about the fact that there are now three witnesses? Well, consider the situation where both ESXi-02 and ESXi-05 suffer a failure. In that case, four components are lost. To have a quorum majority, the two remaining components would require five objects to achieve a majority. This is why there are three witnesses in this configuration. Losing two hosts would still allow the data to be accessible. Note that this behavior is what one would expect with the initial release of VSAN. VSAN 6.0 introduced the concept of votes, where components may have a vote. With this voting mechanism, it is possible that less witness components are needed. However, the scenario described above would still hold true, with witness components replaced by component votes.

Data Integrity Through Checksum

A new enhancement in VSAN 6.2 is the introduction of software checksum. While certain VSAN ready nodes provided support for checksum via certain specific hardware devices in previous versions of VSAN, VSAN 6.2 is the first release to provide it via software. This requires on-disk format V3, which is a new on-disk format with VSAN 6.2.

This feature is policy driven on a per-VM/VMDK basis, but is enabled by default. Administrators will have to create a specific policy that disables checksum (set Disable object checksum to Yes) if they do not want their objects to leverage the feature. Such a policy setting is shown in Figure 5.30.

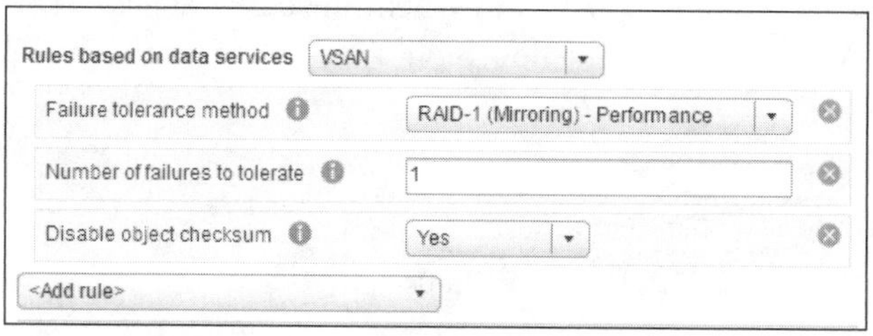

Figure 5.30 Checksum policy setting

Checksum is available on both hybrid and all-flash configurations. The checksum data goes all the way through the VSAN I/O stack. For each 4 KB block of data, a 5-byte checksum is created and stored separately from the data; this occurs before any data are written to persistent storage. In other words, the checksum is calculated before writing the block to the caching layer.

If a checksum error is discovered in the I/O path, the checksum error is automatically repaired. A message stating that a checksum error has been detected and corrected is logged in the VMkernel log.

Checksum also includes a data scrubber mechanism, which validates the data and checksums once every 7 days that will protect your VSAN environment, for instance against data corruption as a result of bit rot. The checksum mechanism also leverages accelerated hardware instructions (Intel c2c32c) that makes the process extremely fast.

Recovery from Failure

When a failure has been detected, VSAN will determine which objects had components on the failed device. These failing components will then get marked as either *degraded or absent*, but the point is that I/O flow is renewed instantaneously to the remaining components in the object. Depending on the type of failure, VSAN will take immediate action or wait for some period of time (60 minutes). The distinction here is if VSAN knows what has happened to a device. For instance, when a host fails VSAN typically does not know why this happened, or even what has happened exactly. Is it a host failure, a network failure, is it transient or permanent, and so on. It may be something as simple as a reboot of the host in question. Should this occur, the affected components are said to be in an *"absent"* state and the repair delay timer starts counting down. If a device such as a disk or

SSD reports a permanent error, it is marked as degraded and it is re-protected immediately by VSAN (replacement components are built and synchronized).

In this case, let's say that we have suffered a permanent host failure in this scenario.

As soon as VSAN realizes the component is absent, a timer of 60 minutes will start. If the component comes back within those 60 minutes, VSAN will synchronize the replicas. If the component doesn't come back, VSAN will create a new replica, as demonstrated in Figure 5.31.

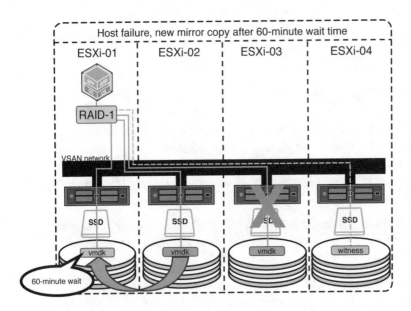

Figure 5.31   Host failure: 60-minute delay

Note that you can decrease this time-out value by changing the advanced setting called *VSAN.ClomRepairDelay* on each of your ESXi hosts in the Advanced Settings section. Caution should be exercised however, because if it is set to a value that is too low, and you do a simple maintenance task such as rebooting a host, you may find that VSAN starts rebuilding new components before the host has completed its reboot cycle. This adds unnecessary overhead to VSAN, and could have an impact on the overall performance of the cluster.

If you want to change this advanced setting, we highly recommend ensuring consistency across all ESXi hosts in the cluster by scripting the required change and to monitor on a regular basis for consistent implementation to avoid inconsistent behavior. The VSAN health check will also verify that the value is set consistently across all hosts in the cluster. (Consult the official VSAN documentation or VMware support before changing this ESXi advanced setting.)

As mentioned, in some scenarios VSAN responds to a failure immediately. This depends on the type of failure and a good example is a magnetic disk or flash device failure. In many cases, the controller or device itself will be able to indicate what has happened and will essentially tell VSAN that it is unlikely that the device will return within a reasonable amount of time. VSAN will then respond by marking all impacted components (VMDK in Figure 5.32) as "degraded," and VSAN immediately creates a new mirror copy.

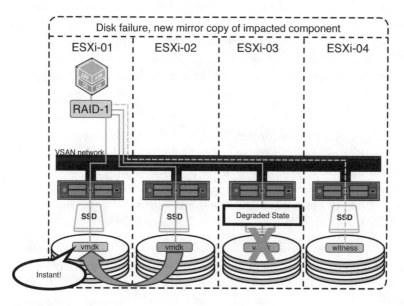

Figure 5.32   Disk failure: Instant mirror copy

Of course, before it will create this mirror VSAN will validate whether sufficient resources exist to store this new copy.

If a recovery occurs before the 60 minutes has elapsed or before the creation of the replica has completed, VSAN will continue to complete the creation of the replica. Once this is complete and the new replica is healthy, the old components are discarded. All of this falls under the concept *reconfiguration*.

Reconfiguration can take place on VSAN for a number of reasons. First, a user might choose to change an object's policy and the current configuration might not conform to the new policy, so a new configuration must be computed and applied to the object. Second, a disk or node in the cluster might fail. If an object loses one of the components in its configuration, it may no longer comply with its policy.

Reconfiguration is probably the most resource-intensive task because a lot of data will need to be transferred in most scenarios. To ensure that regular VM I/O is not impacted by reconfiguration tasks, VSAN has the ability to throttle the reconfiguration task to the extent that it does not impact the performance of VMs.

Problematic Device Handling

VSAN 6.1 introduced a new feature called problematic device handling. There was a significant driving factor behind such a feature, and it is to deal with situations where either an SSD or a magnetic disk drive was misbehaving. In particular, we needed a way to handle a drive that was constantly reporting transient errors, but not actually failing. Of course, in situations like this the drive may introduce poor performance to the cluster overall. The objective of this new feature is to have a mechanism that monitors for these misbehaving drives, and isolate them so that they do not impact the overall cluster.

The feature is monitoring VSAN, looking for significant period of high latency on the SSD or the magnetic disk drives. If a sustained period of high latency is observed, then VSAN will unmount the disk group on which the disk resides. These components in the disk group will be marked as permanent error and the components will be rebuild elsewhere in the cluster. What this means is that the performance of the virtual machines can be consistent, and will not be impacting by this one misbehaving drive.

An enhancement to this feature was added in VSAN 6.2. In this release, there are regular attempts over a period of time to remount caching and capacity tier disks marked under permanent error. This will only succeed if the condition that caused the initial failure is no longer present. If successful, the physical disk does not need to be replaced, although the components must be resynced. If unsuccessful, the disk continues to be marked as permanent error.

What About Stretching VSAN?

With the release of VSAN 6.1, VMware introduced support for VSAN stretched cluster. Using RAID-1 constructs VMs can be deployed on a VSAN stretched cluster with one replica on one site and another replica on another site. If a site fails, a full copy of the data still exists, and vSphere HA can handle the restarting of the virtual machines on the surviving site.

Let's take a look at what this scenario would look like for VSAN in a stretched environment when FTT = 1 has been defined. The scenario shown in Figure 5.33 is what you want VSAN to do when it comes to placement of components.

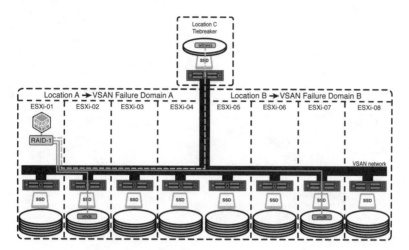

Figure 5.33 VSAN stretched cluster

A number of enhancements were essential to get this stretched cluster functionality.

- **Object placement:** Through the use of fault domains, introduced with VSAN 6.0, the ability to deploy one copy of the data on site A and another copy of the data on site B can now be achieved.

- **Witness placement:** We need to have a third site that functions as a tiebreaker when there is a partition/isolation event. To coincide with the VSAN 6.1 release, a witness appliance was also created which is essentially a stripped down ESXi running in a VM.

- **Support:** VMware has done substantial testing to qualify bandwidth and latency requirements for VSAN stretched cluster. There was also considerable testing done to verify if VSAN stretched cluster could work over L2 and/or L3 networks.

Summary

VSAN has a unique architecture that is future proof but at the same time extensible. It is designed to handle extreme I/O load and cope with different failure scenarios. Key, however, is policy-based management. Your decision-making during the creation of policies will determine how flexible, performant, and resilient your workloads and VSAN datastore will be.

Chapter 6

VM Storage Policies and Virtual Machine Provisioning

This chapter looks at some sample virtual machine (VM) provisioning workflows. You have already learned the various virtual storage area network (VSAN) capabilities that you can add to a VM storage policy and that VMs deployed on a VSAN datastore can use. This chapter covers how to create the appropriate VM storage policy using these capabilities, and also discusses the layout of these VM storage objects as they are deployed on the VSAN datastore.

Policy Setting: Number of Failures to Tolerate = 1

Let's begin by creating a very simple VM storage policy. Then we can examine what will happen if a VM is deployed to a VSAN datastore using this policy. Let's create the first policy to have a single capability setting of number of failures to tolerate (FTT) set to 1. We are going to use RAID-1 mirroring to implement failures to tolerate initially. Later on we shall look at RAID-5 and RAID-6 configurations for the VM objects. This means that any VMs deployed on the VSAN datastore with this policy will be configured with an additional mirror copy (replica) of the data so that if there is a single failure in the VSAN cluster, a full complement of the VSAN storage objects is still available. Let's see this in action, but before we do, let's visualize the expected results as shown in Figure 6.1.

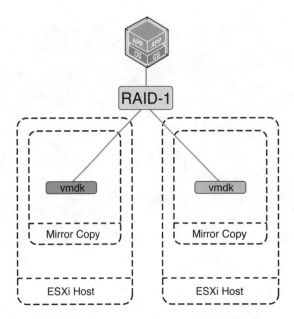

Figure 6.1   VSAN I/O flow: Number of failures to tolerate set to 1

In this VSAN environment, there are a number of ESXi hosts. This is a hybrid configuration, where each ESXi host has a single disk group with a single solid-state disk (SSD) and a single magnetic disk. The VSAN cluster has been enabled, and the ESXi hosts have formed a single VSAN datastore. To this datastore, we will deploy a new VM.

Let's start the process by revisiting the creation of a VM storage policy. This procedure was discussed in significant detail in Chapter 4, "VM Storage Policies on VSAN," where you also learned the various capabilities that you could use for VMs deployed on the VSAN datastore. As you might recall from Chapter 4, the eight capabilities that can be present in a VM storage policy are as follows:

- Number of failures to tolerate
- Number of disk stripes per object
- IOPS limit for object
- Disable object checksum
- Failure tolerance method
- Flash read cache reservation (hybrid configurations only)
- Object space reservation
- Force provisioning

We will keep this first VM storage policy simple, with just a single capability, number of failures to tolerate set to 1.

To begin, click the icon in the VM storage policies page in the vSphere Web Client to create a new policy. This will open the create new VM storage policy screen, as shown in Figure 6.2.

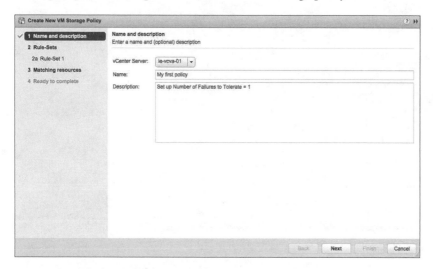

Figure 6.2   Create a VM storage policy

The next screen displays information about rule-sets. Rule-sets are a way of grouping multiple rules together. In this way, VMs can be deployed on different datastores, depending on which selection criteria are satisfied. For the purposes of this exercise, we are creating only a single rule-set. The wizards display additional information about rule-sets, as shown in Figure 6.3.

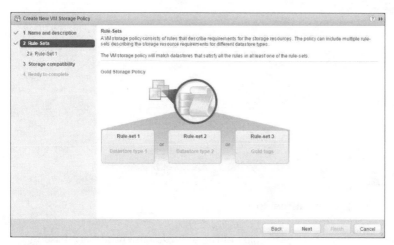

Figure 6.3   Rule-sets

On the next screen, we can begin to add our rule-set for VSAN. First is to change the vendor from none to VSAN, as shown in Figure 6.4. This will add an additional item to the wizard, namely the <Add rule> drop-down. If you click **<Add rule>**, the list of capabilities supported by VSAN is shown.

Figure 6.4   VSAN capabilities

For our first policy, the capability that we want to add is number of failures to tolerate, and we will set this to 1, as shown in Figure 6.5.

Figure 6.5   Number of failures to tolerate set to 1

There are a number of other features on this part of the wizard, namely add tag-based rules and add another rule-set buttons. These are beyond the scope of this book, but you can find additional information in the official vSphere documentation. One additional point to make is the "storage consumption model" shown in the right hand side of the wizard. This gives administrators a good idea on how much space will be consumed depending on the requirements placed in the policy. For example, using a RAID-1 configuration to tolerate one failure will mean that there are two copies of the data created. Therefore a 100 GB VMDK would consume 200 GB of space on the VSAN datastore, as highlighted in the storage consumption model.

Clicking **Next** moves the wizard onto the matching resources window, and at this point the VSAN datastore should be displayed, as shown in Figure 6.6. This means that the contents of the VM storage policy (i.e., the capabilities) are understood by the VSAN datastore.

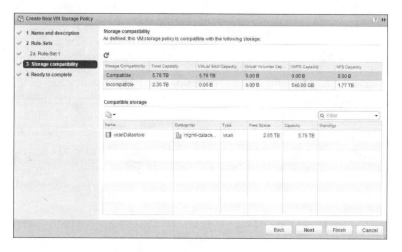

Figure 6.6   Compatible storage resources

Note that in the initial release of VSAN, just because the VSAN datastore is shown in the compatible storage window, it does not mean that the VSAN datastore can provision VMs. It could be that the policy contains an unrealistic stripe width or FTT setting that cannot be met by the VSAN cluster. This screen simply means that VSAN understands the policy contents. This is an important distinction. This was addressed in later versions of VSAN, where the VSAN datastore would also appear as incompatible if the cluster configuration could not meet the contents of the policy.

Review your policy and click **Finish** to create it. Congratulations! You have created your first VM storage policy. We will now go ahead and deploy a new VM using this policy. The process for deploying a new VM is exactly the same as before. The only difference is at the storage-selection step. In the first release of VSAN, by default, no VM storage policy is selected; it is set to none, as shown in Figure 6.7.

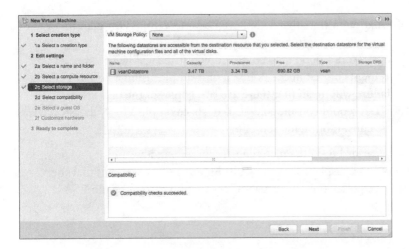

Figure 6.7 No policy selected in VSAN 1.0

This behavior was changed in VSAN 6.0 with the introduction of a default policy for
the VSAN datastore, called the Virtual SAN default storage policy. The rule-set for this
default policy is number of failures to tolerate set to 1 and number of disk stripes per
object set to 1. Now when a VM is created, and the VSAN datastore is selected, a policy
called the datastore default is selected. For VSAN datastores, this is the Virtual SAN
default storage policy, as shown in Figure 6.8.

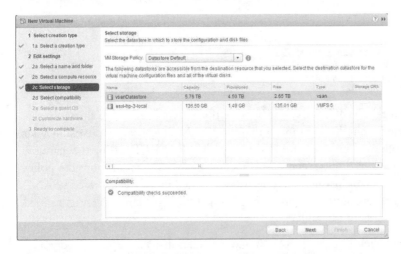

Figure 6.8 Datastore default policy selected in VSAN 6.0

However, when our new VM storage policy (**My first policy**) is selected, you can see that
the VSAN datastore is compatible, as shown in Figure 6.9.

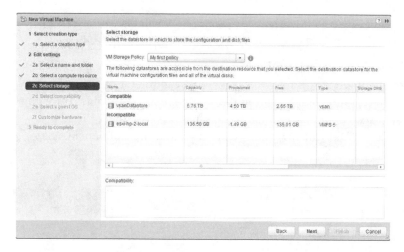

Figure 6.9   My first policy is selected, and the VSAN datastore is compatible

An important point to note here is that in initial release of VSAN, this compatibility check was just like the "matching resources" section of the create new VM storage policy wizard, which simply means that the VSAN datastore understands the contents of the policy. It does not mean that the VSAN cluster can meet the requirements; this will only be known when the VM is actually deployed. Once again, improvements made in VSAN 6.0 now do validation checks to ensure that the VSAN cluster can meet the requirements in the policy. This includes verifying that there are enough hosts in the cluster to meet the number of failures to tolerate requirement and verifying that there are enough capacity devices to meet the number of disk stripes per object.

Once the VM has been deployed, we have the ability to check the layout of the VM's objects. Navigate to the VM view by clicking **Monitor**, and then selecting **Policies**, as shown in Figure 6.10. From here, using the physical disk placement tab, we can see the layout of the VM storage object's VM home namespace, and VM disk files (VMDKs). The VM home namespace is where the .vmx file and other configuration files required by a VM reside. These storage objects that make up a VM on the VSAN datastore are discussed in detail in Chapter 5, "Architectural Details."

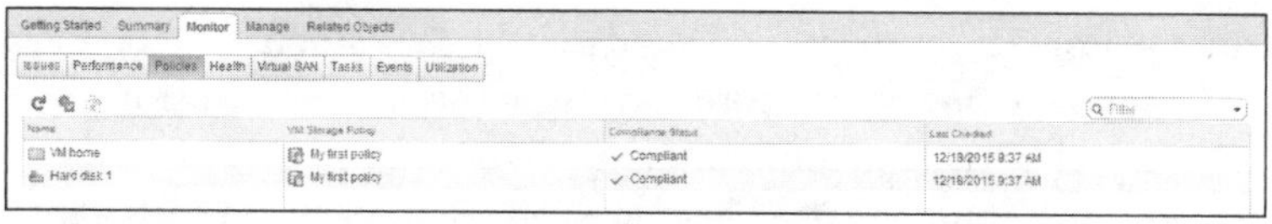

Figure 6.10   Compliance status is compliant

This view is in a different location in the original versions of VSAN. On earlier versions, navigate to the VM view, then click **Manage**, and then select **VM Storage Policies**.

As you can see, both objects are compliant. In other words, they meet the capabilities defined in the VM storage policy. This means that this VM can tolerate a failure in the VSAN cluster and still have a full complement of the storage objects available. If we now select the physical disk placement tab for either of the objects (VM home or hard disk), we can see that there is a RAID-1 (mirror) configuration around the components. See Figure 6.11.

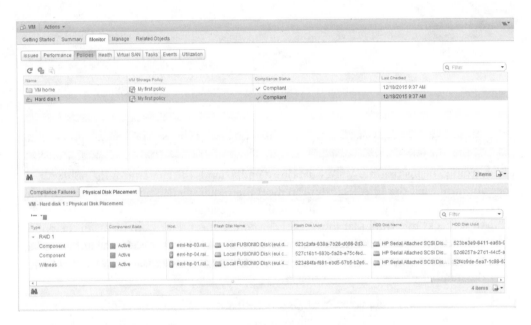

Figure 6.11   Physical disk placement

Policy Setting: Failures to Tolerate = 1, Stripe Width = 2

Let's try another VM storage policy setting that adds another capability. In this case, we will use a cluster with more resources than the first example to facilitate the additional requirements. This time we will explicitly request a number of failures to tolerate set to 1 and a number of disk stripes per object set to 2. Let's build out the VM storage policy and deploy a VM with that policy and see how it affects the layout of the various VM storage objects. In this scenario, we expect a RAID-1 configuration mirrored by a RAID-0 stripe configuration, resulting in four disk components. There are two components in each RAID-0 stripe, which is in turn mirrored in a RAID-1 configuration. Figure 6.12 shows how this will look from a logical perspective.

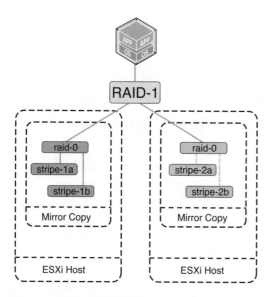

Figure 6.12   VSAN I/O flow: striping, two hosts

Now, let's create the VM storage policy and then provision a VM and see whether the result matches theory.

When creating the new policy, the vendor VSAN is once again selected to display specific capabilities of VSAN in the rule-sets, as shown in Figure 6.13. To meet the necessary VM requirements, we select number of disk stripes per object and set this to 2, and we set number of failures to tolerate to 1. The number of disk stripes defined is a minimum number, so depending on the size of the virtual disk and the size of the capacity tier devices, a virtual disk might end up being striped across multiple disks or hosts.

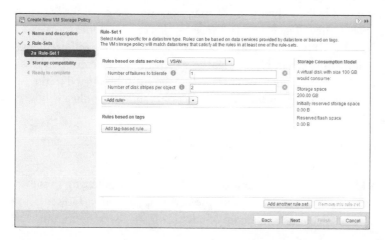

Figure 6.13   VM storage policy with failures to tolerate = 1 and stripe width = 2

Now that we have created a new VM storage policy, let's take a look at the VM provisioning workflow, beginning with Figure 6.14.

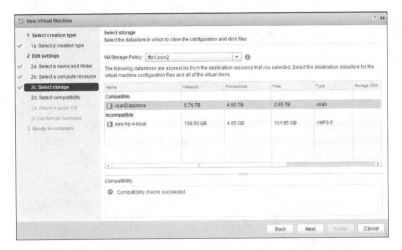

Figure 6.14   The VSAN datastore is compatible for policy ftt=1, sw=2.

In this example, we explicitly select the newly created policy called ftt=1, sw=2. Now you see that the available datastores are split into two distinct categories:

- Compatible
- Incompatible

As you can see, after selecting the newly created VM storage policy, only the VSAN datastore is compatible because it is the only one that can understand the capabilities that were placed in the VM storage policy. The other datastore (in this case, it is local VMFS but it could also be SAN-based VMFS or NFS) do not understand the policy requirements and so are placed in the incompatible category, though these can still be selected should you want to do so. If you do choose an incompatible datastore, you will be alerted to the fact that the datastore does not match the given VM storage policy, and the policy will be shown as not applicable.

After we have deployed the VM, we will examine the physical disk layout again, as shown in Figure 6.15.

As you can see in Figure 6.15, a RAID-1 configuration has been created, adhering to the number of failures to tolerate requirement specified in the VM storage policy. However, now you see that additionally each replica is made up of a RAID-0 stripe configuration,

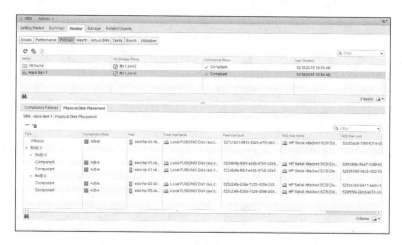

Figure 6.15   Physical disk placement for policy of ftt=1, sw=2

and each stripe contains two components, adhering to the number of disk stripes per object requirement of 2.

We also have a witness component created. Now it is important to point out that the number of witness components is directly related to how the components are distributed across the hosts and disks in the cluster. Depending on the size of the VSAN cluster, a number of additional witness components might have been necessary to ensure that greater than 50% of the components of this VM's objects remained available in the event of a failure, especially a host failure. In the case of a four-node VSAN cluster, because the components are spread out across unique ESXi hosts, it is sufficient to create a single witness disk and keep greater than 50% of the components available when there is a failure in the cluster.

Note that witness components were the only way to configure for a quorum in the initial release of VSAN. Since VSAN 6.0, a new quorum mechanism is available which relies on each component having a vote. This means that there may be occasions when there are no witness components required, and that quorum can be achieved via component votes alone.

An interesting point to note is that the VM home namespace does not implement the number of disk stripes per object requirement. The VM home namespace only implements the number of failures to tolerate requirement. Therefore, if the VM home namespace is examined, we see that the components are not in a RAID-0 configuration, as shown in Figure 6.16.

Figure 6.16   The VM home namespace does not implement stripe width capability

Policy Setting: Failures to Tolerate = 2, Stripe Width = 2

In this next example, we create another VM storage policy that has the number of disk stripes per object set to 2 and the number of failures to tolerate also set to 2. This implies that any VM deployed with this policy on the VSAN cluster should be able to tolerate up to two different failures, be they host, network, or disk failures. Considering the "two-host failure" capability specified and the number of disk stripes of 2, the expected disk layout is as shown in Figure 6.17.

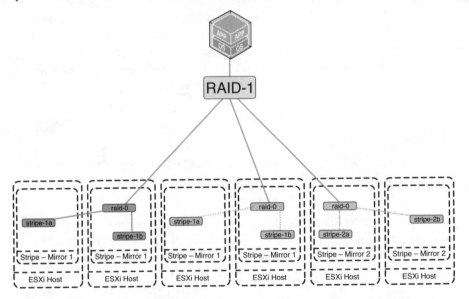

Figure 6.17   VSAN I/O flow: Tolerate two failures and stripe width set to 2

There are a few considerations with regards to this configuration. Because we are continuing with a RAID-1 mirroring configuration to tolerate failures, there needs to be $n + 1$ copies of the data and $2n + 1$ hosts in the cluster to tolerate n failures. Therefore to tolerate two failures, there will be three copies of the data, and there must be a minimum of five hosts in the cluster.

First, the policy is created with the desired requirements, as shown in Figure 6.18.

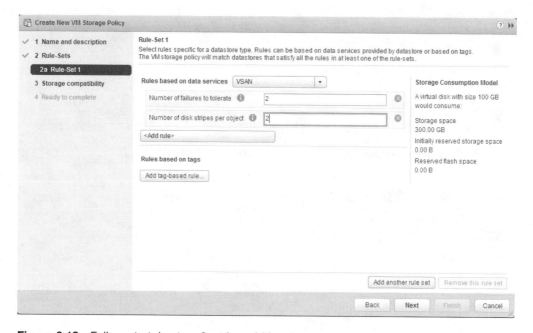

Figure 6.18   Failures to tolerate = 2, stripe width = 2

Next we deploy a new VM with this new policy, and as expected the VSAN datastore is the only one that shows up as compatible when the VM storage policy ftt=2, sw=2 is selected, as shown in Figure 6.19.

Now that we have provisioned a VM, the physical disk placement can be examined to see how the VM storage objects have been laid out across hosts and disks.

First, let's look at the VMDK or hard disk 1 of this VM, as shown in Figure 6.20.

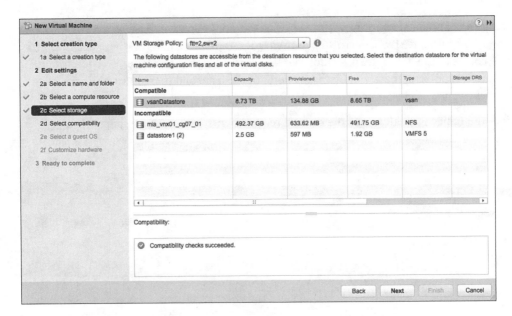

Figure 6.19   The VSAN datastore is compatible with the ftt=2, sw=2 policy

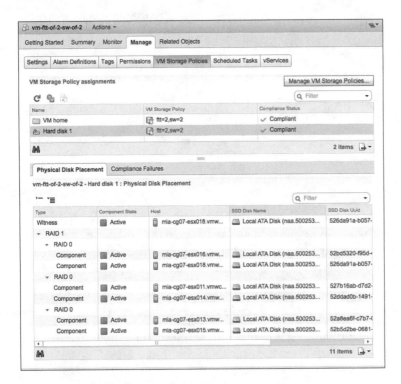

Figure 6.20   Physical disk placement for hard disk using the ftt=2, sw=2 policy

One thing to note is that the location of the physical disk placement has changed between releases. In the original release of VSAN, administrators navigated to the Manage > VM Storage Policies as shown here. In later releases, this view was changed to Monitor > VM Storage Policies. You will see screenshot from the different VSAN versions used throughout this book.

Now we see that for the virtual disk of this VM, VSAN has implemented an additional RAID-0 stripe configuration. For RAID-0 stripe configurations, all components in at least one of the RAID-0 stripe configuration must remain intact. That is why a third RAID-0 stripe configuration has been created. You might assume that if the first component in the first RAID-0 stripe configuration was lost, and the second component of the second RAID-0 stripe configuration was lost, VSAN might be able to use the remaining components to keep the storage object intact. This is not the case. Therefore, to tolerate two failures in the cluster, a third RAID-0 stripe configuration is necessary because two failures might take out the other two RAID-0 stripe configurations. This is also why all of these RAID-0 configurations are mirrored in a RAID-1 configuration. The bottom line with this policy setting is that any two hosts are allowed to fail in the cluster, and the VM's data remains accessible. As you can see in Figure 6.19, components are stored on six different ESXi hosts in this eight-node VSAN cluster: mia-cg07.esx11, mia-cg07.esx13, mia-cg07. esx14, mia-cg07.esx15, mia-cg07.esx16, and mia-cg07-esx018.

Next, let's look at the VM home namespace, as shown in Figure 6.21.

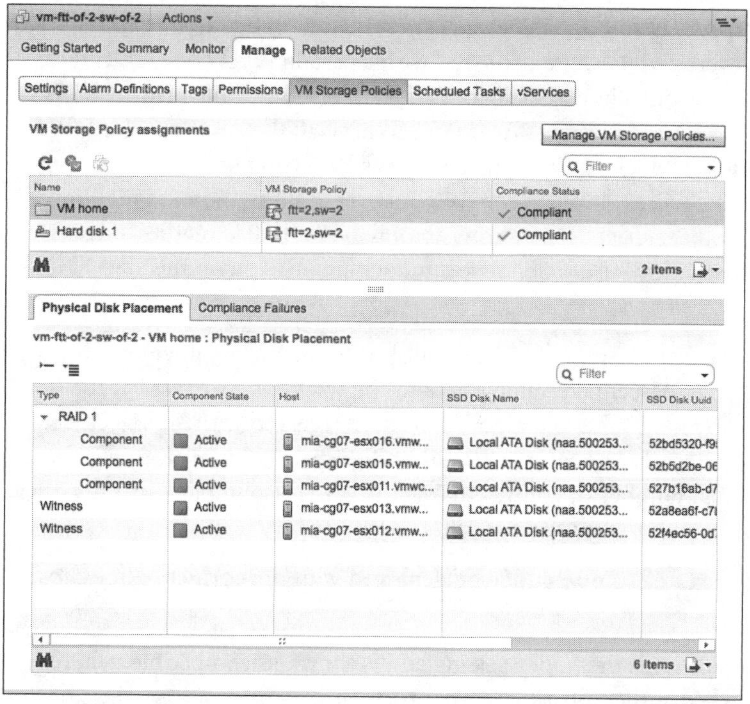

Figure 6.21 Physical disk placement for VM home with the ftt=2, sw=2 policy

Previously, it was stated that the VM home namespace does not implement the number of disk stripes per object policy setting, but that it does implement the number of failures to tolerate. There is no RAID-0 configuration, but we can now see that there are three replicas in the RAID-1 mirror configuration to meet the number of failures to tolerate set to 2 in the VM storage policy. What can also be observed here is an increase in the number of witness disks. Remember that greater than 50% of the components of the VM home namespace object (or 50% of the votes depending on the quorum mechanism used) must be available for this object to remain online. Therefore, if two replicas were lost, there would still be one replica (i.e., copy of the VM home namespace data) available and two witness disks; therefore, greater than 50% of the components would still be available if two failures took out two replicas of this configuration.

Policy Setting: Failures to Tolerate = 1, Object Space Reservation = 50%

This next scenario explores a different capability. As explained in previous chapters, all objects deployed on VSAN are thinly provisioned by default. This means that they initially consume no disk space, but grow over time as the guest OS running inside of the VM requires additional space. Using the object space reservation policy setting in the VM storage policy, however, a VM can be deployed with a certain percentage of its disk space reserved in advance. By default, object space reservation is 0%, which is why VMs deployed on the VSAN datastore are thin. If you want to have all the space reserved for a VM (similar to a traditional "thick" disk), you can do this by setting the object space reservation to be 100%. We will go for somewhere in between. Please note, as highlighted already in this book, that object space reservation can only be set to 0% or 100% if deduplication and compression space efficiency techniques are enabled on the VSAN datastore.

Let's start with an example that reserves 50% of the disk space at VM deployment time, as shown in Figure 6.22. The percentage value refers to the size of the VMDK. If the VMDK is 100 GB at deployment time, the amount of space reserved with an object space reservation value of 50% should reserve 50 GB of disk space. However, as per the storage consumption model, number of failures to tolerate = 1 is also implied in any policy. Therefore the initially reserved storage space is 100 GB.

Once the policy has been created, the VM may be deployed with the correct policy chosen, as shown in Figure 6.23.

The VSAN datastore understands the policy setting and is shown as compatible, whereas the other datastore is marked as incompatible. Now, as already pointed out, we did not

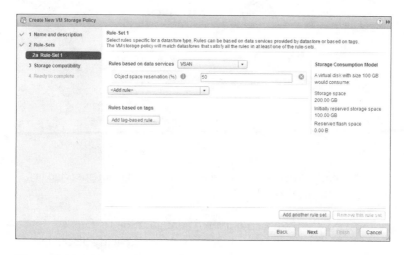

Figure 6.22   Object space reservation

select a requirement of number of failures to tolerate. To reiterate, the number of failures to tolerate setting of 1 is always inferred, even if it is not explicitly specified. Therefore a number of failures to tolerate setting of 1 is implemented if a policy does not specify this requirement. To confirm, the physical disk placement views can be used to check whether a RAID-1 configuration is indeed in place. Only if FTT is explicitly set to 0 in the policy you will not have a RAID-1 configuration.

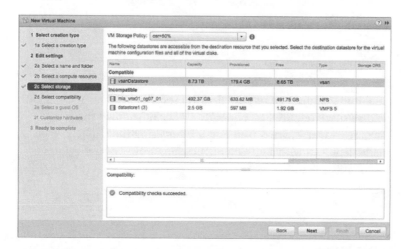

Figure 6.23   The VSAN datastore understands the object space reservation requirement

First, we verify the RAID-1 configuration in the VM home namespace view, as shown in Figure 6.24.

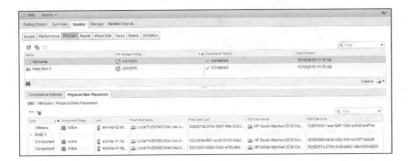

Figure 6.24   VM Home: The number of failures to tolerate is inferred even if not specified in the policy

We can also confirm that the hard disk also has a mirrored configuration to meet a number of failures to tolerate policy setting, even though it was not explicitly placed in the policy, as shown in Figure 6.25.

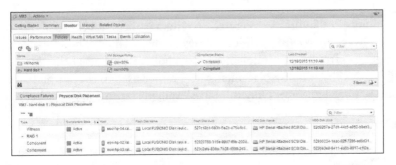

Figure 6.25   VMDK: The number of failures to tolerate is inferred even if not specified in the policy

However, let's return to the initial additional requirement we specified. That requirement was to reserve 50% of the disk space required by our VM. To see how much space the VMDK is consuming, navigate to **Datastore > Manage > Files** using the vSphere Web Client. The VM was initially deployed with a 40 GB VMDK, and now we have requested an object space reservation of 50%, as shown in Figure 6.26.

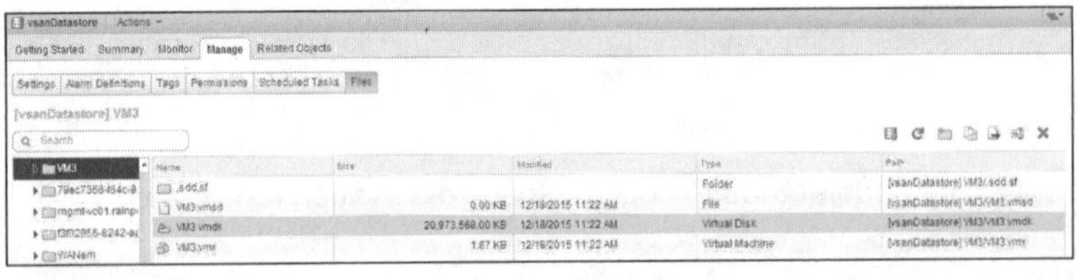

Figure 6.26   Object space reservation = 50% reserves 20 GB out of 40 GB.

As stated, we can see that the 40 GB VM hard disk file deployed with this VM has reserved 20 GB of disk space, equal to the 50% that was requested in the VM storage policy for this VM.

Policy Setting: Failures to Tolerate = 1, Object Space Reservation = 100%

Let's look at one last policy with object space reservation. This is to reserve the full 100% of our VMDK. The same steps are followed as before, which is to create a policy that contains an object space reservation requirement, but this time the value is 100% rather than 50%, as shown in Figure 6.27. This means, as you might have already guessed, that we reserve all of the VM's disk space up front, similar to a thick format VM disk file.

As per the steps that have already been covered in the previous section, the policy requires only an object space reservation setting, but this time set to 100%. As before, a number of failures to tolerate setting of 1 is implied, even though it isn't explicitly stated in the policy.

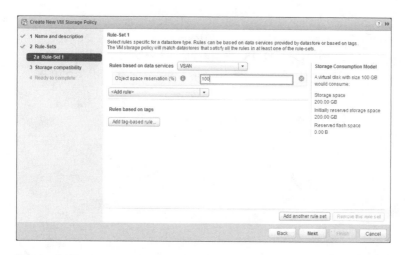

Figure 6.27   Object space reservation = 100%

Note now that the storage consumption model shows that the amount of space that will be initially reserved with this policy is the same as the storage space, for example, 200 GB. When the policy is created, we can once again select this policy during VM deployment.

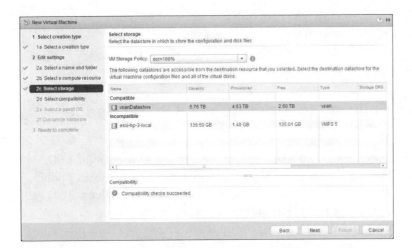

Figure 6.28   The VSAN datastore is compatible with the VM storage policy

We can verify that the VSAN datastore is compatible with our policy selection, as shown in Figure 6.28.

The next step is to determine how much disk space the VMDK file is actually reserving. Once again, you can use the **Datastore > Manage > Files** view to see how much space has been reserved up front for this VMDK, as shown in Figure 6.29. Because the object space reservation value was set to 100%, we should expect the full 40 GB to be reserved.

As expected, the full 40 GB of disk space is reserved up front.

Figure 6.29   40 GB of disk space is reserved

Policy Setting: RAID-5

Let us now look at a new policy introduced in VSAN 6.2, namely RAID-5. To configure a RAID-5 object, select the policy setting "failure tolerance method" and set this to RAID5/6, as shown in Figure 6.30. Note the storage consumption model. For a 100 GB VMDK, this only consumes 133.33 GB, which is 33% above the actual size of the VMDK. Previously when we created a policy for RAID-1 objects, because of the mirror copies, an additional 100% of capacity was consumed.

Since number of failures to tolerate equal to 1 is inferred without us having to add it to the policy, the configuration will roll out a RAID-5. If number of failures to tolerate was set to 2, then a RAID-6 configuration for the objects in implemented. We have added the failures to tolerate policy setting to the example in the Figure 6.30 just for demonstrational purposes.

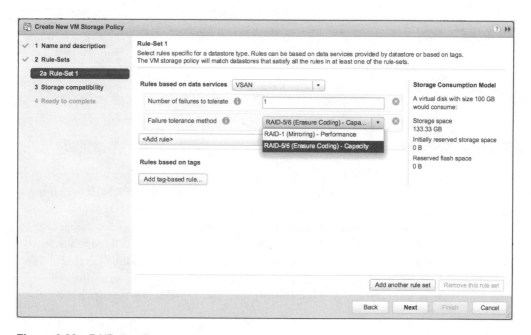

Figure 6.30   RAID-5 policy setup

If a VM is now deployed with this policy, the physical disk placement can be examined as before, and we should now observe a RAID-5 layout across four disks and four hosts.

Figure 6.31 shows the physical disk placement view, and as described, we see a RAID-5 configuration for the object.

Figure 6.31   RAID-5 object as seen from physical disk placement view

Note that the VM home namespace object also inherits a RAID-5 configuration.

Policy Setting: RAID-6

Besides RAID-5, with VSAN 6.2 the option to tolerate two failures in a capacity efficient manner has also been introduced and is called RAID-6. To configure a RAID-6 object, select the policy setting "failure tolerance method" and set this to RAID5/6 and set the policy setting "failures to tolerate" to 2, as shown in Figure 6.32. Note the storage consumption model. For a 100 GB VMDK, this only consumes 150 GB, which is 50% above the actual size of the VMDK. Previously when we created a policy for RAID-1 objects with failures to tolerate set to 2, because of the mirror copies, an additional 200% of capacity was consumed. This means that a 100 GB VMDK required 300 GB of disk capacity at the backend.

If a VM is now deployed with this policy, the physical disk placement can be examined as before, and we should now observe a RAID-6 layout across six disks and six hosts. Figure 6.33 shows the physical disk placement view, and as described, we see a RAID-6 configuration for the object.

Note that the VM home namespace object also inherits a RAID-6 configuration.

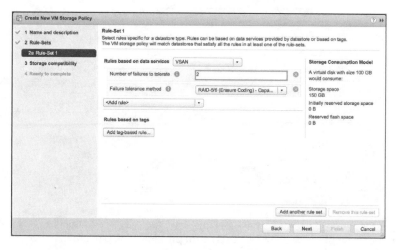

Figure 6.32   RAID-6 policy setup

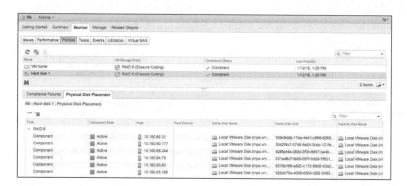

Figure 6.33   RAID-6 object as seen from physical disk placement view

Policy Setting: RAID-5/6 and Stripe Width = 2

It should be noted that using RAID-5/6 does not prevent the use of a stripe width in the policy. All this means is that each part of a RAID-5/6 object will be striped with two components in a RAID-0 configuration. In this next example, a VM was deployed with a RAID-5 configuration as per the previous example, but the policy includes a number of disk stripes per object set to 2. This led to the following object configuration in the physical disk placement view, as shown in Figure 6.34:

Figure 6.34   RAID-5 object with stripe width =2 as seen from physical disk placement view

Note however that the VM home namespace does not implement stripe width, so it continues to have a RAID-5 configuration as per the previous example. Although in the above example we showed how this works with a RAID-5 configuration, the exact same principles apply to a RAID-6 configuration.

Default Policy

As you might imagine, VSAN has a default policy. This means that if no policy is chosen for a VM deployed on the VSAN datastore (VM storage policy left set to none, as per Figure 6.35), a default policy is used for the VM.

The default policy contains the following capabilities:

- Number of failures to tolerate = 1

- Number of disk stripes per object = 1

- Flash read cache reservation = 0%

- Object space reservation = not used

- Force provisioning = disabled

When the VM is deployed, in the initial VSAN release, the VM storage policy is set to none, as shown in Figure 6.35. However, you will also notice that the number of failures to tolerate value of 1 is implemented when the objects are examined via the physical disk

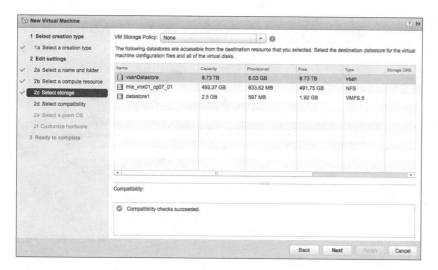

Figure 6.35   No policy selected results in the default policy being used

placement. As you can see in this figure, even though the policy is set to none, a RAID-1 configuration is in place for the VM objects. This means that even if you deploy a VM without a policy, VSAN will automatically provide availability via the default policy.

As shown in Figure 6.36, which is once again taken from the first VSAN release, there is no VM storage policy associated with this VM. However, if we look at the VM home, we can see that it is automatically deployed with a RAID-1 configuration, which is a mirror copy of the data. The two components that make up the RAID-1 mirror are placed on two different ESXi hosts, namely mia-cg07.esx17 and mia-cg07-esx015. This means that if one of the ESXi hosts fails, there is still a full copy of the data available. Another point to make is related to the witness disk. This is placed on a different ESXi host (mia-cg07-esx013) from the data components, too. This is to ensure that greater than 50% of the components remain available should a host failure occur on any single ESXi hosts in the cluster. The witness acts as a vote in this configuration. It allows the VM home object to remain available in the event of a failure in the cluster.

Let's take a look at the hard disk/VMDK next. This is what the VMDK looks like when deployed to the VSAN datastore with a default policy. Because there is only a single VMDK on this VM, it is referred to as hard disk 1 in the user interface in this example. As Figure 6.37 shows, the two components that make up the RAID-1 mirror are placed on two different ESXi hosts, namely mia-cg07.esx12 and mia-cg07-esx013. The witness is placed on ESXi host mia-cg07-esx016.

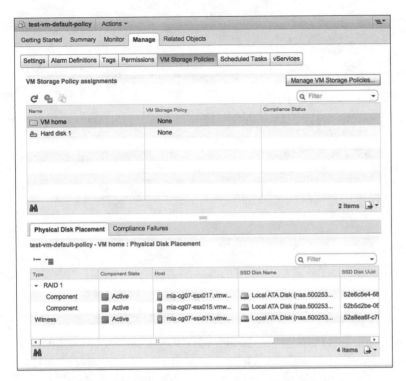

Figure 6.36   Number of failures to tolerate = 1 is part of the default policy

As expected, all components, including the witness, are stored on different hosts to ensure availability.

One final note about the default policy in the initial version of VSAN is the object space reservation setting. This is not included in the default policy (but is included in later releases). Instead, the create VM wizard settings of thick and thin disks are implemented. If no changes are made to the create VM wizard settings during deployment, a lazy zeroed thick (LZT) VMDK will be deployed on the VSAN datastore, similar to having an object space reservation of 100%. This has been a common question in the early days of VSAN in so far as customers did not understand why VSAN was deploying objects that were "thick" and not thin. This is the reason. Although the default policy exists in the initial VSAN release, VMware recommends that administrators create their own policy and not rely on the default policy for deployments. VMware also cautions against editing the default policy in the initial release of VSAN; the recommendation is that if you need to change the default policy, it is much simpler to build a policy via VM storage policies in vCenter to meet those requirements. Also note that editing the default policy can only be

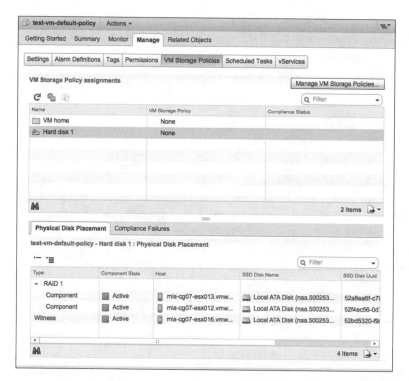

Figure 6.37 Hard disk 1 layout using default policy

done at the command line of the ESXi host in the first release of VSAN, and this editing process needs to be repeated on every ESXi host in the cluster. This can lead to user errors, and so should be avoided if at all possible.

This all became so much easier in VSAN 6.0. In Virtual SAN 6.0, there is now a default policy for the VSAN datastore, called the Virtual SAN default storage policy. If you wish to change the default policy, you can simply edit the capability values of the policy from the vSphere Web Client. The default policy includes the same set capabilities as before, namely tolerate 1 failure, set stripe width to 1, no read cache reservation, no object space reservation, and do not force provision. The failure tolerance method is not specified in the default policy, meaning that it will be by default set to RAID-1 (Mirroring); when using an all-flash VSAN configuration it may be desired to change the policy as such.

Now when deploying a virtual machine, once the VSAN datastore is selected, the VM storage policy is set to datastore default (whereas in VSAN 1.0 it was set to none). You no longer need to explicitly pick a policy. For the VSAN datastore, the datastore default policy is the Virtual SAN default storage policy.

And if you are managing multiple VSAN deployments with a single vCenter Server, different default policies can be associated with different VSAN datastores. Therefore, if you have a "test&dev" cluster and a "production" cluster, there can be different default policies associated with the different VSAN datastores.

Summary

This completes the coverage of VM storage policy creation and VM deployments on the VSAN datastore. One policy setting that we did not include in this chapter was the flash read cache reservation. This is simply because this setting is not visible from a VM layout perspective in the vSphere Web Client. However, it is configured as a percentage value once again, in exactly the same way as object space reservation is configured, as a percentage value of the full VMDK size. For example, if 1% is the flash read cache reservation setting on a 40 GB VMDK, this will reserve 400 MB of flash read cache for that particular VM. As stated, however, there is no way to observe this reservation in the vSphere Web Client. Chapter 10, "Troubleshooting, Monitoring, and Performance," will show how an administrator can use the Ruby vSphere Console (RVC) to examine flash read cache reservation values.

The other policy setting that was not discussed in this chapter was the force provisioning vSphere Replication setting. Again, this is not something that can be readily observed in the vSphere Web Client when it is set in a policy and that policy is used for a VM deployment. If force provisioning is used to deploy a VM, the VM will be deployed on the VSAN datastore as long as one full set of storage objects can be deployed. (The behavior of objects that are deployed with force provision is discussed in more detail in chapter 4.) So even though the policy may contain requirements such as failures to tolerate, or stripe width, or flash read cache reservation, the VM may be deployed without any of these configurations in place when force provisioning is specified. However, the VM will be shown as out of compliance in the vSphere Web Client. When the additional resources become available, this VM will be reconfigured using the additional resources to bring it to compliance. VSAN automatically enforces the policy once the resources are available; no steps are required by the administrator to initiate this process. You should be aware by now that deploying VMs that do not have their requirements met via the use of force provisioning can be dangerous and may result in an unavailable VM should a failure occur in the cluster.

What you would have noticed is that there are a few behaviors with VM storage policies that might not be intuitive, such as the default policy settings, the fact that a number of failures to tolerate set to 1 is implicitly included in a policy, and that some virtual storage objects implement only some of the policy settings. Chapter 5 explained these nuances in greater detail.

## Chapter 7

Management and Maintenance

This chapter covers the common Virtual SAN (VSAN) management and maintenance procedures and tasks. It also provides some generic workflows and examples related to day-to-day management. Management and maintenance of VSAN has changed considerably since the initial version. This chapter will not only look at the original techniques involved, but also discuss in detail the enhancements made along the way to VSAN 6.2.

Health Check

We will begin this chapter with a look at what has become the most valuable tool in an administrator's arsenal when it comes to management and maintenance of Virtual SAN. This is of course the VSAN health check. VSAN health check was introduced in VSAN 6.0 as a plugin for vCenter Server, which in turn pushed out a vSphere installation bundle (VIB) to each of the ESXi hosts in the VSAN cluster. This had to be installed independently from vSphere and VSAN. However since VSAN 6.1, this feature is now embedded into both vCenter Server and ESXi, so very little administrative action is required to leverage this feature now.

Health Check Tests

Possibly the most useful part of the health check is the number of tests that it performs on all aspects of the cluster. It tests to ensure that all of the hardware devices are on the VMware compatibility guide (VCG) (including driver versions), that the network is functioning correctly, that the cluster is formed properly, and that the storage devices do not have any errors. This is invaluable when it comes to troubleshooting VSAN issues and can quickly lead administrators to the root cause of an issue. Administrators should always refer to the health check tests and make sure that VSAN is completely healthy before embarking on any management or maintenance tasks. Figure 7.1 shows a complete set of health checks taken from a 6.1 VSAN cluster. Enhancements are being added to the health check with each release, so expect a different list of health checks depending on the VSAN version. There are also additional health checks for use cases such as VSAN stretched cluster.

Figure 7.1 Health check tests listing

VSAN health check also includes an alerting/alarm mechanism. This means that if a test fails in the health check, an alarm is raised to bring it to the administrator's attention. The other really nice feature of the health check tests is that, through the AskVMware mechanism, all tests are linked to a VMware knowledgebase article which provides details about the nature of the test, what it means when it fails, and how you can remediate the situation. To run the health check tests, first select the Virtual SAN cluster object in the vCenter inventory, then select monitoring, and then select Virtual SAN > Health. The tests can be re-run at any time by clicking the "retest" button. However, the tests are run automatically every 60 minutes. Health check tests will be revisited in Chapter 10, "Troubleshooting, Monitoring, and Performance," when we look at troubleshooting VSAN in greater detail.

Proactive Health Checks

Along with the set of health check tests introduced previously, VSAN health check also provides a set of proactive tests. Typically, one would not run these proactive tests during production. However, these tests can be very useful if you wish to implement a proof-of-concept (PoC) with VSAN, or even as part of the initial deployment of VSAN on site. These proactive tests can give you peace-of-mind that everything is working correctly before putting VSAN into production. The proactive tests include:

- VM creation test

- Multicast performance test

- Storage performance test

Simply select the test that you wish to run, and click the green "start" arrow symbol to begin the test. Figure 7.2 shows the tests as they appear in the vSphere Web Client.

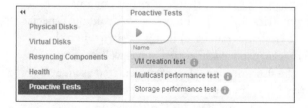

Figure 7.2   Health check proactive tests

The actual tests are well described in the Web Client. The "VM creation test" quickly verifies that virtual machines can be deployed on the VSAN datastore, and once that verification is complete, the sample VMs are removed. The VM are created with whatever policy is the default policy for the VSAN datastore. The "multicast performance test" simply verifies that the network infrastructure can handle a particular throughput using multicast traffic, and highlights if the network is unable to carry a particular load that is desirable for VSAN. This is especially important when there is a complex network configuration that may involve a number of hops or routes when VSAN is deployed over L3. Finally, there is the "storage performance test" which allows administrator to run various storage loads on their VSAN cluster, and examine the resulting bandwidth, throughput, and latency. This is also a very good test for proof-of-concepts or pre-production deployments where administrators can run a burn-in test on their VSAN storage and discover any unstable components, drivers, or firmware on their system. A good recommendation would be to run a storage performance burn-in test overnight as part of any deployment.

Performance Service

One final feature that can be considered part of the health check is the performance service, which was introduced in VSAN 6.2. Since the initial release of VSAN, an area that was identified as needing much improvement was the area of monitoring VSAN performance from the vSphere Web Client. While some information was available in the vSphere Web Client, such as per-VM performance metrics, there was little information regarding the performance of the VSAN cluster at an overall cluster basis, a per-host basis, a per-disk group basis, or even a per-device basis. This information was only attainable via the VSAN observer tool, and was not integrated with vSphere. Nor could the VSAN observer provide any historic data; it could only run in real-time mode. With the release of the performance service, metrics such as IOPS, latency, and throughput (and many others) are now available in the vSphere Web Client at a glance.

The performance service is initially disabled. Administrators will need to enable it via the Web Client. A nice feature of the performance service is that it does not put any additional load on vCenter Server for maintaining metrics. Instead, all metrics are saved on a special VM home object on the VSAN datastore (statistics database) that is created when the performance service is enabled. Now you can also view historic data as well as current system status. The metrics displayed in the user interface (UI) are calculated as an average performance over a 5-minute interval (roll up). Since the statistics are stored in a VM home namespace object, it may use up to a maximum of 255 GB of capacity. Figure 7.3 shows the policy for the statistics database using the VSAN default policy once the performance service is enabled.

Note that the health check also includes a number of tests to ensure that the performance service is functioning normally. These tests are only visible in VSAN 6.2.

Performance Service is Turned ON		Edit
Status	Enabled	
Stats object health	✪ Healthy	
Stats object UUID	06af6a56-69e5-1050-f40c-ecf4bbd59370	
Stats object storage policy	🗐 Virtual SAN Default Storage Policy	
Compliance status	✓ Compliant	

Figure 7.3   Performance service enabled

Now that we have provided an overview of the health check and associated services, let's now turn our attention to some of the more common management tasks an administrator might face with when managing VSAN.

Host Management

VMware VSAN is a scale-out and scale-up storage architecture. This means that it is possible to seamlessly add extra storage resources to your VSAN cluster. These storage resources can be magnetic disks or flash devices for additional capacity, complete disk groups including both cache and capacity devices, but could also be additional hosts containing storage capacity. Those who have been managing vSphere environments for a while will not be surprised that VSAN is extremely simple; adding storage capacity can truly be as simple as adding a new host to a cluster. Let's look at some of these tasks more in depth.

Adding Hosts to the Cluster

Adding hosts to the VSAN cluster is quite straightforward. Of course, you must ensure that the host meets VSAN requirements or recommendations such as a 1 Gb dedicated network interface card (NIC) port (10 GbE being recommended) and at least one cache tier device and one or more capacity tier devices if the host is to provide additional storage capacity. Also, preconfiguration steps such as a VMkernel port for VSAN communication should be considered, although these can be done after the host is added to the cluster. After the host has successfully joined the cluster, you should observe whether the size of the VSAN datastore grows according to the size of the additional capacity devices in the new host. Remember that the flash tier device does not add anything to the capacity of the VSAN datastore. Just for completeness' sake, these are the steps required to add a host to a VSAN cluster using the vSphere Web Client:

1. Right-click the cluster object and click **Add Host**.

2. Fill in the IP address or host name of the server, as shown in Figure 7.4.

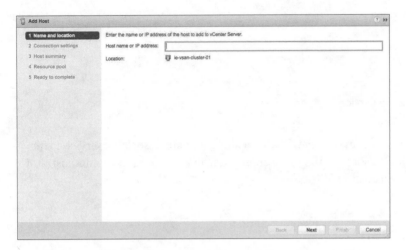

Figure 7.4 Adding a host to the cluster

3. Fill in the user account (root typically) and the password.

4. Accept the **SHA1 thumbprint** option.

5. Click **Next** on the host summary screen.

6. Select the license to be used.

7. Enable lockdown mode if needed and click **Next**.

8. Click **Next** in the resource pool section.

9. Click **Finish** to add the host to the cluster.

That is it; well, you have your VSAN cluster configured to automatic mode, of course. If you do not have it configured to automatic mode, you will need an additional step to create a disk group manually. You will learn how to do that later in this chapter in the disk management section.

Removing Hosts from the Cluster

Should you want to remove a host from a cluster, you must first ensure that the host is placed into maintenance mode, which is discussed in further detail in the next section. After the host has been successfully placed into maintenance mode, you may safely remove it from the VSAN cluster. To remove a host from a cluster using the vSphere Web Client, follow these steps:

1. Right-click the host and click **Enter Maintenance Mode** and select the appropriate VSAN migration option from the screen in Figure 7.5, and then click **OK**. If the plan is to truly remove this host from the cluster, then a full data migration is the recommended maintenance mode option.

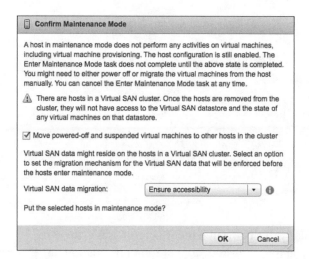

Figure 7.5 Enter maintenance mode

2. Now all the virtual machines (VMs) will be migrated (vMotion) to other hosts. If Distributed Research Scheduler (DRS) is enabled on the cluster, this will happen automatically. If DRS is not enabled on the cluster, the administrator will have to manually migrate VMs from the host entering maintenance mode for the operation to complete successfully.

3. When migrations are completed, depending on the selected VSAN migration option, VSAN components may also be copied to other hosts.

4. When maintenance mode has completed, right-click the host again and select **move to** option to move the host out of the cluster.

5. If you wish to remove the host from vCenter Server completely, right-click on the host once again, and select **remove from inventory**. This might be located under all vCenter actions in earlier versions of vCenter Server.

6. Read the text presented twice, and click Yes when you understand the potential impact.

ESXCLI VSAN Cluster Commands

There are no specific host commands for VSAN. There is a namespace in ESXCLI for the VSAN, however. Using these command-line interface (CLI) commands, you can enable a host to join or leave a cluster. The basic commands as part of esxcli vsan cluster are shown in Example 7.1.

Example 7.1   esxcli vsan Cluster Command Options

```
~ # esxcli vsan cluster
Usage: esxcli vsan cluster {cmd} [cmd options]


Available Commands:
    get        Get the information of the VSAN cluster that this host is
joined to.
    join       Join the host to a given VSAN cluster.
    leave      Leave the VSAN cluster the host is currently joined to.
    restore    Restore the persisted VSAN cluster configuration.
~ #
```

One command that we have used regularly during troubleshooting exercises is the `get` command. The `get` command allows you to get cluster configuration information on the command line, which can be used to compare hosts against each other; a sample is provided in Example 7.2.

Example 7.2   Using the get Command to get Cluster Configuration Information on the Command Line

```
~ # esxcli vsan cluster get
Cluster Information
    Enabled: true
    Current Local Time: 2013-03-18T12:09:11Z
    Local Node UUID: 511b62c3-96e6-434e-6839-1cc1de253de4
    Local Node State: MASTER
    Local Node Health State: HEALTHY
    Sub-Cluster Master UUID: 511b62c3-96e6-434e-6839-1cc1de253de4
    Sub-Cluster Backup UUID: 511cc68b-352a-5cae-cf67-1cc1de252264
    Sub-Cluster UUID: 523845c8-73c9-5d99-0393-9ef20a328714
    Sub-Cluster Membership Entry Revision: 10
    Sub-Cluster Member UUIDs: 511b62c3-96e6-434e-6839-1cc1de253de4,
        511cc68b-352a-5cae-cf67-1cc1de252264,
        511cd526-5682-3688-8206-1cc1de253a92
    Sub-Cluster Membership UUID: 56092451-245f-9c0c-29f6-1cc1de253de4
```

Maintenance Mode

The previous section briefly touched on maintenance mode when removing an ESXi host from a VSAN cluster. With VSAN, maintenance mode includes new functionality that we will elaborate on here. In the past, when an ESXi host was placed in maintenance mode, it was all about migrating VMs from that ESXi host; however, when you implement VSAN, maintenance mode provides you with the option to migrate data as well. The VSAN maintenance mode options relate to data evacuation, as follows:

- **Ensure Accessibility:** This option evacuates enough data from the host entering maintenance mode to ensure that all VM storage objects are accessible after the host goes down. This is not full data evacuation. Instead, VSAN examines the storage objects that could end up without quorum or data availability when the host is placed into maintenance mode and makes enough copies of the object available to alleviate those issues. VSAN (or to be more precise, cluster level object manager [CLOM]) will have to successfully reconfigure all objects that would become inaccessible because of the lack of availability of those component(s) on that host. An example of when this could happen is when VMs are configured with "failures to tolerate" set to 0, or there is already a host with a failure in the cluster, or indeed another host is in maintenance mode. Ensure Accessibility is the default option of the maintenance mode workflow and the recommended option by VMware if the host is going to be in maintenance for a short period of time. If the maintenance time is expected to be reasonably long, administrators should decide if they want to fully evacuate the data from that host to avoid risk to their VMs and data availability. There is one subtle behavior difference to note between the original release of VSAN and later releases. In the first release, when a host was placed in maintenance mode, it continued to contribute storage to the VSAN datastore and components were still accessible. In later releases this behavior was changed. Now when a host is placed into maintenance mode, it no longer contributes storage to the VSAN datastore, and any components on the datastore are marked as ABSENT.

- **Full Data Migration:** This option is a full data evacuation and essentially creates replacement copies for every piece of data residing on disks on the host being placed into maintenance mode. VSAN does not necessarily copy the data from the host entering maintenance mode; however, it can and will also leverage the hosts holding the replica copy of the object to avoid creating a bottleneck on the host entering maintenance mode. In other words, in an eight-host cluster, when a host is placed in maintenance mode using full data migration, then potentially all eight hosts will contribute to the re-creation of the impacted components. The host does not successfully enter maintenance mode until all affected objects are reconfigured and compliance is ensured when all of the component(s) have been placed on different hosts in the cluster. This is the option that VMware recommends when hosts are being removed from the cluster, or there is a long-term maintenance operation planned.

- **No Data Migration:** This option does nothing with the storage objects. If the host is powered off after entering maintenance mode, the situation is equivalent to the host crashing. It is also important to understand that if you have objects that have *number of failures to tolerate* set to 0, you could impact the availability of those objects by choosing this option. There are some other risks associated with this option. For example, if there is some other "unknown" issue or failure in the cluster or there is a maintenance mode operation in progress that the administrator is not aware of, this maintenance mode option can lead to VM or data unavailability. For this reason, VMware only recommend this option when there is a full cluster shutdown planned (or on the advice of VMware support staff).

Note that in the original release of VSAN, if a host enters maintenance mode, VSAN still operates, accesses, and serves data on that host. Only when the host is removed from the cluster or is powered off did VSAN stop using the host (or, of course, when you have decided to do a full data migration, when the data migration has been completed, and the "old" components have been removed). This behavior changed in VSAN 6.0. In VSAN 6.0 and later, when a host is placed into maintenance mode, it no longer contributes storage to the VSAN datastore, and any components that reside on the physical storage of the host that is placed into maintenance mode are marked as absent.

For manual maintenance mode operations (outside of VMware Update Manager), Figure 7.6 shows which options an administrator can select from the UI when a host or hosts are placed into maintenance mode, with Ensure Accessibility being the default preselected data migration suggestion.

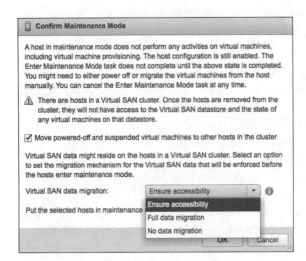

Figure 7.6   Maintenance mode options

Default Maintenance Mode/Decommission Mode

One other important point is the default maintenance mode setting when a product like VMware Update Manager is being used. Before VSAN 6.1, there was no way to control the maintenance mode (decommission mode) option; it was always set to Ensure Accessibility. This was not always the option that customers wished to use. Since the release of VSAN 6.1, customer can now control the default maintenance mode option through an advanced setting. The advanced setting is called VSAN.DefaultHostDecommissionMode, and allows administrators to set the default maintenance mode to an option other than Ensure Accessibility, as listed in Table 7.1.

Table 7.1 VSAN.DefaultHostDecommissionMode Options

Maintenance Mode Option	Description
ensureAccessibility	VSAN data reconfiguration should be performed to ensure storage object accessibility
evacuateAllData	VSAN data evacuation should be performed such that all storage object data is removed from the host
noAction	No special action should take place regarding VSAN data

Recommended Maintenance Mode Option for Updates and Patching

It is best to draw a comparison to a regular storage environment first. When you do upgrades on a storage array, you typically do these upgrades in a rolling fashion, meaning that if you have two controllers, one will be upgraded while the other handles I/O. In this scenario, you are also at risk. The big difference is that as a virtualization administrator *you have a bit more flexibility*, and you *expect certain features* to work as expected, such as vSphere High Availability (HA), for instance. You need to ask yourself what level of risk you are *willing* to take, and what level of risk you *can* take.

From a VSAN perspective, when it comes to placing a host into maintenance mode, you will need to ask yourself the following questions:

- **Why am I placing my host in maintenance mode?** Am I going to upgrade my hosts and expect them to be unavailable for just a brief period of time? Am I removing a host from the cluster altogether? This will play a big role in which maintenance mode data migration option you should use.

- **How many hosts do I have?** When using three hosts, the only option you have is Ensure Accessibility because VSAN always needs three hosts to store objects (two replicas and one witness). Therefore with a three-node cluster, you will have to accept some risk in using maintenance mode, and run with one copy of the data.

- **How long will the move take?**
  - Is this an all-flash cluster or a hybrid cluster?
  - What types of disks have I used (SAS versus SATA)?
  - Do I have 10 GbE or 1 GbE?
  - How big is my cluster?

- **Do I want to move data from one host to another to maintain availability levels?** Only stored components need to be moved, not the "raw capacity" of the host! That is, if 6 TB of capacity is used out of 8 TB, 6 TB will be moved.

- **Do I just want to ensure data accessibility and take the risk of potential downtime during maintenance?** Only components of those objects at risk will be moved. For example, if only 500 GB out of the 6 TB used capacity is at risk, that 500 GB will be moved.

There is something to say for all maintenance mode data migration options. When you select full data migration, to maintain availability levels, your "maintenance window" will be stretched, as you could be copying terabytes over the network from host to host. It could potentially take hours to complete. If your ESXi upgrade including a host reboot takes about 20 minutes, is it acceptable to wait for hours for the data to be migrated? Or do you take the risk, inform your users about the potential downtime, and as such do the maintenance with a higher risk but complete it in minutes rather than hours? Of course, if the maintenance mode takes longer than 1 hour, then you may have components begin rebuild and resync on other nodes on the cluster, which will consume resources (60 minutes is when the clomd timeout expires, and absent components are automatically rebuilt). However, the main risk is if another failure occurred in the cluster during the maintenance window. Then you risk availability to your VMs and your data. One other way to overcome this is to use a number of failures to tolerate = 2, which means that you can do maintenance on one node, and still tolerate another host failing at the same time. The new erasure coding option, which allows customer to implement a RAID-6 configuration, can tolerate two failures but not consume as much capacity as a RAID-1 configuration.

To be honest, it is impossible for us to give you advice on what the best approach is for your organization. We do feel strongly that for normal software or hardware maintenance tasks that only take a short period of time, it will be acceptable to use the Ensure Accessibility maintenance mode data migration option. You should still, however, discuss *all* approaches with your storage team and look at their procedures. What is the agreed service level agreement (SLA) with your business partners and what fits from an operational perspective?

Disk Management

One of the design goals for VSAN, as already mentioned, is the ability to scale out the storage capacity. This requires the ability to add new disks, replace disks with a larger capacity disk, or simply replace failed disks. The next section discusses the procedures involved in doing these tasks in a VSAN environment.

Adding a Disk Group

Chapter 2, "VSAN Prerequisites and Requirements for Deployment," demonstrated how to add a disk group; however, for completeness, here are the steps again. This example shows how to create a disk group on all hosts simultaneously. However, administrators can also create disk groups on a host-by-host basis.

1. Click your VSAN cluster in the left pane.

2. Click the **Manage** tab on right side.

3. Click **Settings** and **Disk Management**.

4. As shown in Figure 7.7, the available devices can be shown on a per device model/size basis or host basis. In this example, the Disk model/size view is shown.

5. Click on the "Claim For" field, and **select** "Capacity tier" for all capacity devices and select "Cache tier" for all the cache devices, then click **OK**.

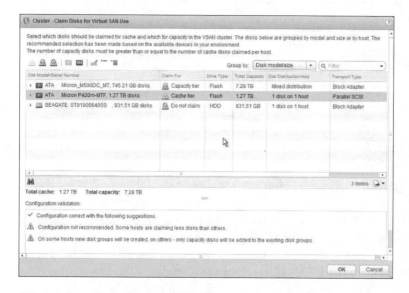

Figure 7.7   VSAN disk management

Now new disk groups are created; this literally takes seconds.

Removing a Disk Group

Before you start with this task, you may want to evacuate the components that are currently in that disk group. In the initial release of VSAN, this could only be achieved by placing the ESXi host with the disk group that you want to remove in maintenance mode. In VSAN 6.0, a new method that allows administrators to evacuate disk groups without placing the host into maintenance mode was introduced.

Evacuating the VM components from a disk group is not a required step for deleting a disk group, but we believe that most administrators would like to move the VM components currently in this disk group to other disk groups in the cluster before deleting the disk group. If you don't do this step, and evacuate the data, you may be left with degraded components that are no longer highly available while VSAN reconfigures these components. And as highlighted many times now, if there is a failure while the objects are degraded, it may lead to data loss.

If you are planning on doing a full data evacuation of a disk group, you should validate first whether sufficient disk space is available within the cluster to do so.

When you complete this step, as shown in Figure 7.8, then you should be able to remove the disk group. However, the icon to remove the disk group may not be visible in the disk groups view depending on how VSAN has been configured.

Disk Groups				
Disk Group	Disks In Use	State	Status	Network Partition Group
▾ 🖥 10.27.51.1	2 of 2	Maintenance M...	Healthy	Group 1
📇 Disk group (01000000003132303444303638394941445249...	2		Healthy	
▾ 🖥 10.27.51.2	2 of 2	Connected	Healthy	Group 1
📇 Disk group (01000000003132313044303931334941445249...	2		Healthy	
▾ 🖥 10.27.51.3	3 of 3	Connected	Healthy	Group 1
📇 Disk group (01000000003132343144430353134494f445249...	3		Healthy	
▾ 🖥 10.27.51.4	3 of 3	Connected	Healthy	Group 1
📇 Disk group (01000000003132313044303932354941445249...	3		Healthy	

Figure 7.8   VSAN disk groups

When VSAN is configured initially, a decision is made about how disks are added to the VSAN datastore. This can be done fully automated, "automatic" mode, or in a manual fashion, "manual" mode. By default, VSAN is configured to automatic mode, which means that if we remove a disk group, VSAN immediately claims the disks again, and as such the option to remove a disk group is not presented to the user. When it is desired to remove a disk group, you need to place the VSAN cluster in manual mode for the remove the disk group icon to appear. This can simply be done through the VSAN cluster settings, as shown in Figure 7.9.

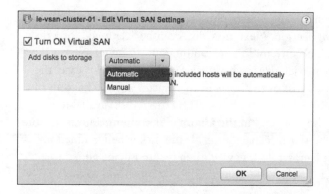

Figure 7.9   Changing mode from Automatic to Manual in the initial release of VSAN

When the VSAN is placed in manual mode, return to the disk management view and you should see that the remove the disk group icon (it has the red *X*) is now visible when you select the disk group on the host that is in maintenance mode. You can now proceed with removing the disk group. If the disk group has already been evacuated, you should see the popup as shown in Figure 7.10, which shows that there is no data left to evacuate. In VSAN 6.0, if there is data still on the disks in the disk group, administrators now have the opportunity to evacuate the components in the disk groups rather than follow the maintenance mode procedure outlined earlier.

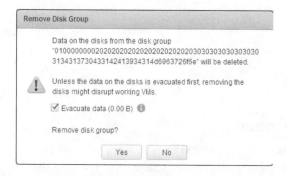

Figure 7.10   Remove disk group from VSAN

Adding Disks to the Disk Group

If your VSAN was configured in automatic mode, adding disks to the disk group is not an issue. New or existing disks are automatically claimed by the VSAN cluster and are used to provide capacity to the VSAN datastore.

However, if your cluster was created in manual mode, you will need to add new disks to the disk groups to increase the capacity of the VSAN datastore. This can easily be done via the vSphere Web Client. Navigate to the VSAN cluster, select the **Manage** tab, and then the **VSAN Disk Management** section. Next, new disks can be "claimed" for a disk group. If your disks do not show up, be sure to do a rescan on your disk controller. Once again, displaying the list of disks by model/size, or by hosts can do this. In this case, the grouping has been changed to hosts. Most of the hosts in this cluster already have all of their disks claimed. However, host esxi-hp-12 still has a HDD (hard disk) available for selection. Select the host and then the disk, and in the **Claim For** column, administrators can choose if the disk is for the cache tier or capacity tier. If the disk is being added to an already existing disk group, or it is not a flash device, then it can only be added to a capacity tier, as shown in Figure 7.11. Select the disks that you want to add to the VSAN cluster and click **OK**.

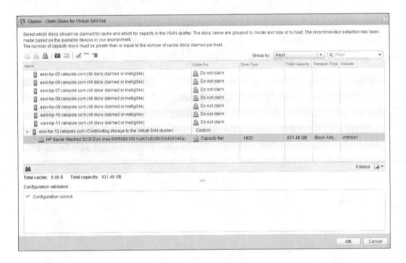

Figure 7.11   Claim disks

Removing Disks from the Disk Group

Just like removing disk groups discussed previously, disks can be removed from a disk group in the vSphere Web Client only when the cluster is placed in manual mode. If the cluster is in automatic mode, the VSAN cluster will simply reclaim the disk you've just removed. When the cluster is in manual mode, navigate to the Disk Management section of the VSAN cluster, select the disk group, and an icon to remove a disk becomes visible in the UI—a disk with a red *X*—as highlighted in Figure 7.12. Note that this icon is *not* visible when the cluster is in automatic mode.

Similar to how the administrator is prompted to evacuate a disk group when the delete disk group option is chosen, administrators are also prompted to evacuate individual disks when a disk is being removed from a disk group. This will migrate all of the components

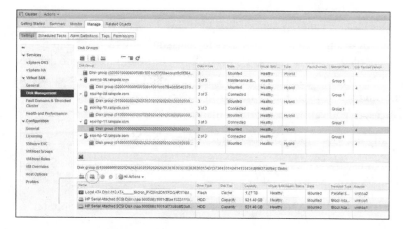

Figure 7.12   Remove a disk from a disk group

on the said disk to other disks in the disk group if there is sufficient space. In the example
in Figure 7.13, the disk is already empty so there are 0 bytes to move, but if there were
still components on this disk, administrators have the opportunity to migrate them before
deleting the disk from the disk group.

There is one important note on removing of individual disk from a disk group. If deduplication and compression are enabled on the cluster, it is not possible to remove the disk
from a disk group. The reason for this is that the deduplicated and compressed data,
along with the associated hash tables and metadata associated with deduplication and
compression, are striped across all the capacity tier disks in the disk group. Therefore it
is not possible to remove a single disk. To remove a single disk from a disk group where
deduplication and compression are enabled on the cluster, the entire disk group should
be evacuated and then the disk may be replaced. Afterwards the disk group should be
recreated and the cluster is balanced via the health check UI.

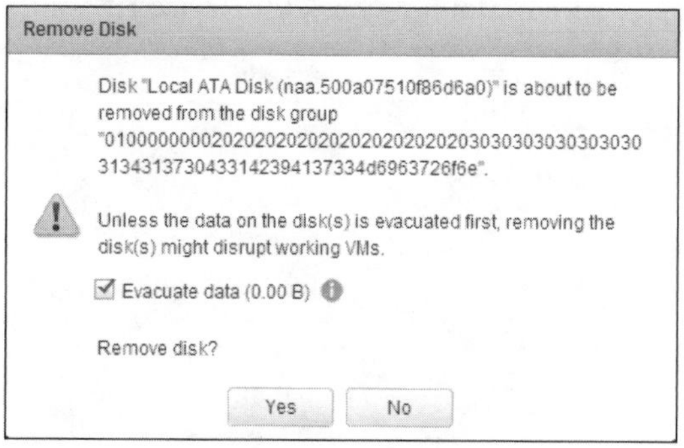

Figure 7.13   Evacuate data

Wiping a Disk

In some cases, other features or operating systems may have used magnetic disks and flash devices before VSAN is enabled. In those cases, VSAN will not be able to reuse the devices when the devices still contain partitions or even a file system. Note that this has been done intentionally to prevent the user from selecting the wrong disks. If you want to use a disk that has been previously used, you can wipe the disks manually.

There are three commonly used methods to wipe a disk before VSAN is used:

- If it was previously in use by VSAN, removing it from the disk group via the vSphere Web Client will remove the partition table.

- If using vSphere 6.0 U1 (and VSAN 6.1), the disk can be erased from the vSphere Web Client directly.

- Using the command `partedUtil`, a disk partition management utility which is included with ESXi.

- Booting the host with the gparted bootable ISO image.

The gparted procedure is straightforward. You can download the ISO image from http://gparted.org/, boot the ESXi host from it, and it is simply a matter of deleting all partitions on the appropriate disk and clicking **Apply**.

> **WARNING**
>
> The tasks involved with wiping a disk are destructive, and it will be nearly impossible to retrieve any data after wiping the disk.

The `partedUtil` method included with ESXi is slightly more complex because it is a command-line utility. The following steps are required to wipe a disk using `partedUtil`. If you are not certain which device to wipe, make sure to double-check the device ID using `esxcli storage core device list`:

Step 1: Display the partition table

```
~ # partedUtil get   /dev/disks/naa.500xxxxxx
15566 255 63 250069680
1 2048 6143 0 0
2 6144 250069646 0 0
```

Step 2: Display partition types

```
~ # partedUtil getptbl /dev/disks/naa.500xxxxxx
```

```
gpt
15566 255 63 250069680
1 2048 6143 381CFCCC728811E092EE000C2911D0B2 vsan 0
2 6144 250069646 AA31E02A400F11DB9590000C2911D1B8 vmfs 0
~ #
```

Step 3: Delete the partitions

```
~ # partedUtil delete /dev/disks/naa.500xxxxxx 1
~ # partedUtil delete /dev/disks/naa.500xxxxxx 2
```

If you are looking for more guidance about the use of partedUtil, read the following VMware Knowledge Base (KB) article: http://kb.vmware.com/kb/1036609.

Blinking the LED on a Disk

In vSphere 6.0, you can blink the LEDs on the front disk drives. Having the ability to identify a drive for replacement becomes very important for VSAN, as clusters can contain tens or even hundreds of disk drives.

You'll find the icons for turning on and off LEDs when you select a disk drive in the UI, as highlighted in Figure 7.14. Clicking on the "green" icon turns the LED on; clicking on the "grey" icon turns the LED off again.

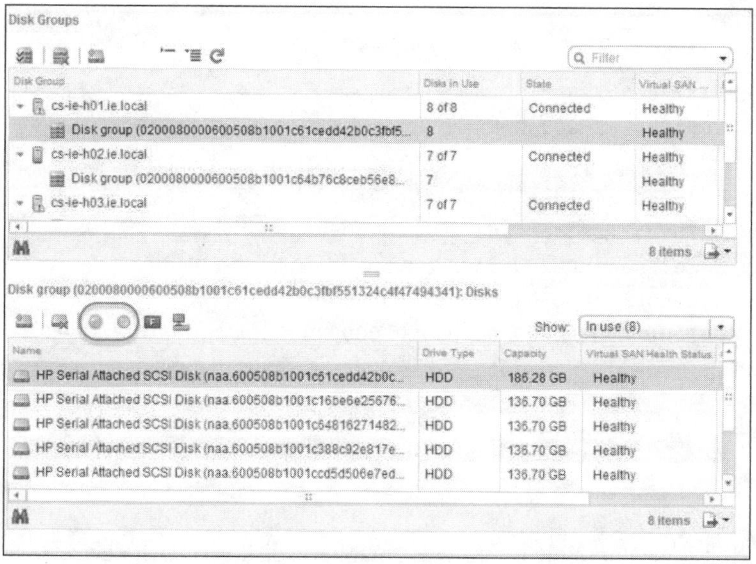

Figure 7.14   Blink a disk LED from the vSphere Web Client

ESXCLI VSAN Disk Commands

From the ESXCLI, a number of disk-related activities might be done. First, you can get and set the manual or automated mode of the cluster. The remaining commands in ESXCLI for VSAN storage relate to disks and disk groups. You can add, remove, or list the disks in a disk group. This will list both SSDs and magnetic disks. Example 7.3 showing `esxcli vsan storage list` highlights for the two devices whether it is a flash device and of which disk group they are part.

Example 7.3   Output of esxcli vsan storage list

```
~ # esxcli vsan storage list
naa.5000c5002bd7526f
      Device: naa.5000c5002bd7526f
      Display Name: naa.5000c5002bd7526f
      Is SSD: false
      VSAN UUID: 52db9f60-57b8-ad88-70eb-889f3c72b5e1
      VSAN Disk Group UUID: 521f9dda-efda-4718-e75d-aec63eb6fbd4
      VSAN Disk Group Name: naa.500253825000c296
      Host UUID: 519f364d-ef04-8d94-8ad4-1cc1de252264
      Cluster UUID: 520bff2a-badc-0cdd-7be7-70e5e5ae032f
      Used by this host: true
      In CMMDS: true
      Checksum: 11848694795517181960
      Checksum OK: true
naa.500253825000c296
      Device: naa.500253825000c296
      Display Name: naa.500253825000c296
      Is SSD: true
      VSAN UUID: 521f9dda-efda-4718-e75d-aec63eb6fbd4
      VSAN Disk Group UUID: 521f9dda-efda-4718-e75d-aec63eb6fbd4
      VSAN Disk Group Name: naa.500253825000c296
      Host UUID: 00000000-0000-0000-0000-000000000000
      Cluster UUID: 00000000-0000-0000-0000-000000000000
      Used by this host: true
      In CMMDS: true
      Checksum: 12800345249350977942
      Checksum OK: true
```

As previously mentioned, it is also possible to remove a magnetic disk or a flash device from a disk group through the CLI; however, this should be done with absolute care and preferably through the UI, as shown on the previous pages.

Failure Scenarios

We have already discussed some of the failure scenarios in Chapter 5, "Architectural Details," and explained the difference between *absent* components and *degraded* components. From an operational perspective, though, it is good to understand how a magnetic disk, SSD, or host failure impacts you. Before we discuss them, let's first shortly recap the two different failure states, because they are fundamental to these operational considerations:

- **Absent:** VSAN does not know what has happened to the component that is missing. A typical example of this is when a host has failed; VSAN cannot tell if it is a real failure or simply a reboot. When this happens, VSAN waits for 60 minutes by default before new replica components are created.

- **Degraded:** VSAN knows what has happened to the component that is missing. A typical example of when this can occur is when an SSD or a magnetic disk has died. When this happens, VSAN instantly spawns new components to make all impacted objects compliant again with their selected policy.

Now that you know what the different states are, let's look again at the different types of failures, or at least the "most" common and what the impact is.

Capacity Device Failure

A disk failure is probably the most common failure that can happen in any storage environment, and VSAN is no different. The reason for this is simple: moving parts. The question, of course, is this: How does VSAN handle disk failure? What if it is doing a write or read to or from that disk?

If a read error is returned from a storage component, be it a magnetic disk in the case of hybrid configurations or a flash device in the case of all-flash configurations, VSAN checks to see whether a replica component exists and reads from that instead. Every object by default is created with number of failures to tolerate set to 1, which means that there are always two identical copies of your object available. There are two separate scenarios when it comes to reading data. The first one is where the problem is recoverable, and the second one is an irrecoverable situation. When the issue is recoverable, the I/O error is reported to the object owner. A component re-creation takes place, and when that is completed, the errored component is deleted. However, if for whatever reason, no replica component exists (an unlikely scenario and something an administrator would have had to create a policy specifically for), VSAN will report an I/O error to the VM.

Write failures are also propagated up to the object owner. The components are marked as degraded and a component re-creation on different disks in the VSAN cluster is initiated. When the component re-creation is completed, the cluster directory (cluster monitoring, membership, and directory service [CMMDS]) is updated. Note that the flash device (which has no error) continues to service reads for the components on all the other capacity devices in the disk group.

In the initial VSAN release, the vSphere Web Client today does not provide an indication of how much data needs to be synced when a component or components are being created as a result of a failure; however, a very useful `vsan.resync_dashboard` Ruby vSphere console (RVC) command does allow you to verify, as shown in Figure 7.15:

```
/localhost/CH-Datacenter/computers/cluster> vsan.resync_dashboard
2013-12-12 16:56:58 +0000: Querying all VMs on VSAN ...
2013-12-12 16:56:58 +0000: Querying all objects in the system from 10.20.177.18 ...
2013-12-12 16:56:59 +0000: Got all the info, computing table ...
+--------------------------------------------------------------------+----------------+--------------+
| VM/Object                                                          | Syncing objects | Bytes to sync |
+--------------------------------------------------------------------+----------------+--------------+
| win1                                                               | 1              |              |
| [vsanDatastore] 9a3f9352-346a-f78d-3360-1cc1de253de4/win1-000001.vmdk |              | 48.00 GB     |
+--------------------------------------------------------------------+----------------+--------------+
| Total                                                             | 1              | 48.00 GB     |
+--------------------------------------------------------------------+----------------+--------------+
/localhost/CH-Datacenter/computers/cluster>
```

Figure 7.15 Using vsan.rsync_dashboard for verification

However, since VSAN 6.0, the vSphere Web Client provides the ability to monitor how much data is being resynced in the event of a failure. Selecting the VSAN cluster object in the vCenter Server inventory, then selecting Monitor, Virtual SAN, and then "resyncing components" can find this information. It will report on the number of resyncing components, the bytes left to resync, and the estimate time for the resyncing to complete.

Cache Device Failure

What about when the cache device becomes inaccessible? When a cache device becomes inaccessible, all the capacity devices backed by that cache device in the same disk group are also made inaccessible. A cache device failure is the same as a failure of all the capacity devices bound to the cache device. In essence, when a cache device fails, the whole disk group is considered to be degraded. If there is spare capacity in the VSAN cluster, it tries to find another host or disk and starts reconfiguring the storage objects.

Therefore, from an operational and architectural decision, depending on the type of hosts used, it could be beneficial to create multiple smaller disk groups versus a single large disk group because a disk group should be considered to be a failure domain, as shown in Figure 7.16.

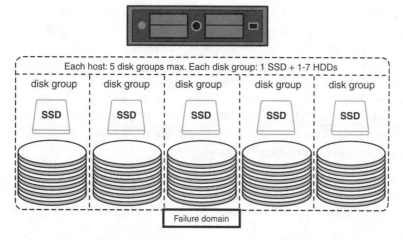

Figure 7.16   VSAN disk groups

Host Failure

Assuming VSAN VM storage policies have been created with the number of failures to tolerate at least set to 1, a host failure in a VSAN cluster is similar to a host failure in a cluster that has a regular storage device attached. The main difference, of course, being that the VSAN host that has failed contains components of objects that will be out of sync when the host returns. Fortunately, VSAN has a mechanism that syncs all the components as soon as they return.

In the case of a host failure, after 60 minutes VSAN will start re-creating components because the likelihood of the host returning within a reasonable amount of time is slim. When the reconstruction of the storage objects is completed, the cluster directory (CMMDS) is once again updated. In fact, it is updated at each step of the process, from failure detection, start of resync, resync progress, and rebuild complete.

If the host that originally failed recovers and rejoins the cluster, the object reconstruction status is checked. If object reconstruction has completed on another node or nodes, no action is taken. If object resynchronization is still in progress, the components of the originally failed host are also resynced, just in case there is an issue with the new object synchronization. When the synchronization of all objects is complete, the components of the original host are discarded, and the more recent copies are utilized. Otherwise, if the new components failed to resync for any reason, the original components on the original host are used.

You probably are wondering by now how this resynchronization of VSAN components actually works. VSAN maintains a bitmap of changed blocks in the event of components of an object being unable to synchronize due to a failure on a host, network, or disk. This allows updates to VSAN objects composed of two or more components to be reconciled after a failure. Let's use an example to explain this. If a host with replica A of object X has been partitioned from the rest of the cluster, the surviving components of X have quorum and data availability, so they continue functioning and serving writes and reads. While A is "absent," all writes performed to X are persistently tracked in a bitmap by VSAN, that is, the bitmap are tracking the regions that are still out of sync. If the partitioned host with replica A comes back and VSAN decides to reintegrate it with the remaining components of object X, the bitmap is used to resynchronize component A.

When a host has failed, all VMs that were running on the host at the time of the failure will be restarted by vSphere HA. vSphere HA can restart the VM on any available host in the cluster whether or not it is hosting VSAN components, as shown in Figure 7.17.

In the event of an isolation of a host, vSphere HA can and will also restart the impacted VMs. As this is a slightly more complex scenario, let's take a look at it in more depth.

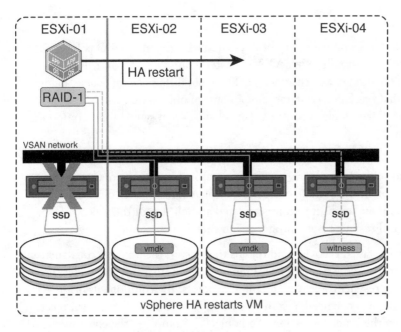

Figure 7.17   VSAN 1 host failed, HA restart

Network Partition

A network partition could occur when there is a network failure. In other words, some hosts can end up on one side of the cluster, and the remaining hosts on another side. VSAN will surface warnings related to network misconfiguration in the event of a partition.

After explaining the host and disk failure scenarios in the previous sections, it is now time to describe how isolations and partitions are handled in a VSAN cluster. Let's look at a typical scenario first and explain what happens during a network partition based on this scenario.

In the scenario depicted in Figure 7.18, VSAN is running a single VM on ESXi-01. This VM has been provisioned using a VM storage policy that has number of failures to tolerate set to 1.

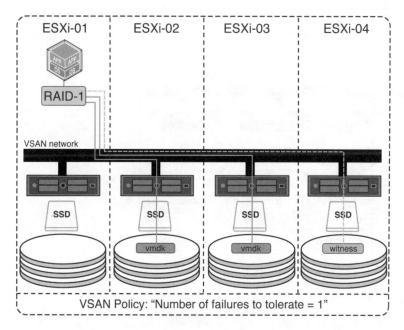

Figure 7.18   VSAN I/O flow: Failures to tolerate = 1

Because VSAN has the capability to run VMs on hosts that are not holding any active storage components of that VM, this question arises: What happens in the case where the network is isolated? As you can imagine, the VSAN network plays a big role here, made even bigger when you realize that it is also used by HA for network heartbeating. Note that the vSphere HA network is automatically reconfigured by VSAN to ensure that the correct network is used for handling these scenarios. Should this situation occur, the following steps describe how vSphere HA and VSAN will react to an isolation event:

1. HA will detect if there are no network heartbeats received from ESXi-01.

2. HA master will try to ping the slave ESXi-01.

3. HA will declare that the slave ESXi-01 is unavailable.

4. VM will be restarted on one of the other hosts (ESXi-03, in this case, as shown in Figure 7.19).

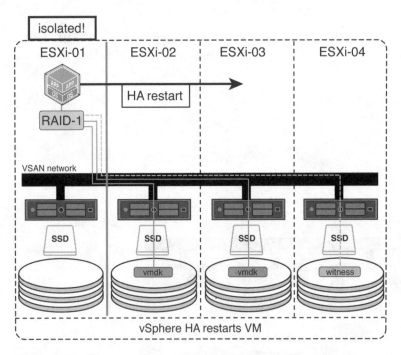

Figure 7.19   VSAN partition with one host isolated: HA restart

Now this question arises: What if something has gone horribly bad in my network and ESXi-01 and ESXi-02 end up as part of the same partition? What happens then? Well, that is where the witness comes into play. Refer to Figure 7.20 as that will make it a bit easier to understand.

Now this scenario is slightly more complex. There are two partitions, one of which is running the VM with its virtual machine disk (VMDK), and the other partition has a VMDK replica and a witness. Guess what happens? Right, VSAN uses the witness to see which partition has quorum, and based on that result, one of the two partitions will win. In this case, partition 2 has more than 50% of the components of this object and therefore is the winner. This means that the VM will be restarted on either ESXi-03 or ESXi-04 by vSphere HA. Note that the VM in partition 1 will be powered off only if you have configured the isolation response to do so.

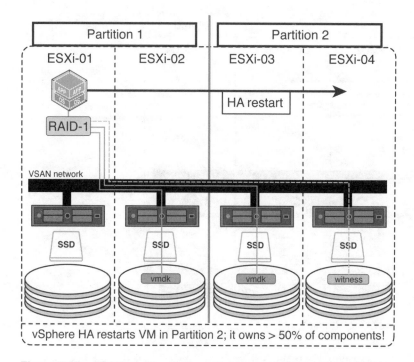

Figure 7.20   VSAN partition with multiple hosts isolated: HA restart

---

TIP

We would like to stress that this is highly recommended! (Isolation response > power off.)

But what if ESXi-01 and ESXi-04 were isolated, what would happen then? Figure 7.21 shows what it would look like.

Remember the rule we discussed earlier?

> *The winner is declared based on the percentage of components available or percentage of votes available within that partition.*

If the partition has access to more than 50% of the components or votes (of an object), it has won. For each object, there can be at most one winning partition. This means that when ESXi-01 and ESXi-04 are isolated, either ESXi-02 or ESXi-03 can restart the VM because 66% of the components of the object reside within this part of the cluster.

To prevent these scenarios from occurring, it is most definitely recommended to ensure the VSAN network is made highly available through NIC teaming and redundant network switches, as discussed in Chapter 3, "VSAN Installation and Configuration."

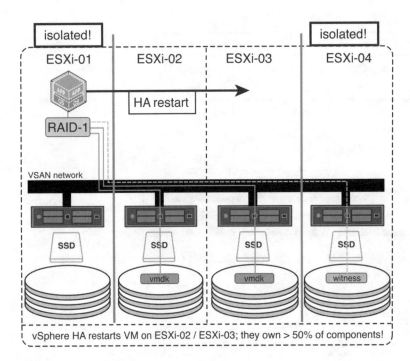

Figure 7.21   VSAN 2 hosts isolated: HA restart

If vCenter is unavailable for whatever reason and you would like to retrieve information about the VSAN network, you can do so through the CLI of ESXi. From the CLI, an administrator can examine or remove the VSAN network configuration. In Example 7.4, you can see the VMkernel network interface used for cluster communication, and also the IP protocol used.

Example 7.4   VMKernel Network Interface and IP Protocol in Use

```
~ # esxcli vsan network list
Interface
      VmkNic Name: vmk2
      IP Protocol: IPv4
      Interface UUID: 06419f51-ec79-0b57-5b3e-1cc1de252264
      Agent Group Multicast Address: 224.2.3.4
      Agent Group Multicast Port: 23451
      Master Group Multicast Address: 224.1.2.3
```

```
Master Group Multicast Port: 12345
Multicast TTL: 5
~ #
```

Disk Full Scenario

Another issue that can occur is a disk full scenario. You might ask, "What happens when the VSAN datastore gets full?" To answer that question, you should first ask the question, "What happens when an individual magnetic disk fills up?" because this will occur before the VSAN datastore fills up.

Before explaining how VSAN reacts to a scenario where a disk is full, it is worth knowing that VSAN will try to prevent this scenario from happening. VSAN balances capacity across the cluster and can and will move components around, or even break up components, when this can prevent a disk full scenario. Of course, the success of this action is entirely based on the rate at which the VM claims and fills new blocks and at which VSAN can relocate existing components. Simply put, the law of physics applies here.

In the event of a disk's reaching full capacity, VSAN pauses (technically called *stun*) the VMs that are trying to write data and require additional new disk space for these writes; those that do not need additional disk space continue to run as normal. Note that VSAN-based VMs are deployed thin by default and that this only applies when new blocks need to be allocated to this thin-provisioned disk. When this occurs, the error message shown in Figure 7.22 appears on the VM's summary screen.

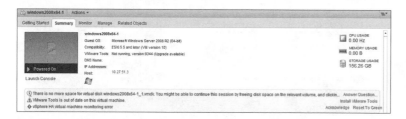

Figure 7.22   No more space message

This is identical to the behavior observed on Virtual Machine File System (VMFS) when the datastore reached capacity. When additional disk capacity is made available on the VSAN datastore, the stunned VMs may be resumed via the vSphere Web Client. Administrators should be able to see how much capacity is consumed on a per-disk basis via the **Monitor > Virtual SAN > Physical Disks** view, as shown in Figure 7.23.

Figure 7.23   Monitoring physical disks

Thin Provisioning Considerations

By default, all VMs provisioned to a VSAN datastore are thin provisioned. The huge advantage of this is that VMs are not taking up any unused disk capacity. It is not uncommon in datacenter environments to see 40% to 60% of unused capacity within the VM. You can imagine that if a VM were thick provisioned, this would not only drive up the cost, but also make VSAN less flexible in terms of placement of components.

Of course, there is an operational aspect to thin provisioning. There is always a chance of filling up a VSAN datastore when you are severely overcommitted and many VMs are claiming new disk capacity. This is not different in an environment where network file system (NFS) is used, or VMFS with thin provisioned VMs. The Web Client interface fortunately has many places where capacity can be checked, of which the summary tab shown in Figure 7.24 is an example.

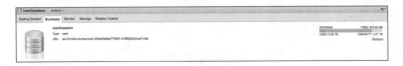

Figure 7.24   Capacity of VSAN datastore

We also have a new set of capacity views introduced in VSAN 6.2, and this makes it very easy to monitor how much space virtual machine objects are consuming.

When certain capacity usage thresholds are reached, vCenter Server will raise an alarm to ensure that the administrator is aware of the potential problem that may arise when not acted upon. By default, this alarm is triggered when the 75% full threshold is exceeded with an exclamation mark (severity warning), and another alarm is raised when 85% is reached (severity critical), as demonstrated in Figure 7.25. (Note that this issue will also raise an alarm in the health check.)

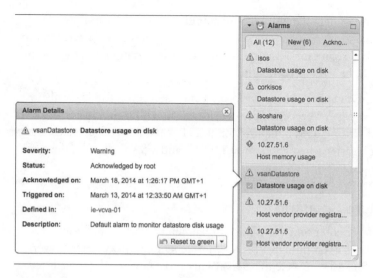

Figure 7.25   Datastore usage warning

vCenter Management

vCenter Server is an important part of most vSphere deployments because it is the main tool used for managing and monitoring the virtual infrastructure. In the past, new features introduced to vSphere often had a dependency on vCenter Server to be available, like for instance, vSphere Distributed Resource Scheduler (DRS). If vCenter Server was unavailable, that service would also be temporarily unavailable; in the case of vSphere DRS, this meant that no load balancing would occur during this time.

Fortunately, VSAN does not rely on vCenter Server in any shape or form, not even to make configuration changes or to create a new VSAN cluster. Even if vCenter Server goes down, VSAN continues to function, and VMs are not impacted whatsoever when it comes to VSAN functionality. If needed, all management tasks can be done through ESXCLI (or RVC for that matter); and in case you are wondering, yes, this is fully supported by VMware.

You might wonder at this point why VMware decided to align the VSAN cluster construct with the vSphere HA and DRS construct, especially when there is no direct dependency on vCenter Server and no direct relationship. There are several reasons for this, so let's briefly explain those before looking at a vCenter Server failure scenario.

The main reason for aligning the VSAN cluster construct with the vSphere HA and DRS cluster construct is user experience. Today, when VSAN is configured/enabled, it takes a single click in the cluster properties section of the vSphere Web Client. This is primarily achieved because a compute cluster already is a logical grouping of ESXi hosts.

This not only allows for ease of deployment, but also simplifies upgrade workflows and other maintenance tasks that are typically done within the boundaries of a cluster. On top of that, capacity planning and sizing for compute is done at cluster granularity; by aligning these constructs, storage can be sized accordingly.

Last but not least: availability. vSphere HA is performed at cluster level, and it is only natural to deal with the new per-VM accessibility consideration within the cluster because vSphere HA at the time of writing does not allow you to fail over VMs between clusters. In other words, life is much easier when vSphere HA, DRS, and VSAN all share the same logical boundary and grouping.

vCenter Server Failure Scenario

What if you would lose the vCenter Server? What will happen to VSAN, and how do you rebuild this environment? Even though VSAN is not dependent on vCenter Server, other components are. If, for instance, vCenter Server fails and a new instance needs to be created from scratch, what is the impact on your VSAN environment?

After you rebuild a new vCenter, you need to redefine a VSAN-enabled cluster and add the hosts back to the cluster. Until you complete this last step, you will be receiving a "configuration issue" warning because the VSAN cluster will not have a matching vSphere cluster (with matching membership) in the vCenter inventory.

One additional consideration, however, is that the loss of the vCenter Server will also mean the loss of the VM storage policies that the administrator has created. Storage policy-based management (SPBM) will not know about the previous VM storage policies and the VMs to which they were attached. VSAN, however, will still know exactly what the administrator had asked for and keep enforcing it. Today, there is no way in the UI to export existing policies, but there is an application programming interface (API) for VM storage policies has been exposed.

One important thing to note about the VM storage policy API is that it is exposed as a separate API endpoint on vCenter Server and it will not be accessible through the normal vSphere API. To consume this API, you must connect to the SPBM server that requires an authenticated vCenter Server session. This API can be leveraged to export and import these policies. You can find an example of how to retrieve information about current VM storage policies in the following article by William Lam: http://www.virtuallyghetto.com/2013/11/restoring-vsan-vm-storage-policy.html. Leveraging this example and the public SPBM APIs, it is possible to develop export and import scripts for your VM storage policies.

Running vCenter Server on VSAN

A common support question relates to whether VMware supports the vCenter Server that is managing VSAN to run in the VSAN cluster. The concern would be a failure scenario where the access to the VSAN datastore is lost and thus VMs, including vCenter Server, can no longer run. The major concern here is that no vCenter Server (and thus no tools such as RVC) is available to troubleshoot any issues experienced in the VSAN environment. Fortunately, VSAN can be fully managed via ESXCLI commands on the ESXi hosts. So, to answer the initial question, yes, VMware will support customers hosting their vCenter Server on VSAN (as it is supported), but obviously in the rare event where the vCenter Server is not online and you need to manage or troubleshoot issues with VSAN, the user experience will not be as good. This is a decision that should be given some careful consideration.

Bootstrapping vCenter Server

If you can run vCenter Server on ESXi, how do you get it up and running in a greenfield deployment? Typically in greenfield deployments, no external storage is available, so VSAN needs to be available before vCenter Server can be deployed.

William Lam of virtuallyghetto.com has described a procedure that allows you to do exactly that. For the full procedure and many more articles on the topic of automation and VSAN, check out William Lam's website (virtuallyghetto.com), who kindly gave us permission to leverage his content. For your convenience, we have written a short summary of the steps required to "bootstrap" vCenter Server on a single-server VSAN datastore:

1. Install ESXi onto your physical hosts. Technically, one host is needed to begin the process, but you will probably want to have two additional hosts ready unless you do not care about your vCenter Server being able to recover if there are any hardware issues.

2. You must modify the default VSAN storage policy on the ESXi host in which you plan to provision your vCenter Server. You must run the following two ESXCLI commands to enable "force provisioning":

```
esxcli vsan policy setdefault -c vdisk -p
    "((\"hostFailuresToTolerate\" i1) (\"forceProvisioning\" i1))"
esxcli vsan policy setdefault -c vmnamespace -p

    "((\"hostFailuresToTolerate\" i1) (\"forceProvisioning\" i1))"
```

3. Confirm you have the correct VSAN default policy by running the following ESXCLI command:

```
~ # esxcli vsan policy getdefault
Policy Class    Policy Value

_____   _____
cluster           (("hostFailuresToTolerate" i1))
```

```
vdisk              (("hostFailuresToTolerate"              i1)
("forceProvisioning" i1))
vmnamespace       (("hostFailuresToTolerate"              i1)
("forceProvisioning" i1))
vmswap             (("hostFailuresToTolerate"              i1)
("forceProvisioning" i1))
```

4. You must identify the disks that you will be using on the first ESXi host to contribute to the VSAN datastore. You can do so by running the following ESXCLI command:

```
esxcli storage core device list
```

5. To get specific details on a particular device such as identifying whether it is an SSD or regular magnetic disk, you can specify the -d option and the device name:

```
esxcli storage core device list -d <disk identifier>
```

6. After you have identified the disks you will be using, make a note of the disk names as they will be needed in the upcoming steps. In this example, we have only a single SSD and single magnetic disk.

7. Before we can create our VSAN datastore, we need to first create a VSAN cluster. To create a VSAN cluster, we will use the following ESXCLI command, note that as of VSAN 6.0 it is no longer needed to generate and specify the UUID using the -u option, but instead you can provide the option "new":

```
esxcli vsan cluster new
```

8. After the VSAN cluster has been created, you can retrieve information about the VSAN cluster by running the following ESXCLI command:

```
esxcli vsan cluster get
```

9. Next we need to add the disks from our ESXi host to create our single-node VSAN datastore. To do so, we need the disk device names from our earlier step for both SSD and HDDs and to run the following ESXCLI command:

```
esxcli vsan storage add -d <HDD-DISK-ID> -s <SSD-DISK-ID>
```

The -d option specifies regular magnetic disks, and the -s option specifies an SSD disk. If you have more than one magnetic disk, you will need to specify multiple -d entries. We also want to point out that in VSAN 6.0/6.1, it is not possible to create an all-flash VSAN datastore without adding the VSAN license first, but in 6.2 this should be possible. Now that you have added the disks to the VSAN datastore you verify which disks are contributing to the VSAN datastore by running the following ESXCLI command:

```
esxcli vsan storage list
```

10. One additional step to save us is that you can also enable the VSAN traffic type on the first ESXi host using ESXCLI, and you can also do this for the other two hosts in advance. This step does not necessarily have to be done now because it can be done later when the vCenter Server is available and using the vSphere Web Client. You will need to either create or select an existing VMkernel interface to enable the VSAN traffic type, and you can do so by running the following ESXCLI command:

    ```
    esxcli vsan network ipv4 add -i <VMkernel-Interface>
    ```

11. At this point, you now have a valid VSAN datastore for your single ESXi host. You can verify this by logging into the vSphere C# client, and you should see the VSAN datastore mounted to your ESXi host. You can now deploy the vCenter Server appliance OVA/OVF onto the VSAN datastore and power on the VM.

12. Once vCenter is deployed, you can create a cluster, enable VSAN on the cluster, and add the bootstrapped host as the first host of the cluster.

13. You can now reset the policies back to defaults.

14. You should add the remaining hosts to the cluster as soon as possible. Also, you need to create a new VM storage policy, and it is recommended to attach this policy to the vCenter Server VM and ensure that the vCenter Server VM becomes compliant with this new policy.

Summary

As demonstrated throughout the chapter, VSAN is easy to scale out and up. Even when configured in manual mode, adding new hosts or new disks is still only a matter of a few clicks. For those who prefer the command line, ESXCLI is a great alternative to the vSphere Web Client. For those who prefer PowerShell, VMware has a wide variety of PowerCLI cmdlets available.

## Chapter 8

Stretched Cluster

This chapter was developed to provide insights and additional information on a very specific type of Virtual SAN (VSAN) configuration, namely stretched clusters. In this chapter we will describe some of the design considerations, operational procedures, and failure scenarios that relate to a stretched cluster configuration specifically. But why would anyone want a stretched cluster in the first place?

Stretched cluster configurations offer the ability to balance virtual machines (VMs) between datacenters. The reason for doing so could be anything, be it disaster avoidance or for instance site maintenance, all of this with no downtime from a VM perspective since compute, storage, and network are available across both sites. On top of that, a stretched cluster also provides the ability to active load balance resources between locations without any constraints.

What is a Stretched Cluster?

Before we get into it, let's first discuss what defines a VSAN stretched cluster. When we talk about a VSAN stretched cluster, we refer to the configuration that is deployed when the stretched cluster workflow is completed in the Web Client. This workflow explicitly leverages a witness host, which can be physical or virtual, and needs to be deployed in a third site. During the workflow the VSAN cluster is set up across two active/active sites, with an identical number of ESXi hosts distributed evenly between the two sites, and as stated with a witness host residing at a third site. The data sites are connected via a high bandwidth/low latency link. The third site hosting the VSAN witness host is connected to both of the active/active data-sites. The connectivity between the data sites and the witness site can be via lower bandwidth/higher latency links. Figure 8.1 shows what this looks like from a logical point of view.

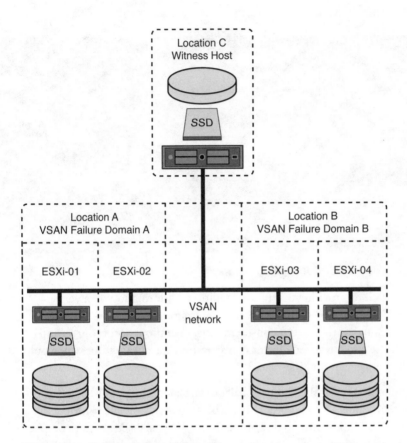

Figure 8.1   Stretched cluster scenario

Each site is configured as a Virtual SAN fault domain. A site can be considered a fault domain. A maximum of three sites (two data, one witness) are supported.

The nomenclature used to describe a Virtual SAN stretched cluster configuration is X + Y + Z, where X is the number of ESXi hosts at data site A, Y is the number of ESXi hosts at data site B, and Z is the number of witness hosts at site C. Data sites are where virtual machines are deployed. The minimum supported configuration is 1 + 1 + 1 (3 nodes). The maximum configuration at the time of writing is 15 + 15 + 1 (31 nodes).

In VSAN stretched clusters, there is only one witness host in any configuration. For deployments that manage multiple stretched clusters, each cluster must have its own unique witness host.

When a VM is deployed on a VSAN stretched cluster it will have one copy of its data on site A, a second copy of its data on site B, and witness components placed on the witness host in site C. This configuration is achieved through fault domains. In the event of a complete site failure, there will be a full copy of the VM data as well as greater than 50% of the components available. This will allow the VM to remain available on the VSAN datastore. If the VM needs to be restarted on the other data site, vSphere HA will handle this task.

Requirements and Constraints

VSAN stretched cluster configurations require vSphere 6.0.0 Update1 (U1) at a minimum. This implies both vCenter Server 6.0 U1 and ESXi 6.0 U1. This version of vSphere includes VSAN version 6.1. This is the minimum version required for VSAN stretched cluster support. However, we strongly recommend implementing the latest available version of VSAN, which at the time of writing was VSAN 6.2.

From a licensing point of view things have changed dramatically over the last 12 months and especially the licensing requirements for stretched clustering have changed. With VSAN version 6.1 a new licensing variant was introduced called "Advanced." This version included both all-flash and stretched cluster functionality. As of version 6.2 however, a new licensing version has been added called "Enterprise" and this version now includes stretched cluster and QoS (limits) functionality. The advanced license includes all-flash, deduplication/compression, and RAID-5/6. Table 8.1 shows what is included in which license edition for completeness. Note that the Enterprise license needs to have been entered and assigned to all hosts in the cluster before the stretched cluster can be formed. Before making any procurement decision, please consult the latest VMware licensing information.

Table 8.1 License editions

	Standard	Advanced	Enterprise
Storage policy-based management	X	X	X
Read/write caching	X	X	X
RAID-1	X	X	X
Distributed Switch	X	X	X
VSAN snapshot and clones	X	X	X
Rack awareness	X	X	X
Replication (5 minutes RPO)	X	X	X
Software checksum	X	X	X
All-flash		X	X

Deduplication and compression	X	X
RAID-5/6 (erasure coding)	X	X
Stretched cluster		**X**
QoS (IOPS Limits)		X

There are no limitations placed on the edition of vSphere used for Virtual SAN. However, for VSAN stretched cluster functionality, vSphere Distributed Resource Scheduler (DRS) is very desirable. DRS will provide initial placement assistance, and can also help in locating VMs to their correct site when a site recovers after a failure. Otherwise the administrator will have to manually carry out these tasks. Note that DRS is now only available in Enterprise Plus edition of vSphere. (Before Q1 of 2016, DRS was also available in Enterprise. Since then VMware has announced that the Enterprise license edition is end of availability.)

When it comes to VSAN functionality, VMware supports stretched clusters in both hybrid and all-flash configurations. In terms of on-disk formats, the minimum level of on-disk format required is v2, which comes by default with VSAN 6.0. (VSAN 6.2 comes with v3.)

Both physical ESXi hosts and virtual appliances (nested ESXi host in a VM) are supported for the witness host. VMware is providing a preconfigured witness appliance for those customers who wish to use it. A witness host/VM cannot be shared between multiple VSAN stretched clusters.

The following are a list of products and features supported on VSAN but not on a stretched cluster implementation of VSAN.

- SMP-FT, the new Fault Tolerant VM mechanism introduced in vSphere 6.0, is supported on standard VSAN 6.1 deployments, but it is not supported on any stretched cluster deployment at this time, be it VSAN or vSphere Metro Storage Cluster (vMSC) based.

- The maximum value for *NumberOfFailuresToTolerate* in VSAN stretched cluster is 1, whereas the maximum value for *NumberOfFailuresToTolerate* in standard VSAN is 3.

- In VSAN stretched cluster, there is a limit of 3 for the number of fault domains. Standard VSAN can go much higher.

- The fault tolerance method capability, introduced in VSAN 6.2, set to capacity (which allows for the use of RAID-5/6) is not supported in a stretched configuration. It must be left at the default setting of performance to use RAID-1.

Networking and Latency Requirements

When Virtual SAN is deployed in a stretched cluster across multiple sites using fault domains, there are certain networking requirements that must be adhered to.

- Between data sites both Layer 2 and Layer 3 are supported.

  - Layer-2 is recommended.

- Between the data sites and the witness site Layer 3 is required.

  - This is to prevent IO to be routed through a potentially low bandwidth witness site.

- Multicast is required between data sites.

  - In the case of Layer 3, protocol-independent multicast (PIM) sparse mode is strongly recommended. Consult with your network vendor for multicast routing best practices and limitations.

- Only unicast is required between data sites and the witness site.

  - Here the multicast requirement is removed to simplify L3 network configurations.

- Maximum round trip latency between data sites is 5 ms.

- Maximum round trip latency between data sites and the witness site is 200 ms.

- A bandwidth of 10 Gbps between data sites is recommended.

- A bandwidth of 100 Mbps between data sites and the witness site is recommended.

Networking in any stretched vSphere deployment is always a hot topic. We expect this to be the same for VSAN stretched deployments. VMware has published two excellent guides that hold a lot of detail around network bandwidth calculations and network topology considerations. The above bandwidth recommendations are exactly that, recommendations. Requirements for your environment can be determined by calculating the exact needs, as explained in the following two documents.

- Virtual SAN 6.1 stretched cluster bandwidth sizing guidance
  https://www.vmware.com/files/pdf/products/vsan/vmware-virtual-san-6.1-stretched-cluster-bandwidth-sizing.pdf

- Virtual SAN 6.1 stretched cluster guide
  https://www.vmware.com/files/pdf/products/vsan/VMware-Virtual-SAN-6.1-Stretched-Cluster-Guide.pdf

- Virtual SAN 6.2 stretched cluster guide
  https://www.vmware.com/files/pdf/products/vsan/vmware-virtual-san-6.2-stretched-cluster-guide.pdf

New Concepts in VSAN Stretched Cluster

A common question is how stretched cluster differs from regular fault domains. Fault domains enable what might be termed "rack awareness" where the components of VMs could be distributed amongst multiple hosts in multiple racks, and should a rack failure event occur, the VM would continue to be available. These racks would typically be hosted in the same data center, and if there was a data center-wide event, fault domains would not be able to assist with VM availability.

Stretched cluster is essentially building on the foundation of fault domains, and now provides what might be termed "data center awareness." VSAN stretched cluster can now provide availability for VMs even if a data center suffers a catastrophic outage. This is achieved primarily through intelligent component placement of VM objects across data sites, site preference, read locality, and the witness host.

The witness host is an ESXi host (or virtual appliance) whose purpose is to host the witness component of VM objects. The witness must have connection to both the master VSAN node and the backup VSAN node to join the cluster (the master and backup were discussed previously in Chapter 5, "Architectural Details"). In steady-state operations, the master node resides in the "preferred site"; the backup node resides in the "secondary site."

Note that the witness appliance ships with its own license, so it does not consume any of your vSphere or VSAN licenses. Hence it is our recommendation to always use the appliance over a physical witness host. The witness appliance also has a different icon in the vSphere Web Client than a regular ESXi hosts, allowing you to identify the witness appliance quickly as shown in Figure 8.2. This is only the case for the witness appliance however. A physical appliance will show up in the client as a regular host and also requires a vSphere license.

Figure 8.2 Witness appliance icon

Another new term that will show up during the configuration of a stretched cluster, and was just mentioned, is "preferred site" and "secondary site." The "preferred" site is the site that VSAN wishes to remain running when there is a network partition between the sites and the sites can no longer communicate. One might say that the "preferred site" is the site expected to have the most reliability.

Since VMs can run on any of the two sites, if network connectivity is lost between site 1 and site 2, but both still have connectivity to the witness, the preferred site is the one that survives and its VSAN components remain active, while the storage on the nonpreferred site is marked as down and the VSAN components on that site are marked as absent. This also means that any VMs running in the secondary site in this situation will need to be restarted in the primary site in order to be usable and useful again. vSphere HA, when enabled on the stretched cluster, will take care of this automatically.

In nonstretched VSAN clusters, a VM's read operations are distributed across all replica copies of the data in the cluster. In the case of a policy setting of *NumberOfFailuresToTolerate*=1, which results in two copies of the data, 50% of the reads will come from replica 1 and 50% will come from replica 2. Similarly, in the case of a policy setting of *NumberOfFailuresToTolerate*=2 in nonstretched VSAN clusters, which results in three copies of the data, 33% of the reads will come from replica 1, 33% of the reads will come from replica 2, and 33% will come from replica 3.

However, we wish to avoid this situation with a stretched VSAN cluster, as we do not wish to read data over the intersite link, which could add unnecessary latency to the I/O and waste precious intersite link bandwidth. Since VSAN stretched cluster supports a maximum of *NumberOfFailuresToTolerate*=1, there will be two copies of the data (replica 1 and replica 2). Rather than doing 50% reads from site 1 and 50% reads from site 2 across the site link, the goal is to do 100% of the read IO from the local site, wherever possible.

The distributed object manager (DOM) in Virtual SAN is responsible for dealing with read locality. DOM is not only responsible for the creation of virtual machine storage objects in the Virtual SAN cluster, but it is also responsible for providing distributed data access paths to these objects. There is a single DOM owner per object. There are three roles within DOM; client, owner, and component manager. The DOM owner coordinates access to the object, including reads, locking, and object configuration and reconfiguration. All objects changes and writes also go through the owner. In VSAN stretched cluster, an enhancement to the DOM owner of an object means that it will now take into account the "fault domain" where the owner runs, and will read 100% from the replica that is in the same "fault domain."

There is now another consideration with read locality for hybrid configurations. Administrators should avoid unnecessary vMotion of virtual machines between data sites. Since the read cache blocks are stored on one (local) site, if the VM moves around freely and ends up on the remote site, the cache will be cold on that site after the migration. Now there will be suboptimal performance until the cache is warmed again. To avoid this situation, soft (should) affinity rules (VM/Host rules) should be used to keep the virtual machine local to the same site/fault domain where possible. Note that this only applies to hybrid configurations, as all-flash configurations do not have a read cache.

Configuration of a Stretched Cluster

The installation of VSAN stretched cluster is almost identical to how fault domains were implemented in earlier VSAN versions, with a couple of additional steps. This part of the chapter will walk the reader through a stretched cluster configuration.

Before we get started with the actual configuration of a stretched cluster we will need to ensure the witness host is installed, configured, and accessible from both data sites. This will most likely involve the addition of static routes to the ESXi hosts and witness appliance, which will be covered shortly. When configuring your VSAN stretched cluster, only data hosts must be in the (VSAN) cluster object in vCenter Server. The witness host must remain outside of the cluster, and must not be added to the vCenter Server cluster at any point.

Note that the witness OVA must be deployed through a vCenter Server. In order to complete the deployment and configuration of the witness VM, it must be powered on the very first time through a vCenter Server as well. The witness OVA is also only supported with standard vSwitch (VSS) deployments.

The deployment of the witness host is pretty much straightforward and similar to the deployment of most virtual appliances as shown in Figure 8.3.

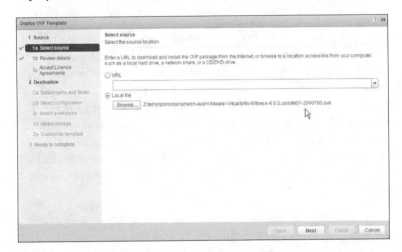

Figure 8.3   Witness appliance deployment

The only real decision that needs to be made is with regards to the expected size of the stretched cluster configuration. There are three options offered. If you expect the number of VMs deployed on the VSAN stretched cluster to be 10 or fewer, select the **Tiny** configuration. If you expect to deploy more than 10 VMs, but less than 500 VMs, then the **Medium** (default option) should be chosen. For more than 500 VMs, choose the **Large** option. On selecting a particular configuration, the resources required by the appliance are displayed in the wizard (CPU, Memory, and Disk) as shown in Figure 8.4.

Figure 8.4   Selection of configuration size

Next the datastore where the witness appliance will need to be stored and the network that will be used for the witness appliance will need to be selected. This network will be associated with both network interfaces (management and VSAN) at deployment, so later on the VSAN network configuration may require updating when the VSAN and management traffic are separated. Lastly a root password will need to be provided and the appliance will be deployed.

If there are different network segments used for management and VSAN traffic (usually the case) then after deployment a configuration change should be made to the VM. This can be done through the Web Client, as shown in Figure 8.5.

At this point the witness appliance can be powered on and the console of the witness should be accessed to add the correct networking information, such as IP address and DNS, for the management network. This is identical to how one would add the management network information of a physical ESXi host via the DCUI. After this has been done the witness can be added to the vCenter inventory as a regular host.

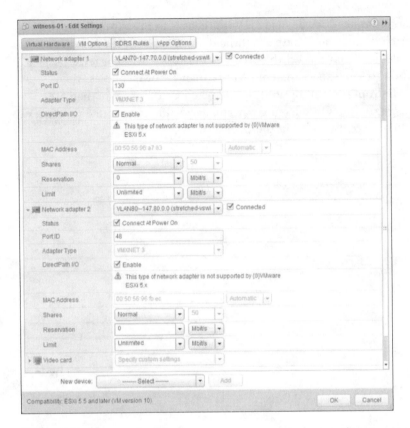

Figure 8.5   Change of networks

> **NOTE**
>
> The "No datastores have been configured" message is because the nested ESXi host has no VMFS datastore. This can be safely ignored.

Once the witness appliance/nested ESXi host has been added to vCenter, the next step is to configure the VSAN network correctly on the witness. When the witness is selected in the vCenter inventory, navigate to Manage > Networking > Virtual Switches. The witness has a port group predefined called *witnessPg*. *Do not remove this port group, as it has special modification to make the MAC addresses on the network adapters match the nested ESXi MAC addresses.* From this view, the VMkernel port to be used for VSAN traffic is visible. If there is no DHCP server on the VSAN network (which is likely), then the VMkernel adapter will not have a valid IP address, nor will it be tagged for VSAN traffic, and this will need to be added and the VMkernel port will need to be tagged for VSAN traffic.

Last but not least, before we can configure the VSAN stretched cluster, we need to ensure that the VSAN network on the hosts residing in the data sites can reach the witness host's VSAN network, and vice-versa. To address this, administrators must implement static routes. Static routes tell the TCP/IP stack to use a different path to reach a particular network. Now we can tell the TCP/IP stack on the data hosts to use a different network path (instead of the default gateway) to reach the VSAN network on the witness host. Similarly, we can tell the witness host to use an alternate path to reach the VSAN network on the data hosts rather than via the default gateway.

Note once again that in most situations the VSAN network is most likely a stretched L2 broadcast domain between the data sites, but L3 is required to reach the VSAN network of the witness appliance. Therefore static routes are needed between the data hosts and the witness host for the VSAN network, but may not be required for the data hosts on different sites to communicate to each other over the VSAN network.

The esxcli commands used to add a static route is:

esxcli network ip route ipv4 add –n <remote network> -g <gateway>

Use the *vmkping –I <vmk> <ipaddress>* command to check that the witness and physical hosts can communicate over the VSAN network. Now that the witness is up and accessible; forming a VSAN stretched cluster literally takes less than a couple of minutes. The following are the steps that should be followed to install VSAN stretched cluster. This example is a 2 + 2 + 1 deployment, meaning two ESXi hosts at the preferred site, two ESXi hosts at the secondary site, and 1 witness host in a third location.

Configure Step 1a: Create a VSAN Cluster Stretched

In this example, there are four nodes available: esx01-sitea, esx02-sitea, esx01-siteb, and esx02-siteb, as shown in Figure 8.6. All four hosts reside in a cluster called stretched-vsan. The fifth host witness-01, which is the witness host, is in its own datacenter and is not added to the cluster, but it has been added as an ESXi host to this vCenter Server.

Depending on how you are configuring your cluster you can decide to either create the stretched cluster during the creation of the VSAN cluster itself, or do this after the fact in the fault domain view. Both workflows are identical and the result will be similar. Note that new VSAN 6.2 functionality like deduplication and compression can also be enabled in a stretched cluster and checksums are fully supported. RAID-5/6 however are not supported in a stretched cluster configuration as this would require 4 or 6 fault domains at a minimum, respectively.

Configure Step 1b: Create Stretch Cluster

If your VSAN cluster has already been formed, it is also possible to create the stretched cluster separately. To configure stretch cluster and fault domains when a VSAN cluster

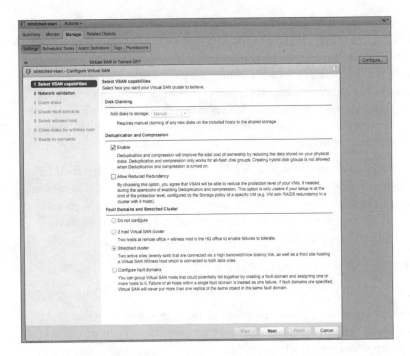

Figure 8.6   Start of stretched cluster creation

already exists, navigate to the Manage > Virtual SAN > Fault Domains view as shown in Figure 8.7, and click on the button "configure" in the stretched cluster section, that begins the stretch cluster configuration.

Figure 8.7   Configure VSAN stretched cluster

Depending on whether you create the VSAN cluster as part of the workflow you may need to claim disks as well when the VSAN cluster is setup in manual mode.

Configure Step 2: Assign Hosts to Sites

At this point, hosts can now be assigned to stretch cluster sites as shown in Figure 8.8. Note that the names have been preassigned. The preferred site is the one that will run VMs in the event that there is a split-brain type scenario in the cluster. In this example, hosts esx01-sitea and esx02-sitea will remain in the preferred site, and hosts esx01-siteb and esx02-siteb will be assigned to the secondary site.

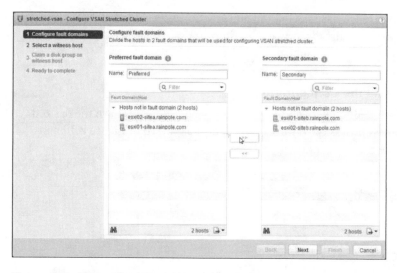

Figure 8.8 Host selection and site placement

Configure Step 3: Select a Witness Host and Disk Group

The next step is to select the witness host. At this point, the host witness-01 is chosen. Note once again that this host does not reside in the cluster. It is outside of the cluster. In fact, in this setup as shown in Figure 8.9, it is in its own data center, but has been added to the same vCenter Server that is managing the stretched cluster.

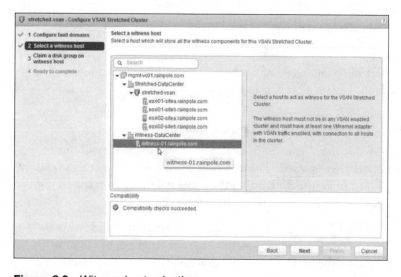

Figure 8.9 Witness host selection

When the witness is selected, a flash device and a magnetic disk need to be chosen to create a disk group. These are already available in the witness appliance (both are in fact VMDKs under the covers, since the appliance is a VM).

Configure Step 4: Verify the Configuration

Verify that the preferred fault domain and the secondary fault domains have the desired hosts, and that the witness host is the desired witness host as shown in Figure 8.10 and click **Finish** to complete the configuration.

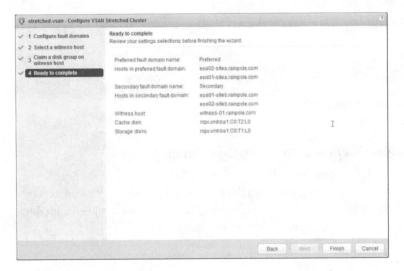

Figure 8.10   Summary of stretched cluster configuration

When the stretched cluster has completed configuration, which can take a number of seconds, verify that the fault domain view is as expected.

Configure Step 5: Health Check the Stretched Cluster

Before doing anything else, use the Virtual SAN health check to ensure that all the stretched cluster health checks have passed. These checks are only visible when the cluster has been configured as shown in Figure 8.11, and if there are any issues with the configuration, these checks should be of great assistance in locating them.

That may seem very easy from a VSAN perspective, but there are some considerations from a vSphere perspective to take into account. These are not required, but in most cases recommended to optimize for performance and availability. The VSAN stretched cluster guide outlines all vSphere recommendations in-depth. Since our focus in this book

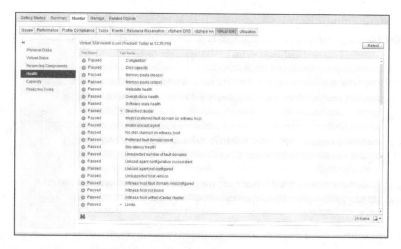

Figure 8.11   Stretched cluster health

is VSAN and as such we will not go to such great level of detail but instead would like to refer you to this guide mentioned previously in this chapter. We will, however, list some of the key recommendations for each of the specific areas:

vSphere DRS:

- Create a host group per data site, containing each of the host of the particular site.

- Create VM groups per site, containing the VMs that should reside in a particular site.

- Create a "should" soft rule for these groups to ensure that during "normal" operations these VMs reside in the correct site.

This will ensure that VMs will not freely roam around the stretched cluster, maintaining read locality, and performance is not impacted due to rewarming of the cache. It will also help from an operational perspective to provide insights around the impact of a full site failure and it will allow you to distribute scale-out services like active directory and for instance DNS across both sites.

vSphere HA:

- Enable vSphere HA admission control and set it to use the percentage-based admission control policy and to 50% for both CPU and memory. This means that if there is a full site failure, one site has enough capacity to run all of the VMs.

- Enable "vSphere HA should respect VM/host affinity rules."

- Make sure to specify additional isolation addresses, one in each site using the advanced setting *das.isolationAddress0* and *das.isolationAddress1*. This means that in the event of a site failure, the remaining site can still pings an isolation response IP address.

- Disable the default isolation address if it can't be used to validate the state of the environment during a partition. Setting the advanced setting *das.usedefaultisolationaddress* to false does this.

- Disable datastore heartbeating, as without traditional external storage there is no reason to have this.

- Select "vSphere HA should respect VM/host affinity rules" so that in the case of a single host failure VMs are restarted within their site.

These settings will ensure that when a failure occurs sufficient resources are available to coordinate the failover and power-on the VMs (admission control). These VMs will be restarted within their respective sites as defined in the VM/host rules. In the case of an isolation event, all necessary precautions have been taken to ensure all of the hosts can validate for isolation locally.

Failure Scenarios

There are many different failures that can occur in a virtual datacenter. It is not our goal to describe each and every single one of them, as that would be a book by itself. In this section we want to describe some of the more common failures, and recovery of these failures, which are particular to the stretched cluster configuration.

In this example, there is a 1 + 1 + 1 stretched VSAN deployment. This means that there is a single data host at site 1, a single data host at site 2, and a witness host at a third site.

A single VM has also been deployed. When the physical disk placement is examined, we can see that the replicas are placed on the preferred and secondary data site, respectively, and the witness component is placed on the witness site as shown in Figure 8.12.

Figure 8.12   VM component placement

The next step is to introduce some failures and examine how VSAN handles such events. Before beginning these tests, please ensure that the VSAN health check plugin is working correctly, and that all VSAN health checks have passed.

Note: In a 1 + 1 + 1 configuration, a single host failure would be akin to a complete site failure.

The health check plugin should be referred to regularly during failure scenario testing. Note that alarms are now raised in version 6.1 for any health check that fails. Alarms may also be reference at the cluster level throughout this testing.

Finally, when the term site is used in the failure scenarios, it implies a fault domain.

Single data host failure—Secondary site

The first test is to introduce a failure on a host on one of the data sites, either the "preferred" or the "secondary" site (see Figure 8.13). The sample virtual machine deployed for test purposes currently resides on the preferred site.

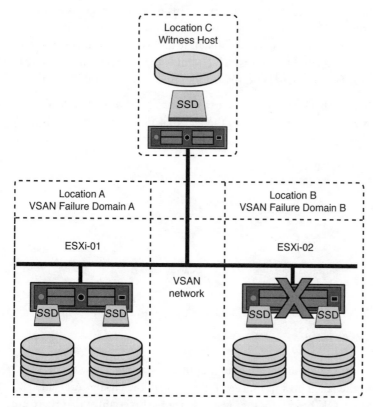

Figure 8.13   Failure scenario—host failed secondary site

In the first part of this test, the secondary host has been rebooted, simulating a temporary outage.

There will be several power and HA events related to the secondary host visible in the vSphere Web Client UI. Change to the physical disk place view of the virtual machine. After a few moments, the components that were on the secondary host will go "absent," as shown in Figure 8.14.

Figure 8.14 VM component absent

However, the virtual machine continues to be accessible. This is because there is a full copy of the data available on the host on the preferred site, and there are more than 50% of the votes available. Open a console to the virtual machine and verify that it is still very much active and functioning. Since the ESXi host which holds the compute of the virtual machine is unaffected by this failure, there is no reason for vSphere HA to take action.

At this point, the VSAN health check plugin can be examined. There will be quite a number of failures, as shown in Figure 8.15, due to the fact that the secondary host is no longer available, as one might expect.

Figure 8.15 Health check tests failed

When going through these tests yourself, please note that before starting a new test it is recommended to wait until the failed host has successfully rejoined the cluster. All "failed" health check tests should show OK before another test is started. Also confirm that there are no "absent" components on the VMs objects, and that all components are once again active.

Single data host failure—Preferred site

This next test will not only check VSAN, but it will also verify vSphere HA functionality, and that the VM to host affinity rules which we recommended are working correctly. If each site has multiple hosts, then a host failure on the primary site will allow vSphere HA to start the virtual machine on another host on the same site. In this test, the configuration is 1 + 1 + 1 so the virtual machine will have to be restarted on the secondary site. This will also verify that the VM to host affinity "should" rule is working (see Figure 8.16).

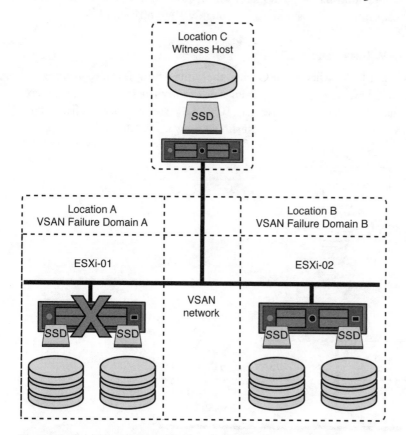

Figure 8.16   Failure scenario—host failed preferred site

After the failure has occurred in the preferred site there will be a number of vSphere HA related events. Similar to the previous scenario, the components that were on the preferred host will show up as "absent."

Since the host on which the virtual machine's compute resides is no longer available, vSphere HA will restart the virtual machine on another host in the cluster. It is important to validate this has happened as it shows that the VM/host affinity rules are correctly configured as "should" rules and not as "must" rules. If "must" rules are configured then vSphere HA will not be able to restart the virtual machine on the other site, so it is important that this test behaves as expected. "Should" rules will allow vSphere HA to restart the virtual machine on hosts that are not in the VM/host affinity rules when no other hosts are available.

Note that if there were more than one host on each site, then the virtual machine would be restarted on another host on the same site as a result of the "vSphere HA should respect VM/host affinity rules" setting. However, since this is a test on a 1 + 1 + 1 configuration, there are no additional hosts available on the preferred site. Therefore, the VM is restarted on a host on the secondary site after roughly 30 to 60 seconds.

Witness host failure—Witness site

A common question that is asked is what happens when the witness host has failed as shown in Figure 8.17? This should have no impact on the run state of the virtual machine since there is still a full copy of the data available and greater than 50% of the votes are also available, but the witness components residing on the witness host should show up as "absent."

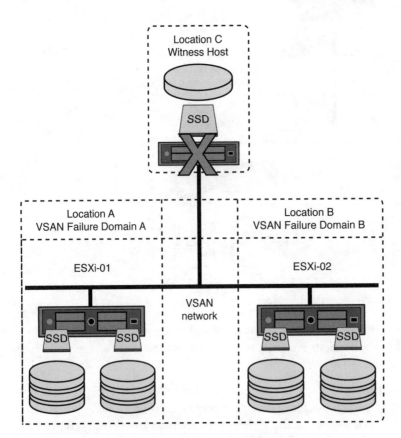

Figure 8.17   Failure scenario—witness host failed

In our environment we've simply powered off the witness host to demonstrate the impact of a failure. After a short period of time, the witness component of the virtual machine appears as "absent" as shown in Figure 8.18.

Figure 8.18 Witness component absent

However the virtual machine is unaffected and continues to be available and accessible. The rule for VSAN virtual machine object accessibility is: at least one full copy of the data must be available, and more than 50% of the components that go to make up the object are available. In this scenario both copies of the data are available and more than 50%, leaving access to the VM intact.

Network Failure—Data Site to Data Site

The last failure scenario we want to describe is a site partition. If you are planning on testing this scenario, which we highly recommend, please ensure before conducting the tests that the host isolation response and host isolation addresses are configured correctly. At least one of the isolation addresses should be pingable over the VSAN network by each host in the cluster. The environment shown in Figure 8.19 depicts our configuration and the failure scenario.

This scenario is special as when the intersite link has failed the "preferred" site forms a cluster with the witness, and the majority of components (data components and witness) will be available to this part of the cluster. The secondary site will also form its own cluster, but it will only have a single copy of the data and will not have access to the witness. This results in two components of the virtual machine object getting marked as absent on the secondary site (see Figure 8.20) since the host can no longer communicate to the other data site where the other copy of the data resides, nor can it communicate to the witness. This means that the VMs can only run on the preferred site, where the majority of the components are accessible.

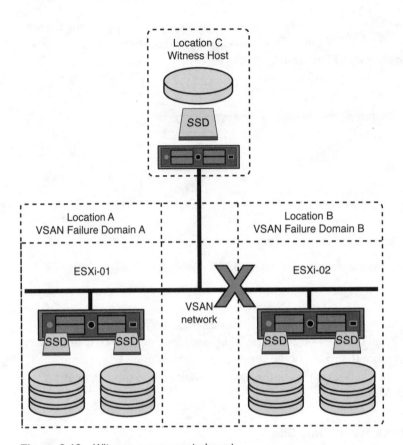

Figure 8.19   Witness component absent

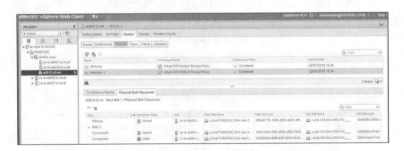

Figure 8.20   Two components absent on the secondary site

From a vSphere HA perspective, since the host isolation response IP address is on the VSAN network and site local, both data sites should be able to reach the isolation response IP address on their respective sites. Therefore vSphere HA does not trigger a host isolation response! This means that the VMs that are running in the secondary site, which has lost access to the VSAN datastore, cannot write to disk but are still running from a compute perspective. It should be noted that during the recovery the host that has lost access to the disk components will instantly kill the VM instances. This however means that until the host has recovered potentially two instances of the same VM can be accessed over the network, of which one is capable of writing to disk and the other is not.

As of VSAN 6.2, a new mechanism has been introduced to avoid this situation. This feature will automatically kill the VMs that have lost access to all VSAN components on the secondary site. This is to ensure that they can be safely restarted on the primary site, and when the link recovers there will not be two instances of the same VM running, even for a brief second. If you want to disable this behavior, you can set the advanced host setting called *VSAN.AutoTerminateGhostVm* to 0. Note that before 6.2 these VMs needed to be killed manually, and VMware even provided a script to take care of this via VMware Knowledge Base Article 2135952.

On the preferred site, the impacted VMs will be almost instantly restarted. By navigating to the policies view after the virtual machine has been restarted on the hosts at the preferred site, and click on physical disk placement, it should show that two out of the three components are available, and since there is a full copy of the data and more than 50% of the components available, the VM is accessible.

Recovering from a Complete Site Failure

The descriptions of the host failures previously, although related to a single host failure, are also complete site failures. VMware has modified some of the Virtual SAN behavior when a site failure occurs and subsequently recovers. In the event of a site failure, Virtual SAN will now wait for some additional time for "all" hosts to become ready on the failed site before it starts to sync components. The main reason is that if only some subset of the hosts come up on the recovering site, then Virtual SAN will start the rebuild process. This may result in the transfer of a lot of data that already exists on the nodes that might become available at some point of time later on, simply because of the boot sequence of the hosts.

It is recommended that when recovering from a failure, especially a site failure, all nodes in the site should be brought back online together to avoid costly resync and reconfiguration overheads. The reason behind this is that if VSAN brings nodes back up at approximately the same time, then it will only need to synchronize the data that was written between the time when the failure occurred and the time when the site came back. If, instead, nodes are brought back up in a staggered fashion, objects might to be reconfigured and thus a significant higher amount of data will need to be transferred between sites. This is also the reason why VMware recommend setting DRS to partially automated mode rather than fully automated mode if there is a complete site failure. Administrators can then wait for the failing site to be completely remediated before allowing any VMs to migrate back to it via the affinity rules.

Summary

A VSAN stretched cluster architecture will allow you to deploy and migrate workloads across two locations without the need for complex storage configurations and operational processes. On top of that it comes at a relatively low cost that enables the majority of VMware users to deploy this configuration when there are dual datacenter requirements. As with any explicit architecture there are various different design and operational considerations. We would like to refer you to the official VMware documentation as the source of the most updated and accurate information.

Chapter 9

Designing a VSAN Cluster

This chapter walks you through all the steps required to enable you to design your perfect VSAN cluster. We will leverage all the insights provided throughout the various chapters to ensure that your VSAN cluster will meet your technical and business requirements. We do want to point out before we go through the various exercises that the *VMware compatibility guide* (VCG) contains a list of predefined configurations that are called VSAN ready nodes. We recommend using these VSAN ready nodes as a starting point for your design. It is less error prone than configuring your own server and selecting each hardware component manually. At the time of this writing, there are 13 different server vendors in the VMware compatibility guide (http://vmwa.re/vsanhcl).

Before running through the design exercises, we would like to discuss some constraints of VSAN but let's discuss the different ready node profiles first.

Ready Node Profiles

With the release of Virtual SAN 6.1 the ready node program was also overhauled. The old profile names "high–medium–low" were deprecated and a more extensive list of different profiles and configurations was introduced. Table 9.1 lists the ready node configurations that were part of the VCG at the time of writing and the different configuration items with each model. In the table below, the hybrid configurations are represented with HY models, and the all-flash configurations are represented with AF models.

Table 9.1   Virtual SAN Ready Node Models

Model	CPU/Memory	Storage Capacity	Storage Performance	VMs per Node
HY-2	1 × 6 core / 32 GB	2 TB	4K IOPS	Up to 20
HY-4	2 × 8 core / 128 GB	4 TB	10K IOPS	Up to 30
HY-6	2 × 10 core / 256 GB	8 TB	20K IOPS	Up to 50
HY-8	2 × 12 core / 348 GB	12 TB	40K IOPS	Up to 100
AF-4	2 × 10 core / 128 GB	4 TB	25K IOPS	Up to 30
AF-6	2 × 12 core / 256 GB	8 TB	50K IOPS	Up to 60
AF-8	2 × 12 core / 348 GB	12 TB	80K IOPS	Up to 120

In the previous version of the ready node program HY-2, HY-6, and HY-8 already existed, but as stated, earlier they were called low, medium, and high. HY-4, AF-6, and AF-8 were introduced with VSAN 6.1, while AF-4 was introduced with VSAN 6.2. HY-4 explicitly was introduced to bridge the gap between the low (HY-2) and medium (HY-6) model and, in our experience, this is what most customers who are looking to implement a hybrid VSAN solution start with.

When it is known what the total amount of required compute and storage capacity is, designers can easily determine which ready node (from your preferred vendor) is the closest match via the VMware compatibility guide. In Figure 9.1 we have selected ESXi 6.0 Update 1 as the version of Virtual SAN that the ready node needs to support, we have selected Fujitsu as our preferred server brand and 8 TB as the total amount of raw storage capacity per host. As shown the HY-6 and AF-6 models are displayed as potential matches.

Figure 9.1   Ready node configuration based on storage capacity selected

Sizing Constraints

As with any platform, VSAN has some constraints that need to be taken into consideration when designing an environment. Some constraints are straightforward, others are less obvious. The following provides a summary of the VSAN 6.2 constraints:

- Maximum of 64 hosts per cluster

- Maximum of 200 virtual machines (VMs) per host

- Maximum of 6,400 VMs per cluster

- Maximum of 5 disk groups per host

- Maximum of 7 disks per disk group

- One cache flash device per disk group

- Maximum of 9,000 components per host

Some of you may wonder what has happened to the "maximum number of vSphere HA protected VMs on a VSAN datastore" item that was originally on this list. This is no longer a concern. vSphere HA had a limitation originally with regards to the number of VMs it could track per datastore in the "power-on list." Changing the design of vSphere HA and accommodating for solutions like VSAN where a single datastore can hold thousands of VMs has removed this limitation. This file no longer has any form of limitation and as such the maximum number of vSphere HA protected VMs per datastore is equal to the maximum number of VMs per datastore.

As said, the majority of these are straightforward. There are two constraints worth explaining further:

- Number of hosts in a cluster

- The maximum number of components

Although 64 hosts per cluster would be a hard limit, we've yet to encounter a customer who experiences this as an actual limit. In all conversations the authors have had with customers, and this is also our recommendation generally speaking, the cluster boundary should be considered the fault domain boundary. Most customers end up with cluster sizes between 3 and 24 hosts, with 8-host and 12-host clusters being most common. What is worth mentioning is that in order to scale up from 32 hosts to 64 hosts, an advanced setting needs to be set on each of the ESXi hosts in the cluster. This option was disabled by default as in order to scale up to 64 hosts, VSAN requires an additional ~200 MB of memory per host. Note that a reboot is required for this setting to take effect. For more details we like to refer to the VMware Knowledgebase Article 2110081— http://kb.vmware.com/kb/2110081. In short, on each host you need to set a couple of advanced settings through the user interface (UI) or through the command-line interface (CLI) as follows on each of the hosts in your cluster:

```
esxcli system settings advanced list -o /CMMDS/goto11
esxcli system settings advanced set -o /Net/TcpipHeapMax -i 1024
esxcli system settings advanced set -o /CMMDS/clientLimit 65
```

The second constraint that is worth discussing is the maximum number of components per host. The maximum number of components in the initial release of VSAN was 3,000 per host; this has been increased to 9,000 per host with VSAN 6.0, and remains the same for VSAN 6.1 and 6.2. Various types of objects may be found on the VSAN datastore that contain one or more components:

- VM namespace

- VM swap

- VM disk

- Virtual disk snapshot

- Snapshot memory

- Witness

As you are no doubt aware at this stage in the book, each VM has a namespace, a swap file, and typically a disk. It is important to understand that the number of failures to tolerate (FTT) plays a critical role as well when it comes to the number of components. The higher you configure FTT, the more components certain objects will have. Meaning that when you configured FTT to 1, and your failure tolerance method is set to RAID-1, this means your disk object will have two mirrors (or in other words, two components) and typically a witness, resulting in three components in total. This also applies to the stripe width. If it is increased to larger than 1, the number of components will also go up. Therefore, if a virtual machine disk (VMDK) object is striped across two disks, you will have two components. For RAID-5, an object will have four components and for RAID-6, an object will have six components.

On top of that, the maximum size of a component is 255 GB, meaning that if you have a 500 GB virtual disk object, the object is configured with one 255 GB component and one 245 GB component. This is important to realize when it comes to scaling and sizing.

Having said that, with the VSAN 6.0 release increasing the limit from 3,000 to 9,000 we have not encountered any customers hitting this constraint or even perceiving it to be a constraint.

Cache to Capacity Ratio

Since the very first version of VSAN, the recommendation from VMware is a 10% ratio of cache versus capacity required before taking *NumberOfFailuresToTolerate* into account. What does this mean?

Let's run through a short scenario as that will make it clear instantly. Let's assume we have the following in our environment:

- 100 VMs

- 50 GB per VM

- FTT = 1

- Failure tolerance method = RAID-1

The math is simple on this one; the required space for the capacity tier and the cache tier will be as follows (not taking any overhead and slack space into account for now):

- Capacity tier: 100 VMs * 50 GB * 2 replicas = 10,000 GB

- Cache tier: 100 VMs * 50 GB = 10% of 5,000 GB = 500 GB

This is the total requirement for the complete cluster by the way. In the case of a 4-node cluster this means that the required amount of cache capacity per host is only 125 GB while the capacity tier would require 2,500 GB.

Designing for Performance

One critical aspect when designing a VSAN infrastructure is, of course, the performance aspect. During the various scenarios described in the examples that follow, our focus is on capacity sizing and partly performance. Performance is mainly a consideration in hybrid configurations. We are, however, slowly seeing a change in terms of all-flash adoption. The prices of flash have come down dramatically (and will continue to do so). With the introduction of RAID-5/6 and deduplication and compression in VSAN 6.2 we expect that, from a total cost of ownership perspective, all-flash configurations will make more sense for the majority of you.

As you have learned throughout the book by this point, VSAN heavily leans on flash devices to provide the required performance capabilities. Flash is leveraged both as a read cache and as a write buffer for hybrid configurations and just as a write buffer for all-flash configurations. Therefore, incorrectly sizing your flash capacity can have a great impact on the performance of your workload. As an example, the difference between a 30 GB read cache and a 150 GB read cache for 30 VMs is huge. Having ~ 1 GB or 5 GB per VM available does make a difference in terms of reducing the need to resort to magnetic disk in the case of a hybrid configuration. But the same applies to the write buffer. Whether you have 600 GB to your disposal to collect writes and destage them when needed or mere 100 GB. It will have an impact on destaging frequency, which in its turn can impact the capacity tier from an endurance point of view. Not only will the size of the flash device make a difference to your VMs, so will the type of flash used!

At the end of the day, all the best practices mentioned are recommendations, and these will apply to the majority of environments; however, your environment may differ. You may have more demanding applications. What truly matters is the aggregate active (hot) data set of the applications executing in the cluster. In practice, you will have to estimate that or leverage the Virtual SAN assessment tool that is available for free and can be requested online by filling out a simple form (http://vmwa.re/vsanass). The result of this assessment will tell you what the active working set is in your environment and, for instance, which VMs are recommended for VSAN. It is possible to run different analysis based on all-flash versus hybrid VSAN for instance, as shown in Figure 9.2.

Figure 9.2   Virtual SAN assessment tooling

Chapter 2, "VSAN Prerequisites and Requirements for Deployment," listed the categories of flash devices that VMware uses to provide an idea around potential performance that can be achieved when using such a device.

The list of the designated flash device classes specified within the *VMware compatibility guide* (VCG) is as follows:

- ~~**Class A**: 2,500–5,000 writes per second~~ (no longer on the VCG)

- **Class B**: 5,000–10,000 writes per second

- **Class C**: 10,000–20,000 writes per second

- **Class D**: 20,000–30,000 writes per second

- **Class D**: 30,000–100,000 writes per second

- **Class E**: 100,000+ writes per second

Just to demonstrate the difference between the various devices, we will list the theoretical performance capabilities of some of the devices in the described classes:

- **Intel P3700, 800 GB, 90k Random Write IOPS, 460k Random Read IOPS—using 4K blocks** (http://www.intel.com/content/www/us/en/solid-state-drives/intel-ssd-dc-family-for-pcie.html

- **Intel S3610, 1.2 TB, 28k Random Write IOPS, 84k Random Read IOPS—using 4K blocks** (http://www.intel.com/content/www/us/en/solid-state-drives/solid-state-drives-dc-s3610-series.html)

- **Micron P320h, 700 GB, 145k Random Write IOPS, 415k Random Read IOPS—using 4K blocks** (https://www.micron.com/products/solid-state-storage/product-lines/p320h#/)

- **Micron M500DC, 800 GB, 24k Random Write IOPS, 65k Random Read IOPS—using 4K blocks** (https://www.micron.com/products/solid-state-storage/product-lines/m500dc)

Now if you would have 400 VMs on four hosts, using Intel P3700 NVMe devices versus regular Intel S3610 devices could make a substantial difference. Just imagine you have 2,000 VMs on 16 hosts. Of course, the price tag on these two examples also significantly varies, but it is a consideration that needs to be taken into account. Whether the device is used for caching or for capacity will also make a difference. Generally speaking, high performance and write optimized drives like the Intel P3700 and the Micron P420m are used for the caching tier, while devices like the Intel S3610 and the Micron M500DC are used for the capacity tier.

Impact of the Disk Controller

A question that often arises is what is the impact of the disk controller queue depth on performance of your VSAN environment. Considering the different layers of queuing involved, it probably makes the most sense to show the picture from VM down to the device, as illustrated in Figure 9.3.

Figure 9.3 shows that there are six different layers at which some form of queuing is done, although in reality there are even more buffers and queues (but we tried to keep it

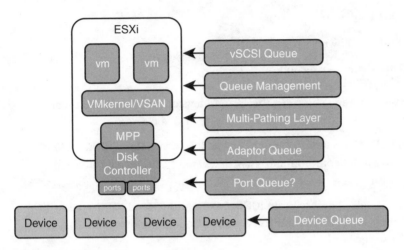

Figure 9.3   Different queuing layers

reasonably simple and depict the layers that potentially could be a bottleneck). Within the guest, the vSCSI adapter has a queue. Then the next layer is VSAN, which, of course, has its own queue and manages the I/O. Next the I/O flows through the multipathing layer to the various devices on the host. On the next level, a disk controller has a queue; potentially (depending on the controller used), each disk controller port has a queue. Last but not least, of course, each device (i.e., disk) will have a queue.

If you look closely at Figure 9.3, you see that I/O of many VMs will all flow through the same disk controller and that this I/O will go to or come from one or multiple devices (usually multiple devices). This also implies that the first real potential "choking point" is the queue depth of the disk controller.

Assume you have four SATA disks, each of which has a queue depth of 32. Total combined, this means that in parallel you can handle 128 I/Os. Now what if your disk controller can handle only 64? This will result in 64 I/Os being held back by the VMkernel/VSAN. As you can see, it would be beneficial in this scenario to ensure that your disk controller queue can hold the same number of I/Os (or more) as your device queue can hold, allowing for VSAN to shape the queue anyway it prefers without being constrained by the disk controller itself.

When it comes to disk controllers, a huge difference exists in maximum queue depth value between vendors, and even between models of the same vendor. Just for educational purposes, Table 9.2 lists five disk controllers and their queue depth to show what the impact can be when making an "uneducated" decision.

Table 9.2   Disk controller queue depth

Manufacturer	Disk Controller	Queue Depth
Dell	PERC H730 Adapter	895
HP	Smart Array P440ar	1,011
Intel	Integrated RAID RS3PC	600
LSI	9271-8i	975
Supermicro	SMC3008	600

For VSAN, it is recommended to ensure that the disk controller has a queue depth of at least 256; do note that all devices on the VCG have a queue depth higher than 256 as that is one of the criteria before they are accepted to the list. Now the disk controller is just one part of the equation, because there is also the device queue. We have looked at various controllers and devices, and here are the typical standards you will find:

```
mpt2sas_raid_queue_depth: int
    Max RAID Device Queue Depth (default=128)
mpt2sas_sata_queue_depth: int
    Max SATA Device Queue Depth (default=32)
mpt2sas_sas_queue_depth: int
    Max SAS Device Queue Depth (default=254)
```

We have highlighted the important parts here. As you can see, the controller in this case has three different queue depths depending on the type of device used. When a RAID configuration is created, the queue depth will be 128. When a SAS drive is directly attached, often referred to as pass-through, the queue depth will be 254. The one that stands out the most is the queue depth of the SATA device; this is by default only 32, and you can imagine this can once again become a choking point. This is one of the reasons there is a very limited number of SATA drives on the VMware compatibility guide for VSAN. Up to vSphere 5.5 Update 3 there are still some devices listed, but these have been removed with the release of VSAN 6.0. Fortunately the shallow queue depth of SATA (and the lack of SATA drives on the VCG) can easily be overcome by using nearline serially attached SCSI (NL_SAS) drives instead, which has a much deeper queue depth.

You can validate the queue depth of your controller using `esxcfg-info Ðs | grep "==+SCSI Interface" -A 18` as it will display a lot of information related to your SCSI interfaces including the queue depth as shown in the following output of this command which was truncated for readability reasons.

```
\==+SCSI Interface :
   |----Name.........................................vmhba0
   |----Driver.......................................lsi_mr3
   |----Queue Depth..................................895
```

Note that even the firmware and driver used can have an impact on the queue depth of your controller and devices. We highly recommend using the driver listed on the *VSAN Compatibility Guide (http://vmwa.re/vsanhcl)* shown on the details page of a specific disk controller, as shown in Figure 9.4. In some cases, it has been witnessed that the queue depth increased from 25 to 600 after a driver update. As you can imagine, this can *greatly impact* performance.

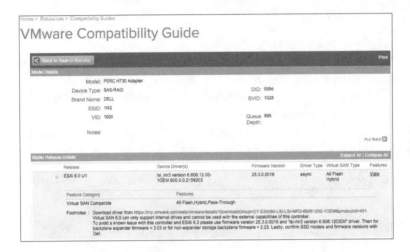

Figure 9.4   Device driver details

The question now that usually arises is this: What about NL-SAS versus SATA drives? Because NL-SAS drives are essentially SATA drives with a SAS connector, what are the benefits? NL-SAS drives come with the following benefits:

- Dual ports allowing redundant paths

- Ability to connect a device to multiple computers

- Full SCSI command set

- Faster interface compared to SATA, up to 20%, no STP (Serial ATA Tunneling Protocol) overhead

- Deeper command queue (depth)

From a cost perspective, the difference between NL-SAS and SATA for most vendors is negligible. For a 4 TB drive, the cost difference on different Web sites at the time of this writing was on average $30. Considering the benefits, it is highly recommended to use NL-SAS over SATA for VSAN.

After reading this section, it should be clear that the disk controller is a critical component of any VSAN design because it can have an impact on how VSAN performs (and not just the disk controller, but even the firmware and device driver used). When deploying VSAN, it is highly recommended to ensure the driver installed is the version recommended in the *VSAN compatibility guide*, or upgrade to the latest version as needed. The easiest way to do this is using the VSAN health check, which we will be covering in Chapter 10. The VSAN health check will check the supportability of the disk controller and driver.

VSAN Performance Capabilities

It is difficult to predict what your performance will be because every workload and every combination of hardware will provide different results. After the initial VSAN launch, VMware announced the results of multiple performance tests (http://blogs.vmware.com/vsphere/2014/03/supercharge-virtual-san-cluster-2-million-iops.html). The results were impressive, to say the least, but were only the beginning. With the 6.1 release, performance of hybrid had doubled and so had the scale, allowing for 8 million IOPS per cluster. The introduction of all-flash however completely changed the game. This allowed VSAN to reach 45k IOPS per disk group, and remember you can have 5 per disk group, but it also introduced sub millisecond latency. (Just for completeness sake, theoretically it would be possible to design a Virtual SAN cluster that could deliver over 16 million IOPS with sub millisecond latency using an all-flash configuration.)

Do note that these performance numbers should not be used as a guarantee for what you can achieve in your environment. These are theoretical tests that are not necessarily (and most likely not) representative of the I/O patterns you will see in your own environment (and so results will vary). Nevertheless, it does prove that VSAN is capable of delivering a high-performance environment. At the time of writing the latest performance document available is for VSAN 6.0, which can be found here: http://www.vmware.com/files/pdf/products/vsan/VMware-Virtual-San6-Scalability-Performance-Paper.pdf. We highly recommend however to search for the latest version as we are certain that there will be an updated version with the 6.2 release of Virtual SAN.

One thing that stands out though when reading these types of papers is that all performance tests and reference architectures by VMware that are publicly available have been done with 10 GbE networking configurations. For our design scenarios, we will use 10 GbE as the golden standard because it is heavily recommended by VMware and increases throughput and lowers latency. The only configuration where this does not apply is ROBO (remote office/branch office). This 2-node VSAN configuration is typically deployed using 1 GbE since the number of VMs running is typically relatively low (up to 20 in total). Different configuration options for networking, including the use of Network I/O Control, are discussed in Chapter 3, "VSAN Installation and Configuration."

Now that we have looked at the constraints and some of the performance aspects, let's take a look at how we would design a VSAN cluster from a capacity point of view.

Design and Sizing Tools

Before we look at our first design, we would like to point you to various tools that can help with designing and sizing your VSAN infrastructure; our preferred tool is the VSAN TCO and sizing calculator. It has been around for a while and can be found at https://vsantco. vmware.com/. The user interface is straight forward, which is shown in Figure 9.5.

Figure 9.5   Official VMware VSAN sizing calculator

This official VMware VSAN sizing calculator enables you to create a design based on certain parameters such as the following:

- Number of VMs

- Size of VM disks (VMDKs)

- Number of VMDKs

- Number of snapshots

- Read versus write I/O ratio

We highly recommend that you use this tool to validate your design scenarios and decisions to ensure optimal performance and availability for your workloads, with http://vsantco. vmware.com being the preferred solution as the official VMware-supported sizing calculator.

Scenario 1: Server Virtualization—Hybrid

When designing a VSAN environment, it is of great importance to understand the requirements of your VMs. The various examples here show what the impact can be of certain decisions you will need to make during this journey. As with any design, it starts with gathering requirements. For this scenario, we work with the following parameters, which are based on averages provided by the (fictional) customer:

- 1.5 vCPU per VM on average
- 5 GB average VM memory size
- 70 GB average VM disk size
- 70% percent anticipated VM disk consumption
- Fault tolerance method: Performance (RAID-1)
- Number of failures to tolerate (FTT): 1

In this environment, which is a green field deployment for a service provider, it is expected that each cluster will be capable of running 1000 virtual machines. Although a Virtual SAN cluster is capable of running more than a 1000 VMs, we want to make sure that we keep the failure domain relatively small and also provide the ability to scale-out the cluster when required.

This means that our VSAN infrastructure should be able to provide the following:

- 1000×1.5 vCPU = 1,500 vCPUs
- 1000×5 GB = 5,000 GB of memory
- $1000 \times 70\%$ of 70 GB = 49,000 GB net disk space

We will take a vCPU-to-core ratio of 8:1 into consideration. Considering that we will need to be able to run 1,500 vCPUs, we will divide that by 8, resulting in the need for 188 cores.

Now let's look at the storage requirements a bit more in-depth. Before we can calculate the requirements, we need to know what level of resiliency will be taken into account for these VMs. For our calculations, we will take a fault tolerance method of RAID-1 (mirroring) and a number of failures to tolerate setting of 1 into account. We also add an additional 30% disk space to cater for metadata and the occasional snapshot. If more disk space is required for snapshots for your environment, do not forget to factor this in when you run through this exercise.

The formula we will use taking the preceding parameters into account looks like the following:

(((Number of VMs * Avg VM size) + (Number of VMs * Avg mem size)) * FTT+1) + 30% slack space

We have included the average memory size because each VM will create a swap file on disk that is equal to the size of the VM memory configuration. Using our industry standard averages mentioned previously, this results in the following:

((((1,000 * 49) + (1,000 * 5)) * 2) = (49,000 + 5,000) * 2 = 108,000 GB + 30% = 140,400 GB

Divide the outcome by 1,024 and round it up; a total combined storage capacity of 138 TB is the outcome. Now that we know we need 138 TB of disk capacity, 5,000 GB of memory, and 188 cores, let's explore the hardware configuration.

Determining Your Host Configuration

We will start with exploring the most common scenario, a 2U host. For this scenario, we have decided to select the Dell R730XD, which is depicted in Figure 9.6. This server has been optimized for storage capacity and hold up to 28 devices in a 2U system including 4 NVMe devices. The Dell R730XD is a dual-socket server and can hold up to 1.5 TB of memory. The dual-socket can be configured with anything ranging from a 4-core to an 18-core CPU. You can find more details on the Dell R730XD at http://www.dell.com/us/business/p/poweredge-r730xd/pd.

Figure 9.6   Dell R730XD server

Our requirements for the environment are as follows:

- Three hosts minimum (according to VSAN)
- 138 TB of raw disk capacity
- 188 CPU cores
- 5,000 GB of memory
- Minimal overcommitment in failure scenarios ($N + 1$ for high availability [HA])

As stated, the Dell R730XD can hold 18 cores per socket, at most resulting in a total of 36 cores per host in a dual-socket configuration. This means that from a CPU perspective, we will need roughly six hosts. However, because we have a requirement to avoid overcommitment in a failure scenario, we need a minimum of seven hosts. From a memory perspective, each host today (using 32 GB DIMMs) can be provisioned with 768 GB of memory. Considering that we require 5,000 GB of memory, we would need seven hosts when it comes to memory. Because we want to have the ability to scale up as needed and have some head room as well and select an optimal configuration from a cost perspective, 512 GB per host is what has been decided on leading to a minimum of 10 hosts per cluster, which also seems to be the most cost-effective configuration from a CPU point of view as cheaper 10- or 12-core CPUs can be used versus top of the line 18-core CPUs.

Of course, price is always a consideration, and we urge you to compare prices based on CPU, memory, and disk configurations. We will not discuss pricing in-depth as this changes so fast, and by the time we are done with this chapter they would have changed again. In this scenario, we have come to the conclusion that 10 hosts were optimal from a CPU and memory point of view, and we will cater for the disk design based on this outcome.

Storage sizing is a bit more delicate. Let's look at our options here. We know we need 138 TB of storage, and we know that we need 10 hosts from a compute point of view. Considering that we have the option to go with either 3.5-inch drives or 2.5-inch drives, we will have a maximum of 240 × 2.5-inch drive slots or 120 × 3.5-inch drive slots total combined for our 10 hosts at our disposal. As each group of disks (seven disks at most in a disk group) will require one flash device, this should be taken into account when deciding the type of disk.

One critical factor to consider is the number of IOPS provided by both magnetic disks and flash devices. Typical 3.5-inch 7200 RPM NL-SAS drives can deliver roughly 80 IOPS, whereas a 2.5-inch 10K RPM SAS drive can deliver 150 IOPS. Do note that in some cases drives with more drive platters and heads may deliver slightly higher IOPS, in some cases NL-SAS drives have been witness to deliver up to 225 IOPS. (IOPS numbers are taken from http://www.techrepublic.com/blog/the-enterprise-cloud/calculate-iops-in-a-storage-array/) From a capacity perspective, NL-SAS drives range from 1 TB up to 6 TB, whereas SAS drives are limited today to 1.2 TB (with VSAN at least). We know we require 138 TB, so let's do some quick math to show the potential impact a decision like this can have. We will use most commonly used disk types for both SAS and NL-SAS to demonstrate the potential impact of going with one over the other:

- 138 TB/4 TB = ~ 35 NL-SAS magnetic disks = 2,800 IOPS from NL-SAS-based magnetic disks.

- 138 TB/1.2 TB = ~ 115 SAS magnetic disks = 17,250 IOPS SAS-based from magnetic disks.

As you can see, a huge difference exists between the two examples provided. Although VSAN has been designed to leverage your flash device as the primary provider of performance, it is an important design consideration because these IOPS are used when data needs to be destaged to magnetic disks or when a read cache miss occurs and the data block has to be retrieved from magnetic disk. In this scenario though, we have decided to use NL-SAS drives as they are more cost effective and will compensate for the loss in performance with a larger flash device.

Let's do the math. In total, as described earlier, we need 35 × 4 TB NL-SAS drives across 10 hosts. This results in a total of 3.5 drives per host, which we will round up to 4.

To ensure that our VSAN cluster provides an optimal user experience, we will use the rule of thumb of 10% flash of anticipated consumed VM disk capacity. In our scenario, we will have a maximum of 1,000 VMs. These VMs have a virtual disk capacity of 70 GB, of which it is anticipated that 70% will be actually consumed. This results in the following recommendation from a flash capacity point of view:

10% of (1,000 VMs * (70% anticipated consumed of 70 GB)) = 4,900 GB

Considering we will require 10 hosts, this means it is recommended to have 4,900 GB/10 = ~490 GB of flash capacity in each host. Note that in our configuration we only have one disk group per host; if we would have two disk groups then we need to take this into consideration as each disk group will also need to have its own flash device. To ensure we can compensate for the lower number of IOPS the capacity tier can deliver, we have decided to use an 800 GB SSD, which will provide us with an additional 310 GB of cache capacity.

Using the *VMware compatibility guide*, we have determined that, for our Dell configuration, we could leverage the following flash devices when taking a performance requirement of a minimum of 20,000 writes per second. (Class D and E qualify for this.) The options we have at our disposal currently are as follows:

- 800 GB SSD SAS Mix Use 12 Gbps

- 800 GB SSD SAS Read Intensive 12 Gbps

- 800 GB SSD SATA Mix Use 6 Gbps

- 800 GB SSD SATA Read intensive 6 Gbps

Note that there is a big price difference in some of these cases, and in our scenario the decision was made to go with the 800 GB SSD SATA Mix Use 6 Gbps flash devices.

The final outstanding item is the disk controller. VMware recommends using a pass-through controller, and Dell offers two variants for the R730XD: the H330 and the H730. The H330 is a standard pass-through controller. The H730 offers advanced functionality such as caching, self-encrypting drives, and other functionality. At the time of writing only the H730 controller is supported with VSAN and as such that controller is selected.

The final configuration is 10 Dell R730XD (3.5-inch drive slot) hosts consisting of the following:

- Dual-socket—12-core E5-2670
- 512 GB memory
- Disk controller: Dell H730
- 4 × 4TB NL-SAS 7200 RPM
- 1 × 800 GB SSD SATA (Mixed Use)

Scenario 2—Server Virtualization—All-flash

In this scenario, we take a slightly different approach than we did in scenario 1. We will use a different type of host hardware form factor, and we use different sizing and scaling input and we will go for an all-flash configuration instead as there are some interesting design considerations around that as well. For this scenario, we will work with the following parameters:

- 2 vCPU per VM on average
- 8 GB average VM memory size
- 20% memory over commitment
- 150 GB average VM disk size
- 100% anticipated consumed VM disk capacity
- Fault tolerance method: Capacity (RAID-5/6)
- Number of failures to tolerate (FTT) = 2

In the environment, we currently have 200 VMs and need to be able to grow to 300 VMs in the upcoming 12 months. Therefore, our VSAN infrastructure should be able to provide the following:

- 300 × 2 vCPU = 600 vCPUs
- 300 × 8 GB = 2,400 GB of memory – 20% = 1,920 GB
- 300 × 150 GB = 45,000 GB disk space

In our sizing exercise, we look at two different server platforms. Our VMs are not CPU intensive but rather memory intensive. We take a vCPU-to-core ratio of 8:1 into consideration. Considering that we will need to be able to run 600 vCPUs, we divide that by 8, resulting in the need for a minimum of 75 cores. From a memory perspective 1,920 GB is required and from a storage point of view we need 45 TB, but that is without taking FTT into account and without any potential savings from deduplication and compression. Before we go through the full design, let's take a look at storage first and the impact of certain decisions.

For storage the requirements are fairly straightforward. If we were going to implement RAID-1 (mirroring), this would mean that by default there would be a 3× storage capacity required. In other words, each 10 GB VM capacity requires 30 GB disk capacity. This is because with RAID-1 and FTT=2 you need two full copies of the data in order to withstand two failures. However, as of VSAN 6.2 it is possible to set a failure tolerance method (FTM) where you have the option to select RAID-1 or RAID5/6. The overhead for RAID-5/6 is significantly lower than in a RAID-1 configuration. The overhead is 1.5 × for FTT = 2 (RAID-6) and 1.33 × for FTT = 1 (RAID-5) instead of the 3 × overhead that RAID-1 has. In this scenario that means the following:

45,000 GB with FTT = 2 and FTM = RAID6 = 1.5 * 45,000 = 67,500 GB

There is a second option to optimize for capacity that can be used on top of RAID-5/6 on all-flash VSAN. This is deduplication and compression. Note that deduplication and compression are enabled or disabled at the same time and the domain for this is the disk group. Results of deduplication and compression will vary per workload type. For a database workload a 2:1 reduction in capacity is a realistic number, whereas virtual desktops are closer to 8:1. What impact does that have in this environment?

In this environment we will be running a mixed server workload ranging from print servers to database servers and anything in between. From a deduplication point of view this will mean that it will not be as efficient as when you would have 300 similar VMs. As such we take a 4:1 data reduction into account. Then there are some other considerations we need to take into account. For instance, we want to be able to rebuild data in the case of a full host failure, even during maintenance. Our requirements are:

- FTT = 2 and FTM = RAID-6 → 45,000 GB * 1.5 = 67,500 GB.

- With a 4:1 data reduction total required capacity is 16,875 GB.

- 10% cache to capacity ratio = 10% of 45,000 GB = 4500 GB.

- Minimum of six hosts to support RAID-6.

- Additional host to allow for full recovery and re-protection (self-healing) after a failure, which means seven hosts minimum.

- Additional host to allow for recovery and re-protection during maintenance, which means eight hosts minimum.

- Assuming one host failure and maintenance mode not impacting recovery we divide 16,875 GB by 6, which means we need 2,812.50 GB per host including the two additional hosts.

- For caching this means we need "4,500 GB/8" per host, which is 562 GB.

- CPU requirement for the environment is 75 cores, divided by six hosts (assuming one host failure and maintenance mode not impacting performance) means we need 12.5 cores per host.

- Memory requirement is 1,920 GB, divided by six hosts is 320 GB of memory per host.

So let's list the outcome to have it crystal clear, each host should have the following resources:

- CPU: 12.5 cores per host

- Memory: 320 GB per host

- Capacity: 2,812.50 GB

- Cache: 750 GB

One thing that stands out immediately is the relatively high amount of cache compared to the amount required for the capacity tier. The reason for this is that deduplication and compression take place when destaging data from the caching tier to the capacity tier, as such the caching tier does not benefit from the reduction. Also, one thing to note is that the caching tier is only used as a write buffer in an all-flash configuration, which means that endurance (wear and tear) is a factor to take into consideration; as such we still recommend the 10% rule.

For this configuration the Supermicro 2U 4-Node TwinPro2 server was selected. This platform provides four nodes in a 2U chassis. We need eight nodes in total to meet the requirements around availability, recoverability, and performance. The model is the SuperServer 2028TP-HC0TR, which is shown in Figure 9.7.

Figure 9.7 Supermicro SuperServer

We will need two units and have decided to use the following configuration which is a great balance between cost and performance:

- Dual six-core Intel E5-2620 v3 2.4 GHz

- 384 GB of memory per host

- SLC SATADOM for booting ESXi

- LSI 3008 SAS controller

- Caching tier: 1 × Intel S3710 – 800 GB

- Capacity tier: 4 × Micron M510DC – 960 GB

We want to leverage as much cache capacity as possible and as such we have purposely included a larger device than VSAN can utilize at the time of writing. VSAN 6.2, and earlier releases, has a limit of 600 GB cache capacity it can utilize. This also means that at the time of maintenance, or during a failure, it may seem that we are slightly under-sized. However, as already mentioned, in an all-flash configuration the most critical aspect of the write cache is the endurance. Additional capacity, beyond 600 GB, will be used by the device for endurance and garbage collection and as such will be very welcome for the caching tier in an all-flash configuration as this. Another decision could be to create a smaller disk group, however it should be noted that a smaller disk group could lead to lower deduplication efficiency and smaller write cache devices with no spare capacity may also have a lower life span as a result of lower endurance.

Summary

As this chapter has demonstrated, it is really important to select your hardware carefully. Selection of a disk type, for instance, can impact your potential performance. Other components, such as disk controllers, can have an impact on the operational effort involved with VSAN.

Think about your configuration before you make a purchase decision. As mentioned earlier, VMware offers a great alternative in the VSAN ready node program. These servers are optimized and configured for VSAN, taking away much of the complexity that comes with hardware selection.

## Chapter 10

Troubleshooting, Monitoring, and Performance

This chapter discusses the extensive suite of tools available to you to monitor and troubleshoot a VSAN environment, and also how to use these tools to investigate and quickly remedy issues on VSAN.

VSAN can leverage already-existing vSphere tools as well as some built-in tools specific to VSAN. This chapter covers the following tools:

- **Health check**: A built-in feature that runs a series of tests on your VSAN cluster and reports any anomalies.

- **ESXCLI**: The command-line interface (CLI) of the ESXi host.

- **Ruby vSphere console (RVC)**: A generic tool for managing vCenter Server instances, but that has also been extended to support VSAN.

- **Performance service:** A new feature available in VSAN 6.2 that provides detailed performance metrics on all aspects of VSAN.

- **VSAN observer**: A web-based performance utility that leverages RVC.

- **ESXTOP**: ESXi host performance monitoring tool.

It should also be noted that prior to VSAN 6.2 and the introduction of the performance service, traditional monitoring utilities, such as the vSphere Web Client, can continue to be used for VSAN, including performance views of individual VMs, and their respective VMDKs.

Health Check

We already introduced the health check in Chapter 7, "Management and Maintenance." In this chapter we will delve into it in far greater detail. This utility should be an administrator's starting point for any troubleshooting activity and most monitoring activities. The health check examines all aspects of a VSAN configuration, and reports back on any configuration issues or failures.

In the initial release of health check, which was made available for VSAN 6.0, administrators had to download the components from VMware and manually install them; first on vCenter Server, and then on the ESXi hosts that formed the VSAN cluster. However since the release of vSphere 6.0 U1, which include VSAN 6.1, the components required for the health check are pre-installed and always on. Administrators do not even need to enable the health check.

The VSAN health check is supported on both the Windows version of vCenter Server as well as the Linux/Appliance version.

All of the health checks that are available via the vSphere Web Client UI are also available via RVC, the Ruby vSphere console. We will discuss RVC in greater detail later on in this chapter.

Ask VMware

Another really useful aspect of the health check is the fact that every test has an "Ask VMware" link. For those of you not familiar with Ask VMware, these links will take administrators directly to a VMware knowledge base article detailing the purpose of the test, reasons why it might fail, and what can be done to remediate the situation. If any of the tests fail, administrators should always click on the Ask VMware button and read the associated KB article. In many cases, steps toward finding a resolution are offered. In others cases, administrators are urged to contact VMware support for further assistance. In Figure 10.1 a complete list of health checks is shown, as well as the location of the Ask VMware button. This can be clicked at any time to learn more about the actual health check.

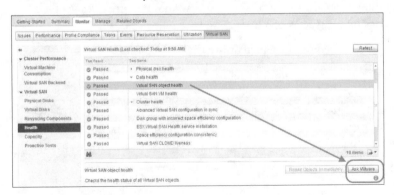

Figure 10.1   Ask VMware

Health Check Categories

In Virtual SAN 6.2, there are a total of seven health check test categories by default. These are:

- Virtual SAN HCL health
- Cluster health
- Network health
- Data health
- Limits health
- Physical disk health
- Virtual SAN performance service

If the VSAN is deployed as a stretched cluster, there is an additional set of health checks associated with that configuration. Let's look at these health checks in more detail.

Virtual SAN HCL Health

The Virtual SAN HCL health (HCL is short for hardware compatibility list) verifies that the storage controller hardware and driver version are on the HCL and are supported for this version of VSAN. If the controller or driver is not on the HCL, or are not supported for this version of VSAN (namely the ESXi version on which VSAN is running), then the health check displays a warning.

Another check is to verify that the Virtual SAN HCL DB is up-to-date. In other words, the checks that you are running are against a valid, up-to-date version of the HCL database. In Figure 10.2 we can see a warning being displayed because the HCL database is not up-to-date.

Figure 10.2   Warning: Virtual SAN HCL DB up-to-date

Since the HCL is updated regularly and frequently, administrators should update the local version of the database of these checks. This can be done online (if your vCenter Server has access to the VMware.com) or alternatively if your vCenter Server is not online, you can download a HCL DB file, and update it.

To update the version of the HCL DB online, simply click on the "Upload from file" or "Get latest version online" as shown in the health check test in Figure 10.2. An alternate method is to navigate to the VSAN cluster object in the vCenter Server inventory, select Manage, select Health and Performance, and then click on the "Get latest version online" button in the HCL database section. The "Last updated" field should now change to "Today," as per Figure 10.3.

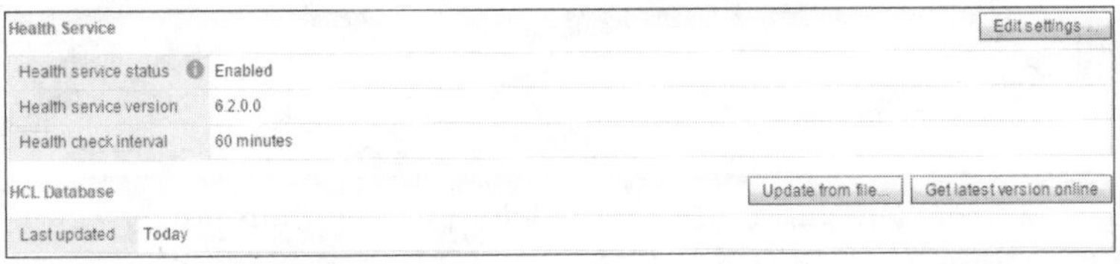

Figure 10.3   Last updated: Today

Once you have the latest version of the HCL DB, the test associated with the up-to-date HCL DB should now pass. You should also retest the health check and see if this update to the HCL DB has addressed any warnings associated with the storage controller hardware support and/or driver version (Figure 10.4).

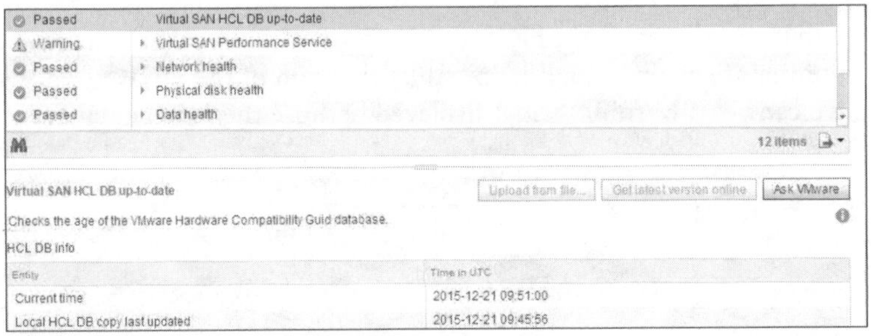

Figure 10.4   Virtual SAN HCL DB up-to-date passed

Note that additional health checks may be displayed in the HCL health if there are issues communicating with one or more hosts in the cluster from vCenter Server.

Cluster Health

The cluster health has a number of different tests associated with it. In the first place, it checks to make sure that the health check service is installed across all the hosts in the cluster. Second, it verifies that all hosts are running with an up-to-date version and finally that the health check service is working successfully.

There is also a health check to ensure that a number of advanced parameters relating to Virtual SAN are consistently set across all the hosts in the VSAN cluster. This will avoid any issues arising with having a subset of hosts using one value and another set of hosts using another value for a particular advanced setting. Note that this test does not validate if the value is a "good" value or if it is even the "default" value. It simply verifies that all ESXi hosts in the VSAN cluster have the same value.

One final check that is worth highlighting is the CLOMD live-ness test. CLOM, the cluster level object manager, runs a daemon called clomd on each ESXi host in the cluster. CLOM is responsible for creating, repairing, and migrating objects, and is critical for handling various workflows and failure handling in VSAN. If the clomd on any host is not responding for some reason, this test will fail.

A number of additional cluster checks were introduced with VSAN 6.2 to handle space efficiency. Amongst the new checks, space efficiency refers to the new deduplication and compression features that are new in VSAN 6.2. These checks basically ensure that all hosts and all disk groups in the cluster are configured correctly with regards to space efficiency and highlights if there are any errors discovered across the cluster. Figure 10.5 shows the complete list of cluster health tests.

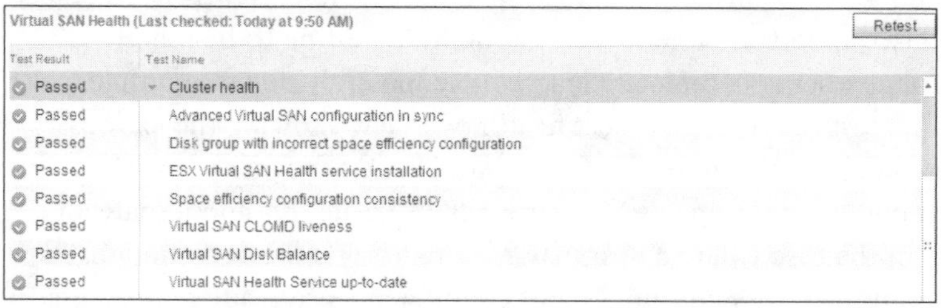

Virtual SAN Health (Last checked: Today at 9:50 AM)		Retest
Test Result	Test Name	
✓ Passed	▾ Cluster health	
✓ Passed	Advanced Virtual SAN configuration in sync	
✓ Passed	Disk group with incorrect space efficiency configuration	
✓ Passed	ESX Virtual SAN Health service installation	
✓ Passed	Space efficiency configuration consistency	
✓ Passed	Virtual SAN CLOMD liveness	
✓ Passed	Virtual SAN Disk Balance	
✓ Passed	Virtual SAN Health Service up-to-date	

Figure 10.5   Cluster health

Network Health

The network section of the health checks contains the most tests. It looks at all aspects of the network configuration, such as ensuring each host in the VSAN cluster has a VMkernel interface configured for VSAN traffic, being able to ping successfully between all hosts on the VSAN network interface, and that all interfaces are having matching multicast configurations.

There are also network checks that ensure all of the ESXi hosts in the VSAN cluster are attached to vCenter Server, that none of the hosts have connectivity issues, and that there are no hosts in the cluster that are not participating in the VSAN cluster.

This is also the first health check to visit if there is a network partition. This health check will tell you which hosts are in which partitions, or if there is a complete network partition and every host is isolated from every other host (the latter is usually an indication of a multicast issue on the network). Figure 10.6 shows the complete list of network health checks.

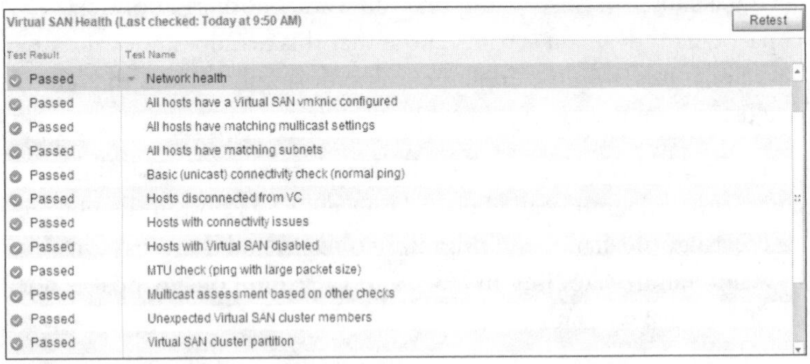

Virtual SAN Health (Last checked: Today at 9:50 AM)		Retest
Test Result	Test Name	
⊘ Passed	▾ Network health	
⊘ Passed	All hosts have a Virtual SAN vmknic configured	
⊘ Passed	All hosts have matching multicast settings	
⊘ Passed	All hosts have matching subnets	
⊘ Passed	Basic (unicast) connectivity check (normal ping)	
⊘ Passed	Hosts disconnected from VC	
⊘ Passed	Hosts with connectivity issues	
⊘ Passed	Hosts with Virtual SAN disabled	
⊘ Passed	MTU check (ping with large packet size)	
⊘ Passed	Multicast assessment based on other checks	
⊘ Passed	Unexpected Virtual SAN cluster members	
⊘ Passed	Virtual SAN cluster partition	

Figure 10.6   Network health

Data Health

Data health contains one test—Virtual SAN object health. This test checks that all of the objects deployed on the VSAN datastore are healthy. This test will highlight unhealthy objects. There are a number of reasons for an unhealthy object. These vary from an object having reduced availability due to components being rebuilt or waiting to be rebuilt. It could also be due to an object being completely inaccessible, possibly due to multiple failures in the cluster. The test provides an object health overview showing the various states of the objects. If VSAN is waiting for the 60-minute CLOMD timer to expire before rebuilding absent components, an administrator can override this and initiate an immediate rebuild (e.g., in the case where a host may have failed and is not coming back soon). It can also show administrators if rebuilding of components is already in progress.

Limits Health

Limits health checks a number of VSAN cluster limits. In the "current cluster situation" test, it checks the component limit, which is currently 9,000 per host. It also checks the disk space utilization and finally checks the read cache reservation, and if any of these are over the limits threshold, a warning is thrown.

An additional limit check examines the impact a host failure will have on the limits in the cluster. If any of the limits are exceeded when a host failure is taken into account, another warning is raised. This is in some ways similar to admission control in vSphere HA, in which it assists administrators in monitoring whether or not there are enough resources for VSAN to self-heal in the case of a failure.

Physical Disk Health

Physical disk health contains a significant number of checks that examines multiple aspects of the VSAN storage. The overall disks health check looks for multiple issues on the physical disk drives, including surface issues, controller issues, driver issues, and issues with the I/O stack. This test will also fail if there are any errors encountered in this health check, such as metadata health, congestion, software state, or disk capacity problems. If this test fails, administrators need to look at what other tests have failed to determine the root cause.

The component limit health test verifies that the upper limit of number of components per disk has not been exceeded. This is quite a large figure, in the region of 50,000, but this health check test will highlight if any disk is reaching saturation from a component count perspective.

Congestion is another interesting test for administrators. This can be an indicator that VSAN might be running at reduced performance. Reasons for congestion are varied, and usually require further investigation. Some examples are an undersized VSAN cluster for the workload running on it, bad hardware/driver/firmware on the storage controller or even software problems.

Disk capacity reports warnings if physical disk usage is starting to become an issue. If the physical disk space is below 80%, then the test reports as OK (green). If the usage of the disk is between 80% and 95%, health will show a warning (yellow). If the usage is above 95%, an alert (red) is thrown by the health check. Threshold is 80% where automatic rebalancing starts to occur.

One last set of tests to mention in the physical disk health is the memory pool tests. Although unlikely to occur, these tests check to ensure that the heaps and slabs used by Virtual SAN are not running low. Should the health check tests show warnings, the advice is to contact VMware support to determine the reason why. Running low on memory pools can lead to performance issues or even operational failures.

Figure 10.7 shows a complete list of physical disk health checks. Other health checks might appear if there is difficulty in communicating with a particular disk.

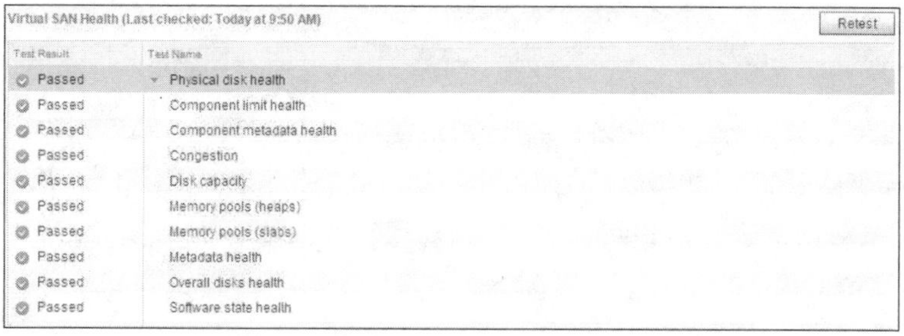

Figure 10.7   Physical disk health

VSAN Stretched Cluster

VSAN 6.1 introduced a set of health checks for the VSAN stretched cluster use case. These looked at all the configuration aspects of stretched cluster and provide guidance if any of the health checks fail. This is an excellent starting point for anyone considering deploying VSAN in a stretched cluster configuration. Further information on VSAN stretched cluster may be found in Chapter 8, "Interoperability."

VSAN Performance Service

The final health check is related to a new feature of VSAN 6.2, namely the performance service. If the performance service has not been configured, this test will throw a warning stating that the Stats DB Object is not found, as per Figure 10.8.

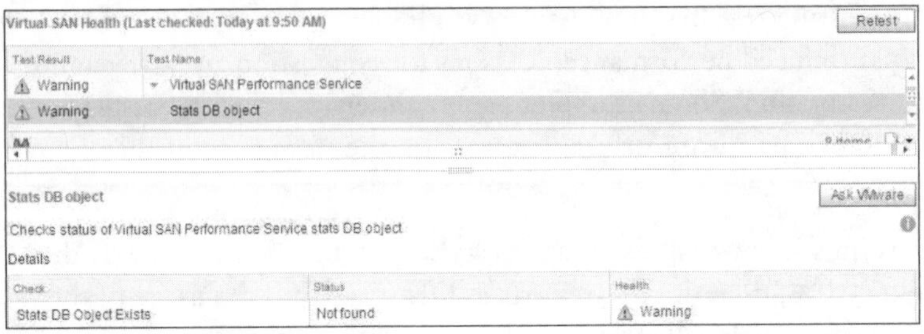

Figure 10.8   Performance service health when disabled

When the performance service has been enabled (we will see how to do this shortly) the Virtual SAN performance service health check now has a number of additional health checks that hopefully all show OK/passed status, as per Figure 10.9. These tests ensure that all hosts are contributing data to the performance service, and that the Stats DB Object (which is in fact a VM home namespace object on the VSAN datastore) is healthy.

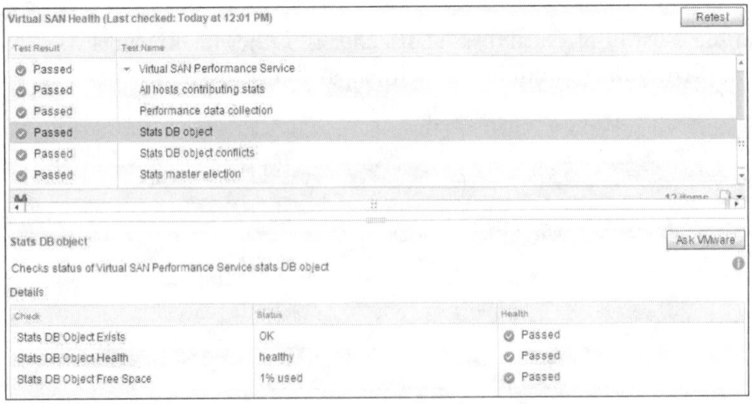

Figure 10.9   Performance service health when enabled

Proactive Health Checks

Before leaving health checks, there is another feature of the health checks that is worth mentioning. This is of course the set of proactive health checks that are also included with the health check feature. These proactive health checks will run a set of tests that give you peace of mind that everything is functioning as expected in your VSAN cluster. Note that VMware does not recommend running these tests in production. These tests are primarily used to ensure everything is working as expected prior to placing VSAN into production, or during a proof-of-concept. There are three proactive tests:

- VM creation test
- Multicast performance test
- Storage performance test

To access the proactive tests, select the cluster object in the vCenter Server inventory, and then select the Monitor tab, then Virtual SAN, and finally proactive tests. This will display the list of proactive tests that can then be selected and started by clicking on the start icon on the UI. When a test is selected, the start icon turns green, which means you can now start the test. Let's look at each of the tests in more detail as shown in Figure 10.10.

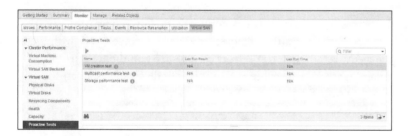

Figure 10.10   Proactive tests

VM Creation Test

The VM creation test takes about 20 to 40 seconds to run, depending on the size of the cluster. The test creates a virtual machine on each host in the cluster, and then deletes the virtual machine afterwards. The task console can be monitoring to track the creation and deletion of virtual machines. This is a very useful test to verify that virtual machines can indeed be created on the VSAN datastore before starting the deployment of actual production-ready virtual machines. If there is an issue with deploying a virtual machine during the VM creation proactive test, the test will either fail immediately or it will timeout within 3 minutes. This test uses the default VM storage policy for the VM. It verifies a number of aspects of VSAN operations. It verifies that the network is configured properly on all the hosts, that the VSAN stack is operational on each host, and that the creation, deletion, and ability to do I/O to VSAN objects is all functioning. The test results will report which hosts failed and which hosts passed the test, and further diagnosis can then be carried out on the problematic host or hosts. Figure 10.11 is the result of a successful run of the VM creation test on a 4-node VSAN cluster.

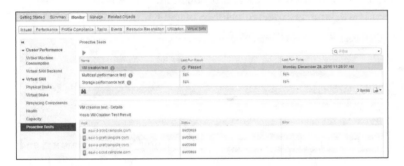

Figure 10.11   VM creation test

Multicast Performance Tests

This next test verifies that there is not only network connectivity between all of the hosts in the VSAN cluster, but also that it has sufficient speed and performance to allow the VSAN cluster to function as expected. The test selects one host to run the tests from, and then reports on the bandwidth (MB/s) achieved. In this 4-node cluster, we can see that VSAN was able to achieve over 80 MB/s on the 10 Gb network. This meets VSAN's network requirements, so the test has succeeded (see Figure 10.12).

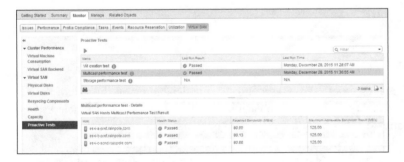

Figure 10.12   Multicast performance test

If the multicast performance test fails, one should examine the network configuration. If some of the hosts succeeded, and others failed, see if there is a configuration pattern that is shared by the hosts that succeeded and the hosts that failed. Are they on different switches for example? Perhaps the link/pipe between switches is not configured correctly, or does not have enough bandwidth. Multicast is an important component of VSAN, and administrators need to ensure it is configured correctly and functioning as expected before placing the VSAN into production.

Storage Performance Tests

It is possible that administrators will make significant use of this last proactive test. The nice thing about the storage performance test is that administrators can control the length of time that this test should run for. This means that administrators can run this overnight when VSAN is first deployed, and in fact there are different workloads that can be chosen for this exact purpose as shown in Figure 10.13.

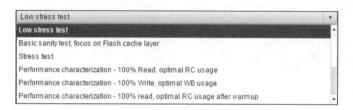

Figure 10.13   Storage performance test workloads

If the test runs overnight, and everything passes, then you have peace of mind that all of the storage components (controller hardware, driver, firmware, cache tier devices, and capacity tier devices) are functioning correctly. If the test fails, then you have also managed to catch the issue before VSAN has been placed into production. As well as selecting a length of time for the test to run, and the type of performance check to run, administrators can also choose a particular VM storage policy. In previous versions of VSAN, it was always a RAID-1 configuration that was tested. With the release of VSAN 6.2, RAID-5 or RAID-6 policies can also now be selected.

It should now be obvious that the health check is the best tool to use when monitoring or troubleshooting a Virtual SAN cluster. This should be the first tool to use when it comes to analyzing anomalies on the VSAN cluster. The integration with Ask VMware, and the multiple KB articles available to describe each test is extremely useful and should empower administrators to root cause many issues on the cluster.

However, there are other tools available for monitoring and troubleshooting VSAN alongside the health check. In the initial release of VSAN, these were the only tools available, as the health check was only made available in VSAN 6.0. We will examine these additional tools next.

ESXCLI

ESXi 5.5 U1 introduced a new ESXi CLI (ESXCLI) namespace: esxcli vsan. This has a selection of additional namespaces that can be used for examining, monitoring, and configuring the VSAN cluster, as demonstrated in Example 10.1:

Example 10.1   esxcli vsan Command Options

```
~ # esxcli vsan
esxcli vsan
Usage: esxcli vsan {cmd} [cmd options]

Available Namespaces:
cluster          Commands for VSAN host cluster configuration
datastore        Commands for VSAN datastore configuration
network          Commands for VSAN host network configuration
storage          Commands for VSAN physical storage configuration
faultdomain      Commands for VSAN fault domain configuration
maintenancemode  Commands for VSAN maintenance mode operation
policy           Commands for VSAN storage policy configuration
trace            Commands for VSAN trace configuration
```

The sections that follow take a look at some of the options available.

esxcli vsan datastore

The esxcli vsan datastore namespace provides commands for VSAN datastore configuration. There is very little that can be done here other than get and set the name of the VSAN datastore. By default, the VSAN datastore name is vsanDatastore. If you do plan on changing the vsanDatastore name, do this at the cluster level via the vSphere Web Client. It is highly recommended that if you are managing multiple VSAN clusters from the same vCenter Server then the VSAN datastores are given unique, easily identifiable names, as shown in Example 10.2.

Example 10.2   esxcli vsan datastore Command Options

```
~ # esxcli vsan datastore
Usage: esxcli vsan datastore {cmd} [cmd options]

Available Namespaces:
   name                     Commands for configuring VSAN datastore name.
```

```
~ # esxcli vsan datastore name
Usage: esxcli vsan datastore name {cmd} [cmd options]
Available Commands:
   get                               Get VSAN datastore name.
   set                               Configure VSAN datastore name. In
general, Rename

                                     should always be done at cluster
level. Across a VSAN

                                     cluster VSAN datastore name should be
in sync.

~ # esxcli vsan datastore name get
   Name: vsanDatastore
```

esxcli vsan network

This namespace provides commands for VSAN network configuration. It is somewhat more useful than the previous *datastore* namespace as it allows you to list the current configuration, clear the current configuration, restore the VSAN network configuration (this is used during the boot process by ESXi, and is not meant for customer invocation), as well as remove an interface from the VSAN network configuration, as shown in Example 10.3.

Example 10.3   esxcli vsan network Command Options

```
~ # esxcli vsan network
Usage: esxcli vsan network {cmd} [cmd options]

Available Namespaces:
   ip          Commands for configuring IP network for VSAN.
   ipv4        Compatibility alias for "ip"

Available Commands:
   clear       Clear the VSAN network configuration.
   list        List the network configuration currently in use by VSAN.
   remove      Remove an interface from the VSAN network configuration.
   restore     Restore the persisted VSAN network configuration.

~ # esxcli vsan network list
Interface
   VmkNic Name: vmk2
```

```
IP Protocol: IP
Interface UUID: a6997656-d456-5d5f-091a-ecf4bbd69680
Agent Group Multicast Address: 224.2.3.4
Agent Group IPv6 Multicast Address: ff19::2:3:4
Agent Group Multicast Port: 23451
Master Group Multicast Address: 224.1.2.3
Master Group IPv6 Multicast Address: ff19::1:2:3
Master Group Multicast Port: 12345
Host Unicast Channel Bound Port: 12321
Multicast TTL: 5
```

What is interesting to view here is the multicast information. If you cast your mind back to the requirements in Chapter 2, "VSAN Prerequisites and Requirements for Deployment," you might remember that there is a requirement to allow multicast traffic between ESXi hosts participating in the VSAN cluster.

Another interesting point to note is that the initial release of VSAN supported IPv4 only. VSAN 6.2 introduces support for IPv6. However, it is the multicast details that are of most interest. The Agent Group Multicast Port corresponds to the *cmmds* port that is opened on the ESXi firewall when VSAN is enabled. The first IP address, 224.2.3.4, is used for the master/backup communication, whereas the second address, 224.1.2.3, is used for the agents. `esxcli vsan network list` is a useful command to view the network configuration and status should a network partition occur.

Additional commands that can be useful for troubleshooting networking problems are as follows:

- `esxcli network diag ping`: Tests the responsiveness of a VMkernel port

- `esxcli network ip neighbor list`: Displays address resolution protocol (ARP) cache entries for all other VSAN nodes on the network

- `esxcli network ip connection list`: Displays the user datagram protocol (UDP) connection information

- `tcpdump-uw`: Sniffs the network traffic

esxcli vsan storage

This namespace is used for storage configuration, and includes options on how VSAN should claim disks, as well as the ability to add and remove physical disks to VSAN.

The command `esxcli vsan storage automode` allows you to get or set the autoclaim option. If it is disabled, the cluster is in manual mode, as shown in Example 10.4:

Example 10.4   esxcli vsan storage Command Options

```
~ # esxcli vsan storage
Usage: esxcli vsan storage {cmd} [cmd options]


Available Namespaces:
  automode          Commands for configuring VSAN storage auto claim mode.
  diskgroup         Commands for configuring VSAN diskgroups
  tag               Commands to add/remove tags for VSAN storage


Available Commands:
  add               Add physical disk for VSAN usage.
  list              List VSAN storage configuration.
  remove            Remove physical disks from VSAN disk groups.
~ # esxcli vsan storage automode
Usage: esxcli vsan storage automode {cmd} [cmd options]
Available Commands:
  get                          Get status of storage auto claim mode.
  set                          Configure storage auto claim mode
```

To display the capacity tier and cache tier devices that have been claimed and are in use by VSAN from a particular ESXi host, you may use the list option. In this particular configuration, which is an all-flash configuration, SSDs are used for the capacity tier devices and a Micron PCI-E device is used for the cache tier. All devices have a true flag against the field Used by this host, indicating that they have been claimed by VSAN and the Is SSD field indicates the type of device (true for flash devices), as shown in Example 10.5.

Example 10.5   esxcli vsan storage list

```
~ # esxcli vsan storage list
naa.500a07510f86d69e
   Device: naa.500a07510f86d69e
   Display Name: naa.500a07510f86d69e
   Is SSD: true
   VSAN UUID: 5229022d-deb5-bced-0efc-a7dc8c38ac45
   VSAN Disk Group UUID: 5253f4bf-1b26-6098-88f5-d8e9ed255359
   VSAN Disk Group Name: t10.ATA_____Micron_P420m2DMTFDGAR1T4MAX_____
___0000000014080C116FB2
   Used by this host: true
```

```
     In CMMDS: true
     On-disk format version: 3
     Deduplication: true
     Compression: true
     Checksum: 10274305517717035587
     Checksum OK: true
     Is Capacity Tier: true


naa.500a07510f86d6ae
     Device: naa.500a07510f86d6ae
     Display Name: naa.500a07510f86d6ae
     Is SSD: true
     VSAN UUID: 522b6fae-7730-bbc4-afd1-64890001d99c
     VSAN Disk Group UUID: 5253f4bf-1b26-6098-88f5-d8e9ed255359
     VSAN Disk Group Name: t10.ATA_____Micron_P420m2DMTFDGAR1T4MAX_____
____0000000014080C116FB2
     Used by this host: true
     In CMMDS: true
     On-disk format version: 3
     Deduplication: true
     Compression: true
     Checksum: 10405036710067954474
     Checksum OK: true
     Is Capacity Tier: true


naa.500a07510f86d683
     Device: naa.500a07510f86d683
     Display Name: naa.500a07510f86d683
     Is SSD: true
     VSAN UUID: 524b8701-1b77-9ff3-015c-87d04769e753
     VSAN Disk Group UUID: 5253f4bf-1b26-6098-88f5-d8e9ed255359
     VSAN Disk Group Name: t10.ATA_____Micron_P420m2DMTFDGAR1T4MAX_____
____0000000014080C116FB2
     Used by this host: true
     In CMMDS: true
     On-disk format version: 3
     Deduplication: true
     Compression: true
     Checksum: 13174218208763526163
     Checksum OK: true
     Is Capacity Tier: true
```

```
t10.ATA_____Micron_P420m2DMTFDGAR1T4MAX_____0000000014080C116
FB2
```

Device: t10.ATA_____Micron_P420m2DMTFDGAR1T4MAX_____00000000140
80C116FB2

Display Name: t10.ATA_____Micron_P420m2DMTFDGAR1T4MAX_____00000
00014080C116FB2

Is SSD: true

VSAN UUID: 5253f4bf-1b26-6098-88f5-d8e9ed255359

VSAN Disk Group UUID: 5253f4bf-1b26-6098-88f5-d8e9ed255359

VSAN Disk Group Name: t10.ATA_____Micron_P420m2DMTFDGAR1T4MAX_____
____0000000014080C116FB2

Used by this host: true

In CMMDS: true

On-disk format version: 3

Deduplication: true

Compression: true

Checksum: 11854951762888586646

Checksum OK: true

Is Capacity Tier: false

If you want to use ESXCLI to *add* new disks to a disk group on VSAN, you can use the add option. There is a different option to choose depending on whether the disk is a magnetic disk (MD) or an SSD (-d|--disks or -s|--ssd, respectively). Note that only disks that are empty and have no partition information can be added to VSAN.

There is also a remove option that allows you to remove magnetic disks and SSDs from disk groups on VSAN. It should go without saying that you need to be very careful with this command and removing disks from a disk group on VSAN should be considered a maintenance task. The remove option removes all the partition information (and thus all VSAN information) from the disk supplied as an argument to the command. Note that when a cache tier device is removed from a disk group, the whole disk group becomes unavailable.

If you have disks that were once used by VSAN and you now want to repurpose these disks for some other use (Virtual Machine File System [VMFS], Raw Device Mappings [RDM], or in the case of SSDs, vSphere Flash Read Cache [vFRC]), you can use the remove option to clean up any VSAN partition information left behind on the disk.

Additional useful commands for looking at disks and controllers include the following:

- esxcli storage core adapter list: Displays the driver and adapter description, which can be useful to check that your adapter is on the HCL

- esxcfg-info -s | grep "==+SCSI Interface" -A 18: Displays lots of information, but most importantly shows the queue depth of the device, which is very important for performance

- `esxcli storage core device smart get -d` *XXX*: Displays SMART statistics about your drive, especially SSDs. Very useful command to display Wear-Leveling information, and overall health of your SSD

- `esxcli storage core device stats get`: Displays overall disk statistics

esxcli vsan cluster

The `esxcli vsan cluster` command allows the ESXi host on which the command is run to get VSAN cluster information, as well as allow the ESXi host to leave or join a VSAN cluster. This can be very helpful in a scenario where vCenter Server is unavailable and a particular host needs to be removed from the VSAN cluster. The restore functionality is not intended for customer invocation and is used by ESXi during the boot process to restore the active cluster configuration from configuration file, as shown in Example 10.6:

Example 10.6   esxcli vsan cluster Command Options

```
~ # esxcli vsan cluster
Usage: esxcli vsan cluster {cmd} [cmd options]

Available Namespaces:
  preferredfaultdomain  Commands for configuring a preferred fault domain
                        for Virtual SAN.
  unicastagent          Commands for configuring unicast agents for Virtual
                        SAN.


Available Commands:
  get                   Get information about the Virtual SAN cluster that
                        this host is joined to.
  join                  Join the host to a Virtual SAN cluster.
  leave                 Leave the Virtual SAN cluster the host is currently
                        joined to.
  new                   Create a Virtual SAN cluster with current host
                        joined. A random sub-cluster UUID will be
                        generated.
  restore               Restore the persisted Virtual SAN cluster
                        configuration.
```

A `get` option to this command is useful for gathering information about the local ESXi hosts (node) health, as well as its role in the cluster. In Example 10.7, you can see that this ESXi host is an *agent* and its status is healthy. Other states, as was discussed in Chapter 5,

"Architectural Details," are *master* and *backup*. These states relate to the role the host plays for the clustering service (CMMDS). Refer to Chapter 5 if you need a refresher on the various roles of hosts in VSAN.

Example 10.7   esxcli vsan cluster get

```
~ # esxcli vsan cluster get
Cluster Information
   Enabled: true
   Current Local Time: 2015-12-28T12:04:04Z
   Local Node UUID: 5676978a-6c3d-28fc-9ea2-ecf4bbd69680
   Local Node Type: NORMAL
   Local Node State: AGENT
   Local Node Health State: HEALTHY
   Sub-Cluster Master UUID: 56703560-1a41-3037-9a8c-ecf4bbd5b260
   Sub-Cluster Backup UUID: 56702cdc-d064-d2a5-8457-ecf4bbd58600
   Sub-Cluster UUID: 5231dfdb-cfe7-aa13-ccfc-2a49e09e85b4
   Sub-Cluster Membership Entry Revision: 3
   Sub-Cluster Member Count: 4
   Sub-Cluster Member UUIDs: 56703560-1a41-3037-9a8c-ecf4bbd5b260,
5676978a-6c3d-28fc-9ea2-ecf4bbd69680, 56702cdc-d064-d2a5-8457-ecf4bbd58600,
56707c8b-3353-d670-c080-ecf4bbd59370
   Sub-Cluster Membership UUID: aad47756-b3ac-e5d8-7fbd-ecf4bbd5b260
```

One additional useful piece of information from this output is the subcluster member UUIDs. There are four entries in this field in total, indicating that this is a 4-node cluster. This is always useful to show how many nodes each host thinks is participating in the cluster when it comes to troubleshooting partition issues. If you want to display which host corresponds to which UUID, you can use the esxcli system uuid get *<uuid>* command.

esxcli vsan faultdomain

Fault domains were introduced in VSAN 6.0, and allow VSAN to be rack aware. What this means is that components belonging to objects that are part of the same virtual machine can be placed not just in different hosts, but in different racks. This means that should an entire rack fail (e.g., power failure), there is still a full set of virtual machine components available so the VM remains accessible.

```
~# esxcli vsan faultdomain
Usage: esxcli vsan faultdomain {cmd} [cmd options]
```

```
Available Commands:
  get            Get the fault domain name for this host.
  reset          Reset Host fault domain to default value
  set            Set the fault domain for this host
```

Fault domains are also used for VSAN stretched cluster and 2-node configurations. These were already discussed earlier in the book. It is unlikely that you will need to use this `esxcli vsan faultdomain` namespace for such a configuration. VMware recommends using the vSphere Web Client UI for all fault domain, stretched cluster, and 2-node (ROBO) configurations.

esxcli vsan maintenancemode

`maintenancemode` is an interesting command option. You might think this would allow you to enter and exit maintenance, but it doesn't. All this option allows you to do is to cancel an in-progress VSAN maintenance mode operation. This could still prove very useful, though, especially when you have decided to place a host in maintenance mode and selected the Full Data Migration option and want to stop this data migration process (which can take a very long time) and instead use the Ensure Access option. Note that you can place a node in maintenance mode leveraging `esxcli system maintenanceMode set -e true -m noAction` where "-m" specifies if components need to be moved or not.

```
~ # esxcli vsan maintenancemode
Usage: esxcli vsan maintenancemode {cmd} [cmd options]


Available Commands:
  cancel            Cancel an in-progress VSAN maintenance mode operation.
```

esxcli vsan policy

Virtual machine (VM) storage policies are something that we have covered in great detail in previous chapters of this book. VSAN associates a default storage policy with the VM's storage objects and esxcli vsan policy namespace shown in Example 10.8 is one way to examine and modify this default storage policy:

Example 10.8   esxcli vsan policy Command Options

```
~ # esxcli vsan policy
Usage: esxcli vsan policy {cmd} [cmd options]
```

```
Available Commands:
   cleardefault                  Clear default VSAN storage policy values.
   getdefault                    Get default VSAN storage policy values.
   setdefault                    Set default VSAN storage policy values.
~ # esxcli vsan policy getdefault

Policy Class   Policy Value
------------   --------------------------------------------------------
cluster        (("hostFailuresToTolerate" i1))
vdisk          (("hostFailuresToTolerate" i1))
vmnamespace    (("hostFailuresToTolerate" i1))
vmswap         (("hostFailuresToTolerate" i1) ("forceProvisioning" i1))
vmem           (("hostFailuresToTolerate" i1) ("forceProvisioning" i1))
```

Here we can see the different VM storage objects that make up a VM deployed on a
VSAN datastore, and we can also see the default policy values. Although the policy value
is called host failures to tolerate, it is actually equivalent to the number of failures to
tolerate in the vSphere Web Client. All the objects will tolerate at least one failure in
the cluster and remain persistent. The class vdisk refers to VM disk objects (VMDKs).
It also covers snapshot deltas. The class vmnamespace is the VM home namespace
where the configuration files, metadata files, and log files belonging to the VM are
stored. The vmswap policy class is, of course, the VM swap. One final note for vmswap
is that it also has a forceProvisioning value. This means that even if there are not
enough resources in the VSAN cluster to meet the requirement to provision both VM
swap replicas to meet the failures to tolerate requirement, VSAN will still provision the
VM with a single VM swap instance. A detailed discussion on force provisioning can
be found in the various chapters throughout this book. The final entry is vmem. This is
the snapshot memory object when a snapshot is taken of a VM, and there is a request to
also snapshot memory. In the initial release of VSAN, the virtual machine memory was
stored in the VM home namespace. In VSAN 6.0, snapshot memory was moved to its
own object.

If you do want to change the default policy to something other than these settings, there
is a considerable amount of information in the help file about each of the policies. The
command to set a default policy is as follows:

```
# esxcli vsan policy setdefault <-p|--policy> <-c|--policy-class>
```

However, VMware recommends avoiding configuring policies from the ESXi host. This is
because you would have to repeat all of the steps on each of the hosts in the cluster. This
is time consuming, tedious, and prone to user error. The preferred method to modify
policies is via the vSphere Web Client, or if that is not possible, via RVC, the Ruby

vSphere client. However, for VM swap, this is the only way to change the default policy as it cannot be changed via the Web Client or RVC.

Of course, we did not cover all of the possible policy settings in the default, but you can certainly include any of the supported policy settings in the default policy if you wish. Take care while changing the default policy, as highlighted a number of times earlier in the book. Setting unrealistic default values for number of failures to tolerate or flash read cache reservation, for example, may lead to the inability to provision any VMs. Using the help output from the `esxcli vsan policy setdefault` command, further details are provided about the policy settings that are displayed here for your information:

- `cacheReservation`: Flash capacity reserved as read cache for the storage object. This setting is only applicable on hybrid configurations; it is not used on all-flash configurations since these configurations do not have a read cache. It is specified as a percentage of the logical size of the object. To be used only for addressing read performance issues. Other objects cannot use reserved flash capacity. Unreserved flash is shared fairly among all objects. It is specified in parts per million. Default value: `0`, Maximum value: `1000000`.

- `forceProvisioning`: If this option is `yes`, the object will be provisioned even if the requirements specified in the storage policy cannot be satisfied by the resources currently available in the cluster. VSAN will try to bring the object into compliance if and when resources become available. Default value: `No`.

- `hostFailuresToTolerate`: Defines the number of host, disk, or network failures a storage object can tolerate. For n failures tolerated, $n + 1$ copies of the object are created, and $2n + 1$ hosts contributing storage are required. Default value: `1`, Maximum value: `3`.

- `stripeWidth`: The number of capacity drives across which each replica of storage object is striped. A value higher than 1 may result in better performance (e.g., on hybrid systems when flash read cache misses need to get serviced from magnetic disk), but there is no guarantee that performance will improve with an increased `stripeWidth`. Default value: `1`, Maximum value: `12`.

- `proportionalCapacity`: Percentage of the logical size of the storage object that will be reserved (similar in some respects to thick provisioning) upon VM provisioning. The rest of the storage object is thin provisioned. Default value: `0%`, Maximum value: `100%`.

- `iopsLimit`: New in VSAN 6.2. This setting defines upper normalized IOPS limit for a disk. The IO rate on a disk is measured and if the rate exceeds the IOPS limit,

IO will be delayed to keep it under the limit. If the value is set to 0, there is no limit. Default value: 0.

- `replicaPreference`: New in VSAN 6.2. This setting is used to select RAID-5 or RAID-6 over the default RAID-1/mirror configurations for objects. If a replication method of capacity is chosen over performance (which is the default), and the number of failures to tolerate is set to 1, then RAID-5 is implemented. If a replication method of capacity is chosen and the number of failures to tolerate is set to 2, then RAID-6 is implemented. Note that capacity is only effective when the number of failures to tolerate is set to 1 or 2. Default value: Performance.

The other argument that needs to be included with the `setdefault` command is the `-c|--policy-class` option. This is the VSAN policy class whose default value is being set. The options are `cluster`, `vdisk`, `vmnamespace`, `vmswap`—one of which must be specified in the command.

Lastly, a word about `cluster`, which is one of the policy class options, but is not a VM storage object like `vmnamespace`, `vdisk`, or `vmswap`. This option is used as a catchall for any objects deployed on a VSAN datastore that are not part of a VM's storage objects. Although we don't envision non-VM storage object types being placed on the VSAN datastore, this is there as a "just in case."

esxcli vsan trace

`esxcli vsan trace` is a troubleshooting and diagnostic utility and should not be used without the guidance of VMware global support services (GSS). It is designed to capture internal diagnostics from VSAN for further analysis. The options are shown in Example 10.9 simply for completeness:

Example 10.9   esxcli vsan trace Command Options

```
~ # esxcli vsan trace
Usage: esxcli vsan trace {cmd} [cmd options]

Available Commands:
   set                     Configure VSAN trace. Please note: This command is not
                             thread safe.

~ # esxcli vsan trace set -h
Usage: esxcli vsan trace set [cmd options]
```

```
Description:
    set                    Configure VSAN trace. Please note: This command is not
                               thread safe.
Cmd options:
    -f|--numfiles=<long>   Log file rotation for VSAN trace files.
    -p|--path=<str>          Path to store VSAN trace files.
    -r|--reset                 When set to true, reset defaults for VSAN trace
                                   files.
    -s|--size=<long>         Maximum size of VSAN trace files in MB.
```

Additional Non-ESXCLI Commands for Troubleshooting VSAN

In addition to the esxcli vsan namespace commands, there are a few additional CLI commands found on an ESXi host that may prove useful for monitoring and troubleshooting.

osfs-ls

osfs-ls is more of a troubleshooting command than anything else. It is useful for displaying the contents of the VSAN datastore. The command is not in your search path, but can be found in the location shown in Example 10.10. In this command, we are listing the contents of a VM folder on the VSAN datastore. This can prove useful if the datastore file view is not working correctly from the vSphere Web Client, or it is reporting inaccurate information for some reason or other:

Example 10.10   osfs-ls Command

```
~ # cd /vmfs/volumes/vsanDatastore
~ # /usr/lib/vmware/osfs/bin/osfs-ls win2k8x64-1_1/

.fbb.sf
.fdc.sf
.pbc.sf
.sbc.sf
.vh.sf
.pb2.sf
.sdd.sf
```

```
.6cc6d752-a00c-ad67-268e-0010185def78.lck
win2k8x64-1.vmdk
win2k8x64-1.nvram
win2k8x64-1.vmx
win2k8x64-1.vmxf
win2k8x64-1.vmsd
win2k8x64-1_2.vmdk
.dvsData
.f6ccd752-5843-0da9-4149-0010185def78.lck
win2k8x64-1_1.vmdk
vmware.log
.d8dad752-a897-8b6a-8a96-0010185def78.lck
```

cmmds-tool

cmmds-tool is another useful troubleshooting command from the ESXi host and can be used to display lots of VSAN information. It can be used to display information such as configuration, metadata, and state about the cluster, hosts in the cluster, and VM storage objects. Many other high-level diagnostic tools leverage information obtained via cmmds-tool. As you can imagine, it has a number of options, as shown in Example 10.11.

Example 10.11   cmmds-tool Command Options

```
~ # cmmds-tool
usage: cmmds-tool <cmd> <options>
commands:
    add                 Adds an entry from stdin. On successful exit the
                            entry is guaranteed to be in the directory
    delete              Deletes matching entries. On successful exit the
                            entry will be deleted from the directory
    dump                Dumps first matching entry to stdout
    find                Finds matching entries
    wait                Waits for a matching entry to appear
    waitdump            Waits for a matching entry to appear and dumps
                            the entry to stdout
    waitformembership   Waits for a membership entry to appear
    whoami                Get the node's uuid as used in the sub-cluster
```

```
    amimember           Check if I am the member in the current sub-cluster
    readdump            Reads a cmmds directory dump from a file
                            (specified with -d/--dumpfile) and
                            o/p to stdout in a given format specified
                            using -f option.
options:
    -o/--owner=<uuid>:        Entry owner
    -u/--uuid=<uuid>:         Entry uuid
    -t/--type=<int>|<name>: Entry type
    -r/--rev=<int>:           Entry revision (-1 for latest)
    -i/--timeout=<int>:       Max time for wait (0 for infinite wait)
    -f/--format=<fmt>:        Output format (fmt should be one of
                                      json/python/simple. Default is
'simple'
    -d/--dumpfile=<file>:     Filename to read the cmmds dump from.
    -p/--print-dump-hdr:      When CMMDS dump is read off the file,
should
                                      the dump file header be
printed as well
    -v/--verbose=<int>:       Verbosity level
    -h/--help:                Print this help text
```

The `find` option may be the most useful, especially when you want to discover information about the actual storage objects backing a VM. You can, for instance, see what the health is of a specific object. In Example 10.12, we want to find additional information about a disk object represented by UUID 52777432-f127-f001-d081-800a04cafb0e.

Example 10.12 cmmds-tool find <uuid>

```
~ # cmmds-tool find -u 52777432-f127-f001-d081-800a04cafb0e
owner=52ca9e00-b362-a040-eb2a-984be1047ad4(Health: Healthy)
    uuid=52777432-f127-f001-d081-800a04cafb0e type=DISK rev=0
    [content = (1587068342272 1100 1+10000000 1200000000 1+0 13400000
    10 i10 i15 11600000 10 116777216 i0
    5214b1a5-b6b1-3a3a-f8b6-ee4ecc7a8d0e
    "52d7b4db-515e86a0-383a-001b21168828")], errorStr=(null)
owner=52ca9e00-b362-a040-eb2a-984be1047ad4(Health: Healthy)
    uuid=52777432-f127-f001-d081-800a04cafb0e type=HEALTH_STATUS rev=0
    [content = (i0 1319401449472)], errorStr=(null)
```

```
owner=52ca9e00-b362-a040-eb2a-984be1047ad4(Health: Healthy)
    uuid=52777432-f127-f001-d081-800a04cafb0e type=DISK_USAGE rev=645
    [content = (118874368 10 10 10 10)], errorStr=(null)
owner=52ca9e00-b362-a040-eb2a-984be1047ad4(Health: Healthy)
    uuid=52777432-f127-f001-d081-800a04cafb0e type=DISK_STATUS rev=645
    [content = (1430420688896 10 10 i10 18 10 1261888 10 10 10 10 10 10
    10 10 1+0 i4)], errorStr=(null)
```

There are, of course, many other options available to this command that can run. For example, a -o *<owner>* will display information about all objects of which *<owner>* is the owner. This can be a considerable amount of output.

Type is another option, and can be specified with a -t option. From the preceding output, types such as DISK, HEALTH_STATUS, DISK_USAGE, and DISK_STATUS can be displayed. Other types include DOM_OBJECT, DOM_NAME, POLICY, CONFIG_STATUS, HA_METADATA, HOSTNAME, and so on.

Example 10.13 shows a list of hostnames taken from a 4-node cluster:

Example 10.13 cmmds-tool find <type>

```
~ # cmmds-tool find -t HOSTNAME

owner=56703560-1a41-3037-9a8c-ecf4bbd5b260(Health: Healthy) uuid=56703560-
1a41-3037-9a8c-ecf4bbd5b260 type=HOSTNAME rev=0 minHostVer=0  [content =
("esxi-c-scnd.rainpole.com")], errorStr=(null)

owner=56707c8b-3353-d670-c080-ecf4bbd59370(Health: Healthy) uuid=56707c8b-
3353-d670-c080-ecf4bbd59370 type=HOSTNAME rev=0 minHostVer=0  [content =
("esxi-d-scnd.rainpole.com")], errorStr=(null)

owner=56702cdc-d064-d2a5-8457-ecf4bbd58600(Health: Healthy) uuid=56702cdc-
d064-d2a5-8457-ecf4bbd58600 type=HOSTNAME rev=0 minHostVer=0  [content =
("esxi-b-pref.rainpole.com")], errorStr=(null)

owner=5676978a-6c3d-28fc-9ea2-ecf4bbd69680(Health: Healthy) uuid=5676978a-
6c3d-28fc-9ea2-ecf4bbd69680 type=HOSTNAME rev=0 minHostVer=0  [content =
("esxi-a-pref.rainpole.com")], errorStr=(null)
```

As you can see, this very powerful command enables you to do lots of investigation and troubleshooting from an ESXi host. In a scenario where a disk has failed in a large cluster, this command can prove helpful when trying to identify which storage objects have been impacted by this failure. Again, exercise caution when using this command. Alternatively, use only under the guidance of VMware support staff if you have concerns.

vdq

The vdq command serves two purposes and is really a great troubleshooting tool to have on the ESXi host. The first option to this command tells you whether disks on your ESXi host are eligible for VSAN, and if not, what the reason is for the disk being ineligible.

The second option to this command is that once VSAN has been enabled, you can use the command to display disk mapping information, which is essentially which SSD or flash devices and magnetic disks are grouped together in a disk group.

Let's first run the option to query all disks for eligibility for VSAN use. Example 10.14 is from a host that does not have VSAN:

Example 10.14   vdq -q

```
~ # vdq -q
[
   {
       "Name"      : "naa.500a07510f86d6c7",
       "VSANUUID" : "",
       "State"     : "Eligible for use by VSAN",
       "Reason"    : "None",
       "IsSSD"     : "1",
"IsCapacityFlash": "1",
       "IsPDL"     : "0",
   },

   {
       "Name"      : "naa.5000c50040e9dd73",
       "VSANUUID" : "",
       "State"     : "Eligible for use by VSAN",
       "Reason"    : "Non-local disk",
       "IsSSD"     : "0",
"IsCapacityFlash": "0",
       "IsPDL"     : "0",
   },
]
```

In the preceding example, the disk is available for VSAN to use. In other words it does not contain preexisting partitions. Example 10.15 shows the output taken from a host that has VSAN already enabled:

Example 10.15   vdq -q

```
~ # vdq -q
 [
   {
       "Name"      : "naa.500a07510f86d693",
       "VSANUUID" : "52db956f-4841-a25e-b20b-14ea25dbb0a5",
       "State"     : "In-use for VSAN",
       "Reason"    : "None",
       "IsSSD"     : "1",
"IsCapacityFlash": "1",
       "IsPDL"     : "0",
   },

   {
       "Name"      : "naa.500a07510f86d69e",
       "VSANUUID" : "5229022d-deb5-bced-0efc-a7dc8c38ac45",
       "State"     : "In-use for VSAN",
       "Reason"    : "None",
       "IsSSD"     : "1",
"IsCapacityFlash": "1",
       "IsPDL"     : "0",
   },

   {
       "Name"      : "t10.ATA_____Micron_P420m2DMTFDGAR1T4MAX_____
__0000000014080C116FB2",
       "VSANUUID" : "5253f4bf-1b26-6098-88f5-d8e9ed255359",
       "State"     : "In-use for VSAN",
       "Reason"    : "None",
       "IsSSD"     : "1",
"IsCapacityFlash": "0",
       "IsPDL"     : "0",
   },
{
       "Name"      : "mpx.vmhba32:C0:T0:L0",
       "VSANUUID" : "",
```

```
     "State"    : "Ineligible for use by VSAN",
     "Reason"   : "Has partitions",
     "IsSSD"    : "0",
"IsCapacityFlash": "0",
     "IsPDL"    : "0",
   },
]
```

As you can see, a number of devices have been claimed by VSAN, while another disk is ineligible because it already has partitions. In this example, the ineligible disk is the ESXi host boot disk. It also points out which disk is an SSD (IsSSD), if a flash device is being used as a capacity device in an all-flash VSAN configuration (IsCapacityFlash), and whether the disk is in a permanent device loss state (IsPDL).

The second useful option to the command is to dump out the VSAN disk mappings; in other words, which flash devices and which magnetic disks are in a disk group. Example 10.16 shows a sample output (which includes the -H option to make it more human readable):

Example 10.16   vdq –i -H

```
~ # vdq -i -H

Mappings:
   DiskMapping[0]:
            SSD:
t10.ATA_____Micron_P420m2DMTFDGAR1T4MAX_____0000000014080C116FB2
            MD:  naa.500a07510f86d693
            MD:  naa.500a07510f86d69e
            MD:  naa.500a07510f86d6ae
            MD:  naa.500a07510f86d6b6
            MD:  naa.500a07510f86d6b8
            MD:  naa.500a07510f86d6bc
            MD:  naa.500a07510f86d683
```

This command shows the SSD relationship to capacity devices, whether they are flash devices in the case of all-flash configurations or magnetic disks in the case of hybrid configurations. Note that even if these are flash devices, they are shown as MD (magnetic disks) in this output. The IsCapacityFlash field would need to be examined to see if these are flash devices (e.g., SSD) or not. This is very useful if you want to find out the disk group layout on a particular host from the command line. This command will quickly tell you which magnetic disks are fronted by which SSDs, especially when you have multiple disk groups defined on an ESXi host.

Although some of the commands shown in this section may prove useful to examine and monitor VSAN on an ESXi host basis, administrators ideally need something whereby they can examine the cluster as a whole. VMware recognized this very early on in the development of VSAN, and so introduced extensions to the RVC to allow a cluster-wide view of VSAN. The next topic delves into RVC.

Ruby vSphere Console

The previous section looked at ESXi host-centric commands for VSAN. These might be of some use when troubleshooting VSAN, but with large clusters, administrators may find themselves having to run the same set of commands over and over again on different hosts in the cluster. In this next section, we cover a tool that enables you to take a cluster-centric view of VSAN. Since version 5.5 U1, VMware vCenter Server contains a new component called the Ruby vSphere console (RVC). The RVC is also included on the VMware vCenter Virtual Appliance (VCVA). As mentioned in the introduction, RVC is a programmable interface that allows administrators to query the status of vCenter Server, clusters, hosts, storage, and networking. For VSAN, there are quite a number of programmable extensions to display a considerable amount of information that you need to know about a VSAN cluster. This section covers those VSAN extensions in RVC.

You can connect RVC to any vCenter Server. On the VCVA, you login via Secure Shell (SSH) and run rvc *<user>*@*<vc-ip>*.

For Windows-based Virtual Center environments, you need to open a command shell and navigate to c:\Program Files\VMware\Infrastructure\VirtualCenter Server\support\rvc. Here, you will find an rvc.bat file that you may need to edit to add appropriate credentials for your vCenter Server (by default, Administrator@localhost). Once those credentials have been set appropriately, simply run the rvc.bat file, type your password, and you are connected.

After you login, you will see a virtual file system, with the vCenter Server instance at the root. You can now begin to use navigation commands such as **cd** and **ls**, as well as tab completion to navigate the file system. The structure of the file system mimics the inventory items tree views that you find in the vSphere client. Therefore, you can run cd *<vCenter Server>*, followed by cd *<datacenter>*. You can use ~ to refer to your current datacenter, and all clusters are in the "computers" folder under your datacenter. Note that when you navigate to a folder/directory, the contents are listed with numeric values. These numeric values may also be used as shortcuts. For example, in the vCenter folder in

Example 10.17 there is only one datacenter, and it has a numeric value of 0 associated with it. We can then cd to 0, instead of typing out the full name of the datacenter:

Example 10.17 Navigating RVC

```
> ls
0 /
1 mia-cg07-vc01/
> cd 1
/mia-cg07-vc01> ls
0 mia-cg07-dc01 (datacenter)
/mia-cg07-vc01> cd 0
/mia-cg07-vc01/mia-cg07-dc01> ls
0 storage/
1 computers [host]/
2 networks [network]/
3 datastores [datastore]/
4 vms [vm]/
```

VSAN Commands

If you want to learn about any command, run *<command>* -help. You can also use help and help *<command-namespace>* (like help vm, help vm.ip) to learn more about commands. Because we are primarily interested in VSAN, let's take a look at what commands are available to us for monitoring and troubleshooting VSAN (see Example 10.18):

Example 10.18 help vsan

```
> help vsan
Namespaces:
health
perf
sizing
stretchedcluster
vsanmgmt

Commands:
apply_license_to_cluster: Apply license to VSAN
check_limits: Gathers (and checks) counters against limits
check_state: Checks state of VMs and VSAN objects
clear_disks_cache: Clear cached disks information
```

cluster_change_autoclaim: Enable/Disable autoclaim on a VSAN cluster

cluster_change_checksum: Enable/Disable VSAN checksum enforcement on a cluster

cluster_info: Print VSAN config info about a cluster or hosts

cluster_set_default_policy: Set default policy on a cluster

cmmds_find: CMMDS Find

disable_vsan_on_cluster: Disable VSAN on a cluster

disk_object_info: Fetch information about all VSAN objects on a given physical disk

disks_info: Print physical disk info about a host

disks_stats: Show stats on all disks in VSAN

enable_vsan_on_cluster: Enable VSAN on a cluster

enter_maintenance_mode: Put hosts into maintenance mode

Choices for vsan-mode: ensureObjectAccessibility, evacuateAllData, noAction

fix_renamed_vms: This command can be used to rename some VMs which get renamed by the VC in case of storage inaccessibility. It is possible for some VMs to get renamed to vmx file path. eg. "/vmfs/volumes/vsanDatastore/foo/foo.vmx". This command will rename this VM to "foo." This is the best we can do. This VM may have been named something else but we have no way to know. In this best effort command, we simply rename it to the name of its config file (without the full path and .vmx extension ofcourse!).

host_claim_disks_differently: Tags all devices of a certain model as certain type of device

host_consume_disks: Consumes all eligible disks on a host

host_evacuate_data: Evacuate hosts from VSAN cluster

host_exit_evacuation: Exit hosts' evacuation, bring them back to VSAN cluster as data containers

host_info: Print VSAN info about a host

host_wipe_non_vsan_disk: Wipe disks with partitions other than VSAN partitions

host_wipe_vsan_disks: Wipes content of all VSAN disks on hosts, by default wipe all disk groups

lldpnetmap: Gather LLDP mapping information from a set of hosts

obj_status_report: Print component status for objects in the cluster.

object_info: Fetch information about a VSAN object

object_reconfigure: Reconfigure a VSAN object

observer: Run observer

observer_process_statsfile: Analyze an offline observer stats file and produce static HTML

proactive_rebalance: Configure proactive rebalance for Virtual SAN

proactive_rebalance_info: Retrieve proactive rebalance status for Virtual SAN

purge_inaccessible_vswp_objects: Search and delete inaccessible vswp objects on a virtual SAN cluster.

VM vswp file is used for memory swapping for running VMs by ESX. In VMware virtual SAN a vswp file is stored as a separate virtual SAN object. When a vswp object goes inaccessible, memory swapping will not be possible and the VM may crash when next time ESX tries to swap the memory for the VM. Deleting the inaccessible vswp object will not make thing worse, but it will eliminate the possibility for the object to regain accessibility in future time if this is just a temporary issue (e.g., due to network failure or planned maintenance).

Due to a known issue in vSphere 5.5, it is possible for Virtual SAN to have done incomplete deletions of vswp objects. In such cases, the majority of components of such objects were deleted while a minority of components were left unavailable (e.g., due to one host being temporarily down at the time of deletion). It is then possible for the minority to resurface and present itself as an inaccessible object because a minority can never gain quorum.

Such objects waste space and cause issues for any operations involving data evacuations from hosts or disks. This command employs heuristics to detect this kind of left-over vswp objects in order to delete them.

It will not cause data loss by deleting the vswp object. The vswp object will be regenerated when the VM is powered on next time.

reapply_vsan_vmknic_config: Unbinds and rebinds VSAN to its vmknics

recover_spbm: SPBM Recovery

resync_dashboard: Resyncing dashboard

scrubber_info: Print scrubber info about objects on this host or cluster

support_information: Command to collect vsan support information

v2_ondisk_upgrade: Upgrade a cluster to latest Virtual SAN

vm_object_info: Fetch VSAN object information about a VM

vm_perf_stats: VM perf stats

vmdk_stats: Print read cache and capacity stats for vmdks.

Disk Capacity (GB):

Disk Size: Size of the vmdk

Used Capacity: MD capacity used by this vmdk

Data Size: Size of data on this vmdk

Read Cache (GB):

Used: RC used by this vmdk

Reserved: RC reserved by this vmdk

whatif_host_failures: Simulates how host failures impact VSAN resource usage

To see commands in a namespace: help namespace_name

To see detailed help for a command: help namespace_name.command_name

>

All the commands shown here must be prefixed by `vsan`. Therefore, to run `enable_vsan_on_cluster`, you must use `vsan.enable_vsan_on_cluster`. Remember that there is command completion, so you only need to type the first couple of characters of each command and then use the Tab key to complete the command (or display which commands match your current types command).

Of course, there is another set of commands in RVC that is also of interest to VSAN administrators. These are the storage policy-based management (SPBM) commands and are used for all things related to VM storage policies. Example 10.19 shows a list of SPBM commands in RVC:

Example 10.19   help spbm

```
> help spbm
Commands:
check_compliance: Check compliance
device_add_disk: Add a hard drive to a virtual machine
device_change_storage_profile: Change storage profile of a virtual disk
namespace_change_storage_profile: Change storage profile of VM namespace
profile_apply: Apply a VM Storage Profile. Pushed profile content to
Storage system
profile_create: Create a VM Storage Profile
profile_delete: Delete a VM Storage Profile
profile_modify: Create a VM Storage Profile
vm_change_storage_profile: Change storage profile of VM namespace and its
disks


To see commands in a namespace: help namespace_name
To see detailed help for a command: help namespace_name.command_name
```

We will return to SPBM commands shortly, but for the moment we will examine the VSAN commands in RVC and how they can help you with monitoring, troubleshooting, and resolving VSAN issues. You must use `vsan.` to precede all VSAN commands.

To get even more help on a particular command, simply precede the full command with `help`.

enable_vsan_on_cluster and disable_vsan_on_cluster

These commands do exactly what they say—enabling and disabling VSAN on the cluster. The only other way to do this is via the vSphere Web Client. You cannot do this via ESXCLI. With ESXCLI, you could get the ESXi host to join or leave the cluster, scaling it in or scaling it out, but there was no way to enable or disable the VSAN service on the cluster. The following commands (where 0 is a numeric representation of the cluster as shown in the ls output) allow you to do this:

```
/vcsa-05/Datacenter/computers> ls
0 Cluster (cluster): cpu 134 GHz, memory 305 GB
/vcsa-05/Datacenter/computers> vsan.disable_vsan_on_cluster 0
ReconfigureComputeResource Cluster: success
 esxi-b-pref.rainpole.com: running []
 esxi-b-pref.rainpole.com: running []
 esxi-b-pref.rainpole.com: running []
 esxi-b-pref.rainpole.com: running []
```

If the command succeeds, the running status changes to success:

```
 esxi-b-pref.rainpole.com: success
 esxi-c-scnd.rainpole.com: success
 esxi-d-scnd.rainpole.com: success
 esxi-a-pref.rainpole.com: success
```

Re-enabling VSAN is just as straightforward:

```
/vcsa-05/Datacenter/computers> vsan.enable_vsan_on_cluster 0
ReconfigureComputeResource Cluster: success
 esxi-b-pref.rainpole.com: success
 esxi-c-scnd.rainpole.com: success
 esxi-d-scnd.rainpole.com: success
 esxi-a-pref.rainpole.com: success
```

host_info

In most cases, it is much easier to navigate to the particular object that you are interested in. If you use the vsan.host_info command, it is easier to navigate to the object in the inventory and then use the numeric shorthand value of the host in the command, as shown in Example 10.20:

Example 10.20   vsan.host_info

```
/vcsa-05/Datacenter/computers> ls
0 Cluster (cluster): cpu 134 GHz, memory 305 GB
/vcsa-05/Datacenter/computers> cd 0
/vcsa-05/Datacenter/computers/Cluster> ls
0 hosts/
1 resourcePool [Resources]: cpu 134.29/134.29/normal, mem 305.31/305.31/normal
```

```
/vcsa-05/Datacenter/computers/Cluster> cd 0
/vcsa-05/Datacenter/computers/Cluster/hosts> ls
0 esxi-b-pref.rainpole.com (host): cpu 2*8*2.40 GHz, memory 102.00 GB
1 esxi-c-scnd.rainpole.com (host): cpu 2*8*2.40 GHz, memory 102.00 GB
2 esxi-d-scnd.rainpole.com (host): cpu 2*8*2.40 GHz, memory 102.00 GB
3 esxi-a-pref.rainpole.com (host): cpu 2*8*2.40 GHz, memory 102.00 GB
/vcsa-05/Datacenter/computers/Cluster/hosts> vsan.host_info 0
2015-12-29 12:42:01 +0000: Fetching host info from esxi-b-pref.rainpole.com
(may take a moment) ...
Product: VMware ESXi 6.0.0 build-3329486
VSAN enabled: yes
Cluster info:
  Cluster role: agent
  Cluster UUID: 5231dfdb-cfe7-aa13-ccfc-2a49e09e85b4
  Node UUID: 56702cdc-d064-d2a5-8457-ecf4bbd58600
  Member UUIDs: ["56703560-1a41-3037-9a8c-ecf4bbd5b260", "56702cdc-
d064-d2a5-8457-ecf4bbd58600", "56707c8b-3353-d670-c080-ecf4bbd59370",
"5676978a-6c3d-28fc-9ea2-ecf4bbd69680"] (4)
Node evacuated: no
Storage info:
  Auto claim: yes
  Checksum enforced: no
  Disk Mappings:
    SSD: Local ATA Disk (t10.ATA_____Micron_P420m2DMTFDGAR1T4MAX_____
____0000000014170C1B9A73) - 1304 GB, v3
    MD: Local ATA Disk (naa.500a07510f86d691) - 745 GB, v3
    MD: Local ATA Disk (naa.500a07510f86d695) - 745 GB, v3
    MD: Local ATA Disk (naa.500a07510f86d69c) - 745 GB, v3
    MD: Local ATA Disk (naa.500a07510f86d69f) - 745 GB, v3
    MD: Local ATA Disk (naa.500a07510f86d6a0) - 745 GB, v3
    MD: Local ATA Disk (naa.500a07510f86d6ba) - 745 GB, v3
    MD: Local ATA Disk (naa.500a07510f86d686) - 745 GB, v3
FaultDomainInfo:
  Not configured
NetworkInfo:
  Adapter: vmk2 (172.200.0.22)
```

In this example, we navigated to the host folder and then when we ran the command, we used the numeric value of 0 that represented the first host in the list, which is esxi-b-pref.rainpole.com. This command shows us a combination of information around cluster, network, and storage. We can see the cluster role and members, the disk mappings showing multiple capacity devices and one micron device marked as an SSD for caching, and networking information related to the VMkernel adapter being used for VSAN traffic on this host. This would have taken a few different `esxcli` commands to display, so immediately we can see the power of the RVC.

host_consume_disks and host_evacuate_data

These next commands are ways of telling a specific host in the VSAN cluster to claim any empty local disks that are not already claimed. This is done via the `host_consume_disk` command. Obviously, this would be with VSAN set up in manual mode; if VSAN were configured in automatic mode, empty, local disks would already be automatically claimed. The command `host_evacuate_data` can be used to move all of the data from a host to other hosts in the cluster prior to removing that host from VSAN.

host_wipe_vsan_disks and host_wipe_non_vsan_disks

However, if you added new disks to a VSAN host, and these disks were already used for VSAN previously, and had residual data or partition information on them, the command `host_wipe_vsan_disks` could be used to create a new, clean, empty disk drive that could be used by VSAN. Similarly, if the disks were used for some other purpose other than VSAN and you wish to use them for VSAN, the command `host_wipe_non_vsan_disks` could be used.

cluster_info

We now meet the first command to give us a cluster-centric view of VSAN. This is probably the best command to start with to get a big picture of the cluster configuration. Once again, navigate to the cluster object in the RVC inventory, or simply type the full path to the cluster object when you run the `vsan.cluster_info` command. This command is equivalent of running the `vsan.host_info` command against every host in the cluster. Previously we saw that `vsan.host_info` display cluster, host, disk, and network info. Now we have a single command to display this information for every host. We won't list all four hosts in this 4-node VSAN cluster, but you should still get the idea from the truncated output shown in Example 10.21:

Example 10.21 vsan.cluster_info

```
/vcsa-05/Datacenter/computers> ls
0 Cluster (cluster): cpu 134 GHz, memory 305 GB
/vcsa-05/Datacenter/computers> vsan.cluster_info 0
2015-12-29 12:50:04 +0000: Fetching host info from esxi-c-scnd.rainpole.com
(may take a moment) ...
2015-12-29 12:50:04 +0000: Fetching host info from esxi-b-pref.rainpole.com
(may take a moment) ...
2015-12-29 12:50:04 +0000: Fetching host info from esxi-a-pref.rainpole.com
```

(may take a moment) ...

2015-12-29 12:50:04 +0000: Fetching host info from esxi-d-scnd.rainpole.com
(may take a moment) ...

Host: esxi-b-pref.rainpole.com

  Product: VMware ESXi 6.0.0 build-3329486

  VSAN enabled: yes

  Cluster info:

    Cluster role: agent

    Cluster UUID: 5231dfdb-cfe7-aa13-ccfc-2a49e09e85b4

    Node UUID: 56702cdc-d064-d2a5-8457-ecf4bbd58600

    Member UUIDs: ["56703560-1a41-3037-9a8c-ecf4bbd5b260", "56702cdc-d064-d2a5-8457-ecf4bbd58600", "56707c8b-3353-d670-c080-ecf4bbd59370", "5676978a-6c3d-28fc-9ea2-ecf4bbd69680"] (4)

  Node evacuated: no

  Storage info:

    Auto claim: yes

    Checksum enforced: no

    Disk Mappings:

      SSD: Local ATA Disk (t10.ATA_____Micron_P420m2DMTFDGAR1T4MAX_____0000000014170C1B9A73) - 1304 GB, v3

      MD: Local ATA Disk (naa.500a07510f86d691) - 745 GB, v3

      MD: Local ATA Disk (naa.500a07510f86d695) - 745 GB, v3

      MD: Local ATA Disk (naa.500a07510f86d69c) - 745 GB, v3

      MD: Local ATA Disk (naa.500a07510f86d69f) - 745 GB, v3

      MD: Local ATA Disk (naa.500a07510f86d6a0) - 745 GB, v3

      MD: Local ATA Disk (naa.500a07510f86d6ba) - 745 GB, v3

      MD: Local ATA Disk (naa.500a07510f86d686) - 745 GB, v3

  FaultDomainInfo:

    Not configured

  NetworkInfo:

    Adapter: vmk2 (172.200.0.22)

Host: esxi-c-scnd.rainpole.com

  Product: VMware ESXi 6.0.0 build-3329486

  VSAN enabled: yes

  Cluster info:

    Cluster role: master

    Cluster UUID: 5231dfdb-cfe7-aa13-ccfc-2a49e09e85b4

    Node UUID: 56703560-1a41-3037-9a8c-ecf4bbd5b260

    Member UUIDs: ["56703560-1a41-3037-9a8c-ecf4bbd5b260", "56702cdc-d064-d2a5-8457-ecf4bbd58600", "56707c8b-3353-d670-c080-ecf4bbd59370", "5676978a-6c3d-28fc-9ea2-ecf4bbd69680"] (4)

```
Node evacuated: no
Storage info:
  Auto claim: yes
  Checksum enforced: no
  Disk Mappings:
    SSD: Local ATA Disk (t10.ATA_____Micron_P420m2DMTFDGAR1T4MAX_____
_____0000000014170C1BA941) - 1304 GB, v3
    MD: Local ATA Disk (naa.500a07510f86d6cf) - 745 GB, v3
    MD: Local ATA Disk (naa.500a07510f86d69d) - 745 GB, v3
    MD: Local ATA Disk (naa.500a07510f86d6ab) - 745 GB, v3
    MD: Local ATA Disk (naa.500a07510f86d6b3) - 745 GB, v3
    MD: Local ATA Disk (naa.500a07510f86d6b4) - 745 GB, v3
    MD: Local ATA Disk (naa.500a07510f86d6bb) - 745 GB, v3
    MD: Local ATA Disk (naa.500a07510f86d6c5) - 745 GB, v3
FaultDomainInfo:
  Not configured
NetworkInfo:
  Adapter: vmk2 (172.200.0.23)
```

Once again, you can see the cluster role and members, the disk mappings showing the cache tier device and capacity tier devices, and networking information related to the VMkernel adapter using for VSAN traffic on this host. We are sure that you will agree that this is a very useful command to get an overview of the cluster configuration.

disks_info

As previously mentioned, VSAN will only automatically claim disks that are local and empty (in other words, have no existing partition table). If you find that VSAN is not claiming a disk for some reason, `disks_info` is a great command to check and see why not. This command will display whether a disk is already in use by VSAN, whether it is available for consuming by VSAN, or whether it is ineligible for use by VSAN. Typically, if the disk is ineligible, `disks_info` displays partition information if the disk is already partitioned. The output can be rather long to display due to some of the disk identifiers and the state of those disks in some cases, hence the reason we've not included the output of this command in the book.

cluster_set_default_policy

This book has previously discussed the concept of a default policy in great detail. In the previous ESXCLI section, we actually saw commands related to the default policy settings. You might remember that we stated that if you used the ESXCLI method of changing the default policy, this would have to be done on a per-host basis. Well, this command allows us to change the default policy across all the hosts in the cluster. Suppose, for instance, that the default policy setting did not meet your requirements. Perhaps you would prefer a default policy that had a higher number of failures to tolerate, or perhaps a higher stripe width. Or perhaps you want to reserve some read cache as part of the default policy. In that case, `cluster_set_default_policy` is the command you would use. First, you would need to create a policy that you want to use as the default. This will then be available under the vmprofiles (profiles was the original name for policies) folder of any VM that is using the policy. The `cluster_set_default_policy` command may then be pointed to that policy and this will become the new default policy for any VMs that are deployed without an explicitly associated VM storage policy.

Having said all of the above, it is now also possible to define in the UI what the default policy should be when a new VM is provisioned. Simply navigate to the datastores view in the Web Client, select the VSAN datastore, select Actions and choose "Change Default Storage Policy," as shown in Figure 10.14. This is a far easier approach than trying to modify the default policy via ESXCLI or RVC.

Figure 10.14   Change default storage policy on the VSAN datastore

object_reconfigure

You can use the RVC command `vsan.object_reconfigure` on already-existing VSAN objects to change their current VM storage policy setting and assign them a new policy. If perhaps you felt that you needed to add a stripe width or increase the number of failures to tolerate of a particular object, this RVC command can do that for you.

object_info, disk_object_info, vm_object_info

These three RVC commands are grouped together as they are in some way related. They all involve displaying detailed information about objects in the cluster, be they disk,

cluster, or VM objects. Let's begin with the `vm_object_info` command because this
is possibly the more intuitive one of the three to begin with. To use this command, you
simply navigate to a VM and provide it as the argument. In Example 10.22, we navigated
to a host that has a single VM and ran the command against it. What then happens is that
RVC checks all ESXi hosts in the cluster to see which ESXi hosts contain objects related
to this VM. At this point, you should be well aware of the fact that VSAN may not place
a VM's storage objects on the same host as the VM compute. In fact, VM storage objects
(including replicas) may be on completely different hosts in the VSAN cluster than the
compute of said VM.

Example 10.22   vsan.vm_object_info

```
/vcsa-05/Datacenter/computers/Cluster/hosts/esxi-c-scnd.rainpole.com/vms>
vsan.vm_object_info 0
2015-12-29 13:01:08 +0000: Done fetching VSAN disk infos
VM R5:
  Namespace directory
    DOM Object: 5ff87756-cdf2-9aa0-05f0-ecf4bbd5b260 (v4, owner:
esxi-c-scnd.rainpole.com, policy: spbmProfileGenerationNumber = 0,
hostFailuresToTolerate = 1, spbmProfileId = 1e65d4c4-40d9-4518-a5d1-
cf1e78505258, proportionalCapacity = [0, 100], replicaPreference =
Capacity, stripeWidth = 1)
      RAID_5
        Component: 5ff87756-403e-0ca1-38af-ecf4bbd5b260 (state: ACTIVE (5),
host: esxi-c-scnd.rainpole.com, md: naa.500a07510f86d6c5, ssd: t10.ATA_____
Micron_P420m2DMTFDGAR1T4MAX_____0000000014170C1BA941, votes: 2,
usage: 0.1 GB)
        Component: 5ff87756-f326-0da1-bab6-ecf4bbd5b260 (state: ACTIVE (5),
host: esxi-a-pref.rainpole.com, md: naa.500a07510f86d693, ssd: t10.ATA_____
Micron_P420m2DMTFDGAR1T4MAX_____0000000014080C116FB2, votes: 1,
usage: 0.1 GB)
        Component: 5ff87756-49be-0da1-d3a3-ecf4bbd5b260 (state: ACTIVE (5),
host: esxi-d-scnd.rainpole.com, md: naa.500a07510f86d6bf, ssd: t10.ATA_____
Micron_P420m2DMTFDGAR1T4MAX_____0000000014170C1B9A6E, votes: 1,
usage: 0.1 GB)
        Component: 5ff87756-c93a-0ea1-5e8e-ecf4bbd5b260 (state: ACTIVE (5),
host: esxi-b-pref.rainpole.com, md: naa.500a07510f86d686, ssd: t10.ATA_____
Micron_P420m2DMTFDGAR1T4MAX_____0000000014170C1B9A73, votes: 1,
usage: 0.1 GB)
  Disk backing: [vsanDatatore] 5ff87756-cdf2-9aa0-05f0-ecf4bbd5b260/R5.vmdk
    DOM Object: 61f87756-db3c-6a7b-5c87-ecf4bbd5b260 (v4, owner:
esxi-c-scnd.rainpole.com, policy: spbmProfileGenerationNumber = 0,
hostFailuresToTolerate = 1, spbmProfileId = 1e65d4c4-40d9-4518-a5d1-
cf1e78505258, replicaPreference = Capacity)
      RAID_5
```

```
        Component: 61f87756-53e6-177c-0a5d-ecf4bbd5b260 (state: ACTIVE (5),
host: esxi-c-scnd.rainpole.com, md: naa.500a07510f86d6cf, ssd: t10.ATA_____
Micron_P420m2DMTFDGAR1T4MAX_____0000000014170C1BA941, votes:
2, usage: 0.0 GB)
        Component: 61f87756-9230-197c-8275-ecf4bbd5b260 (state: ACTIVE (5),
host: esxi-b-pref.rainpole.com, md: naa.500a07510f86d69f, ssd: t10.ATA_____
Micron_P420m2DMTFDGAR1T4MAX_____0000000014170C1B9A73, votes:
1, usage: 0.0 GB)
        Component: 61f87756-0856-1a7c-1ede-ecf4bbd5b260 (state: ACTIVE (5),
host: esxi-d-scnd.rainpole.com, md: naa.500a07510f86d6af, ssd: t10.ATA_____
Micron_P420m2DMTFDGAR1T4MAX_____0000000014170C1B9A6E, votes:
1, usage: 0.0 GB)
        Component: 61f87756-f58b-1b7c-7696-ecf4bbd5b260 (state: ACTIVE (5),
host: esxi-a-pref.rainpole.com, md: naa.500a07510f86d6b8, ssd: t10.ATA_____
Micron_P420m2DMTFDGAR1T4MAX_____0000000014080C116FB2, votes:
1, usage: 0.0 GB)
```

In the preceding listing, the VMs have two objects that are displayed; the VM home namespace directory and the VM disk/VMDK. Both of these storage objects have replicas in a RAID-5 configuration, indicating that they are configured to tolerate one failure in the policy setting, but use "Capacity" over "Performance" in the replicaPreference setting. We can verify that by checking the DOM object line of each object, which explicitly displays the policy settings, and indeed we can see host failures to tolerate = 1 in both cases. Again, although this descriptor specifies host failures to tolerate, it also covers other components such as disk and network.

Of course, possibly the most useful part of this output is that it details where the components are stored. You can see host, capacity disk ID, and the ID of the SSD acting as the cache tier in the disk group. And, finally, you can see whether the components are healthy. In this case, all components appear in the active state, which is normal.

Note that if this was a RAID-1 configuration, we would also have information displayed about the witness components. These should not need explanation at this stage of the book, but suffice it to say that they play a major role when failures occur, and count as a vote to allow storage objects reach a quorum and continue to remain accessible when a failure occurs in the cluster. With RAID-5 and RAID-6 configurations, witness is not required.

Now that we have examined objects related to a VM, sometimes it is also good to know what objects/components are actually on a physical disk. This is where disk_object_ info comes in. With this command, you can display the contents of a physical disk that has been claimed by VSAN and have RVC display the components that are on this disk. This command is run against the cluster, but an additional argument is required whereby the disk identifier must be provided. This is easy to get, and the previous vm_object_ `info` command can provide this information, as can ESXCLI or the vSphere UI. If we use the NAA ID of the capacity device which can be retrieved from the previous command, we can display all the objects and components on that disk drive.

Again, this is another command that provides a lot of useful information. In this example, we have switched to a different VSAN cluster to show some variety to the outputs. The output shown in Figure 10.15 has been truncated for readability; in this case various "DOM objects" have been left out:

```
/localhost/ie-datacenter-01/computers> ls
0 ie-vsan-cluster-01 (cluster): cpu 109 GHz, memory 331 GB
/localhost/ie-datacenter-01/computers> vsan.disk_object_info 0 naa.600508b1001c36662525d1d217c882f87
2014-03-14 11:37:57 +0000: Fetching VSAN disk info from hosts (may take a moment) ...
2014-03-14 11:38:00 +0000: Done fetching VSAN disk infos
Physical disk naa.600508b1001c36662525d1d217c882f87 (525a5dee-1f35-b3b5-cac9-c55d047ea601):
  DOM Object: 16782053-64de-7b11-a685-001517a69c72 (owner: 10.27.51.2, policy: hostFailuresToTolerate = 1, proportionalCapacity =
100)
    Context: Part of VM ie-vdpa-01: Disk: [vsanDatastore] 2e742053-2895-3151-e630-001517a69c72/ie-vdpa-01_2.vmdk
    Witness: 17782053-0097-fb35-a525-001517a69c72 (state: ACTIVE (5), host: 10.27.51.2, md: naa.600508b1001cdb46f505bf98eef9e9b4,
ssd: eui.c68e151fedfa4fcf0024712c7cc444fe)
    Witness: 17782053-9c0b-fa35-cf2a-001517a69c72 (state: ACTIVE (5), host: 10.27.51.2, md:
**naa.600508b1001c36662525d1d217c882f87**, ssd: eui.c68e151fedfa4fcf0024712c7cc444fe)
    Witness: 17782053-2abf-fa35-64b9-001517a69c72 (state: ACTIVE (5), host: 10.27.51.4, md: naa.600508b1001c8119ca0ab3a6fe0d2b19,
ssd: eui.a15eb52c6f4043b5002471c7886acfaa)
    RAID_1
      RAID_0
        Component: 17782053-b020-f935-eb15-001517a69c72 (state: ACTIVE (5), host: 10.27.51.3, md:
naa.600508b1001c784579103bf9baf41797, ssd: eui.d1ef5a5bbe864e27002471febdec3592)
        Component: 17782053-744b-f835-a4ca-001517a69c72 (state: ACTIVE (5), host: 10.27.51.3, md:
naa.600508b1001c034feb6ff087idbl3c4b, ssd: eui.d1ef5a5bbe864e27002471febdec3592)
      RAID_0
        Component: 17782053-2a68-f735-e951-001517a69c72 (state: ACTIVE (5), host: 10.27.51.4, md:
naa.600508b1001c1380cc97bc5345465552, ssd: eui.a15eb52c6f4043b5002471c7886acfaa)
        Component: 17782053-b807-f635-1568-001517a69c72 (state: ACTIVE (5), host: 10.27.51.2, md:
naa.600508b1001cdb46f505bf98eef9e9b4, ssd: eui.c68e151fedfa4fcf0024712c7cc444fe)
```

Figure 10.15   vsan.disk_object_info output

What is nice about this output is that it shows you the object and the context. In other words, you can tell which VM storage object the particular component is a part of. Not only that, it shows all the other components that make up the storage object, and where those other components are located in the VSAN cluster. It also highlights the disk ID that we provided as an argument to the command by including some ** characters at the beginning and the end of the identifier.

What can be deduced from this output is that the disk that we are interested in contains quite a number of components. Some of the components are part of a VM disk/VMDK, whereas other components are used to make up namespace directories of VMs, and others may be part of the VM's swap. This output is extremely useful for troubleshooting once again because it allows you to see the status of components on disks. Once again, in this output, everything appears to be in a good, normal active state.

This brings us to the final `object_info` command. This now uses an actual VSAN object identifier to display the status of a storage object. So, rather than looking at all objects belonging to a VM, or all components storage on a magnetic disk, we can now look in detail at a single storage object in the cluster, be it a namespace directory or a VM disk. This is very useful for tracing the status of a particular object, especially if log files are displaying messages related to an object ID and you are not sure which VM or which magnetic disk has the object in question. In Figure 10.16, we chose a VM disk's ID, and ran the command as follows, with the arguments of cluster and then object ID:

```
/localhost/ie-datacenter-01/computers> vsan_object_info 0 d4502253-e81d-00b8-6351-0010185def78
DOM Object: d4502253-e81d-00b8-6351-0010185def78 (owner: 10.27.51.3, policy: hostFailuresToTolerate = 1, proportionalCapacity = {0, 100})
  Witness: d5502253-10c6-321a-656d-0010185def78 (state: ACTIVE (5), host: 10.27.51.1, md: naa.600508b1001c930aff02e0c5c7971e1d, ssd:
eui.48f8681115d6416c0024717 2ce4df168)
  RAID_1
    Component: d5502253-3461-321a-d275-0010185def78 (state: ACTIVE (5), host: 10.27.51.3, md: naa.600508b1001c034feb6ff0871db13c4b, ssd:
eui.d1ef5a5bbe864e2700 2471febdec3592)
    Component: d5502253-b00b-311a-ff45-0010185def78 (state: ACTIVE (5), host: 10.27.51.2, md: naa.600508b1001c3662525d1d217c882f87, ssd:
eui.c68e151fed8a4fcf0024712c7cc444fe)
  Extended attributes:
    Address space: 43285303296B (40.31 GB)
    Object class: vdisk
    Object path: /vmfs/volumes/vsan:524ed5e9ee77b654-b7895b53dcad7c5e/c2cd2153-24a4-45a5-b0a1-001517a69c72/hbrdisk.RDID-7b82ee6b-b12e-4364-b72c-
c0ba2e4101d0.12.61153313995688.vmdk
```

Figure 10.16   vsan_object_info output

This now gives us a nice detailed view of the makeup of the object. We can see that there is a RAID-1 configuration with two components, indicating that this has a policy setting that has number of failures to tolerate set to 1. All of this can be verified by the DOM object line of the output, which indeed includes hostFailuresToTolerate = 1. We can also see that the object class is vdisk, a VM disk (VMDK). Once again, the command displays useful information about the location of each of the components, and all components are in an active good state.

Using the various object_info commands, an administrator should be able to trace where each of the various storage objects belonging to a VM reside in the cluster and verify that they are in good working order. If issues arise that require an administrator to find components and troubleshoot, these commands are invaluable.

cmmds_find

The cmmds_find command can be extremely useful, especially if an ESXi host posts an error message with the ID of a particular VSAN object and you need to figure out what that said object actually relates to. The vsan.cmmds_find (cmmds for Clustering Monitoring, Membership, and Directory Services) can be used to display information about a particular object in the VSAN cluster.

cmmds_find -t DISK_USAGE

This first option is useful as it displays disk usage information in the cluster. The most important output is the health column; this will immediately tell you whether any disks are in an unhealthy state, as shown in Figure 10.17.

```
/localhost/vsphere5.5-u1> vsan.cmmds_find ~/computers/vsphere5.5-u1/ -t DISK_USAGE

+---+------------+--------------------------------------+-------------+---------+-------------------------------------+
| # | Type       | UUID                                 | Owner       | Health  | Content                             |
+---+------------+--------------------------------------+-------------+---------+-------------------------------------+
| 1 | DISK_USAGE | 52777432-f127-f001-d081-800a04cafb0e | 10.27.51.4  | Healthy | {"capacityReserved"=>18874368,      |
|   |            |                                      |             |         |  "iopsReserved"=>0,                 |
|   |            |                                      |             |         |  "throughPutReserved"=>0,           |
|   |            |                                      |             |         |  "l2CacheReserved"=>0,              |
|   |            |                                      |             |         |  "l1CacheReserved"=>0}              |
| 2 | DISK_USAGE | 5214b1a5-b6b1-3a3a-f8b6-ee4ecc7a8d0e | 10.27.51.4  | Healthy | {"capacityReserved"=>0,             |
|   |            |                                      |             |         |  "iopsReserved"=>0,                 |
|   |            |                                      |             |         |  "throughPutReserved"=>0,           |
|   |            |                                      |             |         |  "l2CacheReserved"=>0,              |
|   |            |                                      |             |         |  "l1CacheReserved"=>0}              |
| 3 | DISK_USAGE | 5269ded0-91a2-4986-4d5e-e946d252730f | 10.27.51.3  | Healthy | {"capacityReserved"=>14680064,      |
|   |            |                                      |             |         |  "iopsReserved"=>0,                 |
|   |            |                                      |             |         |  "throughPutReserved"=>0,           |
|   |            |                                      |             |         |  "l2CacheReserved"=>0,              |
|   |            |                                      |             |         |  "l1CacheReserved"=>0}              |
| 4 | DISK_USAGE | 52f226e9-7664-34a1-b6be-3f27c4d2671e | 10.27.51.3  | Healthy | {"capacityReserved"=>7509901312,    |
|   |            |                                      |             |         |  "iopsReserved"=>0,                 |
|   |            |                                      |             |         |  "throughPutReserved"=>0,           |
|   |            |                                      |             |         |  "l2CacheReserved"=>0,              |
|   |            |                                      |             |         |  "l1CacheReserved"=>0}              |
| 5 | DISK_USAGE | 5251dfbe-2106-16ca-e6eb-c8389a7eebdd | 10.27.51.3  | Healthy | {"capacityReserved"=>0,             |
|   |            |                                      |             |         |  "iopsReserved"=>0,                 |
|   |            |                                      |             |         |  "throughPutReserved"=>0,           |
|   |            |                                      |             |         |  "l2CacheReserved"=>0,              |
|   |            |                                      |             |         |  "l1CacheReserved"=>0}              |
| 6 | DISK_USAGE | 52de5de0-ff71-02fa-b671-558abd3280e1 | 10.27.51.4  | Healthy | {"capacityReserved"=>25165824,      |
|   |            |                                      |             |         |  "iopsReserved"=>0,                 |
|   |            |                                      |             |         |  "throughPutReserved"=>0,           |
|   |            |                                      |             |         |  "l2CacheReserved"=>0,              |
|   |            |                                      |             |         |  "l1CacheReserved"=>0}              |
+---+------------+--------------------------------------+-------------+---------+-------------------------------------+
```

Figure 10.17 cmmds_find –t DISK_USAGE

cmmds_find -t DISK

The -t DISK option is rather useful as it displays details about all the disks in the cluster. There are also some interesting attributes displayed in the Content column, including capacity, and whether the disk is an SSD (isSsd).

cmmds_find -u UUID

The -u UUID option enables an administrator to look at the particular component in even more detail.

From the preceding output, a number of additional types are available. These are HEALTH_STATUS and DISK_STATUS. Any of these can be passed to the vsan. cmmds_find command with the -t option.

We have barely scratched the surface of what this command is capable of. The more observant of you will have noticed that this command is very similar to the -cmmds-tool available in the ESXCLI. That is quite correct, and many of the options used with -cmmds-tool find can also be used here.

fix_renamed_vms

There is not much to add to the description of the `fix_renamed_vms` command. As it states, vCenter Server can rename some VMs if the VSAN datastore access becomes unavailable for whatever reason. This leaves the VMs with a long pathname as the name of the VM, and these are used in the vSphere Web Client as the name of the VM—not very user-friendly. This command renames those VMs from the long pathname to the shorter more human-readable form.

obj_status_report

`obj_status_report` is a nice command to verify that all objects and components in the cluster are in a good, healthy state and that no objects or components have been orphaned (in other words, no longer associated with a VM).

The `obj_status_report` command once again runs against the cluster. The output shown in Example 10.23 is split into two sections; the first displayed nonorphaned objects, and the second displays orphaned objects. It also verifies that any component found is in a healthy state (i.e., has an active state that we observed in the previous outputs):

Example 10.23   vsan.obj_status_report output

```
/mia-cg07-vc01/mia-cg07-dc01/computers> vsan.obj_status_report 0
2014-02-08 12:52:25 +0000: Querying all VMs on VSAN ...
2014-02-08 12:52:25 +0000: Querying all objects in the system ...
2014-02-08 12:52:26 +0000: Querying all disks in the system ...
2014-02-08 12:52:26 +0000: Querying all components in the system ...
2014-02-08 12:52:27 +0000: Got all the info, computing table ...

Histogram of component health for non-orphaned objects
+-----------------------------------+-----------------------------------+
| Num Healthy Comps / Total Num Comps | Num objects with such status |
+-----------------------------------+-----------------------------------+
| 7/7                               |                          1        |
|                                   |                                   |
| 3/3                               |                          7        |
|                                   |                                   |
| 5/5                               |                          2        |
|                                   |                                   |
+-----------------------------------+-----------------------------------+
Total non-orphans: 10
```

```
Histogram of component health for possibly orphaned objects
+-------------------------------------+----------------------------+
| Num Healthy Comps / Total Num Comps | Num objects with such status |
+-------------------------------------+----------------------------+
+-------------------------------------+----------------------------+
Total orphans: 0
```

What you are looking for in the output of this command is any nonorphaned objects that are not in a healthy state, as well as any orphaned objects. Both of these would require further troubleshooting to determine why they are not healthy, and in the case of orphaned objects, how they can be cleaned up.

check_state

check_state is a great command for getting the big picture of your VSAN environment. It carries out a number of fundamental tasks. It checks to make sure all VSAN objects are accessible, it checks to make sure that all VMs are healthy and accessible, and it also checks that any VMs deployed on the VSAN cluster are in sync from both an ESXi host perspective and vCenter Server perspective. Any anomalies are reported when the command is run:

```
/mia-cg07-vc01/mia-cg07-dc01/computers> vsan.check_state 0
2014-02-08 13:00:19 +0000: Step 1: Check for inaccessible VSAN objects
Detected 0 objects to not be inaccessible

2014-02-08 13:00:20 +0000: Step 2: Check for invalid/inaccessible VMs
2014-02-08 13:00:20 +0000: Step 3: Check for VMs for which VC/hostd/vmx are
out of sync
Did not find VMs for which VC/hostd/vmx are out of sync
```

I strongly recommend running this command at regular intervals, perhaps as part of a maintenance cycle. This will ensure that any anomalies are caught early.

This command also has a very useful option for reconnecting orphaned VMs: **--refresh-state**. It runs as shown in Example 10.24:

Example 10.24 vsan.check_state –refresh-state

```
/mia-cg07-vc01/mia-cg07-dc01/computers> vsan.check_state --refresh-state 0
2014-04-30 21:19:18 +0000: Step 1: Check for inaccessible VSAN objects
2014-04-30 21:19:18 +0000: Step 1b: Check for inaccessible VSAN objects,
again2014-04-30 21:19:19 +0000: Step 2: Check for invalid/inaccessible VMs
```

```
Detected VM 'ie-vdpa-01' as being 'orphaned', reloading ...
reloadVirtualMachineFromPath ie-vdpa-01: success


2014-04-30 21:19:23 +0000: Step 2b: Check for invalid/inaccessible VMs
again
2014-04-30 21:19:23 +0000: Step 3: Check for VMs for which VC/hostd/vmx are
out of sync

Did not find VMs for which VC/hostd/vmx are out of sync
```

whatif_host_failures, disk_stats, and vm_perf_stats

Now we come to some statistics and metrics commands. Like the `object_info` command previously, there are stats commands for hosts, disks, and VMs. Let's begin with the `whatif_host_failures` command. This is a very useful command. Not only does it show the current storage capacity configuration (referred to as HDDs or hard disk drives, but also applies to all-flash capacity) in the output, but it also shows you what might happen if a single host in the cluster failed. In Example 10.25 we navigated to the cluster object in the inventory and ran the `vsan.whatif_host_failures` command from there, selecting the full cluster as an argument:

Example 10.25 vsan.whatif_host_failures

```
/vcsa-05.rainpole.com/Datacenter/computers> ls
0 Cluster (cluster): cpu 134 GHz, memory 306 GB
/vcsa-05.rainpole.com/Datacenter/computers> vsan.whatif_host_failures 0
Simulating 1 host failures:


+----------------+--------------------------+------------------------------------+
| Resource       | Usage right now          | Usage after failure/re-protection  |
+----------------+--------------------------+------------------------------------+
| HDD capacity   | 1% used (18402.90 GB free) | 2% used (13738.44 GB free)       |
| Components      | 0% used (35997 available) | 0% used (26997 available)         |
| RC reservations | 0% used (0.00 GB free)   | 0% used (0.00 GB free)            |
+----------------+--------------------------+------------------------------------+
/vcsa-05.rainpole.com/Datacenter/computers>
```

The idea behind the simulation of a host failure is, as it says in the command output, to see whether any disk drive would reach close to capacity if VM storage objects were rebuilt to meet policy requirements in the event of a failure. This is a very useful command to determine whether VSAN could continue to meet the availability requirements of your VMs during a failure. This is a very useful command for capacity planning because if a host failure meant that policy compliance could not be achieved, another failure in the cluster could mean that your VMs become unavailable. This failure could be a host, disk, or even the network.

In the preceding output, there are four hosts in the cluster, but the cluster is very under-utilized, so a host failure has little or no impact on the amount of disk space that my VM storage objects consume. We are nowhere close to filling up the magnetic disks on this cluster.

Now we come to the `vsan.disks_stats` command. Basically, this command can tell you how well your cluster is balanced from a components per magnetic disk basis. It also displays useful information about the amount of disk space that is available and consumed. Other useful information pertains to performance, such as read/write operations and latencies. However, performance will be covered in more detail in the following sections.

Let's look at some outputs, first from a cluster-wide view. The output shown in Figure 10.18 taken from an 8-node VSAN 1.0 cluster, has been truncated for readability, with the output of five hosts removed.

```
/mia-cg07-vc01/mia-cg07-dc01/computers> vsan.disks_stats 0
+------------------------+--------------------------+-------+----------+--------+----------+------+-----------+
|                        |                          |       | Num | Capacity |      |           |      | Device    |
| DisplayName            | Host                     | isSSD | Comp | Total   | Used | Reserved | Used | Latencies |
+------------------------+--------------------------+-------+----------+--------+----------+------+-----------+
| naa.50025385a00c5085   | mia-cg07-esx011.vmwcs.com | SSD  | 0   | 83.47 GB | 0 % | 0 %      | 0r/0w | 0d/0q/0k |
| naa.5000c5006900c7cf   | mia-cg07-esx011.vmwcs.com | MD   | 5   | 1117.75 GB | 0 % | 0 %    | 0r/0w | 0d/0q/0k |
+------------------------+--------------------------+-------+----------+--------+----------+------+-----------+
| naa.50025385a00c5084   | mia-cg07-esx012.vmwcs.com | SSD  | 0   | 83.47 GB | 0 % | 0 %      | 0r/0w | 0d/0q/0k |
| naa.5000c500690142df   | mia-cg07-esx012.vmwcs.com | MD   | 4   | 1117.75 GB | 4 % | 4 %    | 0r/0w | 0d/0q/0k |
+------------------------+--------------------------+-------+----------+--------+----------+------+-----------+
| naa.50025385a00a376a   | mia-cg07-esx013.vmwcs.com | SSD  | 0   | 83.47 GB | 0 % | 0 %      | 0r/0w | 0d/0q/0k |
| naa.5000c50067d8d9f7   | mia-cg07-esx013.vmwcs.com | MD   | 4   | 1117.75 GB | 4 % | 4 %    | 0r/0w | 0d/0q/0k |
+------------------------+--------------------------+-------+----------+--------+----------+------+-----------+
```

Figure 10.18   vsan.disk_stats output

As you can see, there is a somewhat uniform distribution of components across all hosts and all disks in this cluster. VSAN's own initial placement algorithms take control of this. Once again, we have each host listed, and each capacity tier device and flash tier device from those hosts, along with component count, capacity, and various perfor-mance counters. We may also run this command from a host perspective (by traversing to the host object) rather than a cluster perspective, but it doesn't really show any additional data.

There is a slight change in the output in later versions of VSAN. In particular, later versions of this command also include the on-disk format version. In VSAN 1.0, this was version 1, using VMFS-L. In VSAN 6.0, there was a new on-disk format version using VirstoFS (V2). In VSAN 6.2, with the introduction of deduplication and compression features, the on-disk format version has been incremented to V3.

The `disks_stats` is an extremely useful command for verifying that you have a balanced cluster. This is why VMware is making a best practice recommendation to have identically configured ESXi hosts in the VSAN cluster. This will optimally balance the components across ESXi hosts and across the capacity tier disks. If you proceed with building a VSAN cluster with a selection of different ESXi hosts and devices, it may lead to an unbalanced cluster, and certain ESXi hosts in VSAN working harder than other hosts, possibly leading to performance issues.

The final stats command is `vsan.vm_perf_stats`. This command, when run with a VM as an argument, provides input/output operations per second (IOPS), throughput, and latency information on a per-VM basis. This can prove extremely useful for investigating performance issues on individual VMs. The command gathers two sets of performance information, separated by a time gap of 20 seconds. This allows the display to average out the performance over that sample period. However, VSAN provides a much nicer way of examining performance information through the new VSAN 6.2 performance service, or via the VSAN Observer tool, which we will look at in detail very shortly.

resync_dashboard

`resync_dashboard` is an extremely useful command to check how well or quickly storage objects in VSAN are resynchronizing (although this view is also available in the vSphere Web Client UI). This could be occurring for any number of reasons, including a host failure with components being rebuilt elsewhere in the cluster or indeed a change in the policy setting that requires a new object to be re-created and synchronized against the old object. Remember that changes to a VM storage policy may occur on-the-fly. What happens is that a new replica with the new layout is created and is synchronized against the original preexisting components. When this completes, the original components are discarded. And this all takes place while the VM continues to run.

The `vsan.resync_dashboard` command is run against the cluster object in RVC, and it displays all objects that are resynchronizing as well as the number of bytes that are still left to synchronize. Here is an example taken from a cluster when we placed a host into maintenance mode and requested that full data migration takes place. This means that VSAN needs to migrate all the components and objects from the ESXi host entering maintenance mode to other ESXi hosts in the cluster. In Figure 10.19 we see one object to sync with 0.18 GB bytes to sync left:

```
2014-02-10 12:02:47 +0000: Querying all VMs on VSAN ...
2014-02-10 12:02:47 +0000: Querying all objects in the system ...
2014-02-10 12:02:48 +0000: Got all the info, computing table ...
+-------------------------------------------+-----------------+----------------+
|                                           |                 |                |
| VM/Object                                 | Syncing objects | Bytes to sync  |
|                                           |                 |                |
+-------------------------------------------+-----------------+----------------+
|                                           |                 |                |
| vm-ftt-of-1-sw-of-2                       | 1               |                |
|                                           |                 |                |
|    [vsanDatastore] vm-ftt-of-1-sw-of-2.vmx |                 | 0.18 GB        |
|                                           |                 |                |
+-------------------------------------------+-----------------+----------------+
|                                           |                 |                |
| Total                                     | 1               | 0.18 GB        |
|                                           |                 |                |
+-------------------------------------------+-----------------+----------------+
```

Figure 10.19   vsan.resync_dashboard output

enter_maintenance_mode

You can use the `enter_maintenance_mode` command to place the ESXi hosts participating in VSAN into maintenance mode. Refer to Chapter 7, for further information
about what maintenance mode options are available.

lldpnetmap

`lldpnetmap` is an extremely useful RVC command for troubleshooting network issues.
The link layer discovery protocol (LLDP) is a vendor-neutral link-layer protocol used by
network devices to advertise their capabilities. For those of you familiar with cisco discovery
protocol (CDP), this is a vendor-neutral equivalent. When this command is run against a
VSAN cluster, it will display LLDP info for all the hosts in the cluster if such information
exists. Here is an output from a 4-node cluster, showing which uplinks are connected to
which switch. In this case all uplinks on each host are connected to the same switch.

```
/vcsa-05/Datacenter/computers> vsan.lldpnetmap 0

2015-12-29 13:22:40 +0000: This operation will take 30-60 seconds ...

+-------------------------+----------------------------------------+
|                         |                                        |
| Host                    | LLDP info                              |
|                         |                                        |
+-------------------------+----------------------------------------+
|                         |                                        |
| esxi-b-pref.rainpole.com | 04f8b1566a8651: vmnic2,vmnic1,vmnic0 |
|                         |                                        |
| esxi-c-scnd.rainpole.com | 04f8b1566a8651: vmnic2,vmnic1,vmnic0 |
|                         |                                        |
| esxi-d-scnd.rainpole.com | 04f8b1566a8651: vmnic2,vmnic1,vmnic0 |
|                         |                                        |
| esxi-a-pref.rainpole.com | 04f8b1566a8651: vmnic2,vmnic1,vmnic0 |
|                         |                                        |
+-------------------------+----------------------------------------+
```

apply_license_to_cluster

`apply_license_to_cluster` is another straightforward RVC command that can be used to license the VSAN cluster if you did not want to do this task via the vSphere Web Client. It takes an option of `--license-key`.

check_limits

Along with `vsan.check_state`, we recommend running the `check_limits` command at regular intervals when you are running a large number of VMs on your VSAN cluster. Way back in the requirements chapter, a number of VSAN limits were discussed. One of these limits was the number of components that could exist on an ESXi host participating in a VSAN cluster. The number of supported in the initial release of VSAN is 3,000. However this was increased to 9,000 for VSAN 6.0. In the output shown in Figure 10.20, the `vsan.check_limits` is taken from VSAN 1.0. The number of existing components as well as the limit is displayed. Another VSAN limit is the number of socket connections per host that can be carried by the reliable datagram protocol (RDT), VSAN's communication bus. This information is also displayed, along with the number of sockets currently in use. We have truncated some of the output of the command for readability.

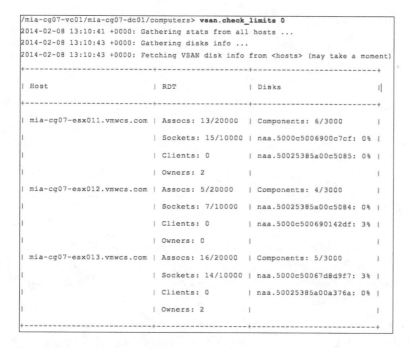

```
/mia-cg07-vc01/mia-cg07-dc01/computers> vsan.check_limits 0
2014-02-08 13:10:41 +0000: Gathering stats from all hosts ...
2014-02-08 13:10:43 +0000: Gathering disks info ...
2014-02-08 13:10:43 +0000: Fetching VSAN disk info from <hosts> (may take a moment)
+-------------------------------+--------------------+----------------------------+
| Host                          | RDT                | Disks                     ||
+-------------------------------+--------------------+----------------------------+
| mia-cg07-esx011.vmwcs.com     | Assocs: 13/20000   | Components: 6/3000         |
|                               | Sockets: 15/10000  | naa.5000c5006900c7cf: 0%  |
|                               | Clients: 0         | naa.50025385a00c5085: 0%  |
|                               | Owners: 2          |                           |
| mia-cg07-esx012.vmwcs.com     | Assocs: 5/20000    | Components: 4/3000         |
|                               | Sockets: 7/10000   | naa.50025385a00c5084: 0%  |
|                               | Clients: 0         | naa.5000c500690142df: 3%  |
|                               | Owners: 0          |                           |
| mia-cg07-esx013.vmwcs.com     | Assocs: 16/20000   | Components: 5/3000         |
|                               | Sockets: 14/10000  | naa.5000c50067d8d9f7: 3%  |
|                               | Clients: 0         | naa.50025385a00a376a: 0%  |
|                               | Owners: 2          |                           |
+-------------------------------+--------------------+----------------------------+
```

Figure 10.20 vsan.check_limits output

Note once again that this is an output taken from VSAN 1.0 and that many of the limits displayed here have been raised significantly in later releases of VSAN. Running this command on your build of VSAN should show what these new limits are. In all likelihood, these limits will continue to rise with newer releases of VSAN.

reapply_vsan_vmknic_config

The `reapply_vsan_vmknic_config` command reconfigures the VSAN network on a particular VMkernel network interface card (NIC) on an ESXi host. This command could prove useful if changes are needed on the physical network layer and you need the VSAN network to recognize these changes. The output shown in Example 10.26 demonstrates what you will see when running this command:

Example 10.26 vsan.reapply_vsan_vmknic_config

```
/vcsa-05/Datacenter/computers/Cluster/hosts> ls
0 esxi-b-pref.rainpole.com (host): cpu 2*8*2.40 GHz, memory 102.00 GB
1 esxi-c-scnd.rainpole.com (host): cpu 2*8*2.40 GHz, memory 102.00 GB
2 esxi-d-scnd.rainpole.com (host): cpu 2*8*2.40 GHz, memory 102.00 GB
3 esxi-a-pref.rainpole.com (host): cpu 2*8*2.40 GHz, memory 102.00 GB
/vcsa-05/Datacenter/computers/Cluster/hosts> vsan.reapply_vsan_vmknic_
config 0
Host: esxi-b-pref.rainpole.com
  Reapplying config of vmk2:
    AgentGroupMulticastAddress: 224.2.3.4
    AgentGroupMulticastPort: 23451
    IPProtocol: IP
    InterfaceUUID: a5227456-06dc-f09d-3390-ecf4bbd58600
    MasterGroupMulticastAddress: 224.1.2.3
    MasterGroupMulticastPort: 12345
    MulticastTTL: 5
  Unbinding VSAN from vmknic vmk2 ...
  Rebinding VSAN to vmknic vmk2 ...
```

recover_spbm

Take a scenario where you have lost your vCenter Server that manages your VSAN cluster. After deploying a new vCenter Server, the one remaining task is to rebuild your VM storage policies. But how do you find out what the policy settings were? This is where the `recover_spbm` command can really help.

First, it displays which VMs are running on VSAN without any policies. By that, we mean running with policies that are not defined in vCenter. The VMs continue to honor their original policy settings where possible, even if the vCenter Server is no longer available.

Once VMs running with policies that are no longer in vCenter Server are discovered by the `recover_spbm` command, you are given options on how to recover them, as shown in Example 10.27:

Example 10.27 vsan.recover_spbm

```
/vcsa-05/Datacenter/computers/Cluster/hosts> vsan.recover_spbm 0
2015-12-29 13:32:30 +0000: Fetching Host info
2015-12-29 13:32:30 +0000: Fetching Datastore info
2015-12-29 13:32:30 +0000: Fetching VM properties
2015-12-29 13:32:30 +0000: Fetching policies used on VSAN from CMMDS
2015-12-29 13:32:30 +0000: Fetching SPBM profiles
2015-12-29 13:32:30 +0000: Fetching VM <-> SPBM profile association
2015-12-29 13:32:30 +0000: Computing which VMs do not have a SPBM Profile ...
2015-12-29 13:32:30 +0000: Fetching additional info about some VMs
2015-12-29 13:32:30 +0000: Got all info, computing after 0.68 sec
2015-12-29 13:32:30 +0000: Done computing
SPBM Profiles used by VSAN:
+----------------------------------+----------------------------+
| SPBM ID                          | policy                     |
+----------------------------------+----------------------------+
| Existing SPBM Profile:           | stripeWidth: 2             |
| R5+SW=2                          | hostFailuresToTolerate: 1  |
|                                  | replicaPreference: Capacity|
+----------------------------------+----------------------------+
| Existing SPBM Profile:           | stripeWidth: 1             |
| R5+SW=2                          | proportionalCapacity: 0    |
|                                  | hostFailuresToTolerate: 1  |
|                                  | replicaPreference: Capacity|
+----------------------------------+----------------------------+
| Existing SPBM Profile:           | stripeWidth: 1             |
| Virtual SAN Default Storage Policy| cacheReservation: 0       |
|                                  | proportionalCapacity: 0    |
|                                  | hostFailuresToTolerate: 1  |
|                                  | forceProvisioning: 0       |
+----------------------------------+----------------------------+
| Existing SPBM Profile:           | hostFailuresToTolerate: 1  |
| R5                               | replicaPreference: Capacity|
+----------------------------------+----------------------------+
| Existing SPBM Profile:           | stripeWidth: 1             |
| R5                               | proportionalCapacity: 0    |
```

```
|                                        | hostFailuresToTolerate: 1  |
|                                        | replicaPreference: Capacity |
+----------------------------------------+----------------------------+
```

In the preceding output, there are no VMs running with undefined policies. vCenter Server has a full list of policies used by all VMs. There are a number of additional options available, such as looking at the missing policies in more details, re-creating the missing policies, and automatically associating the missing policies with VMs. This is a very useful RVC command when there is a vCenter Server failure, or indeed when migrating VSAN to a new vCenter Server.

upgrade_status

This command was a very late additional to RVC when VSAN 6.2 launched. During the on-disk format upgrade from version 2 to version 3, there are a number of steps that need to take place. First, Virtual SAN realigns objects and their components to have a 1 MB address space. Then, Virtual SAN realigns vsanSparse objects to be 4k aligned. These steps could take a considerable amount of time, with the UI progress sitting at 10%, so in order to provide administrators with a view of the alignment and conversion process, this command was added. Once the alignment of objects is completed, the command shows which components are being rebuilt/resynced, due to the evacuation and reformatting of the disk groups with the new on-disk format. Here is a sample (truncated) output, with the status shown every 60 seconds:

```
/vcsa-05/Datacenter/computers/Cluster/hosts> vsan.upgrade_status -r 60 0
2016-03-24 19:18:29 +0000: Upgrade in progress - 15%
2016-03-24 19:18:30 +0000: Updating objects to alignment
2016-03-24 19:18:30 +0000: 0 objects in which need realignment process
2016-03-24 19:18:30 +0000: 49 objects with new alignment
2016-03-24 19:18:30 +0000: 0 objects ready for v3 features
2016-03-24 19:18:30 +0000: Upgrade invovles resyncing objects at times, showing
current resync progress
2016-03-24 19:18:31 +0000: Querying all VMs on VSAN ...
2016-03-24 19:18:31 +0000: Querying all objects in the system from 10.160.54.54
...
2016-03-24 19:18:31 +0000: Got all the info, computing table ...
```

SPBM Commands

Another very useful set of commands that are available in RVC are the SPBM commands. As you might imagine, these are very useful commands for working on storage policies.

Example 10.28 displays a list of the commands available, and most of them should be pretty obvious.

Example 10.28   help spbm

```
> help spbm
Commands:
check_compliance: Check compliance
device_add_disk: Add a hard drive to a virtual machine
device_change_storage_profile: Change storage profile of a virtual disk
namespace_change_storage_profile: Change storage profile of VM namespace
profile_apply: Apply a VM Storage Profile. Pushed profile content to
Storage system
profile_create: Create a VM Storage Profile
profile_delete: Delete a VM Storage Profile
profile_modify: Create a VM Storage Profile
vm_change_storage_profile: Change storage profile of VM namespace and its
disks

To see commands in a namespace: help namespace_name
To see detailed help for a command: help namespace_name.command_name
```

In VSAN, a number of RVC commands to examine the SPBM settings are also available. At this point, you will know that to deploy a VM on VSAN, you create a VM storage policy for the VM, which may stipulate the number of mirror copies of the VM disk (number of failures to tolerate) or indeed a stripe width for the VMDK. SPBM is the underlying technology that controls this aspect of VSAN. In this post, we can look at some of these SPBM extensions in RVC.

Let's first take a look at the SPBM extensions. There are nine in total in the latest version of RVC. The names are pretty self-explanatory:

```
spbm.check_compliance
spbm.device_add_disk
spbm.device_change_storage_profile
spbm.namespace_change_storage_profile
spbm.profile_apply
spbm.profile_create
spbm.profile_delete
spbm.profile_modify
spbm.vm_change_storage_profile
```

If you navigate to a VM in RVC, you can then use these commands against the individual VMs and devices. Let's look at some examples. First, in Example 10.29, I want to check the compliance of a particular VM, named win1:

Example 10.29   spbm.check_compliance

```
/vcsa-05/Datacenter> ls
0 storage/
1 computers [host]/
2 networks [network]/
3 datastores [datastore]/
4 vms [vm]/
/vcsa-05/Datacenter> cd 4
/vcsa-05/Datacenter/vms> ls
0 R5: poweredOff
1 R5+SW=2: poweredOff
/vcsa-05/Datacenter/vms> spbm.check_compliance 0
+-----------------+---------+------------+
| VM/Virtual Disk | Profile | Compliance |
+-----------------+---------+------------+
| R5              | R5      | compliant  |
|    Hard disk 1  | R5      | compliant  |
+-----------------+---------+------------+

Number of 'compliant' entities: 2
/vcsa-05/Datacenter/vms>
```

The next step is to apply a new profile. The profiles can be found in ~/storage/vmprofiles. In Example 10.30, we have two profiles available:

Example 10.30   Display policies via RVC

```
/vcsa-05/Datacenter/storage> ls
0 vmprofiles/
/vcsa-05/Datacenter/storage> ls 0
0 Virtual SAN Default Storage Policy
1 VVol No Requirements Policy
2 R5+SW=2
3 R5
/vcsa-05/Datacenter/storage>
```

We will now change the profile on one of our VMs from R5 (RAID-5) to R5+SW=2 (RAID-5 and number of disk objects to stripe = 2) using the command spbm.vm_change_ storage_profile as shown in Example 10.31:

Example 10.31   spbm.vm_change_storage_profile

```
vcsa-05/Datacenter/vms> ls
0 R5: poweredOff
1 R5+SW=2: poweredOff
/vcsa-05/Datacenter/vms> spbm.vm_change_storage_profile 0 -p ../storage/
vmprofiles/R5+SW=2/
ReconfigVM R5: success
```

Of course, the reconfiguration will take a little time. By issuing the command spbm. check_compliance, it can be observed that hard disk 1 belonging to the VM that uses the storage policy that was just modified is now noncompliant, as shown in Example 10.32:

Example 10.32   spbm.check_compliance

```
/vcsa-05/Datacenter/vms> spbm.check_compliance 0
+-----------------+---------+-----------+
| VM/Virtual Disk | Profile | Compliance |
+-----------------+---------+-----------+
| R5              | R5+SW=2 | compliant |
|    Hard disk 1  | R5+SW=2 | compliant |
+-----------------+---------+-----------+

Number of 'compliant' entities: 2
/vcsa-05/Datacenter/vms>
```

And, of course, we can use the very useful vsan.resync_dashboard command to see how much data is still synching while the reconfiguration is taking place. You can repeatedly run this command, and when the Bytes To Sync is 0, everything is synchronized. Some very useful commands, I'm sure you will agree.

One final note: If you want to use one of the SPBM commands that requires a "device" as an argument, you must use the disk devices as found in ~/vms/<VM>/devices/.

Troubleshooting VSAN on the ESXi

So far, we have looked at a lot of tools that are cluster centric, such as the RVC tool. Although we did discuss some ESXCLI commands available to administrators on an ESXi host, you also need to know where to look to find errors messages and log files. This small section highlights which log files to monitor, as well as some other utilities you might need to use when troubleshooting VSAN.

Log Files

You can find the VSAN log files in the ESXi host locations outlined in Table 10.3.

Table 10.3   VSAN log file locations

Log File Description	Log File Locations
CLOM (cluster-level Object Manager logs)	`/var/log/clomd.log`
OSFS (presents VSAN object storage as a file system)	`/var/log/osfsd.log`
vCenter/ESXi communications	`/var/log/hostd.log` `/var/log/vpxa.log`
VSAN vendor provider	`/var/log/vsanvpd.log`

ESXi log	`/var/log/vmkernel.log`
	`/var/log/vobd.log`
	`/var/log/vmkwarning.log`

You may also find references to the major software components of VSAN, such as LSOM, RDT, DOM, and PLOG. GSS recommends searching the VMkernel log files for entries containing these keywords when troubleshooting VSAN issues. If you are unfamiliar with these software components, revisit Chapter 5. It provides detailed information about the role played by each of the components.

VSAN Traces

We briefly touched on the trace utility back in the ESXCLI section of this chapter. VSAN uses a compressed binary trace format for logging multiple messages per I/O. The traces go into /var/log/vsantraces/. These traces are not human readable and must be extracted before they can be viewed. To decode the VSAN traces into human-readable "log messages," you can run the following commands on the ESXi host:

```
# cd /var/log/vsantraces/
# zcat <file>.gz | /usr/lib/vmware/vsan/bin/vsanTraceReader.py > <file>.txt
```

When this command is run, *<file>*.txt will contain a human-readable form of the trace.

For hosts with less than 512 GB of memory, booting the ESXi image from USB/SD devices is supported. For hosts with a memory configuration larger than 512 GB, ESXi needs to be installed on a local disk or a SATADOM device. The reason for this is that in the event of a critical failure, ESXi is set up to dump its memory state. With memory sizes above 512 GB, there is not enough space on SD/USB devices to capture this state. Therefore a device with a larger capacity is needed. VMware global support services and the VMware engineering teams use this core dump information and relevant VSAN traces for root cause analysis. When installing ESXi on USB or SD, note that you should use a device that has a minimum capacity of 8 GB.

VSAN VMkernel Modules and Drivers

ESXi comes with all of the components required to build a VSAN cluster. No additional VIBs or software components need to be added to the host to successfully create a VSAN cluster and build a scaled-out VSAN datastore.

When VSAN is successfully configured, you will observe new VMkernel modules loaded for the purposes of implementing VSAN. The VMkernel module names are vsan, rdt, plog, and lsomcommon.

When a VM does a write operation, the write goes to SSD, and then VSAN regularly flushes (or evicts) the SSD contents to magnetic disks. The plog module implements the VSAN elevator algorithm. It looks at the physical layout of the magnetic disk and decides when to flush SSD contents to it.

The vsan module can be thought of as the module for both the LSOM and DOM components. As these modules are heavily intertwined, the lsomcommon contains shared code for these components, although these are now separated in VSAN 6.0 and later, and lsom now has its own module.

The rdt module is the reliable datagram transport module responsible for cross-cluster VSAN communication.

Performance Monitoring

One of the most important aspects of managing storage is to be able to monitor and troubleshoot performance issues. VSAN is no different. In this section, we share with you various tools that are at a vSphere administrator's disposal for monitoring and trouble-shooting VSAN performance-related issues.

Introducing the Performance Service

In Virtual SAN 6.2, the issue of being unable to determine the performance of the different parts of VSAN was addressed. With the introduction of the new VSAN 6.2 performance service, administrators can now drill down into the various parts of a VSAN

Cluster and examine the underlying performance. Administrators can now determine how a host, disk group, individual disk, or virtual machine is performing on a VSAN cluster.

Enabling the performance service

Enabling the performance service is quite straightforward. Navigate to the VSAN cluster object in the vCenter Server inventory, click the Manage tab, and click on the Health and Performance section. The performance service will be disabled by default, as per Figure 10.21.

Figure 10.21   Performance service is turned off

To enable the performance service, click on the "Edit" button. When the performance service is enabled, a VM home namespace object, with 255 GB of capacity for the storing of metrics, is created on the VSAN datastore. This requires a policy, but it will choose the VSAN datastore default policy automatically. Administrators can choose a different policy if they wish. Once enabled, the performance service will look similar to Figure 10.22.

Figure 10.22   Performance service is turned on

Now that the performance service is enabled, it may be used for examining VSAN performance.

Using the VSAN performance service

Once the VSAN performance service has been enabled, multiple performance views are now available to the administrators. The views are as follows:

Cluster Performance

Virtual Machine Consumption

Virtual SAN Backend

Host Performance

    Virtual Machine Consumption

    Virtual SAN Backend

Disk Performance

    Disk Group

    Disk

Virtual Machine

    Virtual Machine Performance

    Virtual Disk Performance

To monitor the VSAN performance for any of the above, select the appropriate inventory object (cluster, host, VM), then select the Monitor tab and then select Performance. The performance views will then be available for selection. Figure 10.23 shows an example of the cluster performance view, albeit taken from a very idle, preproduction VSAN system.

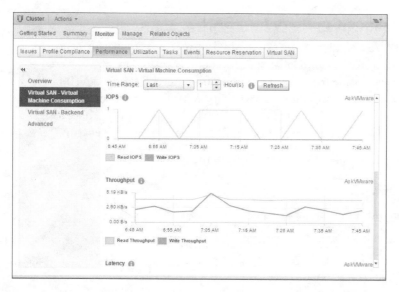

Figure 10.23   Cluster Performance—Virtual Machine Consumption

Performance Service Metrics

Each of the view has a set of metrics which administrators will find useful. These are IOPS, throughput, outstanding IO, latency, and congestion. These can be examined both from a front-end perspective (VM workload perspective) and from a VSAN backend perspective. As previously mentioned, administrators can drill down into the performance from a cluster level, host level, disk group level, disk level, or even to a VM level.

When examining the VSAN backend metrics on a per-host level, some additional counters are available to look at resync/rebuild activity, including the number of resync IOPs and resync throughput.

Further granularity of performance metrics is available in the disk groups and disk views. In the disk group view, read cache hit rate (for hybrid systems) is available, as well as information related to delayed IO. Delayed IO is a good indicator of determining if the amount of outstanding IO is correctly configured, especially for benchmarking. Outstanding IO should be tuned to keep the pipeline full at all times and the device continuously busy. You don't want to go over this and have I/O delayed waiting to get into the queue. This introduces latency. If delayed IO percentage is over 0%, then there is too much outstanding IO in the queue. Delayed IO average latency is telling us how much this delayed IO is adding.

Just like the health check service, the performance service also has the "Ask VMware" capability. Should you need further information on any of the metrics or counters, simply click the "Ask VMware" link and this should provide information related to the metric.

ESXTOP Performance Counters for VSAN

In the initial release of VSAN, there were no VSAN datastore-specific performance counters in esxtop. In VSAN 6.0 and later, specific counters related to VSAN were added to esxtop. However, aside from the VSAN specific counters, esxtop can still be a very useful tool when you want to examine VM activity, VMDK performance, host status, memory usage, adapter queue depth and of course, disk activity on an ESXi host basis. Esxtop is quite easy to use; at a shell prompt on an ESXi host, simply type **esxtop**.

Figure 10.24 shows some sample esxtop output from the initial release.

Figure 10.24 esxtop output

Typing in the character h while esxtop is running can access help. The following display options are available:

- c: CPU

- i: Interrupt

- m: Memory

- n: Network

- d: Disk adapter

- u: Disk device

- v: Disk VM

- p: Power management

- x: VSAN

The VSAN view displays three roles; client, owner, and component manager. These roles were covered in Chapter 5. I/O statistics related to each role may be observed on a per-host basis with esxtop on VSAN 6.0 or later. But what about a deeper view? In VSAN 6.2, the new performance service can also give you this information. However, we also have another tool that provides VSAN-centric performance statistics, namely the VSAN observer tool. We will examine this shortly.

vSphere Web Client Performance Counters for VSAN

Prior to VSAN 6.2, the vSphere client does not have any specific performance counters for VSAN datastore. If you navigate to the VSAN cluster object in the vCenter Server inventory, select the **Monitoring** tab, and then select **Performance** view, there is an option to change the chart options. You will notice that once again nothing specific for the VSAN datastore is available.

However, the performance views available in the vSphere client for both the VMs and the VMDKs work perfectly, even when the VM is deployed on the VSAN datastore. Figure 10.25 shows performance information, in this case highlighting read latency and write latency of VMDKs.

As mentioned in the esxtop section, apart from the new VSAN 6.2 performance service, the VSAN observer tool is what we can use to display information about VSAN performance. In versions of VSAN prior to 6.2, this is really the only tool available for performance monitoring of the underlying VSAN layers. We shall look at this tool next.

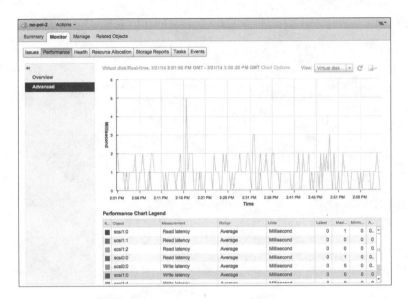

Figure 10.25   vSphere Web Client performance view

VSAN Observer

The vSphere Web Client in vSphere 5.5 U1 ships with a number of built-in VSAN management functions. For example, you will find VSAN datastore as well as VM-level performance statistics in the vSphere Web Client. If you require in-depth VSAN performance, however, down to the physical disk layers, understanding the cache hit rates, reasons for observed latencies, and so on, the vSphere Web Client will not deliver this level of detail in vSphere 5.5 U1. In VSAN 6.2, the new VSAN performance service should now more than fill this gap. However, the performance service was not available in previous VSAN versions. That is where the VSAN observer comes in.

The VSAN observer is part of the RVC, an interactive command-line shell for vSphere management as we have already seen, and RVC is part of both the Windows vCenter Server and VCVA (appliance version of vCenter Server) in vSphere 5.5 U1.

Let's talk a bit about requirements and how to deploy the VSAN observer before delving into what it can do for you.

VSAN Observer Requirements

VSAN observer is a performance tool that has been specifically written to display VSAN performance information. It requires a modern web browser and a working Internet connection (because certain open source software components need to be downloaded for it to work). It also requires vCenter 5.5 U1 Server or later, either the Linux appliance version (VCVA) or the Windows version. RVC is preinstalled in vCenter Server 5.5 U1.

You have two deployment options:

- You can use RVC inside your production vCenter Server that is managing your VSAN clusters.

- You can deploy an additional vCenter Server, just to get RVC and the VSAN observer tool.

In a lab environment, the former is likely more convenient. Administrators need to be aware that the VSAN Observer opens up an unencrypted and unhardened HTTP server. Doing this on your production vCenter Server may very well be against your security policies, which is why VMware created the standalone option. In such a case, deploying an additional server to run RVC may be a better option for you.

Running the `vsan.observer` command with the name of your cluster as an argument will launch VSAN observer. This command will gather statistics from vCenter Server and VSAN every *x* seconds. The default interval value defaults to 60 seconds for statistics collection, but you may specify a smaller or larger interval via the *--interval* parameter. It will currently collect information for a 2-hour period.

Typically, you want to run the command with the `-run-webserver` option, which opens an unencrypted HTTP web server on port 8010. You can change the port number with the *--port* option. Because we have already looked at the steps to launch RVC on a Windows version of vCenter Server in the previous version, let's now look at the steps required to get RVC up and running (and thus launch the VSAN Observer) on the vCenter Server Linux appliance (VCVA):

1. Open an SSH session to your vCenter Server Appliance:

   ssh root@<name or ip of your VCVA>

2. Open RVC using your root account and the vCenter name, in my case:

   rvc root@localhost

3. Now do a `cd` into your vCenter object (you can do an `ls` to see what the names are of your objects on any level), and if you press the <tab> key it will be completed with your datacenter object:

   cd localhost/<Name-of-your-datacenter> /

4. Now do a `cd` again. The first object is computers and the second is your cluster. In my case that looks like the following:

   cd computers/<Name-of-your-VSAN-cluster>/

5. Now you can start the VSAN observer using the following command:

```
vsan.observer . --run-webserver --force
```

6. Now you can see the observer querying stats every 60 seconds, and as mentioned you can stop this by pressing **Ctrl+C**. The collection will stop automatically after a period of 2 hours.

After completing these preparation steps, you can now examine the in-depth VSAN performance data. Begin by opening a web browser and pointing it at http://*<rvc-vc-ip>*:*<observer-port>*. The *<rvc-vc-ip>* is the IP address of the host running RVC, not the IP address of the vCenter Server that you are monitoring (although they could be the same). The port defaults to 8010, but you may have changed it via the `--port` option. We recommend using Google Chrome, but any modern browser should work. Internet Explorer 8 is not considered a modern browser, but may still work to some extent. Older versions of IE will definitely give you problems.

Figure 10.26 shows what the VSAN observer landing page looks like.

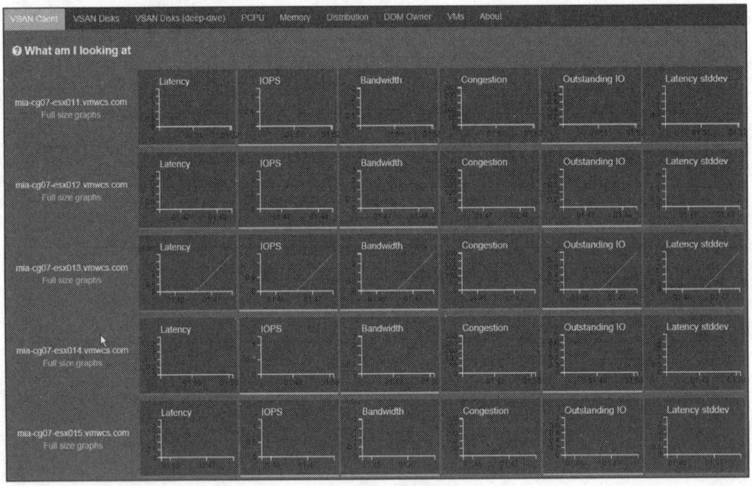

Figure 10.26   VSAN Observer: VSAN Client view

You can also ask the command to generate a stats bundle, a single smaller archive file that contains the same information the web browser would show you, which you can then save, email to colleagues, or email to VMware support. The command option is as follows:

```
vsan.observer <cluster> -generate-html-bundle /tmp
```

This will dump the stats bundle to the /tmp folder on the vCenter Server.

The command will run until you tell it to stop via **Ctrl+C**. Note that it will keep the entire history of your observer session in memory until you press **Ctrl+C**, meaning if you run it for many hours it will use multiple gigabytes of RAM. This is another reason why you may prefer to run the VSAN observer on a dedicated vCenter Server.

Examining VSAN Observer Performance Data

When you first open up VSAN observer, the primary indicator of an issue that is abnormal is that there will be a red underline for the graph in question that is outside normal operating boundaries. Graphs in VSAN observer typically show green for normal state, or gray if there is no information or not enough information yet available. Red is your indicator to start investigating, and is displayed when 20% of the samples taken during the sampling period are outside the configured threshold.

The VSAN Observer UI is organized by subsystem. You should start with the VSAN Client view, which gives you an overview over what level of service the VMs are getting from VSAN. Every host in a VSAN cluster (and hence every "VSAN Client") is consuming storage distributed across all other hosts in the cluster, so seeing a performance issue on the VSAN client on host A may in fact be due to overloaded disks on host B.

The "VSAN disks" view allows you to look at VSAN from that perspective, checking how nodes that contribute storage to the VSAN datastore are doing in terms of servicing I/O from their local disks. You can then further drill down into a deep-dive of the VSAN disks layer on a per-host basis, seeing how VSAN splits I/O among SSDs and HDDs.

Figure 10.27 shows the VSAN disks view. As you can see, there is a lot of information displayed here. This view shows everything from latency, IOPS, bandwidth, congestion, outstanding I/O, and a standard deviation on latency, which shows how much latency has deviated from the average. Once again, you are looking for charts with are underlined in red; these highlight a metric that is outside the norm. That is where investigation into disk-related issues should begin. For latency, the threshold level is set to 30 ms. Bandwidth is measured in kilobytes per second (KB/s). Congestion is a measurement of 1 to 255; 1 means there is no congestion, 255 means it is fully congested. The threshold value for congestion is set to 75.

VSAN shares compute resources with the rest of ESXi; that is, VSAN is consuming a slice of the same CPU and memory resources that the VMs running on a given host are also consuming. VSAN has been designed to consume no more than 10% of CPU resources. You can inspect the VSAN PCPU (physical CPU) and memory consumption in dedicated tabs in the observer, which may also be useful in detecting performance bottlenecks due to CPU or memory limits.

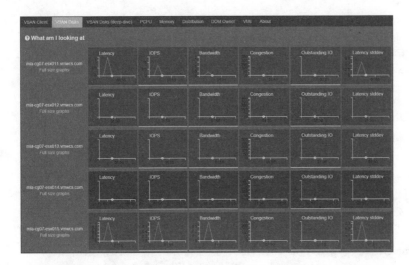

Figure 10.27   VSAN Observer: VSAN disks

Figure 10.28 shows the memory consumption of not just the VSAN components, but also other consumers of memory of the various ESXi hosts participating in the VSAN cluster.

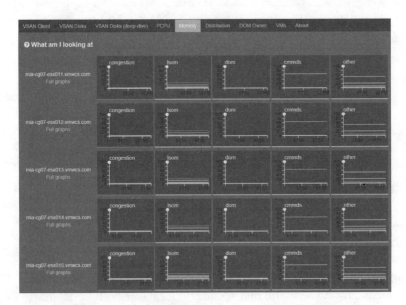

Figure 10.28   VSAN Observer: Memory

Because VSAN is a type of storage that is managed in a very VM-centric way (per-virtual disk using VM storage policies), you can also look at performance on a per-VM or even per-virtual disk level in the VSAN observer. Start in the VMs tab and select the VM that you want to get more detail on.

Figure 10.29 shows the VM Home space from one VM. For each component that makes up the object, information such as latency, IOPS, read cache (RC) hit rate, and cache evictions are all displayed. This is excellent information for determining whether any issues exist with any of the components that make up the storage object of a particular VM that may be exhibiting performance issues. Evictions are a reference to the fact that entries in the cache are being flushed out of cache to magnetic disks. High values here could suggest that there could be contention for cache resources, possibly implying that flash has not been sized correctly. Read cache hit rate is also an interesting graph, because anything below 100% implies that we have had a read cache miss and have had to go to magnetic disk to retrieve a data block, which will increase latency.

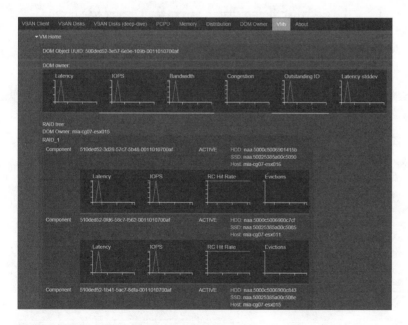

Figure 10.29   VSAN Observer: VMs view

Last but not least, there are tabs for auxiliary information (on cluster balance, distribution of objects, significant cluster events, and so on). Every time you switch tabs, the graphs update automatically and reflect the latest information gathered by RVC in the background.

Most tabs contain information about how to read the information presented in the graphs. However, a lot of them require familiarity with storage performance. Having said that, the more you use the VSAN Observer tool, and the more familiar you get with how your environment should be running in steady state, the more useful this tool will become when you need to troubleshoot issues that occur outside the norm.

As you can imagine, we have only scratched the surface of what you can do with VSAN observer.

Sample VSAN Observer Use Case

As a way of demonstrating the usefulness of VSAN Observer, we reached out to Simon Todd, one of the VMware Support Technical Leads for VSAN, and asked him about how he has used VSAN Observer to troubleshoot a performance issue on VSAN. Simon kindly shared the following scenario, including symptoms and root cause.

The problem statement from the case that Simon shared was this: "During I/O testing, VMs performed slow, and some VMs reported as inaccessible." Troubleshooting began by looking at the log files, after which issues were quickly identified. First, DOM reported TimeTooLong for an operation, as shown in Figure 10.30.

```
2013-12-05T17:21:38.356392 [26141117] [cpu27] [22a870d2 OWNER write]
DOMTraceOpTookTooLong:2645: {'op': 0x4136c85f78c0, 'obj': 0x412eca2b4c40,
'objUuid': '58cc9852-d985-9aae-8bd9-0006f62b11ec', 'time msec': 103129}
```

Figure 10.30   DOMTraceOpTookTooLong

The investigation team also noticed that LSOM was reporting a very high congestion figure of 255, as shown in Figure 10.31.

```
2013-12-05T17:21:35.586223 [27666780] [cpu3] [3184]
LSOMTraceRcLSOMVAAllocFailure:1055: {'status': 'VMK_NO_MEMORY'}
2013-12-05T17:21:35.586224 [27666781] [cpu3] [3184] LSOMTraceRcScanError:
3332: {'rclPacked': 0x0, 'objectSlot': 14000, 'rclIndex': 0, 'rdt': 0x0,
'inFlight': 0x0}
2013-12-05T17:21:35.586224 [27666782] [cpu3] [3184]
LSOMTraceRcDomCompletion:1461: {'status': 'VMK_NO_MEMORY', 'time':
'00:00:00.000003', 'heapCongestion': 0, 'vaCongestion': 0, 'iopsCongestion':
0, 'congestion': 255}
```

Figure 10.31   Congestion at 255

It was now time to turn to VSAN Observer to see whether it could help with locating the root cause of the problems witnessed in the log files. Immediately, when VSAN Observer was launched and the VSAN Client view was opened, it was clear that there were significant latency problems, as shown in Figure 10.32. There were also congestion issues reported, as per the congestion errors found in the logs.

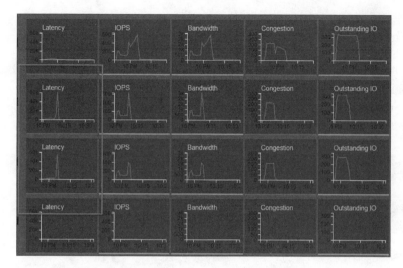

Figure 10.32   Latency issues

The abnormal issues are reported with the red underscores, so this is brought to an administrator's immediate attention. By clicking any of the graphs, it will be enlarged with additional detail. In this case, one of the latency graphs was expanded, and further detail is given about the latency values. As shown in Figure 10.33, the read latency value reported in the graph was extraordinarily high, in the region of 60,000 milliseconds, or 60 seconds.

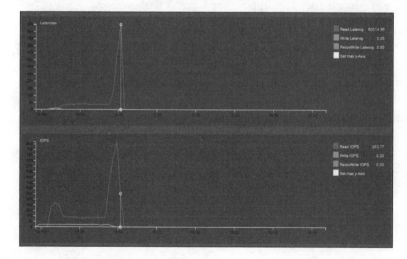

Figure 10.33   Latency and IOPS detail

One thing that stood out was the fact that the IOPS figure was relatively low, but the latency value was high. Why is this? Further investigation was needed. As we have said, there are some other interesting VSAN Observer views to look at. The next interesting view is the VMs. What was observed on this view is that there were a lot of cache evictions occurring for one of the VM's components. Looking at other VMs revealed similar behavior. So, it looks like the root cause of our latency and congestion issues are due to the flash device struggling to deal with the workload. It seems that it has to regularly evict blocks from the cache to make room for new data blocks, as shown in Figure 10.34 by the orange peak in the Evictions graph.

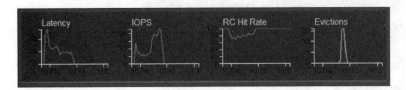

Figure 10.34   Evictions

This led to the support team asking this customer about the type of flash device that was being used in this environment. It turned out that the flash device used in this particular configuration was a Class A flash device, only capable of 2,500 IOPS maximum. The flash devices in each of the hosts were being maxed out by the workload that the customer was trying to deploy on this VSAN cluster resulting in this unwanted behavior. Unfortunately for the customer, it was impossible for VMware support to fix this issue, as this was an unsupported flash device (VMware does not support any Class A flash devices).

Hopefully, this use case showed some of the usefulness of VSAN Observer and how it can be used to identify bottlenecks, but also demonstrated what kind of impact the selection of a flash device can have on performance of your infrastructure. You should familiarize yourself with what is the norm for your environment so that anomalies are readily observed, although the red underscore when values are above the threshold also helps. This use case should also drive home the importance of correctly sizing your VSAN environment; so once again, you should review Chapter 9, "Designing a VSAN Cluster," for guidance on how to correctly size your VSAN cluster and avoid issues like the one discussed here from occurring in your environment.

Summary

As you can clearly see, an extensive suite of tools is available for troubleshooting and monitoring a VSAN deployment. We heard from a lot of VMware customers that they no longer wished for their storage to be a "black box" where visibility into performance was next to impossible. With this extensive suite of CLI and UI tools, customers can drill down into the lowest levels of VSAN behavior.

Index

A

absent components, 185
administrators, views of VSAN, 9–11
admission control, vSphere HA, 50–51
agent role (hosts), 97–98
all-flash VSAN
    read cache in, 101
    VSAN read on, anatomy of, 103
apply_license_to_cluster command, 297
Ask VMware link, 246

B

boot considerations, ESXi, 15
bootstrapping, vCenter server, 197–199

C

cache devices, 14–15, 21–22, 99
    failure, 186–187

cacheReservation command option, 266
cache tier destaging, 117–118
caching algorithms, I/O flow, 100
capacity devices, 14–15, 19–20, 99
    failure, 185–186
check_limits command, 297–298
check_state command, 292–293
checksum
    data integrity through, 130–131
    object, disabling, 73
CLI (command-line interface), 171
CLOM (cluster level object manager), 96–97, 249
cluster_info command, 282–284
cluster level object manager (CLOM), 96–97
cluster monitoring, membership, and directory services (CMMDS), 97, 187
clusters, 10
    adding hosts to, 169–170
    creation of, 48–49
    designing (see design considerations, clusters)

clusters (*Continued*)
  health, 248–249
  removing hosts from, 170–171
  stretched (*see* stretched clusters)
  vSphere HA (*see* vSphere HA (high availability) cluster)
`cluster_set_default_policy` command, 284–285
CMMDS (cluster monitoring, membership, and directory services), 97, 187, 263
`cmmds_find` command, 289–290
`cmmds-tool` command, 269–272
command-line interface (CLI), 171
commands. *see* specific commands
communication network, vSphere HA, 49–50
component protection, vSphere HA, 51
components, 86–87
  absent, 185
  degraded, 185
  limits, 87–88
  management, 95
  replicas, 90–91
  software (*see* software components)
  witness, 87, 90–91
compression, deduplication and, 105–107
configuration
  IGMP snooping querier, 39
  networks
    issues, 38–40
    VDS, 32–37
    VSS, 31–32
  NIOC example, 40–42
  stretched clusters, 202–203, 208–216
congestion test, disks, 251

D

data health checks, 250
data integrity, through checksum, 130–131

data locality, I/O flow, 107–108
  in VSAN stretched clusters, 108–109
data paths, for objects, 95–96
datastores, usage warning, 195
decommission mode, 175
deduplication, compression and, 105–107
default maintenance mode, 175
default policy, 160–164
  hard disk 1 layout, 163
  number of failures to tolerate = 1, 162
  storage, 93–94
degraded components, 185
Dell R730XD server, 238–241
delta disks, 87, 90, 126
design considerations
  clusters
    cache to capacity ratio, 228–229
    ready node profiles, 225–226
    server virtualization (*see* server virtualization)
    sizing constraints, 227–228
    tools, design and sizing, 236
  performance, 229–231
    disk controllers, 231–235
  VDS and NIOC, 42–43
    redundant 10GbE switch with link aggregation, 45–48
    redundant 10GbE switch without link aggregation, 43–45
DHCP (dynamic host configuration protocol), 36
`disable_vsan_on_cluster` command, 279–280
disabling
  IGMP (internet group management protocol) snooping, 39
  object checksum capability, 73

disk controllers
  queue depth, impact of, 231–235
  RAID-0, 18–19
disk failure, 133, 185
disk full scenario, 193–194
disk groups
  adding, 177–178
    disks to, 54–55, 179–180
  creation, example, 55–58
  maximums, 52
  multiple, configuration, 52–53
  removing, 178–179
    disks from, 180–181
  role of, 51–52
  sizing ratio, cache device to capacity
    device, 53–54
disk management, 177
  adding
    disk groups, 177–178
    disks to disk groups, 179–180
  removing
    disk groups, 178–179
    disks from, 180–181
disk_object_info command,
    287–288
disks
  adding to disk groups, 177–178
    automatically, 54–55
    manually, 55
  blinking LED on, 183
  removing from disk groups, 180–181
  wiping, 182–183
  esxcli vsan disk commands, 184
disks_info command, 284
disk_stats command, 294–295
distributed object manager (DOM), 95–96,
    100, 207
distributed port group, creating, 33–34
distributed RAID, 83–85

Distributed Resource Scheduler (DRS), 195,
    204
DOM (distributed object manager), 95–96,
    100, 207
DRS (Distributed Resource Scheduler), 195,
    204

E

enable_vsan_on_cluster command,
    279–280
Ensure Accessibility option (maintenance
    mode), 173
enter_maintenance_mode command, 296
ESXCLI, 245, 256
  esxcli vsan cluster command, 258–259
  esxcli vsan datastore namespace, 256–257
  esxcli vsan faultdomain command,
    263–264
  esxcli vsan maintenancemode
    command, 264
  esxcli vsan network namespace, 257–258
  esxcli vsan policy command,
    264–267
  esxcli vsan storage namespace, 258–262
  esxcli vsan trace command, 267–268
  esxcli network diag ping command,
    258
  esxcli network ip connection list
    command, 258
  esxcli network ip neighbor list
    command, 258
  esxcli vsan cluster command, 171–172,
    258–259
  esxcli vsan disk command, 184
  esxcli vsan faultdomain command,
    263–264
  esxcli vsan maintenancemode
    command, 264
  esxcli vsan network namespace, 257–258
  esxcli vsan policy command, 264–267

esxcli vsan storage, 258–262

esxcli vsan trace command, 267–268

ESXi, 14

  boot considerations, 15

  firewall ports, 26

  NIC teaming in, 25

  troubleshooting VSAN on, 303

    log files, 304

    VMkernel modules and drivers, 305

    VSAN traces, 304–305

ESXTOP, 245

esxtop command, 308–309

ESXTOP performance counters, 308–309

explicit failover order, 44

F

failures

  cache devices, 186–187

  capacity devices, 185–186

  hosts, 187–188

  number to tolerate (*see* number of failures to tolerate)

  recovery from, 131–134

  write failures, 185–186

failure scenarios, 127–130, 185

  cache device failure, 186–187

  capacity device failure, 185–186

  disk full scenario, 193–194

  host failure, 187–188

  network partition, 188–193

  stretched clusters, 216–223

    network failure, 221–223

    preferred site, 219–220

    secondary site, 217–218

    witness host failure, 220–221

  vCenter server, 195

failures to tolerate = 1, object space reservation = 50 percent, 152–155

failures to tolerate = 1, object space reservation = 100 percent, 155–156

failures to tolerate = 1, stripe width = 2, 144–148

failures to tolerate = 2, stripe width = 2, 148–152

failure tolerance method, 66–69, 119–120

fault domains, stretched clusters *vs.*, 206–208

find option (cmmds-tool command), 270

firewall ports, 26

fix_renamed_vms command, 291

flash devices, 21–22

flash read cache reservation, 71

  policy setting, 122

force provisioning, 71–72, 94, 127

forceProvisioning command option, 266

Full Data Migration option (maintenance mode), 173

G

get option (esxcli vsan cluster command), 262

global support services (GSS), 267

GSS (global support services), 267

H

HA (high availability) cluster

  VSAN storage providers, 75

    changing policies on-the-fly, 75–79

  vSphere, 49–51

hard disk 1 layout (default policy), 163

HBA mode, 17
HCL (hardware compatibility list), 4
    health checks, 247–248
health check, VSAN, 165, 245, 246
    Ask VMware link, 246
    cluster health, 248–249
    data health, 250
    limits, 250
    network health, 249–250
    performance service, 168–169
    physical disk, 251
    proactive (*see* proactive health checks)
    stretched cluster, 252
    tests, 165–167
    Virtual SAN HCL health, 247–248
    VSAN performance service, 252
heartbeat datastores, vSphere HA, 50
help command, 276–279, 301
host_consume_disks command, 282
host_evacuate_data command, 282
hostFailuresToTolerate command
        option, 266
host_info command, 280–282
host management, 169
    adding hosts to clusters, 169–170
    esxcli vsan cluster commands, 171–172
    removing hosts from clusters, 170–171
hosts, 10
    adding to cluster, 169–170
    configuration, determination, 238–241
    failure, 132, 187–188
    management (*see* host management)
    removing from cluster, 170–171
    roles, 97–98
    witness, 206
host_wipe_non_vsan_disks command, 282
host_wipe_vsan_disks command, 282
hybrid VSAN

    capacity tier on, 105
    VSAN read on, anatomy of, 102–103
    VSAN write on, anatomy of, 103–104

I

IEEE 802.3ad, 42
IGMP (internet group management
        protocol) snooping, 39
I/O flow, 100
    cache layer, role of, 100–102
        read cache, 100–101
        write cache, 101–102
    caching algorithms, 100
    data locality, 107–108
        in VSAN stretched clusters, 108–109
    deduplication and compression, 105–107
    striping, two hosts, 145
    VSAN read
        on all-flash VSAN, 103
        on hybrid VSAN, 102–103
    VSAN write
        on all-flash VSAN, 104–105
        on hybrid VSAN, 103–104
IOPS (input/output operations per second)
        limit threshold, 70
iopsLimit command option, 266
IP-Hash, 46
isolation response, vSphere HA, 51

J

JBOD mode, 17
jumbo frames, 24–25

L

LACP (link aggregation control protocol), 46
Lam, William, 197

latency issues, VSAN Observer sample use cases, 317

latency requirements, stretched clusters, 205

layer 3 (L3) (routed) network, 23

layer 2 (L2) (switched) network, 23

layout, objects, 91–93

   default storage policy, 93–94

LBT (load based teaming) mechanism, 45

license editions, stretched clusters, 203–204

limits, components, 87–88

limits health checks, 250

lldpnetmap command, 296

local log structured object manager (LSOM), 95, 101

log fi les, troubleshooting VSAN on ESXi, 304

LSOM (local log structured object manager), 95, 101

LUN (logical unit number), 5, 61

M

magnetic disks, 20

maintenance mode, 172–174

   updates and patching, 175–176

master role (hosts), 97–98

migration, for objects, 96–97

multicast heartbeats, 25

multicast performance test, 168

multicast performance tests, 254–255

N

namespaces, 89–90

   esxcli vsan datastore, 256–257

   esxcli vsan network, 257–258

   esxcli vsan storage, 258–262

NAS (network-attached storage), 62

Network file system (NFS), 62

network health checks, 249–250

networking, 29–30

   configuration

      issues, 38–40

      VDS, 32–37

      VSS, 31–32

   redundant 10GbE switch with link aggregation capability, 45–48

   redundant 10GbE switch without link aggregation capability, 43–45

   stretched clusters, 205

   VMkernel network for VSAN, 30–31

network interface card (NIC), 7, 25

network I/O control. *see* NIOC (network I/O control)

network partition, 188–193

network policies, 2

network requirements, VSAN, 22–25

   jumbo frames, 24–25

   layer 2/layer 3 networks, 23

   NIC (network interface cards), 22

   NIC teaming, 25

   NIOC (network I/O control), 25

   switches, 22

   traffic, 24

   VMkernel network, 23, 30–31

NFS (Network file System), 62

NIC (network interface card), 7, 22

NIC teaming, 25

NIOC (network I/O control), 25

   configuration example, 40–42

   design considerations, 42–43

NL-SAS drives, 234

No Data Migration option (maintenance mode), 174

NSX virtualization platform, 2

number of disk stripes per object (SPBM), 69–70

number of failures to tolerate, 65–66, 84, 228
  best practice for, 112–113
  policy setting, 110–112
number of failures to tolerate = 1, 137–144
  default policy, 162

O

object_info command, 285–289
object_reconfigure command, 285
objects, 86–87
  data paths for, 95–96
  delta disks, 87
  layout, 91–93
    default storage policy, 93–94
  namespace, 89–90
  ownership, 96
  placement and migration for, 96–97
  storage (see storage objects)
  VM swap, 90
object space reservations, 71, 152
  policy setting, 122–123
obj_status_report command, 291–292
on-disk formats, 98
  cache devices, 99
  capacity devices, 99
osfs-ls command, 268–269

P

partedUtil method, 182–183
pass-through mode, 17
patching (maintenance mode), 175–176
performance, 245
  cache tier destaging, 116–117
  data (VSAN Observer), 313–316
  designing for, 229–231
    disk controllers, 231–235

monitoring (see performance monitoring)
  and RAID caching, 19
  read cache misses, 115–116
  VSAN capabilities, 235
  writes, 114
performance monitoring, 305
  ESXTOP performance counters, 308–309
  performance service (see performance service)
  VSAN observer (see VSAN observer)
  vSphere Web Client performance counters, 309–310
performance service, 168–169, 305–306
  enabling, 306
  health checks, 252
  metrics, 307–308
  VSAN, 306–307
physical disk health check, 251
physical disk placement
  failures to tolerate = 1, stripe width = 2, 146–147
  failures to tolerate = 2, stripe width = 2, 151
  number of failures to tolerate = 1, 144
PIM (protocol-independent multicast), 205
placement, for objects, 96–97
policy settings
  failures to tolerate = 1, object space reservation = 50 percent, 152–155
  failures to tolerate = 1, object space reservation = 100 percent, 155–156
  failures to tolerate = 1, stripe width = 2, 144–148
  failures to tolerate = 2, stripe width = 2, 148–152
  number of failures to tolerate = 1, 137–144
  RAID-5, 157–158
  RAID-6, 158–159
  RAID-5/6 and Stripe Width = 2, 159–160

ports
    firewall, 26
    VMkernel, building, 34–37
preferred site, 207
    failure scenarios, 219–220
proactive health checks, 167–168, 253–255
    multicast performance tests, 254–255
    storage performance tests, 255
    VM creation test, 253–254
profile-driven storage, 61
proof-of-concept (PoC), 167
proportionalCapacity command
        option, 266
protocol-independent multicast (PIM), 205
provisioning
    force, 71–72, 94, 127
    thin, 194–195

Q

queue depth, disk controllers, 231–235
queuing layers, disk controllers, 231–232

R

Raghuram, Raghu, 1
RAID-0, 18–19, 87, 144
    stripe configuration, 151
    usage, when no striping specified in
        policy, 117
        test 1, 118
        test 2, 119
        test 3, 119
RAID-1, 67, 84, 87, 144, 228
RAID-5, 67–69, 84, 157–158, 228
RAID-6, 67–69, 84–85, 158–159, 228
RAID caching, 19
RAID (redundant array of inexpensive
        disks), 17

distributed, 83–85
RDT (reliable datagram transport), 98
read cache, I/O flow, 100–101
    in all-flash VSAN configurations, 101
ready node profiles, clusters, 225–226
ready nodes, VSAN, 16–17
reapply_vsan_vmknic_config command,
        298
reconfiguration, 133
recover_spbm command, 298–300
recovery, from failures, 131–134, 223
redundant 10GbE switch with link
        aggregation capability, 45–48
redundant 10GbE switch without link
        aggregation capability, 43–45
reliable datagram transport (RDT), 98
replicaPreference command option, 266
replicas, 90–91
    failure scenarios, 127–130
reservations
    flash read cache, 71, 122
    object space, 71, 122–123, 152
resiliency, 11
ROBO (remote office/branch office)
    VSAN 2-node, 26
Ruby vSphere console (RVC), 245, 275–276
    SPBM commands, 300–303
    VSAN commands (see VSAN commands
        (RVC))
rule-sets, 139
RVC. see Ruby vSphere console (RVC)

S

SATA drives, 234
SDDC (software-defined datacenter), 1–2
SDN (software-defined network), 1
secondary site, 207
    failure scenarios, 217–218

server virtualization
   all-flash configuration, 241–244
   hybrid configuration, 237–238
      host configuration, determination, 238–241
service level objective (SLO), 11
sizing calculator, 236
sizing constraints, 227–228
SKU (stock keeping unit), 4
slave role (hosts), 97–98
SLO (service level objective), 11
snapshots, 126
software components, 94
   cluster monitoring, membership, and directory services, 97
   data paths for objects, 95–96
   host roles, 97–98
   management, 95
   object ownership, 96
   placement and migration for objects, 96–97
   reliable datagram transport, 98
software-defined datacenter (SDDC), 1–2
software-defined network (SDN), 1
software-defined storage, 2
software-only storage solutions, 4
space consumption, verifying, 126–127
SPBM (storage policy-based management), 5, 62–65, 109
   commands in RVC, 279, 300–303
   disable object checksum capability, 73
   failure tolerance method, 66–69
   flash read cache reservation, 71
   force provisioning, 71–72
   IOPS limit for object, 70
   number of disk stripes per object, 69–70
   number of failures to tolerate, 65–66
   object space reservations, 71
SSD (solid-state disks), 17

stock keeping unit (SKU), 4
storage controllers, 17–19
storage objects, 80
   virtual machine, 88
   VM swap, 124–126
storage performance tests, 168, 255
storage policies, 11
   changing on-the-fly, 75–79
   example, 11–12
   VM storage policy (see VM storage policy)
storage policy-based management. see SPBM (storage policy-based management)
storage providers
   VASA, 74–75
   VSAN (highly available), 75
      changing policies on-the-fly, 75–79
storage reports, 126–127
storage sizing, 239
storage traffic, 25
stretched clusters, 25–26, 201–223
   configuration, 202–203, 208–216
      procedural steps, 211–216
      size of, 209
   constraints, 203–204
   data locality in, 108–109
   defined, 201–203
   failure scenarios, 216–223
      network failure, 221–223
      preferred site, 219–220
      secondary site, 217–218
      witness host failure, 220–221
   vs. fault domains, 206–208
   health checks, 252
   latency requirements, 205
   license editions, 203–204
   networking, 205
   products/features not supported by, 204

stretched clusters (*Continued*)
  requirements, 203–204
stripe width
  best practices, 122
  chunk size, 121
  configuration error, 120–121
  maximum, 119–120
  policy setting
    cache tier destaging, 117–118
    read cache misses, 115–116
    writes, 114
stripeWidth command option, 266
Supermicro 2U 4-Node TwinPro2 server, 243
switches
  VDS (VMware vSphere Distributed
    Switches), 22, 29–30, 32–37
  VSS (VMware standard switches), 22, 29,
    31–32

T

tcpdump-uw command, 258
-t DISK option (cmmds_find command),
  290
-t DISK_USAGE option (cmmds_find
  command), 289–290
tests, VSAN health check, 165–167
thin provisioning, 194–195
tools, for design/sizing clusters,
  236
troubleshooting
  VSAN, non-ESXCLI commands for
    cmmds-tool, 269–272
    osfs-ls, 268–269
    vdq, 272–275
  VSAN on ESXi, 303
    log files, 304
    VMkernel modules and drivers, 305
    VSAN traces, 304–305

U

updates (maintenance mode), 175–176
upgrade_status command, 300
usage warnings (datastore), 195
-u UUID option (cmmds_find command),
  290

V

VASA (vSphere APIs for Storage Awareness)
  overview, 73–74
  storage providers, 74–75
  vendor providers, 73
vCenter server
  bootstrapping, 197–199
  failure scenario, 196
  management, 195–199
  running on VSAN, 196–197
VCG (VMware Compatibility Guide), 225
VCVA (VMware vCenter Virtual
  Appliance), 275
VDI (virtual desktop infrastructure), 117
vdq command, 272–275
VDS (VMware vSphere Distributed
  Switches), 22, 29–30
  creation, 32
  design considerations, 42–43
  distributed port group, creation, 33–34
  VMkernel ports, building, 34–37
  VSAN network configuration, 32–37
virtual desktop infrastructure (VDI), 117
virtualization layer, 1
Virtual Machine File System (VMFS), 99
virtual machine (VM), 2
  storage objects, 88
Virtual SAN 1.0, 8
Virtual SAN 6.0, 8
Virtual SAN 6.1, 8

Virtual SAN 6.2, 8

Virtual SAN HCL health, 247–248

Virtual SAN object health test, 250

Virtual SAN traffic, 36

virtual storage appliance (VSA), 4

Virtual Volumes (VVols), 62

VM. *see* virtual machine (VM)

VM creation test, 167–168, 253–254

VM disk (VMDK), 84, 89, 90

VMFS-L (VMFS local), 99

VMFS (Virtual Machine File System), 99

VM home namespace, 87, 89–90, 123, 148

VMkernel network, 23, 30–31
    adapter, 34

VMkernel ports, building, 34–37

vm_object_info command, 288–289

vMotion traffic, 40

vm_perf_stats command, 295

VM provisioning, VM storage policy
    assignment during, 81–82

VM storage policy, 5, 61–82, 138, 139
    assignment during VM provisioning,
        81–82
    creating, 81
    default, 93–94
    enabling, 81
    storage policy-based management
        (*see* SPBM (storage policy-based
        management))
    VSAN capabilities and, 63–65

VM swap, 90, 123–124
    descriptor file, 125
    storage objects, 124–126

VM (virtual machine), 2

VMware Compatibility Guide
    (VCG), 225

VMware hardware compatibility guide, 16

VMware standard switches. *see* VSS
    (VMware standard switches)

VMware vCenter Virtual Appliance
    (VCVA), 275

VMware VSAN sizing calculator, 236

VMware vSphere, 13
    ESXi, 14, 15

VSAN capabilities, 109–110
    data integrity through checksum,
        130–131
    delta disks, 126
    failure scenarios, 127–130
    flash read cache reservation policy
        setting, 122
    force provisioning, 127
    number of failures to tolerate
        best practice for, 112–113
        policy setting, 110–112
    object space reservation policy setting,
        122–123
    performance, 235
    problematic device handling, 134
    recovery from failure, 131–134
    snapshots, 126
    storage reports, 126–127
    stretching, 134–135
    stripe width, best practices, 122
    stripe width chunk size, 121
    stripe width configuration error, 120–121
    stripe width maximum, 119–120
    stripe width policy setting, 113
        cache tier destaging, 116–117
        read cache misses, 115–116
        writes, 114
    VM home namespace, 123
    VM swap, 123–126

VSAN commands (RVC)
    apply_license_to_cluster, 297
    check_limits, 297–298
    check_state, 292–293
    cluster_info, 282–284

VSAN commands (RVC) (*Continued*)

    cluster_set_default_policy, 284–285

    cmmds_find, 289–290

    disable_vsan_on_cluster, 279–280

    disk_object_info, 287–288

    disks_info, 284

    disk_stats, 294–295

    enable_vsan_on_cluster, 279–280

    enter_maintenance_mode, 296

    fix_renamed_vms, 291

    help, 276–279

    host_consume_disks, 282

    host_evacuate_data, 282

    host_info, 280–282

    host_wipe_non_vsan_disks, 282

    host_wipe_vsan_disks, 282

    lldpnetmap, 296

    object_info, 285–289

    object_reconfigure, 285

    obj_status_report, 291–292

    reapply_vsan_vmknic_config, 298

    recover_spbm, 298–300

    upgrade_status, 300

    vm_object_info, 288–289

    vm_perf_stats, 295

    whatif_host_failures, 293–294

VSAN datastore, 48

    properties, 58–59

VSAN observer, 245, 310

    performance data, 313–316

    requirements, 310–313

    sample use cases, 316–318

vsan.observer command, 311

VSAN read, I/O flow

    on all-flash VSAN, 103

    on hybrid VSAN, 102–103

VSAN ready nodes, 16–17

VSAN traces, troubleshooting VSAN on ESXi, 304–305

VSAN traffic, 24, 40

VSAN (virtual SAN), 4

    administrator's view, 9–11

    benefits of, 7

    cache and capacity devices, 14–15

    defined, 6–7

    disk groups (*see* disk groups)

    firewall ports, 26

    networking, 29–30

    overview, 4–5

    requirements, 15–22

        cache tier devices, 21–22

        capacity tier devices, 19–20

        hardware compatibility guide, 16

        network (*see* network requirements, VSAN)

        ready nodes, 16–17

        storage controllers, 17–19

    software components (*see* software components, VSAN)

    stretched cluster, 25–26

    troubleshooting on ESXi, 303

        log files, 304

        VMkernel modules and drivers, 305

        VSAN traces, 304–305

    2-node/ROBO, 26

    use cases, 7–8

    VMkernel network for, 30–31

VSA (virtual storage appliance), 4

vSphere APIs for Storage Awareness. *see* VASA (vSphere APIs for Storage Awareness)

vSphere Distributed Switch. *see* VDS (VMware vSphere Distributed Switches)

vSphere HA (high availability) cluster, 49

    admission control, 50–51

communication network, 49–50

component protection, 51

heartbeat datastores, 50

isolation response, 51

vSphere Web Client performance counters, 309–310

VSS (VMware standard switches), 22, 29

VSAN network configuration, 31–32

W

whatif_host_failures command, 293–294

wiping disks, 182–183

esxcli vsan disk commands, 184

Witness appliance

deployment, 208

icon, 206

witness component, 87, 90–91, 111

failure scenarios, 127–130

write cache, I/O flow, 101–102

write failures, 185–186

writes

performance, 114

retiring to capacity tier, 105

REGISTER YOUR PRODUCT at PearsonITcertification.com/register
Access Additional Benefits and SAVE 35% on Your Next Purchase

- Download available product updates.

- Access bonus material when applicable.

- Receive exclusive offers on new editions and related products.
  (Just check the box to hear from us when setting up your account.)

- Get a coupon for 35% for your next purchase, valid for 30 days. Your code will
  be available in your PITC cart. (You will also find it in the Manage Codes
  section of your account page.)

Registration benefits vary by product. Benefits will be listed on your account page
under Registered Products.

PearsonITcertification.com—Learning Solutions for Self-Paced Study, Enterprise, and the Classroom
Pearson is the official publisher of Cisco Press, IBM Press, VMware Press, Microsoft Press,
and is a Platinum CompTIA Publishing Partner—CompTIA's highest partnership accreditation.
At **PearsonITcertification.com** you can

- Shop our books, eBooks, software, and video training.
- Take advantage of our special offers and promotions (pearsonitcertifcation.com/promotions).
- Sign up for special offers and content newsletters (pearsonitcertifcation.com/newsletters).
- Read free articles, exam profiles, and blogs by information technology experts.
- Access thousands of free chapters and video lessons.

Connect with PITC – Visit PearsonITcertifcation.com/community
Learn about PITC community events and programs.

PEARSON IT CERTIFICATION

Addison-Wesley • Cisco Press • IBM Press • Microsoft Press • Pearson IT Certification • Prentice Hall • Que • Sams • VMware Press

ALWAYS LEARNING   PEARSON